Annual Report on Financing Old Age Care in China (2017)

Keyong Dong · Yudong Yao
Editors

Bo Sun
Executive Editor

Annual Report on Financing Old Age Care in China (2017)

SSAP

Springer

Editors
Keyong Dong
School of Public Administration
Renmin University of China
Beijing, China

Yudong Yao
Dacheng Fund
Shenzhen, Guangdong, China

Translated by Simin Tan and Jade Hung

ISBN 978-981-13-0967-0 ISBN 978-981-13-0968-7 (eBook)
https://doi.org/10.1007/978-981-13-0968-7

Jointly published with Social Sciences Academic Press, Beijing, China

The print edition is not for sale in China Mainland. Customers from China Mainland please order the print book from: Social Sciences Academic Press.

Library of Congress Control Number: 2018946674

Revised by Chen Zhaojuan

This Springer imprint is published by the registered company Springer Nature Singapore Pte Ltd.
The registered company address is: 152 Beach Road, #21-01/04 Gateway East, Singapore 189721, Singapore

Members of Editorial Board and Research Group

Editorial Team

Dong Zhang
Wang Zhenzhen
Ma Yuanyuan
Ling Yan
Gong Yuanyuan
Li Jianing

The Research is Generously Supported by

China Banking Association
Asset Management Association of China
Insurance Asset Management Association of China
China Social Insurance Association

Organizations Contributing to the Research (in alphabetical order)

Changjiang Pension Insurance Co., Ltd.
Dacheng Fund Management Co., Ltd.
China Universal Asset Management Company Limited
China Asset Management Co., Ltd.
CCB Pension Management Co., Ltd.
Ping An Endowment Insurance Co., Ltd.
Ruihui-Lize Capital Management Co., Ltd.
MANULIFE TEDA Fund Management Co., Ltd.
Tianhong Asset Management Co., Ltd.
Industrial Bank Co., Ltd.
China Merchants Fund Management Co., Ltd.
Principal Financial Group, Inc.

About COACFF50

Established on December 9, 2015, China Old Age Care Finance Forum CAFF is launched by Prof. Keyong Dong from the Renmin University of China, China Academy of New Supply-side Economics, and several other organizations. It invited prominent scholars on board the advisory committee to provide guidance for the scholarly activities and research of the forum, including Pan Gongsheng, Deputy Governor of the People's Bank of China and Administrator of the State Administration of Foreign Exchange; Yang Ziqiang, former executive assistant of the former Governor at the People's Bank of China; and Wang Zhongmin, Vice Chairman of the National Council for Social Security Fund. Members of the CAFF50 are top decision-makers and experts on financing old age care from political, academic, and industry domains, with great reputation and social influence. Committed to becoming a high-quality and professional think tank, COACFF50 acts to provide research support for policymakers, to build a communication platform for industry professionals, and to be a financial literacy center for the public. The mission of CAFF50 is to promote the development of financing old age care, improve the long-term capital market, impel the building of inclusive financing senior care, and deliver the social responsibility of advancing people's livelihood and well-being in China.

Official website: www.caff50.net
Contact: info@caff50.net
WeChat public account: CAFF50

Contents

About Key Contributors

With a doctoral degree in economics and research focus on pension policies and financing old age care, Prof. Keyong Dong is currently a doctoral advisor at the Renmin University of China and the Secretary-General of CAFF50. He also holds a concurrent post as the special consultant at Ministry of Human Resources and Social Security, Chinese representative at China-EU Social Security Reform Project, member of Pension Project Evaluation Committee of National Development Bank, and Visiting Professor of Ford School of Public Policy, University of Michigan and National School of Administration. His professional experience includes Dean of School of Public Administration and Policy, Dean of School of Labor and Human Resources, Renmin University of China, and Secretary-General of Steering Committee of national MPA education. For decades, he has conducted a number of studies on projects of financing old age care in collaboration with national ministries and commissions, including the National Development and Reform Commission, the Ministry of Finance, the Ministry of Human Resources and Social Security, and other ministries. In addition, as the founder of China Pension Forum, he has also organized several international seminars on financing old age care jointly with Harry Smorenberg, founder of the World Pension Summit. He has published more than one hundred papers in the *Management World*, *Journal of Public Management*, *China Industrial Economics*, and other major journals.

Yudong Yao, a researcher and doctoral advisor with a Ph.D. degree in economics, is currently the Chairman of CAFF50. His research interests include macroeconomics and financial development. He is now the Vice President and Chief Economist of Dacheng Fund, and the Secretary-General of China Small and Medium Banks Development Forum. He also holds a concurrent post of the Vice President of Banking Accounting Society of China, Standing Director of Society of Public Finance of China, and Research Fellow at Finance and Taxation Research Center of Tsinghua University. He was the Former Director of the Institute of Finance at People's Bank of China, Economist of International Monetary Fund, and Deputy Inspector and Deputy Director of Monetary Policy Division of the People's

Bank of China. He has published in *Economic Research Journal*, *Journal of Financial Research*, and other journals.

Bo Sun earned his doctoral degree in management from Renmin University of China and had his postdoctoral training at China Securities Regulatory Commission and the Finance Department of Tsinghua University. As a fellow member of CAFF50 with a research focus on financing old age care, he holds a position at the Huaxia Fund pension management department and also serves as a visiting fellow at human resources and development center of Renmin University of China. He previously worked for the China Securities Regulatory Commission Research Center. Many of his research papers can be found in prestigious journals such as *Tsinghua Financial Review*, *Financial Regulation Research*, *Journal of Public Management*, and *China Social Security*.

Chapter 1
Financing Old Age Care: Definition, Theoretical Framework and Trend

Keyong Dong and Bo Sun

Abstract Financing old age care is an umbrella term which includes pension finance, financial services for the elderly and finance for the elderly care industry. Pension finance is to manage pension assets in a way to preserve and increase their value; financial services for the elderly are to serve the elderly population's needs for various financial products; finance for the elderly care industry is to assist the industry in investment and financial activities. Financing old age care is not only significant to an ageing society but also to economic transformation and upgrade. China's pension finance is seriously lagging behind, calling for greater efforts to close the gap.

Keywords Financing old age care · Pension finance · Financial services for the elderly · Finance for the elderly care industry

With the aggravating trend of population ageing, life after retirement is becoming a topic of wide concern. Retirement involves many aspects in which financial intermediaries play an important role. In recent years, such terms as pension finance and financing old age care have become quite popular, but they are often elusively defined, making it difficult for people to tell the differences or relations between them. This paper aims to analyze the related concepts so as to define the conceptual framework and to explore the trend in financing old age care.

K. Dong
Renmin University of China, Beijing, China

B. Sun (✉)
Pensions Management Department, China Asset Management, Beijing, China

K. Dong and Y. Yao (eds.), *Annual Report on Financing Old Age Care in China (2017)*, https://doi.org/10.1007/978-981-13-0968-7_1

1 Conceptual Framework

1.1 Definition of Pension Finance

The term pension finance is coined by the British scholar Professor David Black and discussed in his monograph *Pension Finance.* "Pension finance" is to study how pension funds invest in financial assets, real estate, derivatives and alternative investments. Therefore, pension finance here refers to pension asset management. Different from other countries, China has "financing for old age" in addition to "pension finance", though there is no clear distinction between the two concepts. He (2011) argues that China should establish a system of financing old age care, that is, a whole range of financial services including basic old age insurance, enterprise annuity, endowment insurance, old age savings, "home for care" for seniors, pension trusts and pension funds. Here, "finance for old age" is actually pension finance. Hu (2013) also equates pension finance with finance for old age which, according to him, is a field of study that explores how pension investment is made in direct or indirect financing market in order to realize value preservation and appreciation while promoting the development of financial markets. Yang (2015) argues that financing old age care refers to the financial services that manage the pension assets in the form of cash, fixed assets and equity.

Overall, "pension finance" and "finance for old age" are interchangeable in China and their essential idea is consistent with "pension finance" used in the rest of the world, that is, pension asset management. The only difference is the extended implications in China: one is related to the impact of pension on the capital market; the other is concerned about the pension system.

1.2 Definition of Old Age Finance

Deng Junwu and others employ the concept of old age finance, which refers to the preparation of various assets for retirement when young, and the financial operating mechanisms to replace these assets with the products or services available at old age. He believes that "although old age financing is a new concept, its implications are not so." He also notes that the meaning of *yanglao* ("provision for the elderly" in Chinese) is too broad and the term *yanglao jinrong* ("finance for old age") cannot reflect the needs for society to get financially ready for the challenges of an ageing population. Wu (2014) pointed out that financing old age care refers to the saving and investment mechanism related to the financial preparation for old age, which mainly includes basic old age insurance, enterprise annuity, endowment insurance, old age savings, housing mortgage loans, pension trusts, pension funds and other financial services. Overall, the core concept of old age finance is still savings and asset management for old age, similar to the pension finance, but taking into account of the impact of population ageing.

Some scholars refer to "old age finance" as "the financial activities in response to ageing". This definition has even broader implications. As we all know, any concept should have a clear connotation and delineation. Connotation alludes to the unique attributes while the delineation specifies the scope. In this sense, the concept of "financial activities in response to ageing" has specific connotations but lacks delineation, that is, there is no clear conceptual boundary. In the context of an ageing society, any financial activity is directly or indirectly related to the problem of ageing, which makes "old age finance" such an all-encompassing term that we can hardly tell what financial activities do not fit the category. In addition, if old age finance is considered to be "financial activity in response to ageing," there is another theoretical paradox: If an economy does not have the pressure of ageing, will there be no such financial activities and the need to promote their development? The answer is obviously no, because in any society, everyone must make financial preparations for old age. Thus, the above definition is theoretically flawed as it focuses more on society as a whole than the needs of individuals. In this sense, "financing old age care" has a better defined scope and connotations.

1.3 Financing Old Age Care Re-defined

Chinese scholars are divided in a number of terms related to old age, or they tend to use different names for the same thing, such as old age security, old age insurance and pension, or social relief and social assistance. This is not conducive to research and may cause confusion in public perception. Therefore, in the field of finance for old age, we should clarify the actual scope of and boundary between the relevant concepts. Only in this way can we deepen our understanding, solidify the theoretical foundation and promote the sound development of services for the elderly. This paper proposes the use of "financing old age care" as defined below.

In terms of provision for old age, the financial services that a society and its members need include not only the pensions but also other activities and services aimed at the elderly. The existing literature does not have a term that rightly and fully captures the meaning of finance for old age. We propose the use of "financing old age care" which, as an umbrella term, refers to the totality of financial activities that are centered on the various financial needs of members of society in order to meet the challenges of ageing. Such a system includes three aspects: First, the pension finance, referring to a series of financial activities to build up pension assets, including the pension system and pension asset management; second, financial service for the elderly, referring to financial services provided by institutions to meet the needs of the elderly for financial products; third, the finance for elderly care industry, referring to the financing activities to support industries related to elderly care.

Apparently, financing old age care covers not only pension finance - now an important topic in public discussions, but also the financial services for the elderly and finance for the elderly care industry. The three components mentioned above constitute the financing old age care but each has its own focus: pension finance focuses on pension money with the aim of accumulating pension assets and preserving and increasing the asset value through reasonable institutional arrangements; financial services for the elderly focus on the financial needs of the elderly; finance for the elderly care industry is to assist businesses dedicated to the elderly in their investment and financial activities.

2 The Significance of Improving the Financing of Old Age Care

First, promoting financing old age care is an important measure to address the challenge of ageing population. Financing old age care covers both the process in which people save for old age as well as various financial services provided for the elderly and the businesses dedicated to them. Without the development of financing old age care, on the one hand, there may not be enough businesses and services to meet the demands. On the other hand, there may also be a lack of sufficient pension to purchase related products and services. Second, financing old age care is one of the cores in the modern financial system. On the one hand, pension assets are often huge. The total pension assets of the United States reached USD 26.8 trillion at the end of 2015, about 153% of GDP that year. In OECD countries, the average pension assets account for more than 80% of the country's GDP and the size of the assets is still increasing. On the other hand, the financing old age care is targeting at all people over the age of 30, which is a broad demographic coverage. Huge pension assets and large population speak the importance of this segment in modern finance.

2.1 Pension Finance Addresses Financial Security at Old Age and Facilitates Economic Restructuring

Pension finance mainly covers how pension programs are designed and pension assets are managed. With a global trend in population ageing, the pension plans are becoming more important, as they are related to the sustainable development of the pension system as well as the sound development of a society. In recent years, the pension system in Europe has failed to pace with the demographic and economic changes, and its sustainability is thus called into question. What is even worse is that in countries such as Greece, the unreasonable pension system has not only resulted in a national dilemma but also exacerbated the sovereign debt crisis and social turmoil, almost leading to state insolvency. In China, the population ageing outpaces financial readiness, which calls for a reform to optimize the pension system and ensure the financial security at old age.

Pension asset management has a far-reaching impact on the financial industry and the real economy. The international experience shows that the huge volume of pension assets has become one of the major sources for the asset management industry. By the end of 2015, the size of the pension vehicles in American financial markets reached USD 24.8 trillion, representing 143% of the U.S. GDP in that year. Pensions which try to keep their money from devaluation have become important institutional investors in the capital market, with the equity investment in stocks, VCs, and PEs accounting for as much as 60%. This effectively supports the real economy and helps promote the emerging industries and industrial innovation and upgrade.

In addition, pension finance can help promote economic restructuring. Household consumption has long been inadequately motivated in China. One of the most important reasons is that the social security system, especially the pension scheme, is yet to be improved, and a large amount of household income is thus set aside in preventive savings. In contrast, the abundant pension assets of the United States have curbed the residents' interest in saving to some extent. In recent years, the savings rate of U.S. residents has remained at only around 5%. Therefore, citizens can spend large amounts of their income on consumption. It is foreseeable that the continuous development of pension finance in China will drive the national consumption and facilitate economic restructuring.

2.2 *Financial Services for the Elderly Benefit the Elderly Population and the Financial Industry*

The senior citizens have a wide range of financial needs. In addition to the traditional services such as savings, insurance and loans, they also need new services such as wealth management, "home for care" loan and will-trusts. The financial services designed for them meet their financial needs in all aspects, and are thus more targeted, effective and efficient. In addition, financial services for the elderly differ from traditional financial services in that the ultimate goal of the old age social security is to take care of the life of the senior members, including their needs of financial management, loans, endowment insurance, medical and health care, elderly home care and nursing institutions, among others. All these need institutions that could cater to the needs of the elderly for financial and other products and provide more targeted services, and the financial institutions are thus required to adapt themselves to the change, combining the virtual financial services and the real economy.

2.3 *Finance for the Elderly Care Industry Is an Important Impetus to the Growth of These Industries*

First, since senior housing and other segments of the elderly care industry need large and long-term investment, it is difficult for businesses to finance their operations completely on their own. Financing and funding support are thus important for them. Second, finance for the elderly care industry has significant social benefits. The elderly care industry is to serve the elderly with diminishing income and spending power. In order to ensure the availability of services, many countries impose price restrictions on some of the service providers. Therefore, they serve the public interests to some extent. In this sense, finance for the elderly care industry has both social and financial benefits. Third, the elderly care industry is an important area for pension investment. Retirement savings could last for decades, and during this process a reasonable investment must be made in order to preserve and increase their values. However, pensions, which are a crucial source of income for people after retirement, demand high investment safety. Good elderly care businesses, such as retirement communities, can provide a stable cash flow, and they are an ideal investment option for pension funds given the latter's low-risk investment preference.

3 How Old Age Care Is Financed: Current Situation and Trends

3.1 Pension Finance: A Focus of Public Attention

Since the aggravating trend of ageing has posed a challenge to the sustainability of the pension system in China, the pension finance has drawn much attention from all walks of life. And studies have shown the current pension system will face a serious gap in the long run. In addition to population ageing and other factors, the unreasonable institutional structure is another constituent that undermines a sustainable pension system. Overall, a public consensus on the reform of the pension system is to focus on occupational annuities as the second pillar and personal tax-deferred pensions as the third pillar; to establish a market-oriented pension investment and operation system; and to gradually reduce the payment burden on enterprises and to delay the retirement age. For the asset management industry, pensions are generally regarded as a "blue ocean" of uncontested market spaces. The United States has more than 90% of the USD 24.8 trillion market-oriented pension funds in investment. Currently, China has over RMB 5 trillion in pension funds, and the domestic pensions market is expected to approach RMB 10 trillion in 2020. Even so, pensions account for less than 20% of GDP in China, far away from the average of 80% in OECD countries. This shows that there is huge potential for the pension asset management industry to develop in China. Therefore, financial institutions such as banks, securities and insurance companies attach great importance to pension management, deeming it a strategic area for their future growth. This will surely be a driving force for pension finance.

3.2 Financial Services for the Elderly: The Early Development

As China gradually becomes an ageing society and the financial needs of the senior citizens have become increasingly prominent, the financial industry begins to attach importance to financial services for the elderly. Some banks proclaimed the strategic goal of being a specialist in this area and established specialized branches to develop services exclusively for the senior citizens. There are also banks that have developed financial services programs for the elderly that cover wealth management products, value-added services and easy settlement. In general, various financial institutions have started to explore the financial services for the elderly and the possible ways to integrate them with pension asset management and elderly care. For example, the newly established pension company of China Construction Bank aims to participate in the pension management as well as to diversify financial service for the elderly in order to meet the financial demands of the community in such areas as retirement, medical care, housing and education. The insurance industry, in addition to traditional types of insurance, such as life insurance and endowment insurance, expands into retirement community and elder care sectors through newly established senior service agencies. Overall, the financial services for the elderly in China are still at the preliminary stage, and a mature financial format is not yet formed. In the future, with the increase of the elderly population, the financial service for this demographic segment will grow faster and gradually extend into the entire the elderly care industry and advance the financial services to the real economy.

3.3 Finance for Elderly Care Industry: Much to Be Improved

The elderly care industry is by nature less attractive to financial capital. There are two reasons for this. First, the elderly have shrinking income and limited spending power, and most businesses dedicated to them can thus only operate at a marginal profit. The average profit of the elderly care industry in the United States and Japan stands at only 5%, which is not attractive to financial capital. Second, elderly care in China is a new industry, which has greater uncertainty in earning performance that debases investment. However, the elderly care industry brings about significant economic and social benefits. Both policy and market-oriented measures should be taken to develop finance for the industry.

Policy-based financial support refers to the non-profit financial support provided by the government and government-run financial institutions to the elderly care industry and businesses as a compensation for the social benefits they have brought. Such support mainly includes policy-based lending and guarantees, government-guided funds and special support funds. As mentioned earlier, since it is difficult for the elderly care industry to attract market-oriented capital, policy-based finance is crucial for its development. Japan, Germany and other countries provide varying degrees of tax relief, loan concessions and other measures to support institutions engaged in elderly care. In recent years, China has also promulgated a series of policies, aiming to support the industry through policy-based financing by supporting local governments to set up special funds and exploring such models as industrial funds and PPPs to support the elderly care industry. Overall, China has already promulgated a number of financial policies in this regard but hasn't had specific implementation model yet.

Market-based financing refers to the financial support provided by market players for the elderly care industry, in accordance with the market mechanism and through direct or indirect financing means. Such financing can enhance the efficiency in allocating financial resources. Overall, market-oriented financing for the elderly care industry is relatively advanced in western countries. In addition to the conventional credit, IPO, bond financing, there are some innovative financing vehicles, such as the most representative REITs (real estate investment trusts) and private equity funds. The retirement communities or institutions in the United States are financed primarily through REITs; and five of the top ten retirement communities are held by REITs. In addition, private equity funds also play an important role in financing the elderly care industry. In 2009, after acquiring a retirement community operator, Blackstone becomes the 12th largest retirement community owner in the United States. The elderly care industry in China is at early stage of development. Most of the businesses are of a small or medium size; and the highly competitive environment adds to the risks of investments. Moreover, the risk-free interest rates were kept at a high level in China a few years ago, which in turn made the elderly care industry less attractive to financial capital. Therefore, finance for the elderly care industry lags behind that of foreign countries and the needs of the industry. Of the components of financing old age care, it is in need of improvement, which can be achieved by policy or market means.

4 Conclusion

In China, financing old age care lags behind; the pension scheme is below the international standards; and the pension management is also at the initial stage of development. In addition, as population ageing occurred later in China than in the developed countries, its financial services for the elderly and finance for the elderly care industry are underdeveloped. However, due to the influence of family planning and other factors, China is ageing much faster than other countries and will soon become an "aged" or "super-aged" nation. In this context, we must attach importance to financing old age care, and through policy and other support, foster the development of the sector, and get people financially ready for the challenges of an ageing society.

References

He, Q. (2011). To establish pension finance: an imperative task for China, International Financing, (4).
Hu, J. (2013). Financing old age care: theoretical definition and several practical issues, Finance and Trade Economics, (6).
Yang, Y. (2015). Report on the development of China's ageing society and old age security, Tsinghua University Press.
Wu, Y. (2014). Old age and retirement industry development, China Social Sciences Academic Press.

Keyong Dong, Professor of Renmin University of China, advisor of doctoral program, honorary recipient of the state funding, Secretary-General of CAFF50, former Dean of School of Labor and Human resources and School of Public Administration and Policy, Renmin University of China, Secretary-General of the National MPA Advisory Board, with a research interest in the pension policy and aging finance.

Bo Sun, Ph.D in Management Science, Postdoctoral Fellow in Finance, invited member of CAFF50, a staff member of the Pensions Management Department of China Asset Management, with a research interest in financing old age care.

Chapter 2
Survey Report on the Financing of Old Age Care in China

Keyong Dong and Li Gan

Abstract The CAFF50 Survey is designed to obtain a better understanding of citizens' plans for their old age and their needs for financing old age care. It focuses on respondents' perception of financing old age care, their participation in such scheme and willingness to participate. Results show that most of the respondents have some basic ideas about retirement savings, and own some retirement assets through diversified channels. However, on the whole, their savings are not enough. In terms of pension investment, the majority of respondents show a keen interest and are prudent in making investment decisions. However, the risk prevention and fraud control still need to be addressed in this area. In addition, the majority of the respondents show a strong interest in participating in the third pillar of pensions, that is, personal tax-deferred pension. In the future, based on the continuous reform of the pension insurance system and improvement of the multi-pillar pension insurance system, we should further raise the general public's awareness of retirement savings, continuously make innovations in products designed to finance old age care, optimize the market of financing old age care, and meet the investment needs of different demographic groups.

Keywords Perception of financing old age care and participation
Retirement savings · Personal tax-deferred pension

K. Dong
Renmin University of China, Beijing, China

L. Gan (✉)
Department of Economics, Texas A&M University, College Station, TX, USA

K. Dong and Y. Yao (eds.), *Annual Report on Financing Old Age Care in China (2017)*, https://doi.org/10.1007/978-981-13-0968-7_2

1 Introduction

1.1 Purpose and Implication of the Survey

Since China became an ageing society in 2000, the speed of population ageing has been accelerating. At the same time, we are also facing the problem that ageing is outpacing financial readiness, seriously affecting the effectiveness of our pension system and the economic security of the elderly. Therefore, using financial instruments and technologies to improve the income security of the elderly is the only way to adapt to the change of the traditional retirement planning and meet the growing needs of the ageing population. In this context, to promote ageing financing, which is related to the social stability and security, has increasingly become the focus of attention of all sectors of society.

In 2016, President Xi Jinping gave instructions twice on the work concerning the ageing population; the Central Economic Work Conference also proposed to speed up the introduction of the pension reform. However, the lack of basic data on financing old age care affects the scientific support for policy-making and restricts further research. At the same time, the lack of micro-base data is not conducive for the financial institutions to develop related products to meet the public needs of old age care.

In this context, the China Old Age Care Financing Forum (CAFF50) COACFF and Survey and Research Center for China Household Finance jointly organized the CAFF50 survey project. The participating agencies include CAFF50 member institutions, such as Institute of Social Security of Renmin University of China, Tianhong Asset Management Co., Ltd., Industrial Bank, CCB Pension Management Co., Ltd. The survey aims to understand the needs of the general public in old age planning and financing old age care from perspectives of the public awareness of and willingness to participate in financing old age care so as to provide a scientific basis/reference for policy-making, high quality micro-data for research and financial product development.

1.2 Methodology and Data Processing

1.2.1 Survey Methodology

The CAFF Survey is a national sampling survey built upon previous surveys conducted by Survey and Research Center for China Household Finance. The design is based on the demographic characteristics of each province and municipality with special focus on such factors as gender, age groups, income level, and regional differences. The survey is administered by Tianhong Asset Management Co., Ltd. and Industrial Bank through a combination of online platform and offline research to targeted population with uniform copies of questionnaires given out in 31 provinces (autonomous regions and municipalities directly under the Central Government) in China. Data were collected through the survey system, and distilled, merged and processed by CAFF50 and experts from Survey and Research Center for China Household Finance. This report was developed based on the analysis of the valid data derived from the survey.

1.2.2 Data Processing

This survey gave out 46,000 copies and collected 45,482 effective copies, 35,706 from Tianhong Asset Management Co., Ltd., and 9776 from Industrial Bank. The effective recovery rate reaches 98.88%.

In order to further ensure the representativeness of the sample data, we adjusted the data of this survey in two areas - education level and total family assets- based on the survey data of 2015 China Household Finance Survey (CHFS). The sample is divided into 7 * 13 groups according to the level of education (i) and the total of family assets (j),—The weights needed for the adjustment of groups i and j are calculated as follows,

$$w_{i,j} = \frac{CHFS\%_{i,j}}{sample\%_{i,j}}$$

Wherein, CHFS% (i, j) is the proportion of the i and j groups of the total CHFS samples; sample% i, j is the ratio of the i and j groups to the total survey samples. For each sample, there is a weight coefficient for its corresponding group. The following data are based on adjusted weight analysis.

1.3 Demographic Information of the Respondents

See Table 1.

Table 1 Basic information of the respondents

	Categories C	Proportion (%)		Categories	Proportion (%)
Age	Under 29 (29 incl.)	37.1	Monthly income (RMB)	Less than 800	7.7
	30–39	21.7		801–1500	9.8
	40–49	16.4		1501–4000	37.1
	50–59	13.4		4001–8000	27.4
	Over 60 (60 incl.)	11.3		8001–15,000	9.0
Gender	Male	60.8		More than 15,001	4.7
	Female	39.2		No	4.2
Property ownership (unit)	0	27.7	Household assets	Less than 100,000	21.0
	1	42.4		100,000–300,000	24.1
	2	19.7		300,000–500,000	14.8
	3 or more	10.2		500,000–700,000	10.3
Residency	Urban area	60.0		700,000–1,000,000	8.6
	Rural area	40.0		1,000,000–1,500,000	8.0
Employment	Retired	28.2		1,500,000–3,000,000	8.0
	Employed	71.8		3,000,000–5,000,000	2.8
				More than 5,000,000	2.5

2 Perception of the Financing of Old Age Care

Financing old age care is an umbrella term that encompasses all financial activities centering on various needs in old age in order to meet the challenge of an ageing society. It includes not only the financial supports but also the spending services and related products of the pension/retirement industries. This is a crucial system to ensure the basic living standards and social services for the elderly in the future.

2.1 Expected Age and Amount for Retirement Savings

2.1.1 When to Start Savings

According to the survey data, more than 60% (61.8%) of the respondents agree that one should start retirement savings before the age of 40 by purchasing old age insurance or other investment savings. Among them, 26.4% consider one should start

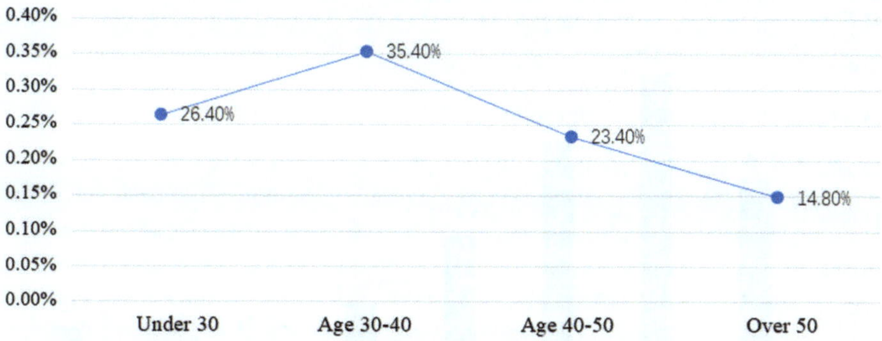

Fig. 1 Respondents' perception of time to start retirement savings

the savings by the age of 30, while 14.8% indicate after the age of 50, as shown in Fig. 1.

The data show that the Chinese people have a relatively high awareness of retirement savings, and most of the respondents think that the savings should be started at an earlier age rather than right before retirement. On the one hand, this may be because that most of the respondents have realized that in an ageing society, it has become increasingly unrealistic to rely on "offspring who will in turn support the aged parents." Instead, it requires personal savings to obtain a higher quality of life after retirement. It also may be because China's current social security system needs improvement and the pension is not enough, the majority of respondents thus hope to increase their personal pension funds through some other ways.

2.1.2 How Much Should Be Saved

According to the survey, 76.2% of the respondents think that the pension assets needed for the entire retirement period is within RMB 1 million; among them, 55.8% think RMB 0.5 million is needed. Nearly a quarter, or 24.3% of the respondents think RMB 300,000 should be enough and only 23.8% of respondents think it needs over RMB 1 million to cover the entire retirement period. See Fig. 2.

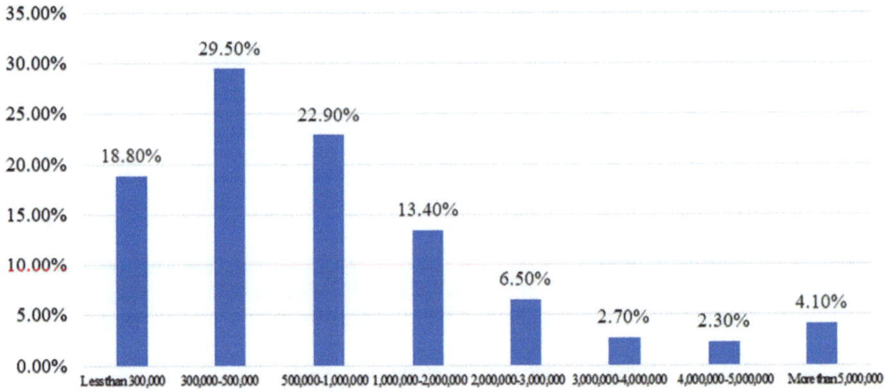

Fig. 2 Expected amount of retirement savings

Table 2 Different views on the amount of retirement saving among different age groups

Age groups savings (RMB)	Under 29 (29 incl.) (%)	Age 30–39 (%)	Age 40–49 (%)	Age 50–59 (%)	Over 60 (60 incl.) (%)
Below 300,000	29.2	25.7	21.5	17.4	19.0
300,000–500,000	31.1	33.3	34.4	28.0	28.9
500,000–1,000,000	18.0	20.4	21.3	23.4	22.9
1,000,000–2,000,000	9.6	9.9	10.6	16.3	14.8
2,000,000–3,000,000	4.0	4.3	5.1	8.6	7.0
3,000,000–4,000,000	2.0	1.7	1.9	2.7	3.0
4,000,000–5,000,000	2.3	1.6	1.8	1.5	2.1
Above 5,000,000	3.7	3.1	3.4	2.1	2.2

Different age groups also have different views on the amount of retirement savings. The data shows that the amount of expected retirement savings is lower in the younger age groups but higher in those groups closer to the retirement age (Table 2). To some extent, this reflects that people near retirement age have a clearer picture of their post-retirement needs and expect higher savings.

2.2 *Participation in Financing Old Age Care and Retirement Savings*

2.2.1 Current Retirement Savings

The survey shows that more than 70% (71.0%) of the respondents have a retirement saving within RMB 500,000; among them, 28.9% have a retirement saving no more than RMB 100,000 and 26.2% have savings RMB 100,000-300,000. Only 24.5% of

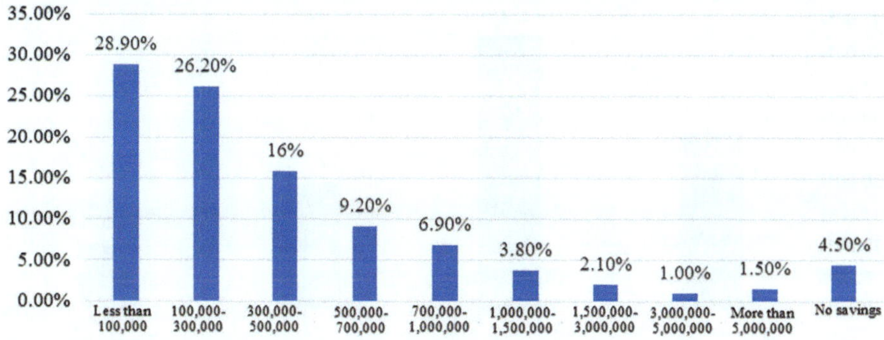

Fig. 3 Current retirement savings of the respondents

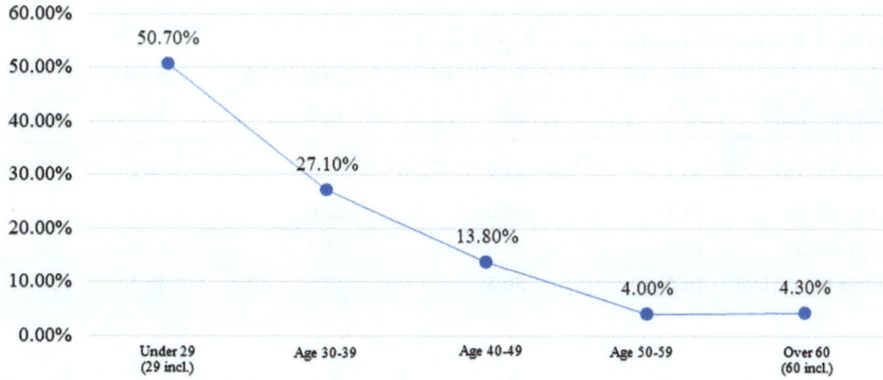

Fig. 4 Respondents without retirement savings by age groups

the respondents have a retirement saving over RMB 500,000. It is noteworthy that 4.5% of the respondents have not yet started saving for their retirement. See Fig. 3.

A further analysis on the demographic characteristics of those without any retirement savings shows that nearly 80% (77.8%) of them are under the age of 39 and 50.7% are under 29. At the same time, nearly 18% of them are between the age of 40 and 59; this age group is relatively near the retirement age and may face a greater challenge in their old ages. See Fig. 4.

2.2.2 Property Ownership

In addition to special retirement funds, fixed assets such as real estate is also an important source of retirement savings. The survey shows that 72.3% of the respon-

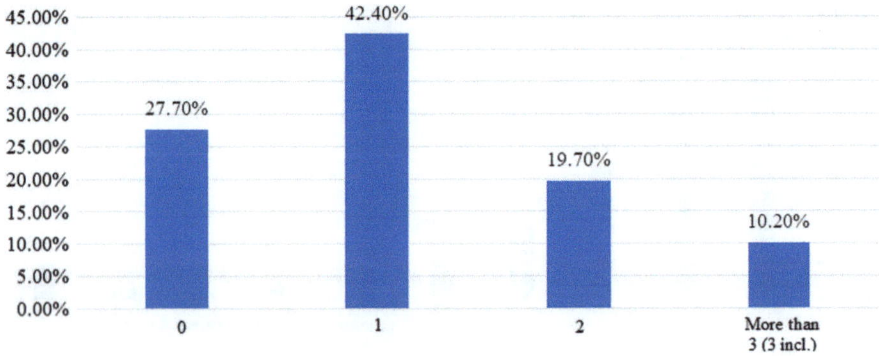

Fig. 5 Property owned by the respondents (by units)

Table 3 Respondent's property ownership by age group

Age	0 unit (%)	1 unit (%)	2 units (%)	3 units (%)
Under 29 (29 incl.)	35.4	35.9	16.2	12.6
Age 30–39	30.3	44.8	18.6	6.4
Age 40–49	24.7	45.0	22.6	7.7
Age 50–59	16.0	46.9	25.3	11.8
Over 60 (60 incl.)	16.5	50.5	22.5	10.5

dents currently have one or more than one piece of property[1], as shown in Fig. 5, surpassing their counterparts of the United States, Japan, Germany and many other developed countries[2].

A further analysis on the property ownership among different age groups shows that the population with property ownership increases as the age increases. Over 80% of those who are aged 50 and over own property; among them, 83.5% of the population over the age of 60 have their own properties, with 50.5% having one piece of property and 33% possessing two or more pieces of property, as shown in Table 3. This shows that at present the elderly population in China has a relatively high property ownership rate, which to a certain extent increases the readiness for the old age after retirement.

[1]Note: Due to the difference between the sampling plan and sample population, there is some discrepancy between this data and the survey of the Survey and Research Center for China Household Finance.

[2]Gan et al. (2015).

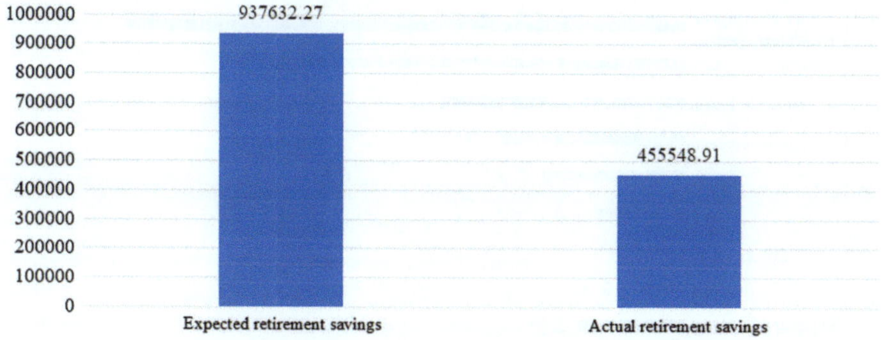

Fig. 6 Comparison of the respondents' expected and the actual retirement savings (yuan)

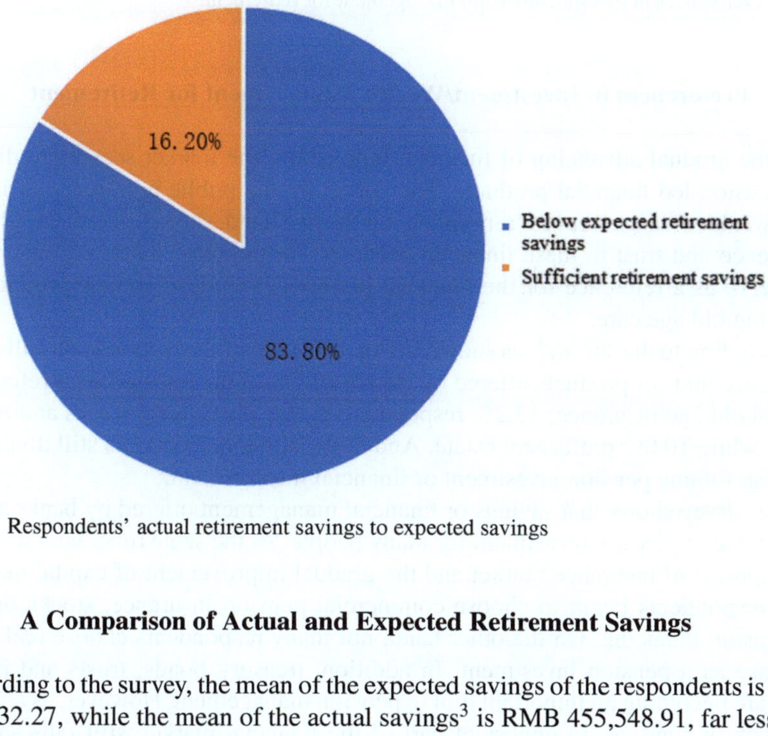

Fig. 7 Respondents' actual retirement savings to expected savings

2.2.3 A Comparison of Actual and Expected Retirement Savings

According to the survey, the mean of the expected savings of the respondents is RMB 937,632.27, while the mean of the actual savings[3] is RMB 455,548.91, far less than expected, as shown in Fig. 6.

In addition, although 95.5% of the respondents have started saving for retirement, over 80% (83.8%) have not yet reached the expected amount of saving for the old age, as shown in Fig. 7. To a certain extent, it reflects that financing old age care still has great potential for development in China.

[3]Note: excluding real estate and other fixed assets.

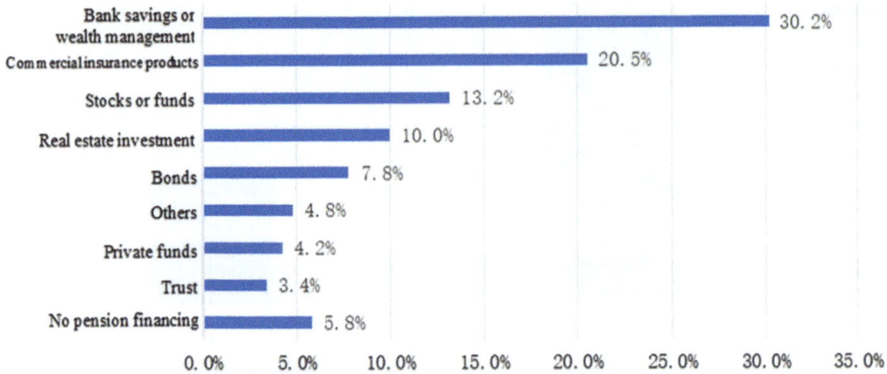

Fig. 8 Preferences in investment/wealth management for retirement

2.2.4 Preferences in Investment/Wealth Management for Retirement

With the gradual advancing of financial innovation, the market sees more diversified pension-led financial products. The survey of the public preference in investment/wealth management for retirement, on the one hand, sheds light on the Chinese preference and trust in these financial products; on the other hand, the survey can also serve as a reference for the financial institutions to develop new products for financing old age care.

According to the survey[4], as shown in Fig. 8, 30.2% of the respondents still prefer saving accounts or products offered by banks; 20.5% of the respondents prefer commercial old age insurance; 13.2% respondents prefer purchasing stocks and mutual funds, while 10.0% prefer real estate. And 5.8% of the respondents still don't have any plan for any pension investment or financial management.

The survey shows that savings or financial management offered by banks are the first choice of pension investment for many people. At the same time, with the rapid development of insurance market and the gradual improvement of capital markets, more respondents begin to choose commercial pension insurance, stocks or fund for pension financing. On the other hand, not many respondents choose real estate purchase as a pension investment. In addition, treasury bonds, trusts and private funds are becoming an important tool in pension management. However, as a whole, the stock or fund, as an important part of the financial market, still falls short of the respondents' preference when compared to the products offered by banks and insurance companies. Therefore, in the future, the securities and fund industry need to develop products that better meet the demand of pension management.

[4]This question is a multiple-choice question; in order to more clearly reflect the respondents' selection, the data is processed by using SPSS multiple response sets so that the sum of the options is 100%.

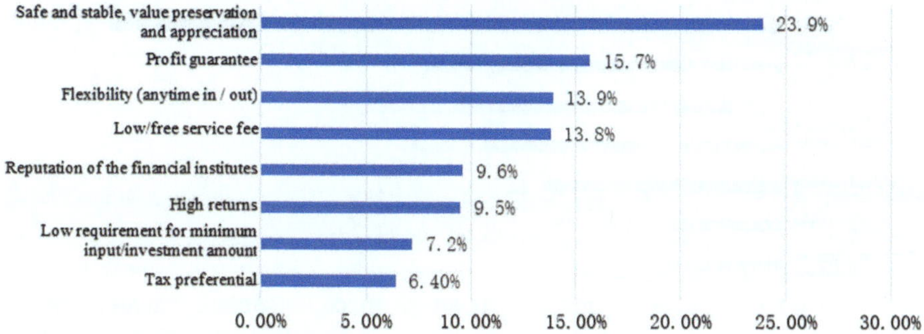

Fig. 9 Factors affecting retirement investment/wealth management decisions

2.2.5 Factors Affecting Retirement Investment/Wealth Management

In order to gain a better understanding of the demand for products designed to finance old age care, the survey asks respondents about "factors that affect your decision on retirement investment/wealth management".

According to the results of the survey, as shown in Fig. 9, the most important factors in the retirement investment/wealth management decisions are security, stability and investment returns. In addition, there is a clear guarantee of profit, flexibility (anytime in/out) and credibility of financial institutions. These are all important factors affecting the respondents' decisions.

2.2.6 Access to Retirement Investment/Wealth Management Products

Before people choose retirement investment/wealth management products, they usually try to understand the corresponding products through different channels. Knowing these channels can provide reference for the financial institutions in promoting and launching their related products.

The survey shows that the bank is still the primary channel for the respondents to obtain information of retirement investment/wealth management products, accounting for 31.5%, followed by the recommendation from family and friends, network (information shared by online wealth management communities or pushed via mobile phone, etc.), insurance companies and fund companies, as shown in Fig. 10. This suggests that under the background of a gradual diversified financial market, the respondents also have more extensive channels in choosing products designed to finance old age care.

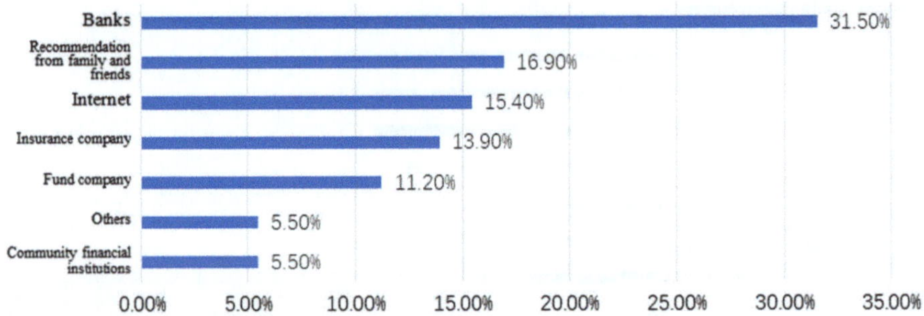

Fig. 10 The channels from which the respondents receive information about the retirement investment/wealth management products

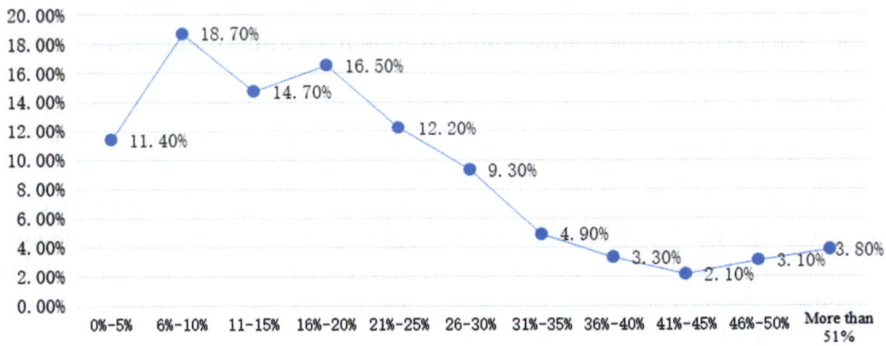

Fig. 11 The amount of income set aside for financing old age care

2.3 *Willingness to Engage in Banking Activities Aimed at Financing Old Age Care and Level of Participation*

2.3.1 The Portion of Income Set Aside for Financing Old Age Care

How much the respondents are willing to set their income aside for wealth management products designed to finance old age care, to some extent, reflects their readiness and actual participation in the banking activities in this regard.

The survey shows that more than 61.3% of the respondents are willing to put aside less than 20% of their income toward wealth management products used specifically to finance old age care; among them, 11.4% are only willing to put aside less than 5% of their income for that purpose, and 18.7% are willing to put aside 6–10% of their income for the same. Less than 40% (38.7%) of the respondents are willing to spend more than 20% of their income on financing old age care, as shown in Fig. 11.

In terms of the share of personal income used for wealth management products designed to finance old age care, the mean of the respondents' ideal proportion is 16.63%, with a median of 13%. The overall distribution is more concentrated on the

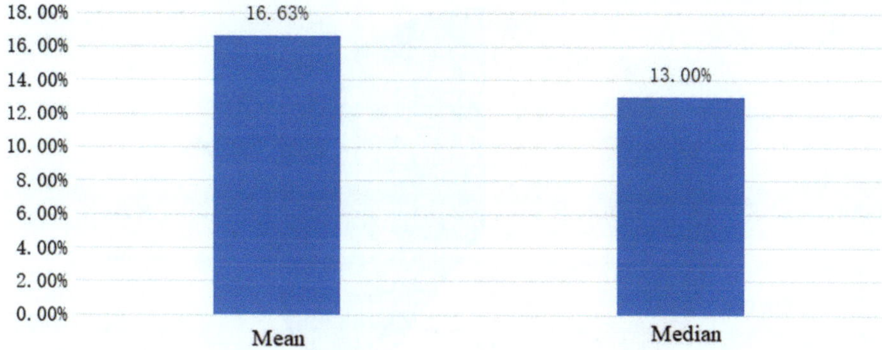

Fig. 12 Mean and median of amount of income to be spent on wealth management products designed to finance old age care

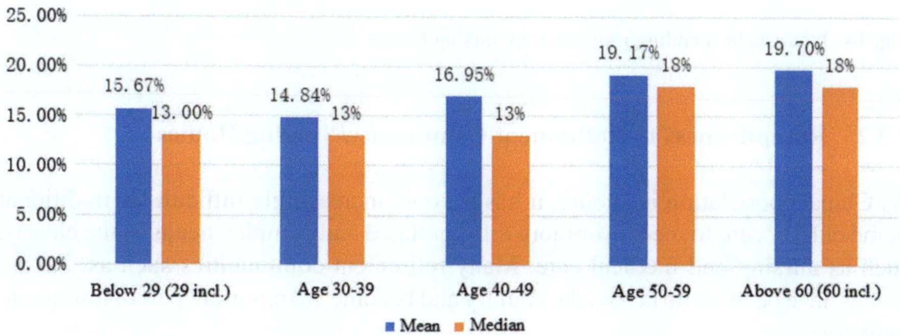

Fig. 13 Mean and median of the share of retirement savings in total income among different age groups

left rather than a normal curve. Therefore, the median is more representative. The respondents mainly agree to spend about 13% of income on wealth management products designed to finance old age care, as shown in Fig. 12.

A further analysis on the mean and median of the income share spent on wealth management products designed to finance old age care among different age groups shows that the share is higher among the group aged above 50 (50 incl.) than the group aged below 49 (49 incl.), as shown in Fig. 13. On the one hand, the former group may spend less on housing and children's education and could afford such expenditure. On the other hand, it is likely that some of these groups are about to enter or have already entered old age, and have stronger sense about the living standard after retirement. Thus, they are willing to invest a greater portion of their income on wealth management products designed to finance old age care.

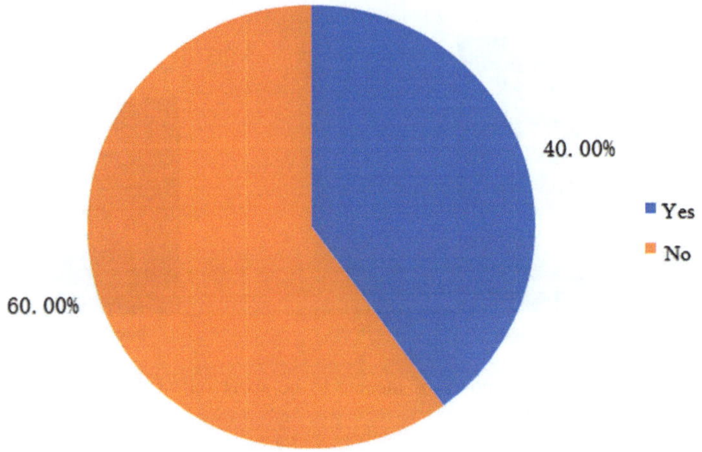

Fig. 14 Interests in spending retirement in nursing homes

2.3.2 Receptiveness to Retirement Community/Nursing Homes

As China's population is ageing, it has become increasingly difficult for traditional home elderly care to meet ever more differentiated and complex needs of the elderly, such as nursing and medical care. Many retirement communities such as nursing homes have been set up across the country and become an important part of retirement industry.

According to the data, 40.0% of the respondents indicated that they are willing to spend their future retirement at the nursing homes, as shown in Fig. 14. This suggests that to some extent, the Chinese have a relatively positive understanding of the community-based retirement and old age care.

From the demographic characteristics, as the age increases, the interest to choose nursing homes for retirement displays an inverted-U trend. The younger groups don't show a mild interest in the nursing homes. The middle-aged populations (40–49 years old), who are the "sandwich generation" as they are responsible for bringing up their own children and for the care of their ageing parents, show a stronger interest. With the further advance in age, the interest declines (see Fig. 15).

Overall, those respondents with higher education are more receptive of elderly care at nursing homes. This indicates that to some extent, the higher level of education better prepares the respondents to accept the modernized retirement living. See Fig. 16.

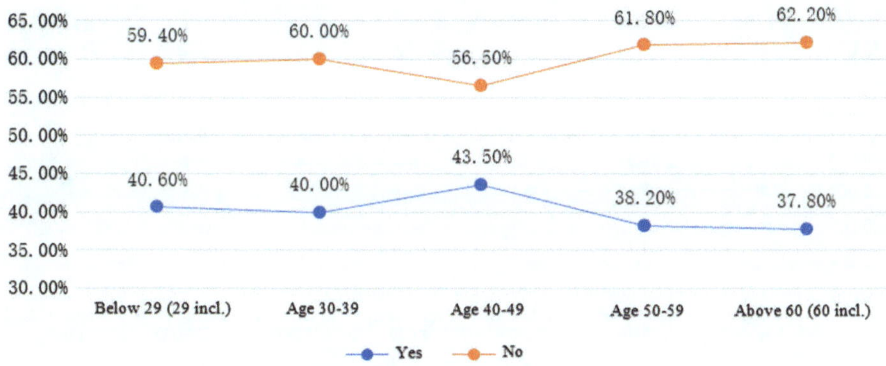

Fig. 15 Different age groups and their interests in spending retirement in nursing homes

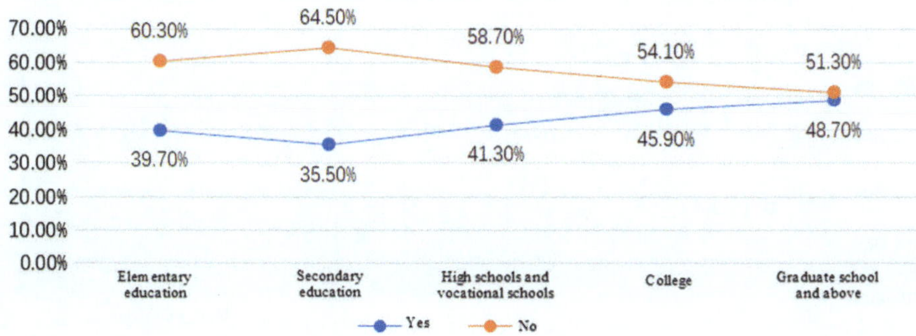

Fig. 16 Groups of different educational background and their interest in spending retirement life in nursing homes

In terms of income, the general trend is that the higher the income level, the higher the respondents' receptiveness to the idea of living in nursing homes, as shown in Fig. 17. This suggests that the cost is an important factor in this decision. However, those who have a monthly income of over RMB 15,001 show diminishing interest in this option. This may be because they are more financially capable to stay with family at home, such as better housing arrangement and in-home care assistance.

For the perceived reasonable cost for nursing home, nearly half (47.4%) of the respondents are willing to pay no more than RMB 2000 per month; 18.4% are willing to pay RMB 1000 per month; 23.5% are willing to pay a monthly fee of RMB 2001–3000; only 29.1% of the respondents are willing to pay more than RMB 3000 per month. See Fig. 18.

For the population currently above the age of 60, different levels of pensions is a major factor in determining the acceptable costs to pay for the nursing homes. The data show that the lower the level of pension benefits, the lower the amount that people are willing to pay for retirement at nursing homes; the higher the level of pension benefits, the higher the amount people are willingness to pay. See Table 4.

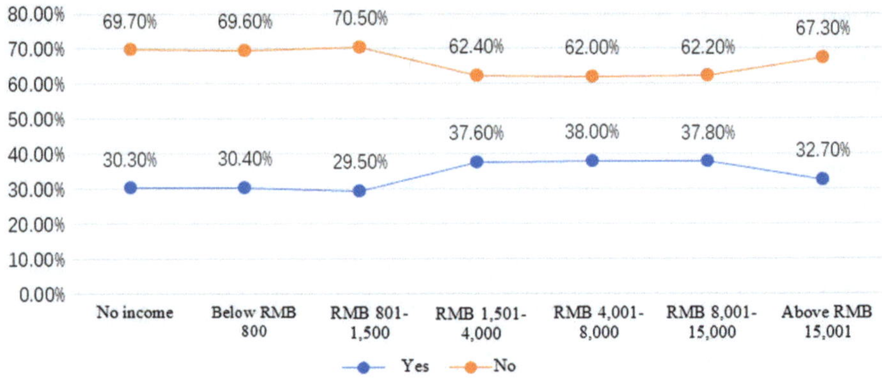

Fig. 17 Different income groups and their interests in spending retirement life in nursing homes

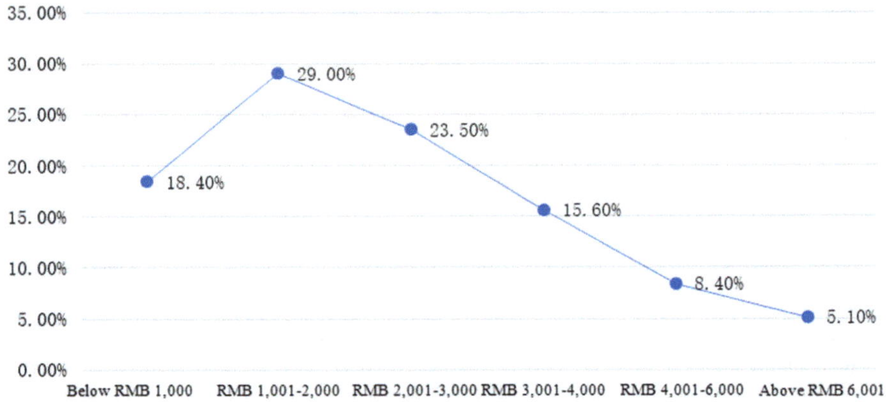

Fig. 18 Acceptable fees for nursing homes among respondents

Table 4 Different pension plans and the acceptable nursing home costs for people aged 60 and above

Pension (RMB)	Acceptable costs (RMB)					
	Below 1000	1001–2000	2001–3000	3001–4000	4001–6000	Above 6001
Below 800	29.8%	36.2%	19.6%	8.4%	3.6%	2.5%
800-1500	5.9%	37.5%	30.1%	14.0%	10.3%	2.2%
1500-3000	4.6%	25.8%	39.4%	16.2%	6.3%	7.6%
3000-5000	2.6%	23.3%	22.8%	29.1%	18.0%	4.2%
Above 5000	0.0%	2.3%	18.6%	18.6%	20.9%	39.5%

Fig. 19 The respondents' experience with financial fraud

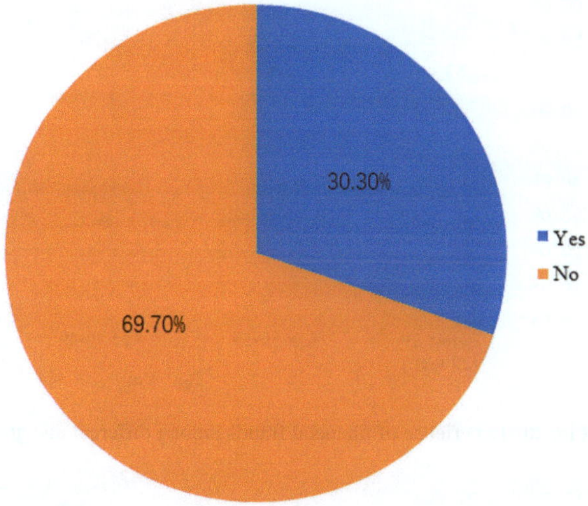

2.4 *Victimization in the Financial Frauds and Scams*

2.4.1 Prevalence of Financial Frauds

With the gradual development of financial industry, China sees rapid growth of criminal activities in the financial sector. Financial fraud and scams have become one of the most damaging economic crimes.

According to the survey, 30.3% of respondents have experienced financial fraudulence, and 69.7% of the respondents have no such experience, as shown in Fig. 19. In terms of age, the proportion of respondents experiencing financial fraud decrease as the age declined, but the share increases to 26.1% among those aged 60 and above (see Fig. 20). The reason is possibly that people of this age group are more vulnerable to the ongoing and modern financial crimes as they are gradually distant from social development and lack financial education.

2.4.2 Respondents' Monetary Loss in Financial Frauds

About 58.3% of the respondents who experienced financial scams suffer the monetary loss of less than RMB 10,000; 41.7% lost more than RMB 10,000 and 9.2% lost more than RMB 100,000. See Fig. 21.

By the age groups and their victimization in financial frauds, the data show that the young and middle-aged groups under age 49 lost relatively small amount of money in such crimes, mainly less than RMB 10,000. For a monetary loss of more than RMB 10,000, the age group over 50 accounted for a higher percentage than other age groups. In particular, for the loss of more than RMB 100,000, the population over the age of 50 accounted for a higher percentage than other groups. (See Table 5.)

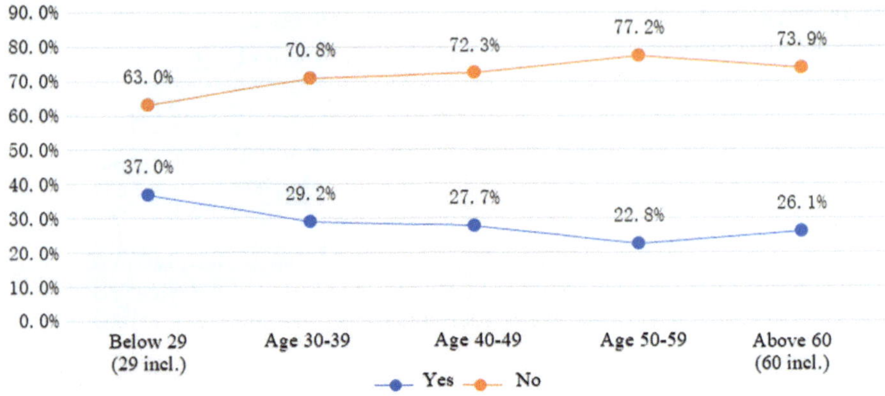

Fig. 20 Experience of financial frauds among different age groups

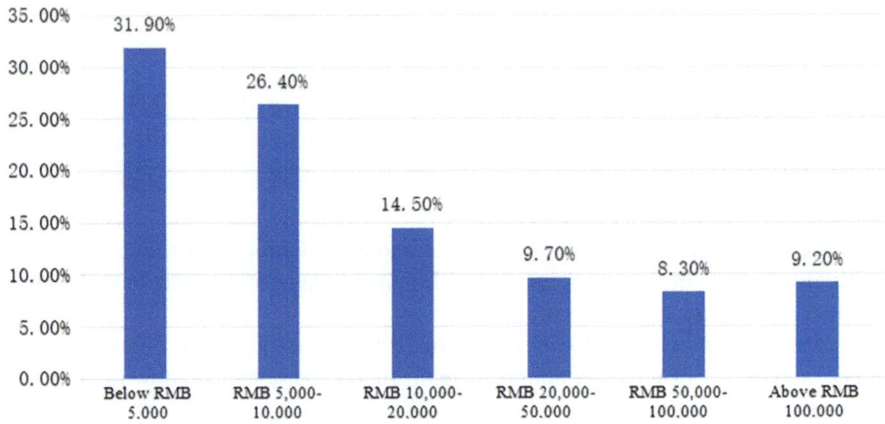

Fig. 21 The amount of money lost in financial frauds

The survey shows that the current criminal activities in the financial sector are very serious. On the one hand, it reflects that there are still many loopholes in the current financial regulations. On the other hand, it reflects the majority of respondents need to raise their awareness financial fraud prevention.

Table 5 Monetary losses in financial frauds among different age groups

	Below 29 (29 incl.) (%)	Age 30–39 (%)	Age 40–49 (%)	Age 50–59 (%)	Above 60 (60 incl.) (%)
Below RMB 5000	44.6	41.1	37.2	27.1	32.4
RMB 5000-10,000	24.0	28.8	28.3	27.3	22.6
RMB 10,000-20,000	12.0	11.3	12.2	14.3	18.8
RMB 20,000-50,000	7.9	8.3	7.6	10.4	9.6
RMB 50,000-100,000	5.7	5.7	6.8	10.0	7.1
Above 100,000	5.9	4.8	7.9	10.9	9.5

2.5 *Summary*

2.5.1 Awareness of Retirement Savings Developed, yet Savings Insufficient for Retirement

According to the results of the survey, most of the respondents have already had the awareness of early retirement savings; more than 60% of the respondents think that retirement savings should begin before the age of 40 instead of right before the retirement. At the same time, we found that, at present, only 16.2% of the respondents reach the expected savings to meet the needs in their own retirement. This suggests that at present the actual retirement savings are not enough in China, and there is still much room for the development of financial market for old age care.

2.5.2 Investment Diversified for Old Age Care, Traditional Financial Management Still Dominant

With the gradually improved financial market, China has seen ever-innovative and diversified financial products for old age care. The respondents' choices suggest that the traditional financial management is still the mainstay of retirement savings; saving accounts or wealth management products offered by banks account for nearly one third of the market. Products, stocks and funds from for-profit insurance have also become an important vehicle for the pension management. It is foreseeable that with the gradual development of market for financing old age care, the diversified retirement saving plans will also be favored by most Chinese people.

2.5.3 Investing More Wisely for Retirement, Safe and Sound Financial Products Preferred

The factors that influence financial product selection somehow reflect investors' risk assessment. According to the survey, the major factors in selecting investment in/wealth management for old age care are the safety, stability and value-added. In addition, there is a clear guarantee of profit, flexibility (anytime in/out) and credibility of financial institutions. These are all important factors when the respondents make decision for investment in/wealth management for old age care. However, the high-yield is not the most important factor for the majority of people when making investment in financing old age care, indicating that the majority of investors are relatively conservative and prudent in investment, instead of blindly pursuing high returns.

2.5.4 Showing Interest in Care Facilities, Willingness to Pay Remained Low

With the growing ageing population, the traditional elderly care supported by individual family gradually weakens. Against this background, nursing homes and other care facilities have gradually developed. According to the survey data, 40% of the respondents, in particular those with a higher education level and with higher incomes, are open to the idea of living at nursing homes and other care facilities after retirement. However, in terms of acceptable cost, nearly half of the respondents are willing to pay less than RMB 2000 per month. This level of payment may compromise the quality of care services, which, to a certain extent, will affect the final decisions of retirees.

2.5.5 Diverse Access to Wealth Management, and Measures Needed to Prevent Financial Frauds

Overall, the respondents have diversified channels to access to investment/wealth management products designed to finance old age care. Banks, Internet, friends and family, insurance companies and fund companies are important channels for them to obtain such investment/wealth management products. 95.5% of the respondents are currently (or plan to be) engaged in investment/wealth management products designed to finance old age care through different ways, reflecting the strong interest in financial management for retirement. However, it is noteworthy that 30.3% of the respondents have experienced financial frauds, either in wealth management products designed to finance old age care or other financial activities. Some of them even suffer great loss in such crimes. It serves as a good reminder to prevent such risks.

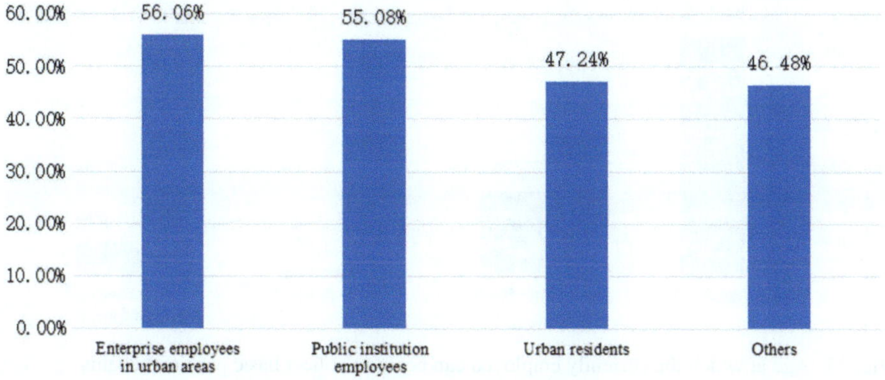

Fig. 22 Employees' Expected Replacement Rate for Old Age Insurance

3 The State of Participation in Old Age Insurance and Overall Awareness

3.1 Participation of Current Employees in Old Age Insurance and Their Expected Pension Benefits

3.1.1 Current Employees' Expected Replacement Ratio of Their Old Age Insurance

In order to understand the respondents' expectation on the pension benefits after retirement, the research team develops the question "What is your expected replacement ratio of old age insurance to your salary before retirement?"

According to the survey, the expected replacement ratio from the old age insurance is higher among the employees who work for enterprises and the public institutions in urban areas, at 56.6 and 55.08%, respectively, as shown in Fig. 22. This expected replacement ratio falls within the target replacement ratio of 59.2% but higher than the actual ratio of 45% in China. At the same time, the expected replacement ratio is slightly above the international warning line of 40–50%, but far away from the internationally accepted replacement ratio of 70–80%, which is considered enough to maintain the same living standard after retirement.

3.1.2 Age at Which the Currently Employed Can Start to Collect Basic Pension Benefits

The eligible age for receiving basic pension benefits refers to the age at which retirees can start collecting pension benefit. The study on the expected value of such an age can shed light on the respondents' specific views on policies related to old age

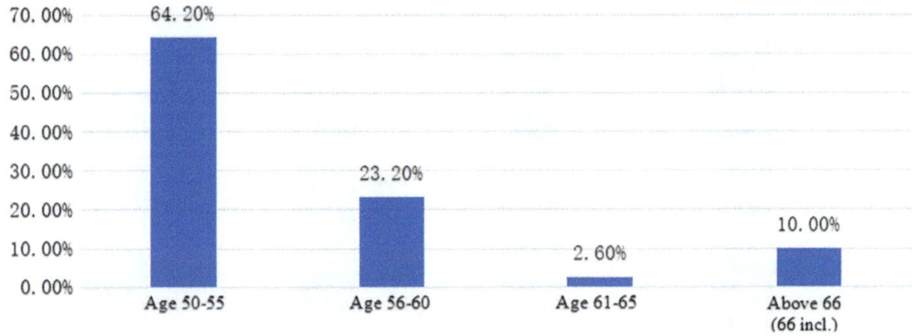

Fig. 23 Age at which the currently employed can begin to collect basic pension benefits

insurance and deferred retirement. Data show that currently nearly 90% (87.4%) of the respondents hope to receive pension benefit before age 60. More than 12.6% of the respondents are also willing to start receiving pensions at the age of 60 and beyond (See Fig. 23).

3.2 Personal Tax-Deferred Pension Plan: Interest in Participation and Preferred Investment

The personal tax-deferred pension plan is the third pillar of the pension system, following the basic old age insurance system (pillar 1) and occupational pensions (pillar 2). It is an important part of a sound pension system. It features a fully accumulated system model: a private, voluntary pension scheme supported by state tax incentives and independent from employers.

3.2.1 The Incentive to Participate in the Personal Tax-Deferred Pension Plans

In the 20th century, China proposed to study and launch the third pillar personal tax-deferred pension policy, which was further specified during the Third Plenary Session of the 18th Central Committee of the Communist Party of China. The National Thirteenth Five-Year Plan also put forth the "development of personal tax-deferred pension insurance." However, the specific policy has not been introduced yet. On the whole, the policy makers have already given prominence to the third pillar of personal tax-deferred pension system. A study on the incentive to participate in such pension plan can shed lights on the respondents' perceptions and acceptance of the scheme and provide reference for the policy makers in advancing the third pillar plan.

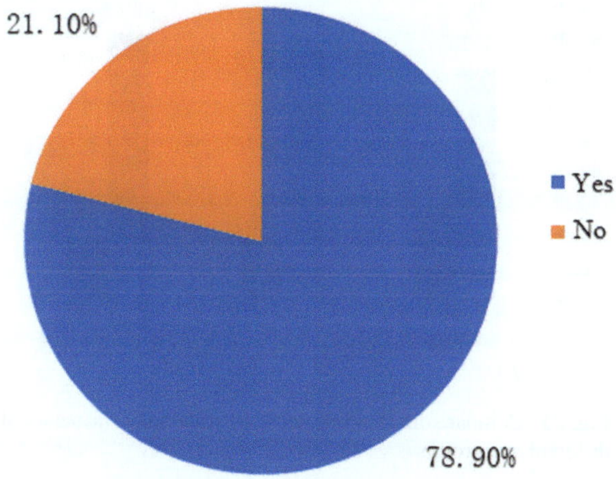

Fig. 24 Responses to the third pillar pension plan

The task force designed the question "If China establishes a voluntary personal pension account system, which allows you to make a reasonable contribution from your pre-tax income to this account, but the fund will become available after your retirement. Will you be interested in participating?" The survey shows that nearly 80% (78.9%) of the respondents are for the personal tax-deferred pension plan, only 21.1% of the respondents indicate otherwise, as shown in Fig. 24.

In terms of age groups, the interest to participate in personal tax-deferred pension plans marks an inverted U shape. The middle age group (30–49 years old) shows stronger incentive than those groups who are under 29 (29 incl.) and over 50 of age. This may be because the majority of people under the age of 29 are mostly in the early stage of their career, when their incomes are too low to afford or consider participating in the third pillar pension plan. Most of the people after 50 already have had a retirement plan and expressed slightly lower interest in participating in the plan (see Fig. 25).

Considering different levels of education, those who with higher levels of education show stronger interest in the third-pillar personal tax-deferred pension plans (see Fig. 26). This may be because those who receive more education are relatively more aware of the importance of retirement savings. It may also be because these people with higher education have higher income and can allocate a higher proportion of their income for retirement savings. Coupled with the tax incentives, they are obviously more motivated to join the plan.

In terms of income, the interest in participating in personal tax-deferred pension plans marks an inverted U shape, as shown in Fig. 27. The middle-and high-income groups show significantly higher interest in participating in the third pillars of pension insurance than the group with a monthly income less than RMB 1500 and high-

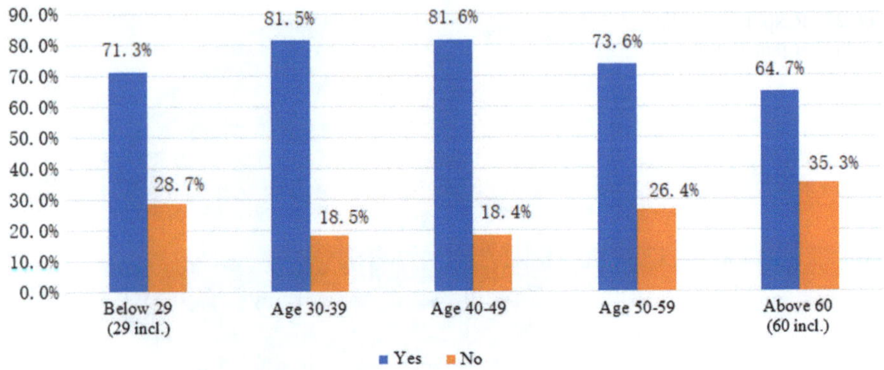

Fig. 25 Comparison of willingness to participate in personal tax-deferred pension plan among different age groups

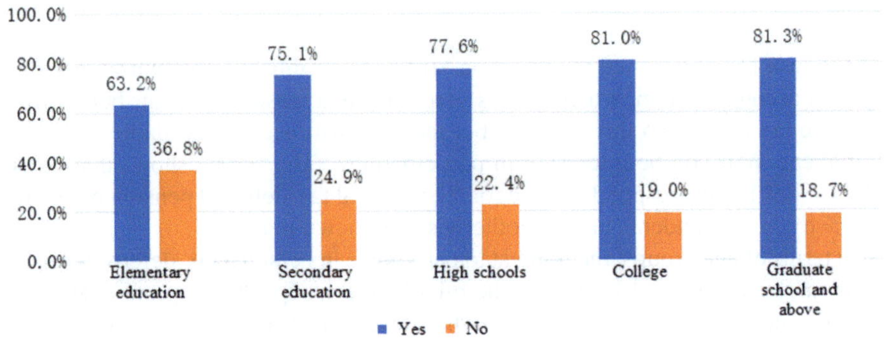

Fig. 26 Comparison of willingness to participate in personal tax-deferred pension plan among population with different educational backgrounds

income groups (with a monthly income over RMB 15,001). This may be because the low-income groups have limited capacity to participate in the third pillar pension plan, while the high-income groups are able to independently handle their retirement savings through diverse channels.

3.2.2 The Voluntary Contribution for the Third Pillar Personal Tax-Deferred Pension Plan

A survey on the voluntary contribution for personal pension plans can shed light on the willingness of people to participate in the third pillar plan and thus provide data support for the system planning.

According to the survey, more than 90% of the respondents (90.6%) are willing to contribute no more than RMB 1000 to the personal tax-deferred pension account per month; among them, 68.4% are willing to set aside less than RMB 500 per month,

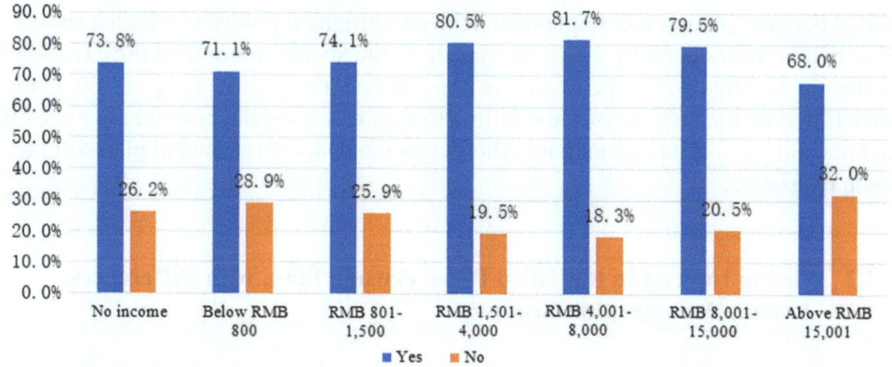

Fig. 27 Comparison of interest in the third pillar pension plan among different income groups

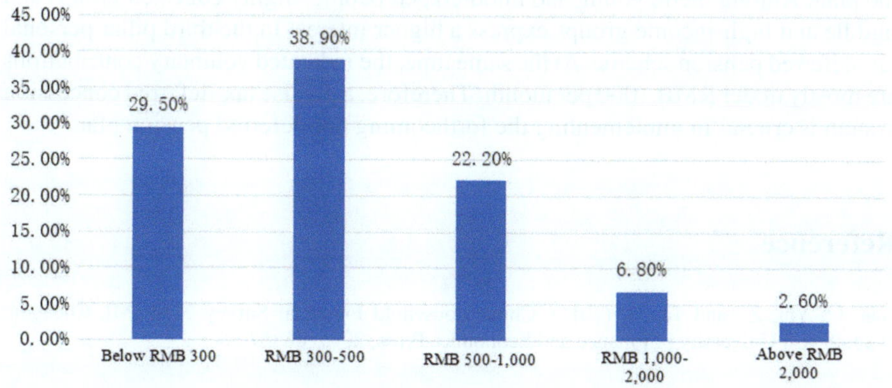

Fig. 28 Willingness to participate in the third pillar pension plan

and 29.5% intend to contribute RMB 300 monthly. Only 9.4% of the respondents are willing to contribute more than RMB 1000 per month to the third pillar personal tax pension (see Fig. 28).

3.3 Conclusion

3.3.1 People Hope to Receive Basic Pension at a Younger Age and Delayed Retirement Policy Faces Resistance

In recent years, with the population ageing, China encounters rapidly increasing pressure on the income and expenditure of the pension system. In addition to other factors, the delayed retirement has become a key issue that stirs up many discussions in academic and political circles. According to Ministry of Human Resources and

Social Security, China will implement delayed retirement policy, to which a specific plan will be introduced by 2020. According to the survey, more than 90% (87.4%) of the respondents now hope to receive pension benefits before the age of 60, while only 12.6% of the respondents are willing to start receiving the pension after age 60 and beyond. To a certain extent, this shows that the delayed retirement plan will face some resistance.

3.3.2 Strong Interest in the Third Pillar Pension Plan, with Differences Among Demographic Groups

The survey shows that respondents express a strong interest in the third pillar tax-deferred pension plan. Nearly 80% of the respondents are willing to participate in the plan. Among them, young and middle-aged people, highly educated groups and middle and high-income groups express a higher interest in the third pillar personal tax-deferred pension scheme. At the same time, the indicated voluntary contributions are mostly under RMB 1000 per month. Therefore, a precise tax-deferred concession system is crucial in implementing the forthcoming tax-deferred pension plan.

Reference

Gan, L., Yin, Z., and Tan, J. (2015). China Household Financial Survey 2014 [M]. Chengdu: Southwest University of Finance and Economics Press, 2015: 66–67.

Keyong Dong, Professor and doctoral advisor at Renmin University of China, and Secretary-General of China Ageing Finance Forum (CAFF50). He has been granted a special allowance by the State Council, and used to be Dean of School of Labor and Human Resources and School of Public Administration at Renmin University of China, and Secretary-General of National MPA Education Steering Committee, specializing in pension policy and finance for old age.

Li Gan, Professor at Department of Economics, Texas A&M University, USA; Senior Researcher at the National Bureau of Economic Research (NBER) of USA; Dean at Economics and Management Institute, Southwest University of Finance and Economics; Director of Survey and Research Center for China Household Finance; Guest Lecturer of Changjiang Scholars Program of Ministry of Education, Distinguished Specialist of the "Thousand Talents Program" the "2016 Sun Yefang Financial Innovation Award" recipient. He is mainly dedicated to research on microeconomics.

Chapter 3
Macroeconomic Effects and Policy Challenges of Population Ageing in China

Yudong Yao and Haiming Tan

Abstract With the gradual ageing of population, reduced labor force and savings, China's economic growth will significantly slow down and trigger a series of problems such as falling real estate prices, old age and health care endowment deficit, which all call for preventive measures and in-depth analysis. Based on the systematical analysis of the domestic and global trend, this study explores the impact of ageing population macro-economy in China by comparing with Japan and other countries. A series of measures are proposed, including to increase the total fertility rate, guide the population flow with new urbanization, promote "excellent leverage" rather than simple "deleverageing", encourage innovation, support "intellectual capital" and more humanitarian care for the elderly to meet the challenges posed by an ageing society.

Keywords Population ageing · Macro economy · Business cycle · Adaptive strategies

Population and technology are decisive forces in the economic cycle. Compared to scientific and technological advances, changes in the population are easier to predict and their longer-term economic impact is more easily quantified. The economic "long-swing" theory, put forward by Nobel Prize laureate Simon Kuznets in 1971, connected the great prosperity with the big population boom in the United States in the late 19th century. Paul Krugman, the 2008 Nobel laureate, employs an municipal hierarchy model to accurately deduce a city's development caused by population flow.

China has the largest population in the world. The ageing population and urbanization will be a major issue both domestically and globally in the coming decades. According to the United Nations Population Division (UNPD), China will have 34% of its total population over the age of sixty in 2050, higher than the global average by 12 percentage points and reaching the same level of population ageing as

Y. Yao
Dacheng Fund, Beijing, China

H. Tan (✉)
People's Bank of China, Beijing, China

K. Dong and Y. Yao (eds.), *Annual Report on Financing Old Age Care in China (2017)*, https://doi.org/10.1007/978-981-13-0968-7_3

the developed countries in Western Europe. With the gradual ageing population, the diminishing labor force and savings rate, China's economic growth will significantly decline in the future and trigger a series of problems such as the drop in real estate prices and deficits in pension and health care fund. If stimulated from the demand side, the aggregate leverage ratio will continue to rise and thus increase financial risks. Faced with the foreseeable problems, we should take precautions and find solutions with in-depth analyses.

1 Global and Domestic Trends in Population Ageing

1.1 Population Ageing: A Global Trend

The declining birth rate and extended life expectancy are direct causes of increasing population ageing around the world. In the 1950s, people aged sixty and over accounted for only 8% of the world's total population. By 2015, this proportion has risen to 12.3% and is expected to reach 21.5% in 2050. Globally, the population aged sixty and over is expected to double, from 900 million in 2015 to 2.1 billion in 2050. By that time, the elderly population will exceed the population under the age of fifteen.

Among all continents, Africa will boast the world's youngest population in thirty-five years and Europe will have the oldest population. South America and Asia currently have a relatively younger population, but their ageing rate is faster than that in Europe and North America. The main reason why population in underdeveloped African, South American and Asian population remain relatively young is that these continents enjoy higher birth rates and lower life expectancy, which is particularly true in Africa, as shown in Fig. 1.

According to the prediction of the United Nations Population Division (UNPD), although Africa's population is less than one quarter and less than one half of Asia's population in 2015 and 2050, respectively, the number will be almost the same as the Asian's in 2100, as shown in Fig. 2.

Among major countries, Nigeria will have the world's youngest population in the next thirty-five years and Japan will remain the oldest. India and China currently have a relatively younger population. However, the Chinese population is now rapidly ageing and India will see accelerated population ageing after 2040, as shown in Fig. 3.

In terms of population size, India, China, the United States and Nigeria will be the four most populous countries in the world. Among them, India will have a population of 1.42 billion in 2022, surpassing China; then it will reach 1.71 billion by 2050, 1.26 times of China's population; India will still have 1.66 billion in 2100, while China will have only one billion. In 2015, Nigeria will have a population of 180 million, 56% of the US population; but in 2049, Nigeria's population will reach 390 million, surpassing that of the United States; and then in 2100, Nigeria will have 750 million while the United States will have only 450 million, as shown in Fig. 4.

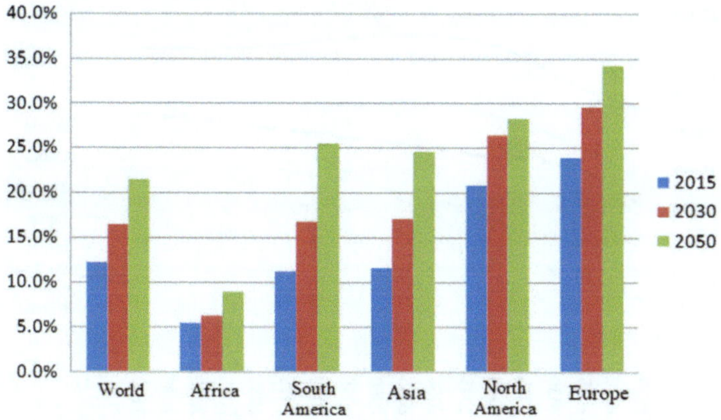

Fig. 1 Projected share of the persons aged sixty and above of the total population by regions [*Data Source* UN (2015)]

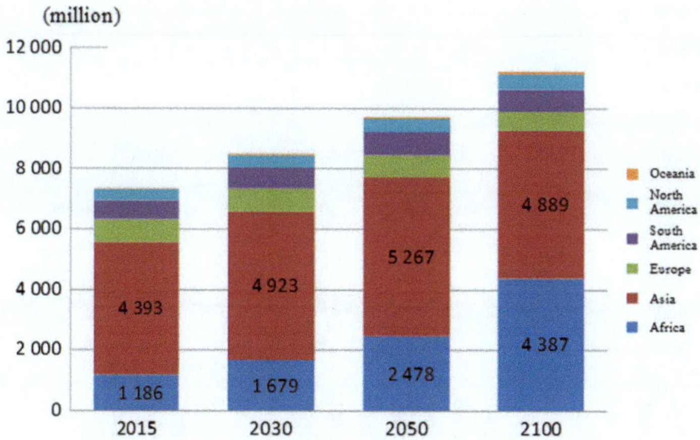

Fig. 2 Projected population by region [*Data Source* UN (2015)]

China leads the way in population ageing globally as the whole world enters into an ageing society. In terms of median age, in 2015, India was twenty-seven, China thirty-seven, the United States thirty-eight, Japan forty-six and the world's average was 29.6; in 2020, India will be twenty-eight, China 38.7, the United States 38.6, Japan 48.3; in 2050, India will be thirty-seven, China 49.6, the United States 41.5, Japan 53.3 and the world's average 36.1. In terms of the proportion of the 60-year-old and above in the total population, in 2015, the number is 15.2% in China, 4.5% in Nigeria, 8.9% in India, 20.7% in the United States and 33.1% in Japan; China will reach 29%, surpassing the United States, in 2035 and 36.5%, surpassing Europe in 2050, as shown in Fig. 5.

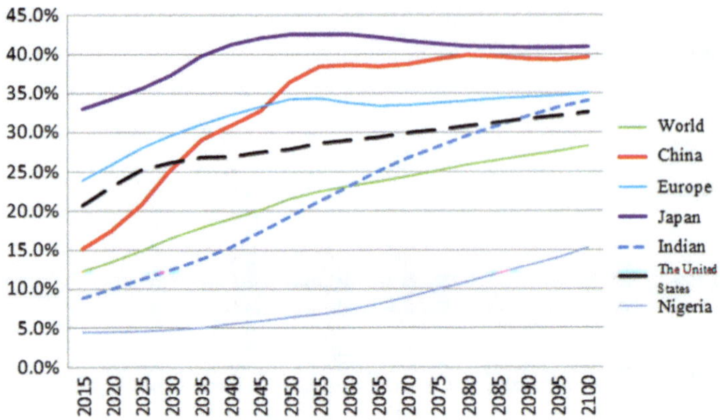

Fig. 3 Distribution of older population aged sixty and above (percentage) by major countries [*Source* UN (2015)]

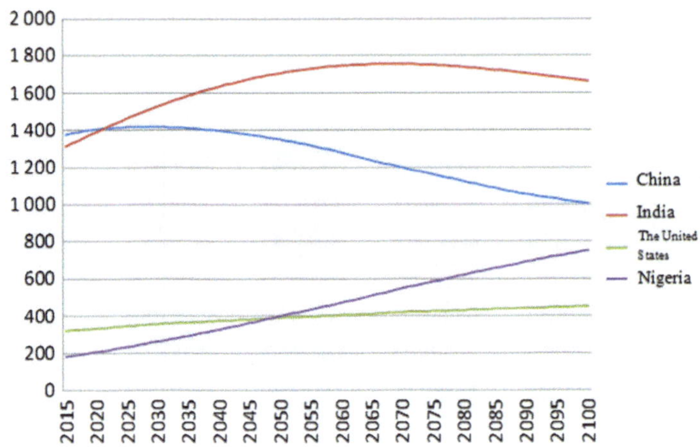

Fig. 4 Projected population growth of the most populous countries in the world [*Data Source* UN (2015)]

1.2 China's Ageing Population

In order to predict the impact of population ageing on China's economy, China Ageing Finance Forum has established a general equilibrium model to study the long term Chinese population growth (hereinafter referred to as COACFF50 macroeconomic model). Based on the data from the Sixth National Census in 2010, the model divides the nation into five tiers of geographic regions,[1] including the first-, second-,

[1](1) Tier-1 cities include Beijing, Tianjin, Shanghai, Guangzhou and Shenzhen. (2) Tier 2 cities, including provincial capital cities other than Tier 1 cities and the four cities at sub-provincial level directly administrated by the State Council. (3) Small and medium-sized cities: other cities than the

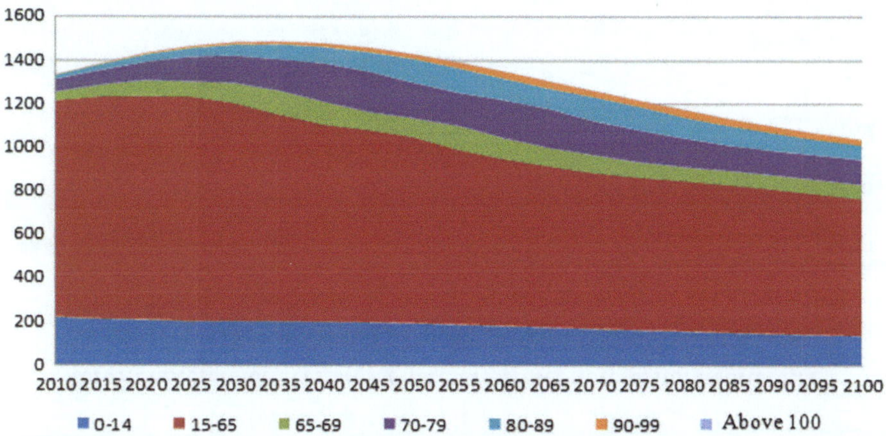

Fig. 5 Population of various age groups in China (*unit* million) (*Data Source* UN (2015), author's computation)

third-, and fourth-tier cities, and rural areas. Such variables as fertility rate, population migration, leverage ratio, economic growth, and house prices, are simulated in a unified model. The results show three major characteristics of China's ageing population in the future: rapid ageing rate; more female elders; and more rural elders.

(1) **Rapid Ageing**. China's rapid ageing is mainly caused by the accelerated rate of ageing, as discussed in the previous comparison with other major countries around the world. In 2015, the Chinese aged over sixty-five is 150 million, accounting for 11.6% of the total population. By 2030, the size will reach 280 million, accounting for 20.2%, and will peak at 400 million, accounting for 27.2% of the total population in 2055. During this time frame, the fastest ageing period will occur before 2040 when the population aged over sixty-five will increase by an average of 0.5 percentage points per year, as shown in Fig. 6.

(2) **More Female Elders**. The main reason why there will be more female senior citizens than male is that female life expectancy is greater than that of male. The amount of older men and women are basically the same or a little less among the sixty-five to sixty-nine age groups. However, the women population over the age of seventy is obviously bigger than men, which means the older the age, the greater the share of woman population. See Fig. 7.

(3) **More Rural Elders**. Population in rural areas is ageing mainly due to the continuous outflow of young and middle-age groups. By 2040, the population aged sixty-five and over in rural areas will increase by one percentage point every year, twice the rate of the entire country. If the current trend of population flow stays the same, people over the age of sixty-five will constitute 40% of the rural population,

---

Tier 1 and Tier 2 cities; (4) towns and townships; and (5) rural areas. The definition of townships and rural areas is the same as that of the "Sixth Census."

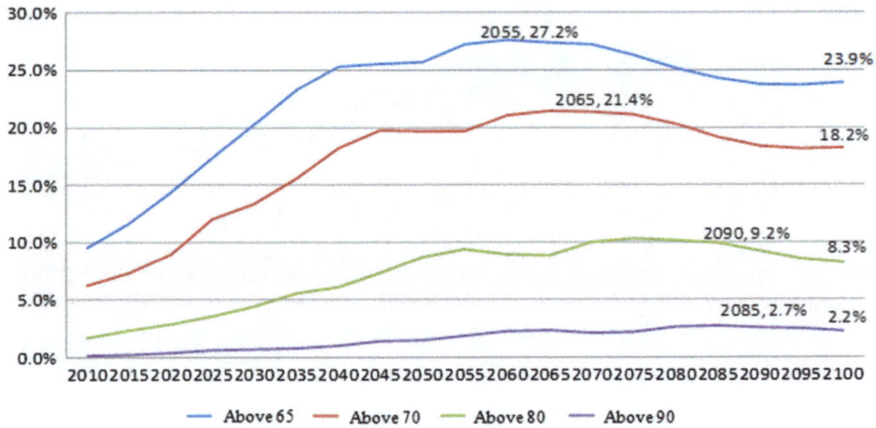

Fig. 6 Rate of ageing in China (*Source* UN (2015), author's computation)

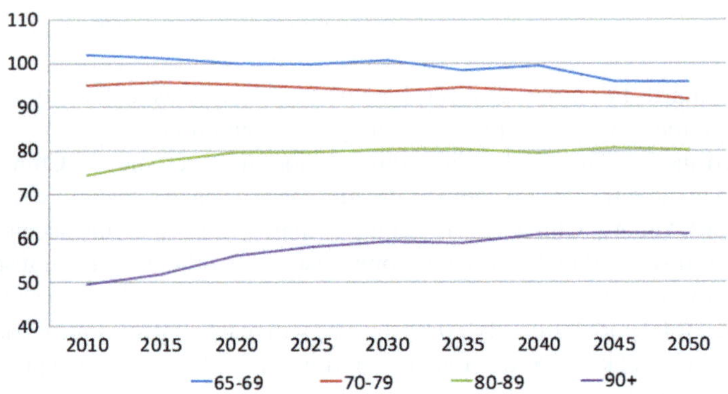

Fig. 7 Sex ratio for different age groups in China (Female = 100) (*Source* UN (2015), author's computation)

which will lead to a huge economic and social problem by 2040. Among all levels of cities, the larger the city, the slower the ageing rate, especially the first-tier cities (Beijing, Shanghai, Guangzhou, Shenzhen and Tianjin) will be relatively young with the people aged sixty-five and above, accounting for 21.9% of the total population in 2040, as shown in Fig. 8.

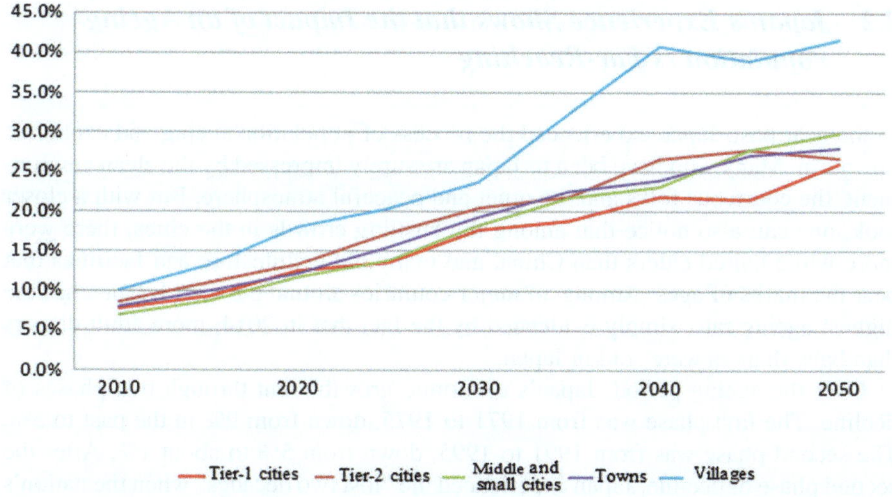

Fig. 8 Rate of ageing by administrative division (65+) (*Source* UN (2015), author's computation)

2 The Macro-economic Impact of Population Ageing

2.1 The Impact of Population Ageing on the Economy: More Harm Than Benefit

The United Nations Population Division study (2015) points out that, on the one hand, ageing population poses financial challenges to the sustainability of pension and healthcare systems. In developing countries, 342 million elderly people didn't have sufficient income in 2009 and by 2050 this figure could rise to 1.2 billion if coverage of pension schemes remains the same. On the other hand, decrease in birth rate will allow women to spend more years to workforce, and families will have more financial resources to invest in health, education and old age care. Thus, population ageing is also, to a certain extent, conducive to economic growth. However, these results would only be possible when concerned institutions adopt effective policies to promote the accumulation of human and establish material capital. The major scholars of population research, such as Cai (2010) and Hu et al. (2012), believe that China's ageing population will slow down the economic growth.

2.2 *Japan's Experience Shows that the Impact of an Ageing Population Is Far-Reaching*

In the near past, Japan experienced the process of population ageing and economic downturn. Many who have been to Japan are surely impressed by the clean environment, the courteous folks and the quiet and peaceful atmosphere. But with a closer look, one can also notice that among the bustling crowds in the cities, there were more white-haired elders than China, and many old architecture and facilities that bear the marks of ages. Among all major countries around the world, Japan has the highest ageing rate, simply evidenced by the fact that in 2014, more adult diapers than baby diapers were sold in Japan.

Over the ageing period, Japan's economic growth went through two phases of decline. The first phase was from 1971 to 1975, down from 9% in the past to 5%. The second phase was from 1991 to 1995, down from 5% to about 1%. After the second phase of decline, Japan experienced the "lost two decades" when the nation's average annual GDP growth rate was only 0.75%, while the price level of the same period was a negative growth of 0.8% per year. As a result, the total GDP of JYP470 trillion in 2011 was JYP 5 trillion lower than that of 1991, as shown in Fig. 9.

In order to salvage the economy, the Japanese government actively adopted stimulus measures such as cutting taxes and increasing investment to stimulate economic growth. With the expansion of fiscal policy, coupled with the increasing pension and healthcare burden, the government debt rose steadily. The ratio of the government debt to GDP was 63% in 1991, up to 148% in 2001 and 225% in 2011. See Fig. 10 for details. Although Japan's corporate sector is de-leverageing and its corporate debt-to-GDP ratio dropped from 147% in 1991 to 119% in 2001 and to 105% in 2011, the aggregate leverage ratio is still on the rise.

After the government's vigorous stimulating efforts, Japan's economy still saw no improvement due to the ageing population. By carefully analyzing Japan's GDP structure, it is found that the decline in corporate equipment investment is the main

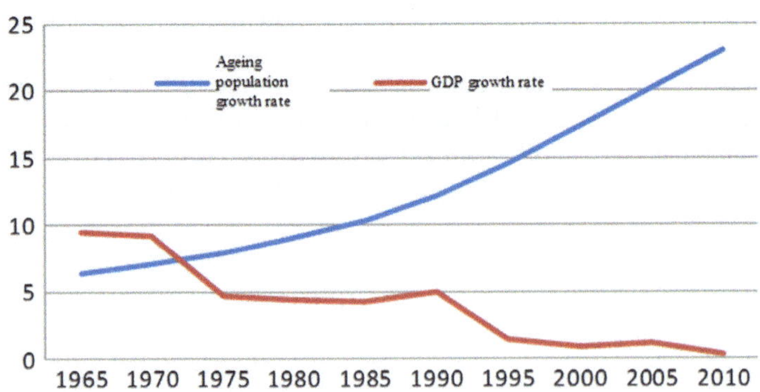

Fig. 9 The decline of economic growth rate with population ageing (%) [*Source* Japan Statistical Yearbook (2013)]

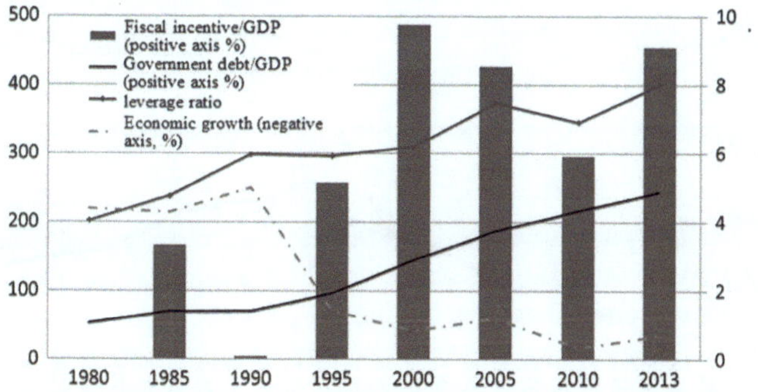

Fig. 10 Fiscal incentives and government debt in Japan [*Source* Japan Statistical Yearbook (2013)]

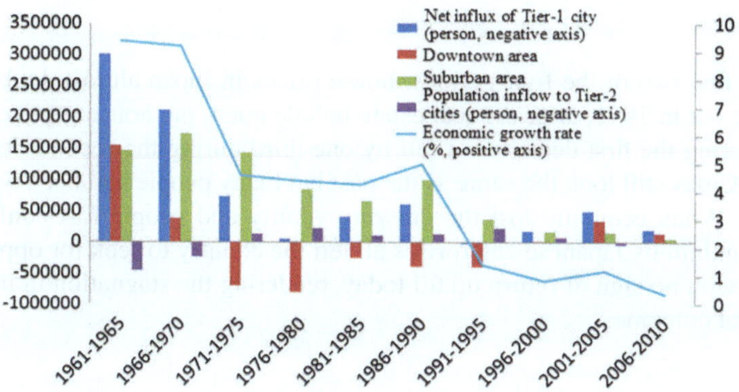

Fig. 11 Population migration and economy growth in Japan [*Source* Japan Statistical Yearbook (2013)]

reason. Japan's capital formation for enterprises equipment accounted for 20% of GDP in 1991 and fell to 14% in 1998, then stayed at that level till today. In terms of investment volume, the capital formation of equipment for enterprises in 2011 was only 70% of that in 1991; in the same period, Japan's private consumption remained stable and its government spending even doubled. Even residential investment, believed to be sluggish, only dropped for two percentage points as a share of GDP in twenty years. Behind the downturn in corporate investment is the declining saving rate caused by an ageing society. In 1991, the savings rate for Japanese residents was 16%, but down to 5% ten years later.

Influenced by population ageing and economic recession, fluctuations were also seen in population migration and house prices. Japan's population flow experienced four major periods after World War II: the population migrated to major metropolitan centers before 1970; from 1970 to 1990, the population of metropolitan areas spread to the suburbs; from 1990 to 1995, people returned to second-tier cities; and afterwards, the population flowed back to big cities again, as shown in Fig. 11.

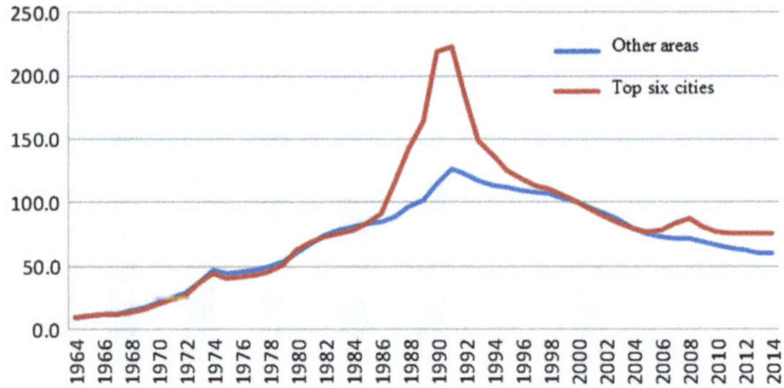

Fig. 12 Japan's real estate index (2000 = 100) [*Source* Japan Statistical Yearbook (2013)]

In the first two of the four periods, house prices in Japan almost doubled every ten years; but in 1991, after the real estate bubble burst, the housing prices was cut in half during the first decade and fell by one third during the second decade (see Fig. 12). Cities still look the same as the past but many people had been worn down by debts. When economy lost the growing vitality and people lost confidence in fortune, ambitious Japanese enterprises all left the country to seek for opportunities overseas with no sign of return up till today, rendering the stagnation in investment is a logical outcome.

2.3 *The Strong Similarities in Population Growth Between China and Japan*

According to the United Nations Population Division (UNPD), Japan is thirty years older and forty years ahead of economic development than China. The present day China resembles the Japan in 1985. The economic depression in Japan in the 1990s serves a good lesson on the economic problems that China may face after achieving the first centennial goal in 2020. The commonality between China and Japan is the ageing population. Moreover, China is ageing more rapidly than Japan, as it takes twenty years for Japan's population aged sixty-five and above to grow from 10% in 1985 to 20% in 2005, while it will only take fifteen years for the same age group in China to grow from 10% in 2014 to 20% by 2029.

Studying the correlation between the working-age population of China and Japan, GDP per capita and housing prices, we can see the patterns as shown in Fig. 5. As shown in Figs. 13, 14, 15, and 16, in the period of similar economic development (1980 in Japan and 2012 in China), both China and Japan show that the higher the per capita GDP, the higher the labor force ratio, and the higher the housing prices, indicating strong correlation.

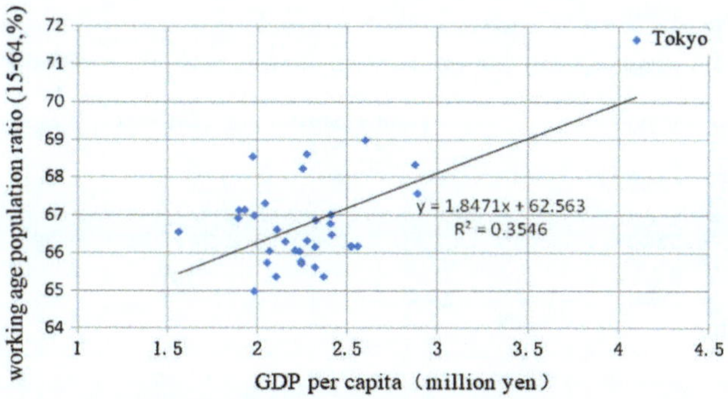

Fig. 13 Correlation between the working-age population and GDP per capita (Japan 1980) [*Data Source* Japan Statistical Yearbook (2013), China Statistical Yearbook (2013)]

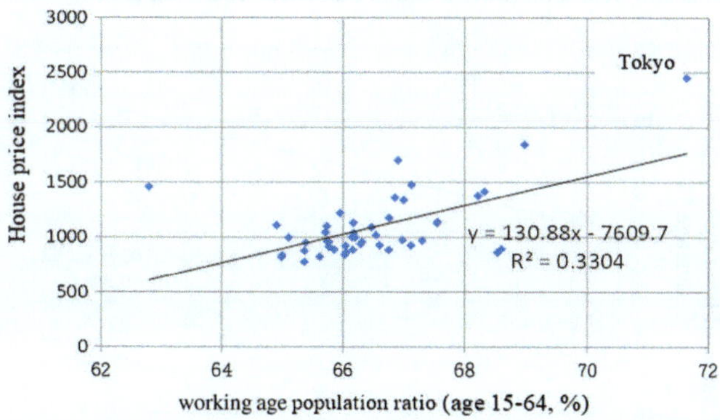

Fig. 14 Correlation between the working-age population and housing prices (Japan 1980) [*Data Source* Japan Statistical Yearbook (2013), China Statistical Yearbook (2013)]

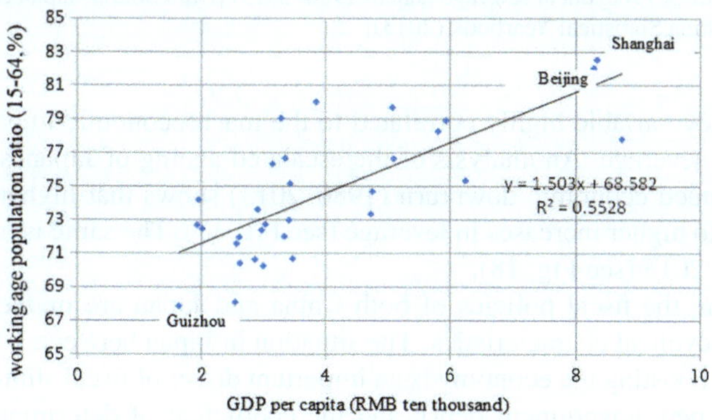

Fig. 15 Correlation between the working-age population and GDP per capita (China 2012) [*Data Source* Japan Statistical Yearbook (2013), China Statistical Yearbook (2013)]

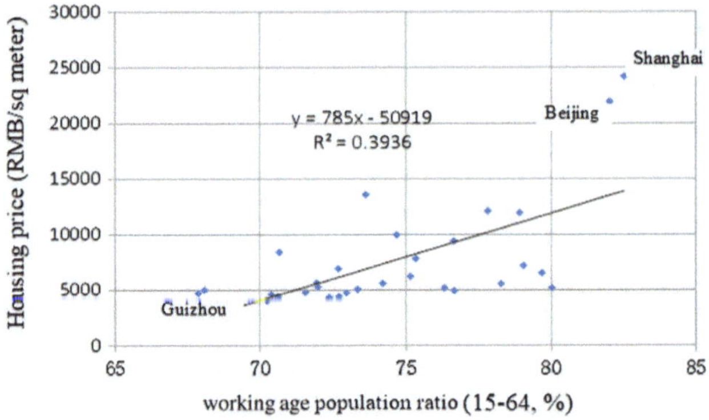

Fig. 16 Correlation between the working-age population and housing prices (China 2012) [*Data Source* Japan Statistical Yearbook (2013), China Statistical Yearbook (2013)]

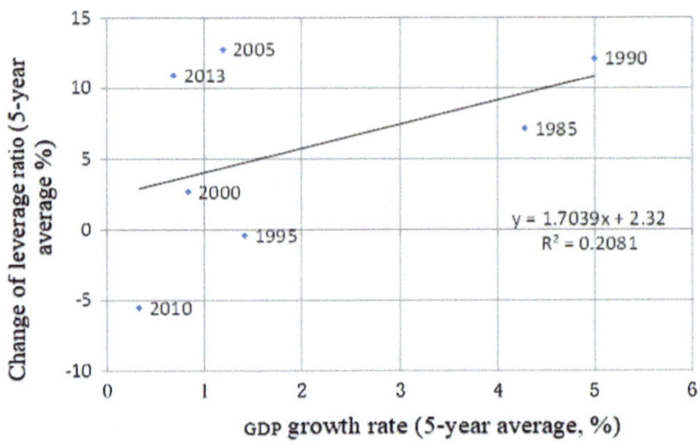

Fig. 17 Changes of Procyclical leverage (Japan 1980–2013) [*Data Source* Japan Statistical Yearbook (2013), China Statistical Yearbook (2013)]

Another key variable highly correlated to the macroeconomic impact of ageing population is leverage. An analysis of the escalated ageing of Japanese population and its continued economic downturn (1980–2013) shows that higher growth rate corresponds to higher increases in leverage (see Fig. 17). The same is true for China from 2000 to 2013 (see Fig. 18).[2]

In addition, the fiscal policies of both China and Japan are marked by prominent counter-cyclical characteristics. The situation in Japan between 1980 and 2013 suggests that boosting the economy is an important driver of fiscal stimulus (as indicated by the new government debt), and the coefficient of determination (R^2) of single regression is as high as 0.74 (see Fig. 19). The situation in China from 2000 to 2013 is quite similar (see Fig. 20).

[2]Due to the large number of data points on Japan, 5-year data are used; since China has fewer data points, annual data is used (but the economic growth rate uses 5-year moving average).

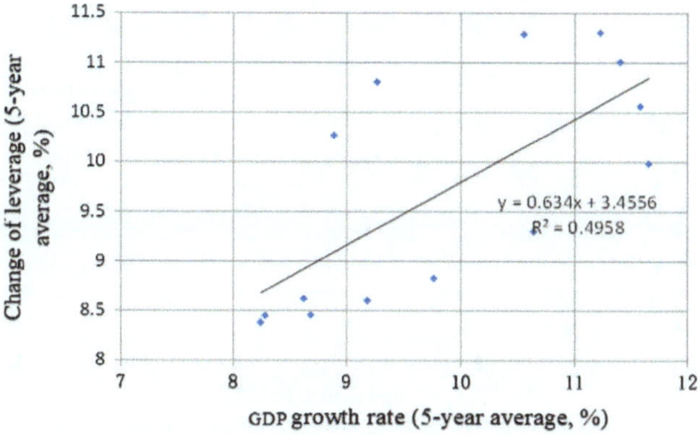

Fig. 18 Changes of Procyclical leverage (China 2000–2013) [*Data Source* Japan Statistical Yearbook (2013), China Statistical Yearbook (2013)]

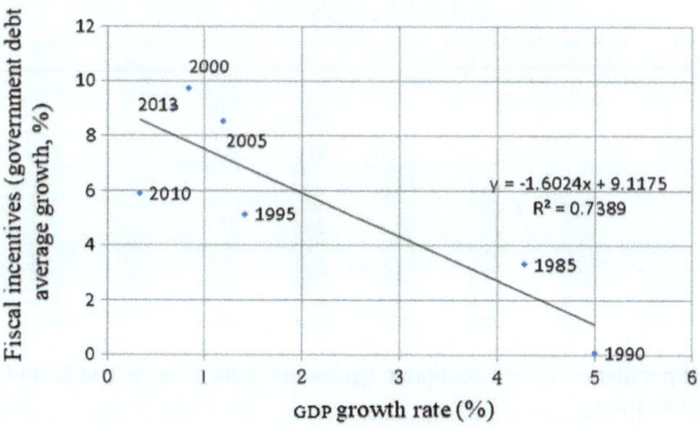

Fig. 19 Countercyclical fiscal policies in Japan (1980–2013) [*Data Source* Japan Statistical Yearbook (2013), China Statistical Yearbook (2013)]

It should be noted that the past three decades are the phase when China sees the full development of demographic dividend. At present, since the proportion of the working population in China just began to decline, the negative impact of population ageing on economic growth remains to be seen (Fig. 21). After synthesizing the patterns of population flow, changes in housing prices and leverage ratio, this paper attempts to predict the development trajectory of China's economy in the coming decades through theoretical and empirical models and the Japanese "experience and lessons".

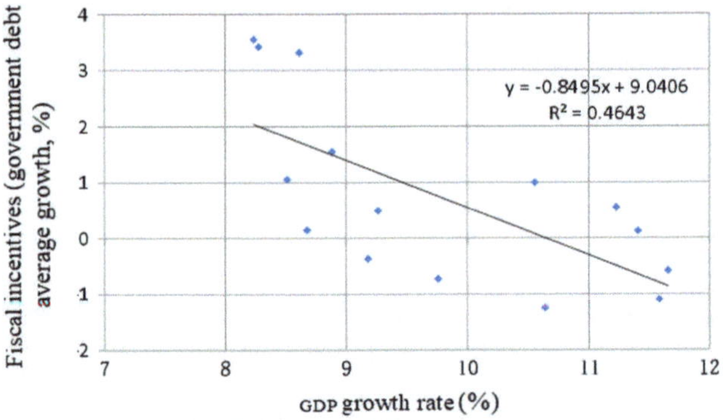

Fig. 20 Countercyclical finance policies in China (2000–2013) [*Data Source* Japan Statistical Yearbook (2013), China Statistical Yearbook (2013)]

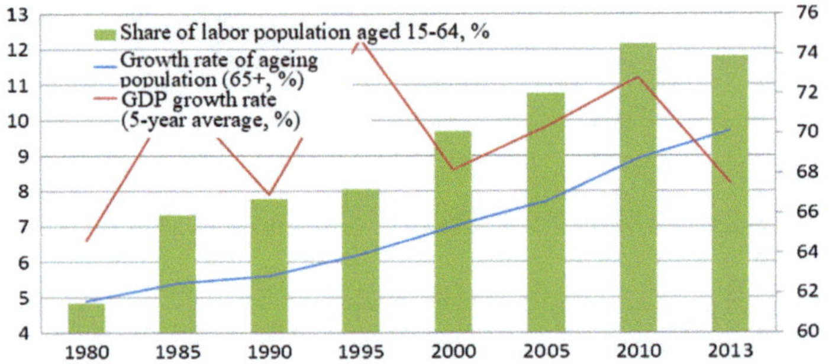

Fig. 21 Current population-driven economic cycles in China (*Source* The Sixth Census Bulletin, the authors' computation)

2.4 *Features of China's Macroeconomy in the "long-swing"*

Based on the COACFF50 macro model simulation, the analysis shows[3] that with the ageing population, China's long-term macroeconomy possesses the following six characteristics:

First, the continuous decline of potential growth rate. There will be a hurdle between 2021 and 2025 when the economic growth rapidly down from the previous 6.5% to the next level of 3–4% and basically maintain at this rate till 2035, then it will slightly rise to about 4% (see Fig. 22). However, according to this growth trajectory, China's per capita GDP will reach RMB 206,000 (unchanged at 2010) by 2050, or about today's USD 32,000. China will become a highly developed country by that time.

[3]See Tan, H., et al., "Population Aging, Migration, Financial Leverage and the Economic Long-Swing," Economic Research, No. 2, 2016.

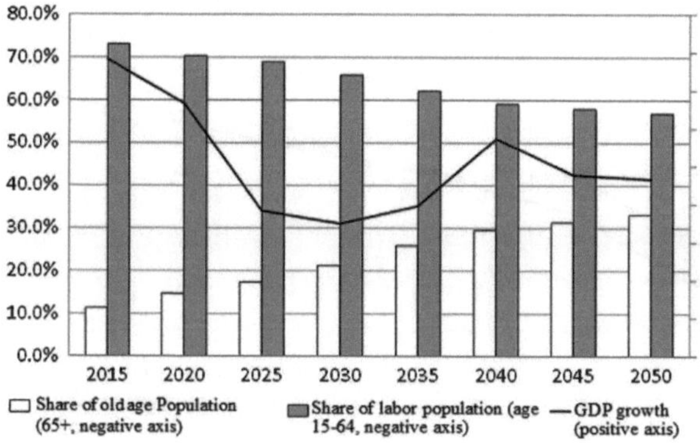

Fig. 22 Population ageing and GDP growth rate in the baseline scenario (*Sources* The Sixth Census Bulletin, and the authors' computation)

Second, high leverage. To achieve the goal of a doubled per capita GDP by 2020, a relatively loose fiscal and monetary policy will be implemented. With the stimulus on the demand side, especially by the government's increased leverage, the level of aggregate leverage measured by debt-to-GDP ratio will continue to rise. The average annual leverage ratio will rise by 12.2 percentage points to 260% by 2020, equivalent to that of Japan's average in 1985–1990. After then, the annual average growth rate of leverage will drop to 4.7 percentage points in 2020–2050 and reach about 400% in 2050, similar to Japan's current leverage (see Fig. 23). It is noteworthy that Japan's asset bubble burst in the early 1990s when its leverage rate reached 300%, a similar range when the United States also experienced a subprime crisis.

Third, the "tidal" flow of population. The population moves from rural and lower-tier cities to higher-tier cities are mainly affected by both income growth and housing prices. In a booming economy, the relatively rapid income growth of urban residents has a greater positive impact on population inflows than the negative impact of rising house prices, resulting in a net inflow of population. During the economic depression, the rapid or even absolute decreased income growth of urban residents doubled with the high housing prices will force the population "out" from the higher-tier cities and develop a "deurbanization". The period between 2011 and 2015 sees a relatively slow urbanization, which will increase in 2016–2020 but the subsequent two economic downturns in 2021–2025 and 2031–2035 will trigger respective "deurbanization". See Fig. 24 for details.

Fourth, periodical fluctuation of asset prices. This is mainly impacted by per capita income (positively related to economic growth) and population flows. For example, as people move from second-tier to first-tier cities where high housing prices and living costs will drive them back to the second-tier cities, this is when the housing prices fluctuate. With the economic recession in 2021–2025, the housing prices in the 2-, 3-, and 4-tier cities will all drop. Their five-year cumulative decreases will be 15, 26, 33 and 58% respectively. Then Chinese people will suffer from the sluggish economy and falling house prices, a situation similar to what happened

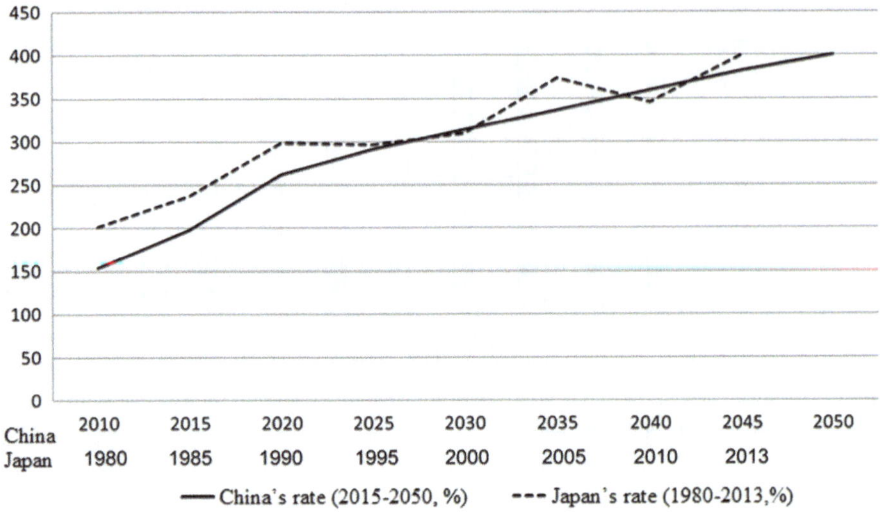

Fig. 23 Leverage ratio of the baseline scenario (*Sources* The Sixth Census Bulletin, the authors' computation)

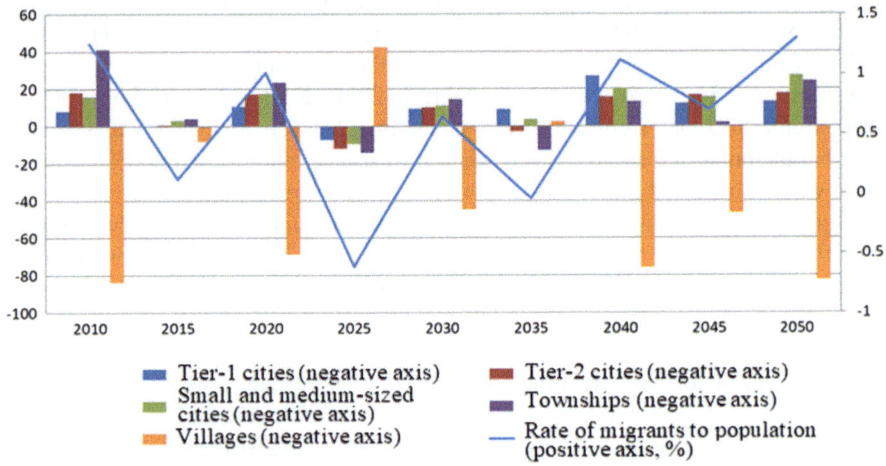

Fig. 24 Population migration in the baseline scenario (*unit* 10,000 persons) (*Sources* The Sixth Census Bulletin, China Statistical Yearbook (2013), and the authors' computation)

when Japan's economic bubble burst in the early 1990s. After that, house prices will recover somewhat and fall again in 2030–2035. Such fall will put the entire economy, already at high leverage, into greater risk. If not properly handled, a Chinese-style "subprime mortgage crisis" is likely to happen in 2025 and 2035, as shown in Fig. 25.

Fifth, tremendous pressure on the pension gap. With the advent of hyper-ageing society, many provinces now have seen deficits in basic pension. In the future, the

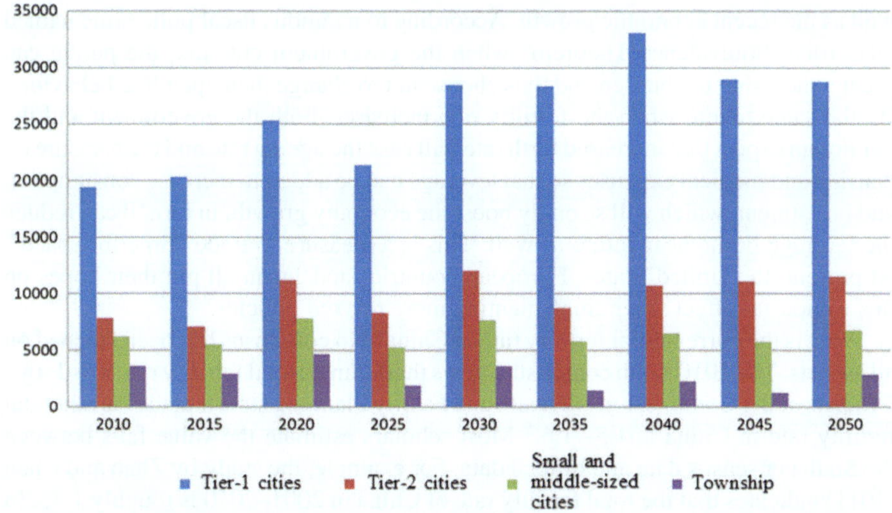

Fig. 25 Housing price of the baseline scenario (*unit* RMB/m^2) (*Sources* The Sixth Census Bulletin, China Statistical Yearbook (2013), and the authors' computation)

ageing population will postpone their retirement or "work after retirement" like the Japanese. We projected that 30% of the funding shortage can be resolved by the re-employment of the people over the age of sixty-five. In the future, we may need to redefine the "elder" as a person who is eighty years old and above. It may gradually become more commonplace for people to stay in workforce until the age of eighty, which may also help to fill the pension gap.

Sixth, the long-standing gap in medicare funding. With rapid population ageing, the cost of medical care is rising rapidly too. At the same time, advances in medical technologies will greatly increase the average life expectancy, which in turn aggravates the medical insurance gap. The international experience shows that it is very difficult to close the medical insurance funding gap. Even with the Obama Medical Reform Act, the United States still cannot completely solve the problem.

3 Countermeasures to Population Ageing

3.1 Raising the Total Fertility Rate

Traditionally, it has been argued that simply raising fertility rate does not necessarily promote economic growth, as it will, instead, increase the burden of dependency and reduce the labor force ratio in the near future. What is more, it takes decades for its positive impact on population ageing to be felt. However, our model, after introducing the rational expectation factors, found that raising fertility rate benefits the future as well as the recent economic growth. According to a famous fiscal policy rule named "Ricardian Equivalence Theorem" when the government cuts tax, the public can predict the rising tax burden and thus choose not to change their spending behaviors. By the same token, when the fertility rate increases, both the government and the public can expect that increased birth rate will ease the ageing rate and the pressure on pension and medical expenses so that leverage can be added to increase consumption and investment, which will strongly boost the economy growth, in turn, it can reduce the leverage in the near future as well. This is a measure to trade "time for space". At present, the United States, European countries and Japan all pin their hopes on this wonderful effect when implementing more relaxed policies.

What is the current total fertility rate in China? No consensus has been reached on all aspects. The 2010 Sixth consensus shows that China's total fertility rate was 1.18.[4] Officials of the Commission of Health and Family Planning state that the current total fertility rate in China is 1.5−1.6.[5] Most scholars estimate the value falls between the Sixth consensus data and official data. For example, the study by Zhao and Chen (2011) indicates that the total fertility rate of China in 2001–2010 is roughly 1.45. In order to verify this data, with the help of Tianhong Fund Management Company, we conducted a special survey after the Spring Festival in 2015. This survey was given to 130,000 people, including 33,164 women with a marital history; among them, 16,586 women have given birth, the average age of them was 30.1 years old, and the total fertility rate was 1.27; as for the 16,578 people who haven't given birth, their average age was 27.8 and the total fertility desire rate was 1.26; with the weighted average of the both, we derived the total fertility rate of 1.26.

This paper uses the Sixth Census data as the assigned valuation of the national total fertility rate and takes into account the fact that the fertility rate among the fifteen to nineteen years old female is very low. The total fertility rate of women of reproductive age twenty to fifty is calculated to be 1.25, a value pretty close to that derived from the survey conducted by Tianhong Fund. On this basis, Six Census data is used to calculate the respective total fertility rates of the five tier cities and the total fertility rate of first-tier cities, second-tier cities, small and medium-sized cities, townships and rural areas in 2010–2050 are 0.85, 0.80, 1.14, 1.17 and 1.49, respectively. The COACFF50 model assumes that the total fertility rates of these five geographic hierarchy will remain unchanged from 2015 to 2050, but urbanization and the women of childbearing age moving to areas of low fertility rate will still result in a declining national total fertility rate, as shown in Fig. 26.

Based on COACFF50 macro-model simulation analysis, when the total fertility rate increases by every 0.1 percentage point, economic growth will increase by 0.15 percentage points from 2020 to 2100. If the total fertility rate increases from the current 1.25 to 2.1, China's economic growth will increase by 1.3 percentage points per year (see Figs. 27 and 28).

---

[4]See "Sixth Census Data", China Statistics Press, April 2012.

[5]See press release Wang Pei'an, deputy director of the State Health and Family Planning Commission, on implementing the two-child policy. November 16, 2013. National Health and Family Planning Commission, www.moh.gov.cn.

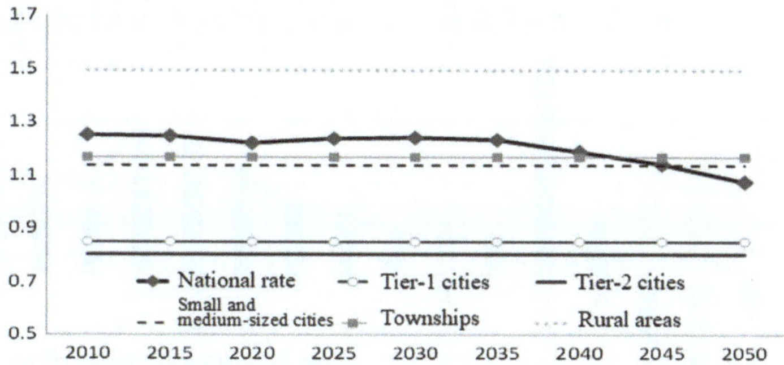

Fig. 26 Total fertility rates in the baseline scenario (*Sources* The Sixth Census Bulletin, and the authors' computation)

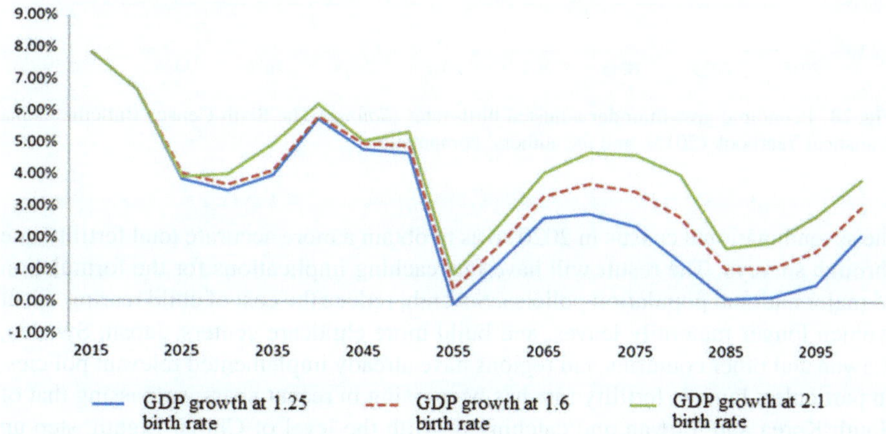

Fig. 27 Economic growth at different birth rates (*Sources* The Sixth Census Bulletin, China Statistical Yearbook (2013), and the authors' computation)

Based on the above discussions, the following eight suggestions are proposed. First, start from the top-level blueprint/outline and drop the promotion such as "maintain the low birth rate" for population development in the "13th Five-Year Plan". Second, gradually change the existing policies to encourage more childbirth, because family planning does not always mean plan for fewer children in a family, it can mean more children in a household instead. Third, increase financial subsidies to encourage childbirth. The Chinese government currently gives generous export duty rebate to support processing trade, which doesn't bring about high added value, and to a certain extent, leads to environmental pollution. To properly reduce export tax rebate and increase childbirth subsidies in the long run are more conducive to the healthy economic and social development. Fourth, prevent the divorce rate from rising too fast. Fifth, consider the necessity and feasibility of encouraging immigration, starting with skilled immigrant workers. Sixth, come up with a careful planning for

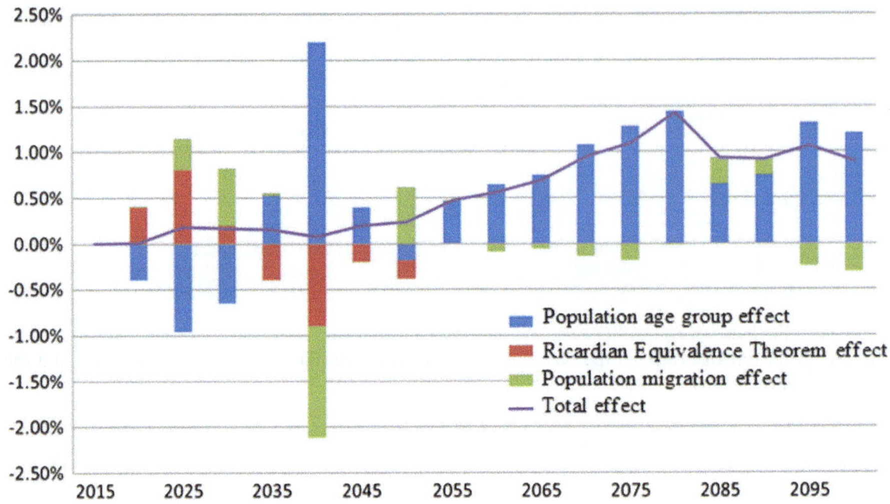

Fig. 28 Economic growth under adjusted birth rates (*Sources* The Sixth Census Bulletin, China Statistical Yearbook (2013), and the authors' computation)

the seventh national census in 2020 so as to obtain a more accurate total fertility rate through surveys. The result will have far-reaching implications for the formulation of major national population policies. Seventh, reduce the cost of child rearing, grant women longer maternity leaves, and build more childcare centers. Japan, Sweden, Taiwan and other countries and regions have already implemented relevant policies. In particular, Japan's fertility rate has been rising in recent years, surpassing that of South Korea and Taiwan and catching up with the level of China. Eighth, step up in promotion and appeal to the whole society to fully recognize the importance of population crisis and strive to form a public consensus.

3.2 Guiding Population Flow According to New Urbanization

The current trend of urbanization and population flows shows that young people tend to migrate to cities and participate in economic activities where labor productivity is higher, which is conducive to economic growth.

COACFF50 macro-model simulation analysis indicates that limiting the population inflow to first-tier cities is a "double-edged sword". Since tier-1 cities represent the highest productivity in China, restricting the population inflow will impede the combination of advanced productive forces and the most talented and economically viable labor force. Such limitation not only hinders China's economic upgrading but also drives down economic growth, eventually leading to the national GDP growth rate decreased by an average of 0.25 percentage points in 2021–2050 (Fig. 29). How-

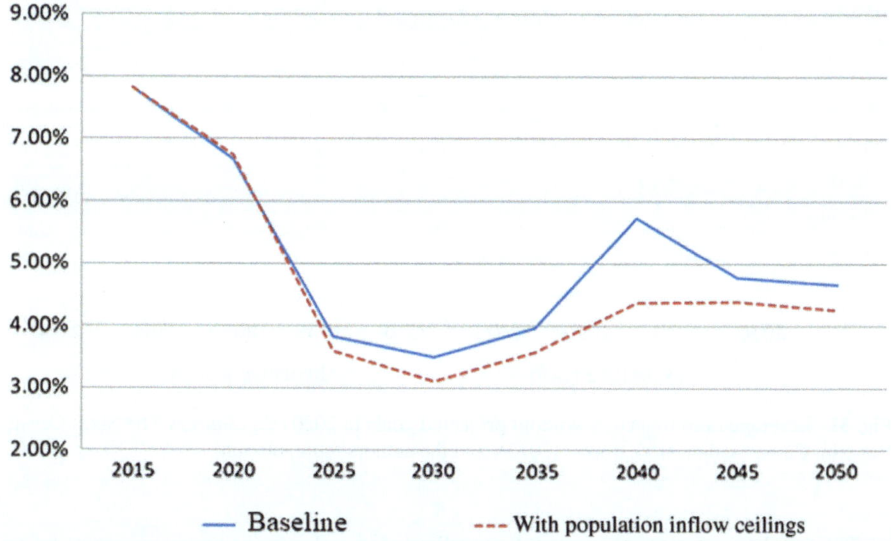

Fig. 29 Tier-1 cities' limits on population inflows and economic growth rate (*Sources* The Sixth Census Bulletin, China Statistical Yearbook (2013), and the authors' computation)

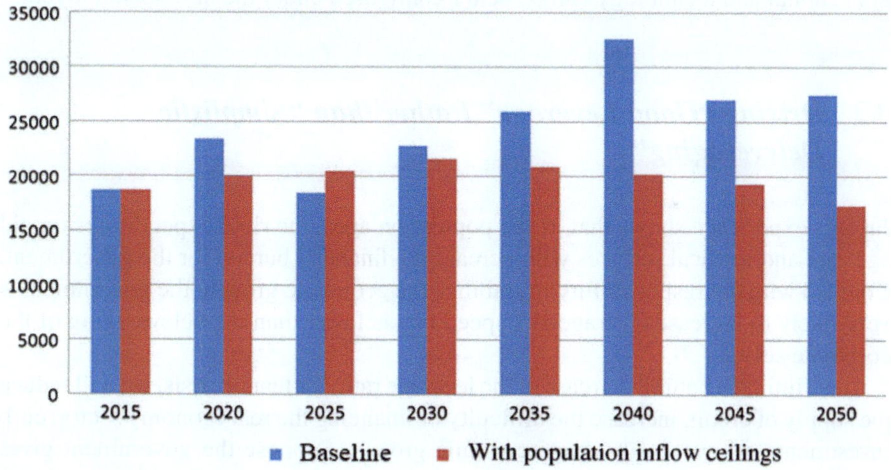

Fig. 30 Tier-1 cities' limits on population inflows and house prices (*Sources* The Sixth Census Bulletin, China Statistical Yearbook (2013), and the authors' computation)

ever, limiting population inflows in first-tier cities can reduce the volatility of housing prices (Fig. 30), thus fostering financial stability.

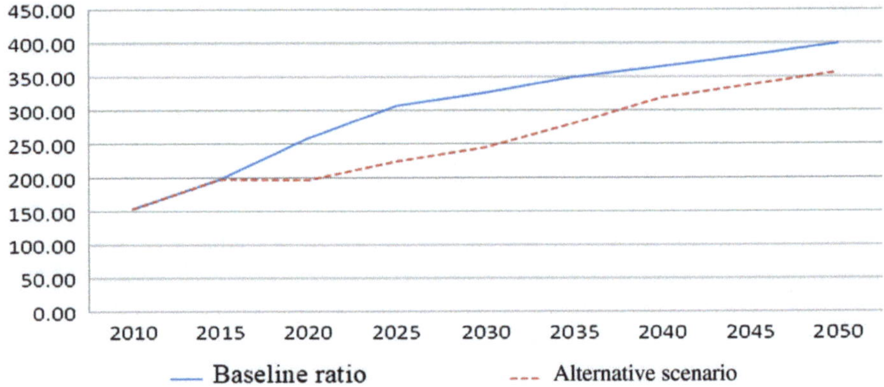

Fig. 31 Leverage ratio trajectory without projected goals in 2020 (%) (*Sources* The Sixth Census Bulletin, China Statistical Yearbook (2013), and the authors' computation)

The implementation of regional coordinated development programs may be an ideal approach that serves many purposes. For example, the "Beijing-Tianjin-Hebei Integration Plan" expands the spatial limitation of the first-tier cities so that population, capital and technology can be better configured under the new spatial layout.

3.3 Driving "Good Leverage" Rather than "Simplistic Deleveraging"

Japan's experience shows that as the population ages, the rigid expenditures on old age care and medical services will increase the financial burden for the government. Coupled with the responsibility to stabilize the economic growth, the government is very likely to increase leverage at a speed that is faster than the deleveraging of the corporate sector.

If we limit the natural increase of the leverage ratio for fear of crisis, we will reduce the supply of credit, increase the difficulty of financing the real economy sector, curb investment and eventually drag economic growth. Suppose the government gives up its goal of an average annual GDP increase of 6.5% for 2016–2020 in order to control the increase in leverage ratio, the economy will develop lower-growth-rate equilibrium even though the leverage ratio drops significantly (see Fig. 31).

Although the leverage rate declines, economic growth also drops dramatically, hitting nearly 2% during 2021–2025 and 2031–2035, creating the two "lost five years" (see Fig. 32). The average economic growth rate between 2015 and 2050 will reduce from the baseline of 4.23–3.40%. Housing prices will also be sluggish. Housing prices in both big and small cities will substantially decrease while maintaining the original volatility. During 2021–2025, the prices in the 1st-, 2nd-, 3rd-, and 4th-tier cities will drop by 40, 55, 61 and 89%, respectively (see Fig. 33). Admittedly,

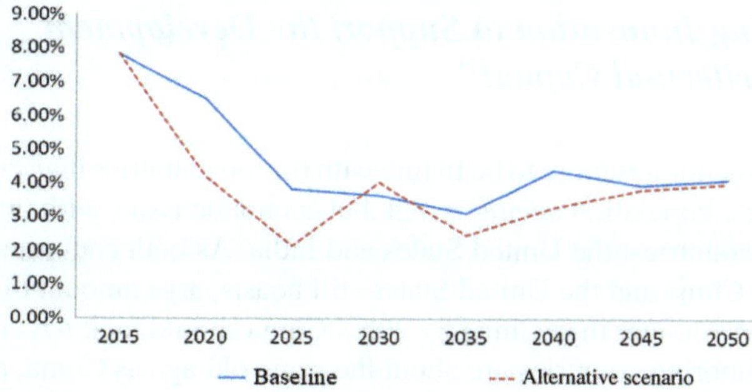

Fig. 32 Economic growth rates without double the per capita income by 2020 target (*Sources* The Sixth Census Bulletin, China Statistical Yearbook (2013), and the authors' computation)

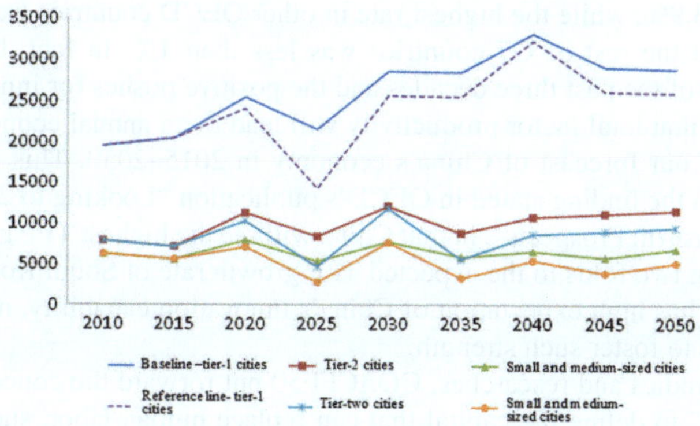

Fig. 33 House prices without double the per capita income by 2020 target (*Unit* RMB/m^2) (*Sources* The Sixth Census Bulletin, China Statistical Yearbook (2013), and the authors' computation)

such a pessimistic result may be caused by the models' limited consideration of the economic growth brought about by technological progress. However, based on the regression studies and the OECD research results, the TFP (total factor productivity) of this model is set at 3.13%, the highest level around the world, indicating the direct impact of technological progress on economic growth have been fully considered.

In response to the financial crisis since 2008, the United States also used the re-leveraging strategies of issuing additional government bonds, cutting taxes and taking over bankrupt private enterprises. The current implementation of local debt conversion and asset securitization in China is a "good leverage" strategy that maintains the level of total social financing, reduces the debt interest burden, and enhances the debt sustainability.

3.4 Fostering Innovation to Support the Development of "Intellectual Capital"

The global competition is more to be in line with the top countries than comparable to the average ones. Population ageing is a global economic issue, with two exceptions among the big countries: the United States and India. As both countries have higher birth rates than China and the United States still boasts large amount of immigrants, they will remain younger than China by 2050. China should look beyond East Asia, where the neighboring countries are about the same old age as China, and be aware of the youthful United States and thriving India. In addition, another leading country is South Korea, whose accelerated technological progress makes it stand out among the OECD countries. From 1985 to 2011, the annual average TFP to GDP growth in Korea was 3.9%, while the highest rate in other OECD countries was only 1.7% in Finland and the rest of G7 countries was less than 1%. In fact, based on the empirical data of the past three decades and the positive pushes for innovations, we have assumed that total factor productivity will lead to an annual economic growth of over 3% in our forecast of China's economy in 2015–2050. This projection is consistent with the finding stated in OECD's publication "Looking to 2060—Long-term Global Growth Prospects", in that China will see the highest TFP growth rate in the world, even two folds to the expected TFP growth rate of South Korea. It shows that the world has high expectation of China's innovation capability, motivating us to take actions to foster such strength.

Based on studies and researches, COACFF50 put forward the concept of "intellectual capital" to define the capital that can replace human labor, such as robots, automated factories and AI networks. In our definition, the most important attribute of intellectual capital is its ability to replace human labor to participate in economic production and people's living. In our opinion, these intellectual capitals can effectively solve a series of problems arising from a hyper-ageing society, such as the shortage of labor force, the drop in economic output, the decline in the rate of capital return and the rise of labor costs. It is recommended to establish a number of industrial funds to attract private capitals into the intellectual capital industry and to provide necessary funding for capital R&D; support a number of intellectual capital-generating enterprises with developmental potentials, and gradually substitute relatively low-skill labor by introducing intellectual capitals; keep "made in China" in China and set up a compensation mechanism to manage the unemployment caused by intellectual capital, such as to provide training opportunities for re-employment for those who are negatively affected or replaced by intellectual capitals.

3.5 Providing More Humanistic Care to the Elderly

The "Great Harmony" promoted by the Chinese Confucianists and the "Uniformity of All Things" proposed by the Taoists convey the same wisdom, that is, to treat everyone/everything with equal respect without discrimination. Overly differentiating the thinking and behaviors of the elders from the younger groups will alienate them from the society. Once the differentiation is established in society, the elders themselves will also reinforce such perception, manifesting the so-called Symbolic Interaction Theory. Therefore, it is suggested that one should refrain himself/herself from overemphasizing the difference between the elders and the young to avoid strengthening such discrimination. In many cases, equal treatment is the epitome of true respect.

As a matter of fact, the effective inheritance of spiritual legacy is in essence the ultimate pursuit of humane care. Humanity, in fact, is "to preserve and carry on the civilization/marks by human activities" which is also a sincere expectation and blessing from the COACFF50 for an ageing Chinese society.

References

Cai, F. (2010). Population changes, demographic dividend and Lewis Turning point. *Economic Research*, (4).

Hu, A., Liu, S., and Ma, Z. (2012). Population ageing, population growth and economic growth - Empirical evidence from provincial panel data of China. *Population Research*, (5).

Zhao, Z., and Chen, W. (2011). How low is China's fertility rate?. *Social Sciences in China*, (3).

Yao Yudong, Ph.D. in economics, chief economist of Dacheng Fund, former director general of the Financial Research Institute of the People's Bank of China, core member of the COACFF50 and Chairman of the Academic Committee.

Tan Haiming, CPA of China, Chartered Financial Analyst, Director of Monetary Policy Department II of the People's Bank of China, invited member of COACFF50 and member of Academic Committee. This article represents only personal point of view and is not an official opinion.

Chapter 4
A Strategic Rethink on Pension Reforms in China

Keyong Dong

Abstract China's population is ageing quickly, and its current pension system is facing many significant challenges and institutional drawbacks caused by the failure of the system to clearly define government, corporate and individual responsibilities. At the core of China's pension reform is the three-pillar design with Chinese characteristics: basic public pension based on the social pooling account (pillar 1); the occupational pension system consisting of financing deficit in the individual account by transferred state-owned assets, enterprise annuities and occupational annuities (pillar 2); and voluntarily contributed pension plans based on personal choice (pillar 3), supported by tax concessions. The government has overall responsibility for system establishment, service management and funding of Pillar I, and plays a regulatory role in system establishment and operation of the 2nd and 3rd pillar.

Keywords Three-pillar pension system · Public pension · Occupational pension Personal tax-deferred pension

China's rapidly ageing population poses significant challenges to the existing pension systems in the country, especially the pension for urban employed workers established in accordance with social security principles. Such challenges include the desire of the citizens to increase pension benefits and the increasing financing burden on the state, empty individual accounts, the implicit debt arising from institutional transition and the huge funding gap faced by the country's existing pension system over the long term. Therefore, further pension reforms are necessary. According to the third Plenary Session of the 18th CPC Central Committee, China will "adhere to the basic old age insurance system that combines social pools with individual accounts, improve the individual accounts system, complete the incentive mechanism in which those who contribute more will get more, guarantee the rights and interests of the insured"; "strengthen management of and supervision over investment of social insurance funds, and encourage the funds to be invested into diversified sectors in the market"; "enact preferential policies, such as tax exemption and deferral, and encourage the development of enterprise annuity, occupational

K. Dong (✉)
Renmin University of China, Beijing, China

K. Dong and Y. Yao (eds.), *Annual Report on Financing Old Age Care in China (2017)*, https://doi.org/10.1007/978-981-13-0968-7_4

annuity and for-profit insurance, so as to bring into shape a multi-level social security system." The above statements set out a clear direction for the design of China pension system. However, because the problems faced by the pension system are intertwined with each other, China's pension reform is hindered by many factors and the views of stakeholders are not uniform. This study examines China's pension practice and international pension reforms, analyzes the evolution and problems of China's pension system, reviews pension reform proposals, and puts forward some suggestions to revamp China's pension systems. This study is based on the following premises.

First, the scope of the study is limited to the pension scheme for urban employees, which covers employees of enterprises and public institutions. It does not discuss the pension scheme for urban and rural residents. This is because there are huge differences between the two branches of China's pension system—the pension scheme for urban and rural residents and the pension scheme for urban employees—in terms of payment methods, benefits, management, and the insured population. This study only discusses the pension scheme for urban employees.

Secondly, the academic circles have agreements as well as disagreements on how to address problems in the pension scheme for urban employees. This study focuses on issues on which people have split views. We will not further discuss topics on which there is broad agreement (delaying the retirement age, etc.).

Thirdly, among the many challenges faced by the existing pension scheme for urban employees, the most significant issue is the scope and speed of population-ageing in China makes the present pension system unsustainable in the long term. Therefore, this study focuses on discussing how China's pension system can achieve sustainability over the long term. Correspondingly, the proposals put forward hereunder also aim to work in the mid-to-long terms.

1 Institutional Infrastructure and Achievements of the Existing Pension System

1.1 Institutional Infrastructure

1.1.1 Pillar 1: Basic Pension

(1) **Basic old age insurance system for urban employees**. The formulation of related policies, including the State Council's *Decision on Reforming the Old Age Insurance System for Enterprise Employees (1991)*, *Decision of the CPC Central Committee on Some Issues Concerning the Establishment of a Socialist Market Economy* adopted at the Third Plenary Session of the 18th CPC Central Committee in 1993, and the *Notice of the State Council on Deepening the Reform of the Old Age Insurance System for Enterprise Employees* (1995), unveiled China's old age insurance reform. The State Council's *Decision on Establishing a Unified Pension System for Enterprise*

Employees (1997) and *Decision on Improving the Basic Old Age Insurance System for Enterprise Employees (2005)* marked the establishment of a basic pension system combining social pools with individual accounts.

The present basic old age system combines social pools with individual accounts. The basic design consists of two components: the social pooling component is operated on a pay-as-you-go basis which uses contribution by current employees to pensioners (intergenerational transfer) and redistributes income between high- and low-income people; the second component is accumulated amounts in individual accounts, which will be used to address the pension crisis brought about by population ageing. The individual account scheme also provides incentives for retirement savings. It, on the one hand, allows employees to supervise employers' contribution and, on the other hand, ensures "those who contribute more will get more". The basic pension system aims to provide retirees with the means by which they can maintain a reasonable living standard. The target replacement rate set by the policy is about 60%. As of the end of 2016, the number of people participating in the pension scheme for urban employees reached 379.3 million, among which there were 278.26 million participating employees and 101.03 million retirees. The annual revenues of the pension fund were RMB 3.5058 trillion, and its annual expenditures were RMB 3.1854 trillion. At the end of the year, the balance of the pension fund was RMB 3.8580 trillion.

(2) **Pension system for employees of public institutions**. The pension system for employees of public institutions in China is undergoing an overhaul. Prior to this reform, the retirement benefits of employees of government agencies and public institutions were linked to their years of service and salaries. The policy is based on the provision of the *Implementation Measures of the Pension System and Other Systems of Public Institutions* promulgated by the former Ministry of Personnel and the Ministry of Finance in 2006 (G.R.B.F. [2006] No. 60): The pension benefits for civil servants are paid in proportion to the sum of position-based salary and grade-based salary. According to related reports, as of the end of 2013, the number of civil servants employed was about 7 million and the number of employees of public institutions was over 30 million. There is currently no official data on the pension benefits for civil servants. According to the *Green Paper on Social Security* published by the Chinese Academy of Social Sciences in 2012, the pension benefits for civil servants were generally higher than RMB 4000 per month. In January 2015, the State Council issued the *Decision on the Reform of the Pension System for Employees of Public Institutions*, at the core of which is a unified basic old age insurance system for both public institutions and enterprises. The policy abolishes the dual-track pension system and requires both employers (corporate employers and government agencies) and employees to contribute to the pension system. Precisely because of the merging of the two tracks, more and more attention has been paid to the problems in the pension system for corporate employees, which has undergone an overhaul before other pension systems.

1.1.2 Pillar 2: Occupational Pension

(1) **Enterprise annuities**. Since the late 1980s, some Chinese enterprises have started to implement enterprise annuity plans. In 1991, the *Decision on Reforming the Old Age Insurance System for Enterprise Employees* issued by the State Council explicitly encouraged (for the first time) enterprises to establish supplementary pension plans for their employees. On December 25, 2000, the State Council promulgated the *Pilot Program on Improving the Social Security System in Urban Areas* (hereinafter referred to as the "Program") which was the first document that mentioned enterprise annuities. Article 10 of the second part of the Program provides that "Qualified enterprises may establish market-oriented enterprise annuity plans for employees. They are contributed by both corporate employers and employees. These contributions accumulated in individual employee accounts until retirement. Employer contributions not exceeding 4% of the aggregate salaries of all employees can be treated as a deductible expense. Personal retirement savings are also encouraged." On May 1, 2004, China issued the *Trial Implementation Measures for Enterprise Annuities* and the *Trial Administration Measures for of Enterprise Annuity Funds* to guide the development of enterprise annuities and regulate the operation of enterprise annuity funds. In 2011, the revised *Measures for the Administration of Enterprise Annuity Funds* further improved the basic structure of China's enterprise annuity system. These two measures provide the principal laws and regulations governing enterprise annuities in China.

The *Trial Implementation Measures for Enterprise Annuities* stipulates: "Enterprise annuities, also known as supplementary pension insurance plans for employees, refer to voluntary supplementary pension plans with contributions made by both corporate employers and employees. They are established by companies voluntarily based on their business performance to supplement the basic pension scheme which has an insufficient replacement rate and to improve the living standard of employees after retirement." The objective of the enterprise annuity system is to meet the needs of employees who wish to maintain a higher living standard after retirement whereas the basic pension system aims to provide employees with means to maintain a basic living standard. They pay benefits at levels consonant with pre-retirement living standards. Enterprise annuities are voluntarily established by enterprises with contribution made by both employers and employees. The annual contribution made by an enterprise should not exceed one twelfth of the previous year's total payroll of the enterprise. The aggregate contributions paid by an enterprise and their employees generally does not exceed one sixth of the previous year's total payroll of the enterprise.

(2) **Occupational annuities**. Occupational annuities, as part of Pillar II, are established for public institution employees to help make up for the decline in the basic pension benefits after the merging of the two tracks. Occupational annuity policy and the basic pension policy for public institutions were introduced to supplement each other. The *Implementation Measures for Occupational Annuities of Government Agencies* promulgated by the State Council in March 2015 stipulate that government agencies must start to implement the occupational annuity system on October 1,

2014 and the cost of occupational annuities should be borne jointly by employers and employees. The proportion of the employer's contribution is 8% of its total payroll, and employees should contribute 4% of their own salaries. The occupational annuity system will supplement and perfect the structure of China's overall pension system.

1.1.3 Pillar 3: Personal Tax-Deferred Pension

Personal tax-deferred pension plans form the third tier of China's pension system. Personal tax-deferred pension was proposed in the last century and further defined at the Third Plenary Session of the 18th CPC Central Committee. The *Opinions of the State Council on Accelerating the Development of Modern Insurance Services* issued in 2014 proposed that China should timely introduce a personal tax-deferred pension system. The 2015 work plan of the China Insurance Regulatory Commission (the "CIRC") specified a pilot program would roll out during the year. China's 13th Five Year Plan also sets out the task of developing personal tax-deferred pension schemes, but no specific policies related to personal tax-deferred pension have been in place so far. However, the implementation of the pillar 3 is only a matter of time.

1.2 Achievements

1.2.1 It Facilitated the Transition of China's Economy from a Planned Economy to a Market Economy

Under the old planned economic system, state-owned enterprises were the mainstay of the economy and undertook the provision of old age insurance benefits. During the transition of China's planned economy to a market economy, the pension burden on state-owned enterprises was heavier than that of private enterprises. The reform built a unified pension system that combines social pools with individual accounts, for all enterprises, including state-owned enterprises and private companies. The system created conditions for equal competition between state-owned and private enterprises in a market economy and laid a solid foundation for the establishment of a modern enterprise system in China. Moreover, under the historical background of the restructuring of state-owned enterprises in the 1990s, the pension reform has distributed pension obligations throughout the society, creating conditions for the reorganization of enterprises and the reform of state-owned enterprises.

1.2.2 It Meets Current Social and Economic Needs

The old pension system is segmental and hindered the flow of human resources between enterprises with varied ownership structures as well as between different regions. The socialized pension system meets the requirement for free movement of labor force. In particular, the reform put forward the concept of sharing the pension burden between the government, enterprises and individuals, and set up an individual account system which requires individuals directly assume part of the responsibility of providing for the aged. The breakaway from the traditional idea that pension burden should be completely borne by the state is conducive to the transformation of the government under the market economy and lays the foundation for further improvement of the pension system.

1.2.3 It Ensures Wide Coverage and Basic Security

As one of the core features of the current pension system, the number of employees participating in the pension scheme for urban employees was 379.30 million by the end of 2016, including 278.26 million participating employees and 101.03 million retirees. Unlike the old basic pension system which only covered the employees of state-owned enterprises and collectively-owned enterprises, the new scheme covers the majority of urban employees. On the one hand, the pension reform has changed the method for calculation and release of benefits and lowered the replacement rate by 70%. Its main goal is to ensure basic security of retirees, thus easing the financing pressure of the system. On the other hand, the reform has put a pension adjustment mechanism in place. Since 2005, the pension system has been adjusted annually for 12 consecutive years. The average pension benefits across the country in 2016 were RMB 2362 per month, which is able to guarantee an acceptable standard of living for the elderly.

1.2.4 It Is a Means to Address the Pension Crisis Caused by Population Ageing

If measured by international standards, China has become an ageing society since 1999. The old pension system is a pay-as-you-go system which is unable to cope with the pension crisis brought about by population ageing. In response, countries across the world have generally adopted a multi-pillar pension system. The current pension system in China consists of the basic pension system solely funded and run by the government, the individual account system contributed by individuals, and enterprise annuities and occupational annuities (pillar 2 2) which are designed to supplement the basic pension system. The personal tax-deferred pension system (pillar 3) is also about to roll out. All in all, the pension reforms in China over the past 20 years is in line with the development trend of pension in the world today and has a significance to the attempts of the countries across the world to cope with the crisis of population ageing.

2 Risks and Institutional Predicaments Faced by China's Pension Systems Over the Long Term

2.1 Risks Over the Long Term

2.1.1 Due to the Massive Funding Gap, China's Current System Is Unable to Cope with the Crisis Brought About by Ageing Population

The pension gaps discussed hereunder can be divided into two types: annual gaps and total gaps. Annual gaps are the shortfall between pension revenues and expenditures each year. The total gap refers to the aggregate shortfall between pension revenues and expenditures over the years. According to data of the data of the Ministry of Human Resources and Social Security (MOHRSS) of China, the deficit of the basic pension fund in 2016 was up to RMB 330.7 billion, not including RMB 651.1 billion of financial subsidies. In fact, since 2001, the number of employees of state-owned or collective-owned enterprises in urban areas covered by basic pensions has been growing at a rate of 4.04%, lower than the average growth rate of retirees which stands at 6.64%. The funding of basic pensions mainly relies on the working population which means the pension gap will continue to widen.

The total gap over a long period is related to the length of the period, economic situation and population development. Opinions vary on the size of the total gap. Different agencies and scholars have given different estimates. Ma Jun and others of Deutsche Bank believe that China's annual pension gap will reach 0.2% of GDP by 2020 and 5.5% of GDP by 2050. The present value of the total pension deficit over the next 38 years, calculated at the nominal GDP growth rate, is equivalent to 75% of current GDP. According to Cao Yuanzheng and others, the total pension gap will reach RMB 68.2 trillion by 2033, accounting for 38.7% of the GDP of that year (Table 1).

2.1.2 Unreasonable Pension Structure Overburdens the Government

Most OECD countries adopt the three-pillar pension model, which aims to rationally split pension responsibility between the state, employers and individuals. The pillar 1 of public pension is intended to ensure the minimum level of income for the elderly. The pillar 2 is the occupational pension. The state provides tax incentives to motivate employees to save a portion of his or her earnings for retirement, all or part of which is matched by the employer. Occupational pension funds are invested to preserve and increase the value of pension assets. The pillar 3 offers a supplementary source of income to the aged. It is voluntary private pensions. To encourage people to make use of this pillar, tax incentives are provided by the government. The purpose of this pillar is to provide supplementary sources of retirement income for self-employed and higher-income earners. Overall, among the three pillars of the pension system, the 2nd and pillar 3s play an increasingly important role in providing old age security.

In the United States, for example, the pillar 2 (i.e., occupational pensions) occupies the largest proportion of the country's total pension assets, followed by the pillar 3 (i.e., private pensions) and public pensions. In terms of benefits, the average replacement rate of public pensions is about 30–40%, and the replacement rate of the 2nd and pillar 3s together is about 40–50%, which means the pension burden on the U.S. government pension burden is small but old age security provided by the pension system remains adequate (Table 2).

Compared to the U.S., due to high contribution of basic pensions and the lack of tax incentives, enterprise annuities have been developing slowly in China. By the end of 2016, 76,300 enterprises nationwide had set up enterprise annuities, covering 23.25 million employees, accounting for only 6.63% of the employees participating in the basic employee pension. Most employees in China are unable to participate in enterprise annuities. As of the end of 2015, the total value of enterprise annuity funds was RMB 1.1075 trillion, accounting for 28.71% of the assets of the basic pension fund, and per capita enterprise annuity assets were RMB 47,600, which

Table 1 Estimation of basic pension gaps in China

Estimator	Year of estimation	Deadline	Size
Ma Jun	2012	2050	Accounting for 75% of GDP in 2050
Cao Yuanzheng	2012	2033	Accounting for 38.7% of GDP in 2033
Gao Peiyong	2011	2050	Accounting for 95% of GDP in 2050

Table 2 Comparison of the structure of the U.S. and Chinese pension systems (2016)

U.S.				
Name	Pillar I Public pension	Pillar II Occupational pension	Pillar 3 Personal pension	Total
Total assets (USD trillion)	2.8	15.4	7.9	26.1
Percentage of the total pension assets (%)	10.7	59.0	30.3	100

(continued)

Table 2 (continued)

China				
Name	Basic pension	Enterprise annuity	Personal tax-deferred pension	Total
Total assets (RMB trillion)	4.0	1.04	0	5.04
Percentage of the total pension assets (%)	79.4	20.6	0	100

Source ICI, and the Ministry of Human Resources and Social Security of China (MOHRSS)

was rather inadequate in terms of old age security for participating employees. In the meanwhile, the pillar 3 of personal tax-deferred pensions has not yet been set up. As a result, the basic pension is the largest source of retirement income. Those who have already retired also completely rely on the basic pension to maintain a reasonable standard of living after retirement. In the long run, the state treasury will face tremendous pressure.

2.1.3 The Low Level of Pension Benefits Cannot Help the Elderly Maintain an Adequate Standard of Living

In the current old age insurance system, the basic pension scheme is intended to guarantee the minimum income at retirement, and enterprise annuities are a supplement to the basic pension scheme. Therefore, the replacement rate of the basic pension is rather low, about 60% of the average salary of the general public. However, because only less than 10% of the enrollees of the basic pension have been covered by enterprise annuities and most Chinese citizens do not have much personal saving, the basic pension scheme is the only source of retirement income for most employees. Therefore, when the pension system was just set up, the replacement rate of the basic pension about 70%, which was rather high. However, since 2000, the replacement rate of the basic pension scheme has dropped. It declined from 73% in 1997 to 43% in 2016, as shown in Fig. 1. The International Labor Organization (ILO) Conventions requires the minimum replacement rate to be at about 40–50%. Although China has spent more than one decade to adjust pension benefits, the replacement rate of the basic pension scheme remains low and inadequate to fund a modest standard of living.

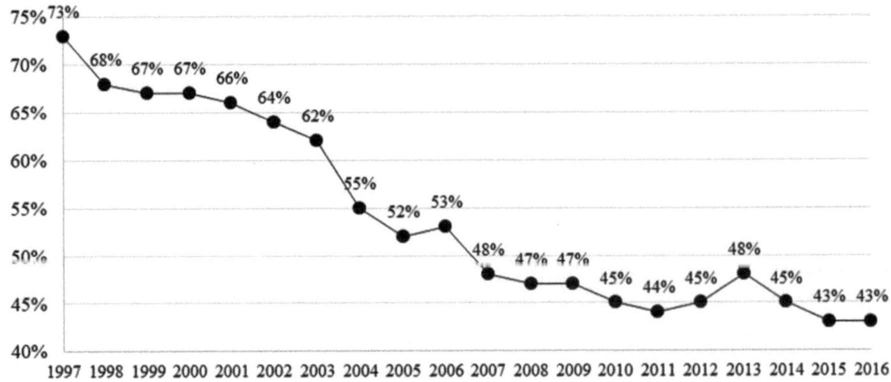

Fig. 1 Changes in the replacement rate of China's basic pension. *Source* Labor and Social Security Statistics Report 1997–2016

2.2 *Institutional Predicament*

2.2.1 The Basic Pension Scheme Is Still Operating on a Pay-as-You-Go Basis and Fails to Achieve the Goal of the Reform

China's current basic old age insurance system combines social pools with individual accounts. The part of social pools is operated on a pay-as-you-go basis and redistributes income through transfers of funds among citizens. Individual accounts are prefunded and invested to increase the value of pension assets, intended to address the expected pension crisis in the future. An efficient combination of social pools and individual accounts should be able to achieve inter-generational redistribution and provide incentives and represent collective and individual responsibility. However, since there is no specific institutional design for financing reform costs and invisible debts, when the contributions from social pools are insufficient to pay current benefits, the Chinese government "borrows" money from the individual accounts in order to pay the benefits promised to current retirees. This is widely called the problem of "empty accounts." This means, in reality, China's basic pension system is still operated on a pay-as-you-go basis which uses current receipts from workers to pay current benefits to retirees. The system design that combines social pools and individual accounts fails to achieve the expected goal and falls short in dealing with the pension crisis caused by an ageing population.

2.2.2 The Size of the Pension Hole Dubbed "Empty Individual Accounts" Will Continue to Grow

In addition to the pay-as-you-go social pooling account, the basic pension system in China also includes prefunded individual accounts intended to introduce personal pension obligations and reduce the burden on the state. However, due to the lack of a clear system design for the funding the reform of the basic pension, the social pooling account is used to pay current pension benefits after the reform. In fact, the current beneficiaries do not make contributions to the social pooling account. As a result, the new social pooling account does not have sufficient fund to pay current pension benefits. Therefore, local authorities have "borrowed" from the individual accounts to pay the benefits promised to current retirees. This is widely called the problem of "empty accounts." Moreover, the deficit in individual accounts has grown from RMB 740 billion in 2004 to RMB 4.4 trillion in 2015 and will continue to grow.

In 2001, the three northeastern provinces (i.e., Liaoning Province, Jilin Province and Heilongjiang Province) carried out a pilot project to finance deficit in the individual accounts. In 2005, the State Council decided to implement the pilot project at the national level. However, in 2009, the pilot project was halted when the State Council approved the request of Liaoning government to "borrow" money from individual accounts to pay for current pension benefits. The "empty account" problem has discouraged Chinese citizens from contributing to the basic pension.

2.2.3 The Pension System Is Bedeviled by the Issue of Under-Declaration of Income and High Contribution Rate

At present, the contribution rate China's basic pension stands at 28%, compared to about 20% of public pensions in OECD countries. If considering China's "social security contributions" as a whole, the social insurance contribution rate totals 58.2% in China, with 40.3% being paid by enterprises and 18.2% paid by individuals[1]. High contribution rates not only affect the competitiveness of enterprises, but also affect employees' current income.

As the contribution rate is stipulated by law and cannot be changed, many companies under-declare the salary of their employees to reduce their contribution obligations. The policy stipulates that the contribution base can be set between 60 and 300% of the average local salary. Many companies opt to make the minimum contribution. The purpose of setting a high contribution rate is to raise more fund for pensions, but under-declaration of income has put a damper on the intended effect of the high contribution rate. In addition, since pension contributions are linked to average salary, if the average salary is higher than the contribution base, it will increase pension expenditure and thus affect the financial sustainability of pension funds.

[1]China's social security contributions include pension fund (employer at a rate of 20% and employee at a rate of 8%), medical insurance fund (employer at a rate of 10% and employee at a rate of 2%), unemployment insurance fund (employer at a rate of 1% and employee at a rate of 0.2%), maternity insurance fund (employer at a rate of 0.8%) and work-related injury insurance fund (employer at a rate of 0.5%) as well as the housing provident fund (employer at a rate of 8% and employee at a rate of 8%).

2.2.4 Linking Basic Pension Benefits to Average Is a Deficient Mechanism in Itself

Linking basic pension benefits and the average salary has a negative impact on the sustainability of the system. At present, the main component of China's basic pension system is the social pooling account. Basic pension benefits are linked to "the previous year's average salary in the pooling area." This design has led to several problems. First of all, it has a negative impact on the fiscal sustainability of the system. This is because, in the contribution period of basic pension, enterprises can choose to contribute at a rate between 60 and 300% of the average wage. The reason for setting a dynamic range is that different enterprises have different profitability and wage levels. However, in fact, most enterprises, especially private-owned enterprises, irrespective of their actual wage levels, choose to make social security contributions at the lowest base allowed by the law. However, pension benefits are linked with the average wage. As a result, the inconsistency between contributions and benefits will damper the enthusiasm of contributors. More importantly, it will increase the pressure on basic pension funds. Secondly, this mechanism will hinder the implementation of the national overall plan for basic pensions. Under unified national management, if pension contributions and benefits are calculated on the basis of the national average wage, pension benefits of retirees in some underdeveloped areas may be higher than the average salary of working citizens, thus inducing early retirement; if the average local salary is used as the base, pension benefits in developed areas will be higher than underdeveloped areas, causing a reverse distribution of income which means a transfer of wealth from the underdeveloped areas to developed areas.

2.2.5 The Implicit Pension Debt Has not Been Paid off

The implicit pension debt (IPD) refers to the current value of pension benefits promised to retirees and "in-between" workers who have not yet retired if the current pension insurance system should cease to operate immediately. In China, the IPD is the value of pension obligations arising from the transition of the old pension system to the new pension system that combines social pools and individual accounts in 1997. The Social Security Department under the former Ministry of Labor of China, the World Bank and the former Economic System Reform Office of the State Council estimated China's IPD in 1995, 1996 and 2000, which was at RMB 2.8 trillion, 1.9 trillion and 6.7 trillion, respectively. The important reason for the growth in the IPD is that China's pension reform coincided with its economic reform as well as the monetization reform of the employee remuneration system. The low-wage and high-welfare remuneration system of the planned economy was replaced by a market-oriented one. The average wage of Chinese workers grew at a high rate. Because pension benefits are positively related to the level of average wage, pension liabilities increased with the average wage over a certain period of time.

3 Goal of China's Pension Reform: Three-Pillar System

3.1 The Evolution of the Three-Pillar Pension Model

3.1.1 The Definition of the Three-Pillar Pension Model

The choice between pay-as-you-go and fund accumulation schemes is a much-debated issue in the academic circle. International practice proves that the pay-as-you-go system has certain advantages in a country with a relatively young population structure, fast economic growth and high wage growth. It will face enormous challenges in the context of slow economic growth, slow wage growth and especially population ageing. Funded pensions show their superiority in maintaining the sustainability of the pension system and improving citizens' ability to fend for themselves after retirement when the income level of the society reaches a certain level and its capital market is relatively well-established. However, the funded system also faces investment risks. Therefore, single pillar systems are not the optimal choice, especially in the context of population ageing. As the population continues ageing and the capital market continues to develop, more and more countries choose the multi-pillar pension system.

Affected by the onset of the population ageing crisis in the 1980s, the pension systems dominated by the pay-as-you-go model were unable to maintain financial sustainability, placing greater financial burden on governments and posing great challenges to the welfare after senior citizens' retirement. In this context, the World Bank summarized pension reform experience in Chile and other countries and proposed a three-pillar pension model in 1994 in an attempt to address the above-mentioned issues. The core idea is not to seek a single pillar solution to the plight brought by population ageing, but to adopt a multi-pillar approach. The overall framework includes:

1st Pillar—mandatory, state-run public pensions with the objective of providing the minimum level of protection to retirees. The government bears ultimate responsibility for the pillar 1. Generally speaking, it is operated on a pay-as-you-go basis, which uses contributions made by current workers through taxation or other means to pay pension benefits promised to current retirees and thus achieve inter-generational redistribution. Contribution rates are actuarially determined based on replacement rates of the pension regime established in light of macroeconomic policies.

2nd Pillar—occupational pensions. It is generally funded by employers and individuals and reflects the shared pension obligations of enterprises and individuals. In some countries, it is the main part of the three-pillar pension system. Unlike the pillar 1 financed on a pay-as-you-go basis, occupational pensions are generally on a funded basis. More and more occupational pension plans are converted from defined benefit (DB) to defined contribution (DC). The value of the benefits payable from a DC scheme after retirement depends on the amount of contributions paid and the investment return achieved. The level of benefit payable after retirement

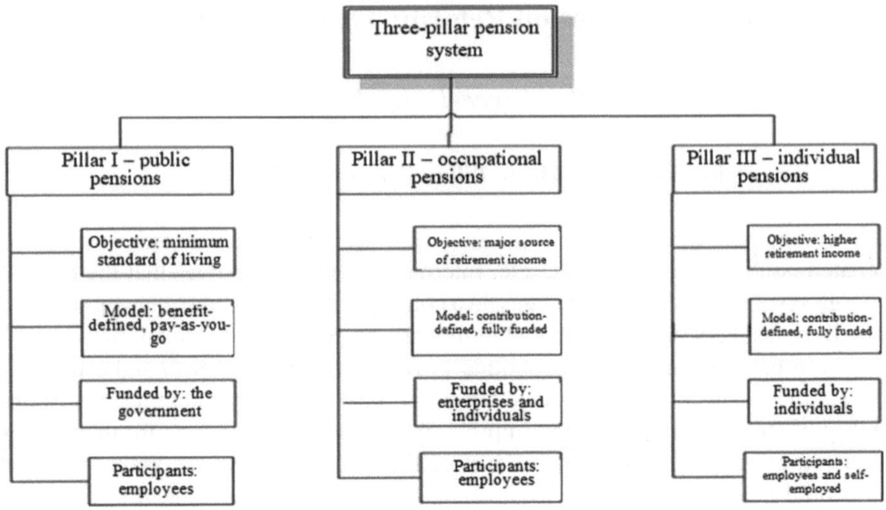

Fig. 2 Framework of the three-pillar pension system

depends on the accumulation of funds during employees' working lifetimes, which is consistent with the principle of actuarial balance. DC pensions can better cope with problems brought by population ageing. A fully funded system can also promote the accumulation of capital and the development of financial markets and reduce people's reliance on the pillar 1. It should be pointed out that in some countries, including the United States, the pillar 2 of occupational pensions are voluntary and the state introduces a set of tax measures to support the pillar 2. There are compulsory occupational pensions as well in many countries.

Pillar 3—fully funded, voluntary private retirement saving plans, supported by the state through tax incentives. It reflects personal obligations to provide for himself/herself after retirement. The objective is to provide additional sources of retirement income to those who need them (Fig. 2).

3.1.2 International Practice

After the introduction of the three-pillar pension model by the World Bank in 1994, most OECD countries have established a multi-pillar pension system. Due to different national conditions and existing pension systems, the multi-pillar pension reform varies from country to country. For example, the financing and management models of the pillar 1 and the pillar 2 may be different in different countries; the payout model of no pillar may also be different. However, in a broad sense, all major economies across the world have established a multi-pillar pension system (see Table 3).

Table 3 Composition of the three-pillar pension system by country/region

	No Pillar Non-contributory pensions	Pillar I Public pensions	Pillar II Occupational pensions	Pillar 3 Personal pensions
U.S.		OASDI	401K and 403b	Individual retirement accounts
Australia	Age pension		Superannuation	Individual retirement accounts
Canada		Public pensions	Retirement pensions	Private retirement savings
UK		Basic state pension State second pension	Occupational pensions	Personal pensions
Chile		Public pensions	Private individual retirement accounts	Supplementary private pensions
Netherlands		Basic state pension (AOW)	Occupational pensions	
Hong Kong, China			MPF	
Singapore			CPF	
China		Social pools Individual accounts	Enterprise annuities	

3.2 *Principles and Functions of China's Three-Pillar Pension System*

3.2.1 Principles of China's Three-Pillar Pension System

We believe China's pension reform should comply with the following four principles: **First, sustainability**. Due to accelerated population ageing, existing pension reserves are insufficient. One of the core challenges facing the employee pension system is financial sustainability in the long run. Therefore, promoting the sustainable development of the system is one of the principles of the pension reform. **Second, universal coverage**. Pensions are a tool to guarantee the old age welfare. To achieve the core objectives of the pension system, it must cover as many people as possible. **Third, adequacy**. Since 2006, China's basic pension have been rising for 11 consecutive years, but the pension replacement rate in China remains at 40–50%, lower than the international warning line. Although faced by a long-term pension gap, the pension system should still provide a reasonable level of benefits. **Fourth, equitability**. Pension systems have a redistribution function. Equitability is a factor that must be considered in the design of pension systems. In particular, the basic pensions serve as a social safety network to prevent old age poverty and a way of income redistribution, therefore, equitability shall be made the starting point for institutional design. Based on the above principles, taking into account China's national conditions and drawing on international experience, we believe that China should adopt a three-pillar pension system.

3.2.2 Pillar 1: Public Pensions

The pillar 1 should be reconstructed on the basis of the current social pooling component. A pay-as-you-go model should be adopted to realize intergenerational redistribution of income. The level of guarantee provided by the pillar 1 should not be too high, aiming to prevent old age poverty. The government should shoulder the ultimate responsibility of Pillar I and ensure the financial security at old age.

3.2.3 Pillar 2: Occupational Pension

The pillar 2 plays an important supplementary role to basic pensions and helps retirees improve their living conditions. The state should introduce tax measures to provide citizens with an incentive for participating in the pillar 2 which is a fully funded pension scheme sponsored by employers and contributed by individuals. In addition, from employers' perspective, occupational pensions are also an important means of profit sharing and incentive to retain human capital. From the perspective of capital formation, because occupational pensions are funded and important long-term property, they can provide stable and long-term fund for the capital market and thus contribute to the development of a sound capital market and support economic growth.

3.2.4 Pillar 3: Personal Pensions

The pillar 3 is designed for freelancers who cannot participate in the pillar 2 and high-income earners who wish to have an additional source of retirement income other than the pillar 2. It is fully funded by individuals on a voluntary basis and incentivized by the state through tax measures. Since the participation in the pillar 3 is entirely voluntary and free from employer influence, it is highly flexible. It not only is an effective retirement saving tool for individuals but also can help reduce the burden on public pensions.

4 Framework and Reform Path of China's Three-Pillar Pension System

4.1 Framework of China's Three-Pillar Pension System

In accordance with the guidelines set out at the Third Plenary Session of the 18th CPC Central Committee, China should "adhere to the basic old age insurance system that combines social pools with individual accounts, improve the individual accounts system, complete the incentive mechanism in which those who contribute more will get more, guarantee the rights and interests of the insured." To realize these goals, we believe it is necessary to reform the existing basic old age insurance system for urban employees. The focus of the reform is to separate social pooling from individual accounts of the pillar 1. The social pooling component should become the pillar 1. The tasks of this reform are "strengthening contribution base regulation, improving the record filing system, complying with actuarial principles and ensuring financial security at old age." Existing enterprise annuity and occupational annuity policies should be merged to form the second pillar. The key tasks of this reform are "smoothly integrating enterprise annuity and occupational annuity policies, improving policy support, standardizing the investment system and sharing the fruits of development." In addition to improving the 1st and pillar 2s, we should also accelerate the development of the pillar 3. The key tasks are "promoting voluntary private pensions, introducing preferential tax policies, entrusting agencies for implementation, and effectively supplementing other pillars." In addition, individual accounts of the basic pension can be incorporated into the pillar 3 as its mandatory component. In short, the three-pillar pension reform should "separate social pools from individual accounts, clearly define the functions of each pillar, set up multiple mechanisms, and strengthen supervision."

4.2 Redefining the Pillar 1 as the Social Pooling Portion of the Basic Pension

Under any three-pillar model, the core function of the pillar 1 is to promote social redistribution with the goal of preventing old age poverty. The pay-as-you-go system is an effective means of promoting social redistribution. Therefore, we suggest that the current social pooling pension of the basic old age insurance should become the first pillar of the multi-pillar pension system.

4.2.1 Adjusting the Replacement Rate of the Public Pension and Reducing the Pension Gap

Replacement rates of public pensions under all three-pillar pension systems across the world are relatively low because its objective is to prevent poverty in old age. In 2012, the average contribution rate of public pensions of OECD countries was 20.7%, and their average replacement rate was 42.2%.[2] In 2016, the contribution rate of the social pooling portion of the basic pension in China is 20%, which was in the neighborhood of that of OECD countries; the replacement rate was about 48%, which was about 6% higher than that of OECD countries, leaving room for downward adjustment.

It is recommended that the contribution rate of the social pooling portion of the public pension should be maintained at 20%. After completing Pillar 2 and Pillar 33 reforms, the benefit level of the pillar 1 should be adjusted to about 40%, similar to that of OECD countries. Under such circumstances, the replacement rate of China's basic pension will be lower than now, which will help reduce the future pension gap and financial burden of the state. According to our calculations, after adjustment of the contribution rate and the benefit level, there won't be a financing gap in the public pension until 2040. The decline in public pension benefits will be offset by an increase in individual account savings.

4.2.2 Strengthening Regulation on Contribution and Ensuring Enrollees Paying Due Contributions in Full

The current policy stipulates that contributions should be between 60% and 300% of the average local wage. Many companies opt to make minimum contributions. We must address the underfunding problem in the public pension system. Otherwise, the sustainability of the public pension will be greatly affected, which will hinder the evaluation of the pension. Full funding means higher funding efficiency which will help reduce the financing burden of the public pension.

In China's case, to solve the above problem, **firstly, the government should improve the contribution management system**. Tax authorities can collect credible information on employers' wage bills. At present, in many regions across the country, social security contributions are managed by human resources and social security authorities. Information on employers' wage bills reported to tax authorities and social security authorities is often inconsistent. We suggest that, to ensure full funding of the public pension, a policy should be introduced to keep employers' social security contribution base and tax base consistent. **Secondly, an incentive mechanism should be established in China**. In many countries, pension benefits are calculated as percentage of the average salary one earned during his/her certain most highly-paid consecutive years of service. For example, if the service period lasts 40 years, the pension benefit is calculated on the basis of the average salary of

[2]OECD, Pension at glance 2013

the employee during his/her 10 mostly highly-paid consecutive years. This system design links pension benefits to the contribution base, which can motivate enrollees to contribute more. It is recommended that incentives that strengthen the link between pension benefits and individual contributions should be introduced. This requires an improved record-filing system.

4.2.3 Reforming the Benefit Calculation Method of the Public Pension to Achieve Integration of Incentives and Redistribution

One of the core functions of the pillar 1 is to redistribute income, which is mainly achieved through distribution of pension benefits. At present, benefits from the social pool is "calculated based on the average local monthly salary of the previous year and the indexed taxable salary of the employee and the accrual rate is 1% for each contribution year." This calculating method links pension benefits to the average local wage and redistributes income within the pooling region. However, as social average wages vary from region to region, there is a huge regional difference in the amount of benefits received by enrollees and thus this design cannot achieve income redistribution between different pooling regions. This also makes it very difficult for workers to transfer their pension when they work in another city.

Therefore, to achieve income redistribution in a larger scope and increase the portability of the basic pension, it is necessary to adjust the way basic pension benefit is calculated. The following is the general path to the reform: benefit of the basic pension should only be linked to the employee's average indexed wage and decoupled from the local average wage so as to avoid regional differences at the level of pension benefit; benefits are calculated at different rates determined based on the employee's average indexed wage, then replacement rates for higher income earners will be relatively lower, while replacement rates for lower income earners will be relatively higher, thus redistributing income between the rich and the poor.

4.3 Vigorously Promoting the Development of Pillar 3

4.3.1 Providing Sufficient Tax Incentives

Take IRAs in the United States for example. In 1974, to encourage individuals to save more for retirement, reduce the state's future pension burden and, in particular, provide a retirement saving tool for self-employed individuals and workers who are not a participant of a 401(k) plan, the Congress of the United States enacted the Employee Retirement Income Security Act, allowing contributions to individual retirement accounts (IRAs) and investments to be tax-deferred until employees take withdrawals after retirement. In 2014, for example, the maximum tax-deferred IRA contribution was USD 5000 for those under the age of 50 and USD 5500 for those above the age 50. Furthermore, the management mechanism of IRAs is very flexible. For example, if an employee leaves a company and the new employer does not sponsor a 401(k) plan, the employee can rollover the 401(k) balance into his/her IRA. These arrangements have driven the development of IRAs which is the largest individual pension plan in the United States. Therefore, to support pillar 3, China should offer adequate tax incentives to motivate employees.

4.3.2 Bringing into Full Play the Role of Pension Funds in Investment

Since individual accounts are long-term assets, the pension fund can be invested in proper ways to be protected against inflation and improve its value, increase the assets. First, underlying assets must be suitable for individual pensions. In foreign countries, individual accounts can invest in a wide range of assets, but funds are generally chosen for most individual accounts. In recent years, the introduction of target date funds and target risk funds suitable for pensions has enriched the investment choices for personal pensions. Therefore, to promote the development of pillar 3 in China, a policy should be adopted to allow individuals to choose according to their risk preference from a wide array of investment products such as insurance products, financial products, funds, and stocks. Secondly, the government should support the development of intermediaries. Since most citizens lack the professional knowledge to make reasonable investment decisions, they need specialized investment advisory agencies to provide them with professional advice. Intermediaries will play a huge role in promoting the development of Pillar 3 in our country.

4.4 Funding Individual Accounts and Incorporating Them into the Pillar 3 as Its Mandatory Component

Individual accounts of the basic pension are funded entirely by individuals and thus are owned by individuals. Individual accounts of pillar 3 are also privately owned. Due to the same nature of ownership, they can be integrated and invested through one single account. Individual accounts of the basic pension are used only for retirement benefit withdrawal by individuals and are in fact mandatory retirement savings, while individual accounts of pillar 3 are also individual retirement saving plans, so the two can be integrated due to their inherent nature. To be more specific, individual accounts of the basic pension can become a mandatory part of pillar 3 and the current contribution rate (8%) can be maintained. They should be fully funded and invested in a market-oriented manner to preserve and potentially increase their value.

4.4.1 Appropriating State-Owned Assets to Make up the Shortfall in Individual Accounts

The Chinese government has borrowed RMB 4.4 trillion from employees' individual accounts to pay the amounts due to current retirees. To finance deficit in individual accounts, the government has to appropriate state-owned assets. At present, the market capitalization of SOEs listed in China and foreign markets is about RMB 20 trillion,[3] and the amount of fund needed to finance deficit in individual accounts is about RMB 5 trillion, which means this solution is feasible. The logic behind the solution is to use state-owned assets to repay government debts and it won't increase the government's financial burden. Therefore, the appropriation of state-owned assets can become the main approach to financing deficit in the individual accounts.

4.4.2 Investing Rationally to Preserve and Increase the Value of Pension Assets

The deficits in individual accounts, funded through multiple channels, can be merged with enterprise and occupational pensions to form pillar 2 as its mandatory component and voluntary component respectively. The current contribution rate (8%) of individual accounts can be maintained. Individual accounts should be fully funded and invested in a market-oriented manner to preserve and potentially increase their value.

In fact, after many years of development, China's capital market has matured enough for pension investment. First, the market size and specialization of the asset management industry have been improving. At present, China's asset management industry holds more than RMB 50 trillion, accounting for about 80% of the GDP. Historic rates of return of collective trusts are between 7 and 10%, and historic rates of return of equity securities are between 10 and 15%. The concept of using capital markets to preserve and increase asset value has been widely accepted. Secondly, capital market can generate long-term investment value. The key factor that determines investment returns in a stock market is the profitability of listed companies. Generally, the overall profitability of listed companies is positive. In the long run, the gradual accumulation of profits will lead to the gradual rise of the overall market price index, resulting in stable long-term investment income. Since 1991, China's stock index has risen by more than 700% and its enterprise annuities and national social security fund have performed very well. The annualized rate of return of enterprise annuities is 7.97% and that of the national social security fund is 8.38%. Provided that individuals participating in pension insurance receive pension benefits for about 14 years after they have contributed premiums for 35 years, benefits of

[3]Including SOE shares held by the State-owned Assets Supervision and Administration Commission of the State Council (SASAC), the Ministry of Finance, and local state-owned assets supervision and administration commissions, including H shares listed in overseas markets and some red chips. Source: Public information.

individual accounts can reach 30% should the annualized rate of return of long-term investment reached 6% (determined based on annualized rate of return of long-term investment in foreign capital markets). The combined benefits (with public pension benefits being 40%) will amount to 70%, which is close to the level of income in the pre-retirement period. For employees participating in enterprise annuities, the total benefits will even higher.

4.5 The Advantages of the Three-Pillar Pension System in China

4.5.1 It Can Help Deal with the Population Ageing Crisis and Reduce the Pension Gap

China is entering into an ageing society before it gets rich, which is the most significant demographic trend in the country. China's pension system faces a huge financing gap, placing the Chinese government under tremendous financial stress. The most significant problem in the current pension system is that it is difficult for the Chinese government to afford the great amount of pension benefits. The root cause for this problem is that the pension system is dominated by pillar 1 which is financed on a pay-as-you-go basis, making the system unable to cope with the population ageing crisis. Under the three-pillar pension system, the government's financing responsibility is limited to pillar 1. After the reforms, both the contribution and benefit levels of pillar 1 will be lowered and the future pension gap will be narrowed. The decline in the level of benefits of the insured will be offset by benefits of fully funded pillar 2 and pillar 3s.

4.5.2 It Can Help Clarify the Relationship Between the Government and the Market and Split Responsibilities for Old Age Care Among the State, Enterprises and Individuals

Under the three-pillar pension system, the government bears the ultimate responsibility for the pillar 1. The pillar 2 is jointly funded by employers and individuals, and the pillar 3 is funded entirely by individuals. The three-pillar design reduces the funding responsibility of the government which is much heavier under a single-pillar pay-as-you-go system and splits responsibilities for financing old age care among the state, enterprises and individuals.

4.5.3 The Three-Pillar Design Makes It Possible to Integrate Both Income Redistribution and Incentives

The current pension system design seeks to integrate the income redistribution effect of the pay-as-you-go model and the incentive effect of a fully funded model into one system, but this goal has not been achieved due to the flaws of institutional design and difficulty in implementation. The three-pillar pension system does not pursue the integration of pay-as-you-go and full funding in one pillar. Instead, the two functions are performed by different pillars. Pillar 1 is financed on a pay-as-you-go basis and helps retirees to maintain the basic standard of living through social pooling, reflecting the strength of the pay-as-you-go system in the redistribution of income across generations. Occupational pensions of pillar 2 and individual pensions of pillar 3 are fully funded and provide individuals with tools to save for their own retirement and improve their standard of living after retirement. They demonstrate the strength of the fully-funded model in self-incentive.

4.5.4 It Accentuates the Role of Pension Fund in Investment and Thus Reducing the Burden of Employers and Employees

Multiple comparative studies show that pension contribution rates in China are very high compared to the world's average level. There is little room left to enhance financial sustainability of China's basic pension by increasing contributions. In the three-pillar pension system after reform, emphasis will be placed on the investment value of pension money. In particular, those of pillar 2 and pillar 3 will be invested heavily in capital markets to preserve and increase asset value, which will enrich sources of pension money and enhance the financial sustainability of the pension system.

4.5.5 Pension Reforms Can Be Achieved Through a Smooth Transition Process and Thus Cost Less

Instead of reconstructing the existing system in a disruptive manner, a multi-pillar design advances and deepens the existing pension system. Therefore, during the building of a multi-pillar system, policy makers have taken into full consideration the connection between the new and old systems and their transition. Under a multi-pillar system, pillar 1 is transformed from the current social pools of the basic old age insurance system. Both of them adopt a pay-as-you-go model and thus no structural adjustment is required. Pillar 2 is composed of the individual accounts of the basic pension and enterprise annuities. Considering existing policies, only the individual accounts of occupational annuities will be mandatory and enterprise annuities will remain voluntary. This institutional framework aims at smoothing the transition and retaining useful features of the existing system as much as possible, which can effectively reduce the resistance to the reforms as well as reform costs.

5 Evaluation of and Solution to Key Problems in the Reform

5.1 *Public Pension Revenue and Expenditure Evaluation*

One of the core objectives of the three-pillar reform design is to reduce the public pension gap and the government's financial burden. Therefore, it is necessary to evaluate post-reform revenue and expenditure of public pension.

5.1.1 Revenue and Expenditure Evaluation Model

(1) Revenue Model:

Revenue of the year = urban working age population × labor force participation rate × employment rate × coverage of the pension scheme among current workers × average wage of the year × contribution rate.

(2) Expenditure Model:

Expenditure of the year = retired urban population × labor force participation rate × coverage of the pension scheme × average pension contribution of the year.

5.1.2 Basic Parameters

See Table 4.

5.1.3 Balance Evaluation

According to the results of this study, under the assumption that the demographic policy will not change, if China continues to implement the current basic pension system, the social pooling portion will face an annual financing gap in 2025 and run out of funds in 2028 or also. Under the most recent reform design, the social pooling portion will face an annual financing gap in 2034 and run out of funds in 2047. Clearly, the reform of the public pension system design can effectively reduce the annual financing gap faced by the basic pension, enhance the sustainability of public pension and reduce the government financial burden.

Table 4 Parameter setting basis

Parameter	Value	Basis
Urban working age population		Calculated according to the demographic model of Bo Sun and data from the fifth national census[a]
Retired urban population		Calculated according to the demographic model of Bo Sun and data from the fifth national census
Labor force participation rate	72.6%	According to Cai Fang, the labor participation rate in China has been maintained below 70% since 2000 and will continue to decline[b] According to the World Bank, China's labor force participation rate from 2007 to 2011 was 72.6%. That of developed economies such as high-income countries or OECD members is around 72%, so it is set at 72.6% in this study
Employment rate	90%	According to the 2009 Blue Book of China's Society published by the Chinese Academy of Social Sciences, the urban unemployment rate in China was 9.4%. This article sets the urban employment rate at 90%[c]
Coverage among current workers	61.9% in 2012 90% in 2020	According to the 2012 National Statistical Communiqué, there were 371.02 million urban employees in 2012, and 229.81 million employees participated in the basic pension scheme, accounting for 61.9% of the employees in urban areas. This paper assumes that the coverage will reach 90% by 2020, which is close to 100% coverage
Labor force participation rate among retirees	5.8% in 2012 Declining to 2.6% in 2020	In 2005, the percentage of retirees covered by the basic pension was 85.8%.[d] In the long run, it should be consistent with the labor force participation rate of current workers and maintained at 72.6% after 2020
Coverage rate among retirees	90%	This paper assumes that the number of retirees covered by the basic pension accounted for 90% of the total number of retirees in 2012
Average contribution base	RMB 28,752	In 2012, the average annual wage of urban employees in the public sector in China was RMB46,769, and that of urban employees in the private sector was RMB28,752. Average contribution base is determined based on the lower one of the two
Growth rate of salary	10% in 2012 5% in 2020 Average annual growth −0.63%	Before 2012, China's average wage growth rate was above 10%. Taking into account China's goal to double income growth by 2020, we assume the average wage growth rate was 10% in 2012 and the economy will gradually enter a steady state, with wage growth reaching 5% in 2020
Contribution rate	28%	According to Document 38, the contribution rate of the individual accounts of the basic old age insurance is 8%, that of the social pooling account is 20%, and the total contribution rate is 28%

[a]Sun et al. (2011, pp. 31–36)
[b]Ma et al. (2010, pp. 11–28)
[c]Task force of the Institute of Economics, Chinese Academy of Social Sciences (2009, pp. 12–15)
[d]Cai (2007, pp. 8–9)

5.2 *Evaluation of Benefits from Individual Accounts*

The three-pillar reform design in this paper recommends a lower replacement rate of the basic pension to reduce the financing pressure on the government and makes up for the decline in the level of public pension benefits by fully funding individual accounts and proper investment of pension assets. Therefore, whether the benefits from individual accounts can make up for the decline in the benefits from the public pension is the key to the reform design. The following simulation model is used to evaluate whether this reform proposal can achieve the above goal.

5.2.1 Basic Model and Parameter Setting

According to Wu et al. (2011)[4], we assume the pension replacement rate of individual accounts[5] is the same as that of enterprise annuities. The contribution rate and the replacement rate of individual accounts have the following relationship:

$$c = \frac{rs \cdot (1+p)^m (b-p)\left[(1+b)^n - (1+r)^n\right]}{(1+b)^n (b-r)\left[(1+b)^m - (1+p)^m\right]}$$

where, *rs* is the replacement rate. For the value of other related parameters, see Table 5.

5.2.2 Simulation Modeling of Benefits from Individual Accounts

In general, after the contribution rate is determined and assuming the values of other variables are constant, the replacement rate can be calculated using the above model. If the value of any variable (for example, nominal return on investment) changes, the replacement rate will also change. According to the calculation results, under the recent scheme which sets the contribution rate of individual account at 8%, if the return on investment can reach 6%, the replacement rate of individual accounts can reach 30.8%, assuming all the current requirements, including the years of benefit payment, remain the same. Taking into consideration the replacement rate of the public pension (40%), the total replacement rate will be about 70%, which is basically close to the current replacement rate. Under the mid- to long-term design which sets the contribution rate of individual account at 8%, if the return on investment can reach 7%, the replacement rate of individual accounts can reach 39%. Taking into consideration the replacement rate of the public pension (30%), the total replacement

[4]Wu et al. (2011).

[5]The replacement rate has different definition. It may refer to the ratio of the average pension benefits to the average wage or the ratio of individual pension benefits to pre-retirement wage. In the study of Wu Zhong, the replacement rate refers to the ratio of pension benefits to contribution base, which is consistent with the level of pension benefits in the study.

Table 5 Parameter setting for calculation of the replacement rate of individual accounts

Parameter	Definition of the parameter	Value	Basis
c	Contribution rate of individual accounts	8%	Contribution rate of individual accounts, baseline scenario. The contribution rate can be changed depending on the change in the replacement rate provided that the values of other parameters have been set
m	Years of contribution or average years of service	35 years	The longer years of contribution one has, the higher the replacement rate he/she will get. Generally, the years of contribution are 30 years and the minimum years of contribution are 15 years
p	Growth rate of average salary	5%	The growth rate of average salary is consistent with the growth rate of GDP
n	Expected years of benefit payment	13.67 years	Years of individual account benefit payment The baseline scenario in this study assumes the retirement age is 56 and the years of benefit of payment total 13.67 years (164 months)
b	Average nominal return on investment	6%	6% in the baseline scenario
r	Inflation rate	2%	2% in the baseline scenario

Table 6 Replacement rate of individual accounts under different designs

Benefit level (replacement rate)	Contribution rate of individual accounts	Average years of contribution	Growth rate of average salary	Expected years of benefit payment	Average nominal return on investment	Inflation rate
rs (%)	*C* (%)	*M*	*P* (%)	*n*	*b* (%)	*r* (%)
30.8	8.0	35	5.0	13.67	6.0	2.0
46.2	12.0	35	5.0	13.67	6.0	2.0
39.0	8.0	35	5.0	13.67	7.0	2.0

rate will be about 69%, which is basically close to the current replacement rate. For detailed calculation results, see Table 6.

5.3 *Ways to Materialize the Plan to Appropriate State-Owned Assets to Fund Individual Accounts*

Considering that the direct appropriation of shares in state-owned enterprises to individual accounts may have a great impact on the market and that there are also other specific issues such as equity allocation of each account, a step-by-step alternative approach that involves transfer and sale of shares can be adopted.

5.3.1 Transfer of State-Owned Assets

The first step in the appropriation of state-owned assets is to transfer shares in SOEs to pension administration authorities. To maintain the ownership nature of state-owned stocks, the State-owned Assets Supervision and Administration Commission of the State Council (SASAC) may transfer shares of some listed companies to the basic pension administration authorities (which may be the National Council for Social Security Fund, or the new pension fund management agency, hereinafter referred to Social Security A). It should be pointed out that after the transfer, to ensure the stable and steady development of the governance structure of state-owned listed companies, the shareholders' rights of the state-owned listed companies will remain with the SASAC.

5.3.2 Sale of State-Owned Assets

The second step is to borrow money from the Ministry of Finance or commercial banks to finance deficit in the individual accounts by pledging stock rights, issuing bonds, taking commercial loans and other methods. There are two main solutions:

Solution 1: The Ministry of Finance directly issues special government bonds to the People's Bank of China or commercial banks to finance deficit in the individual accounts. Social Security A turns proceeds from sale of SOE shares and dividends over to the Ministry of Finance. The Ministry of Finance uses the above proceeds to redeem the special bonds when they mature. After individual accounts are fully funded, the assets should be immediately allocated for market-oriented operation.

However, there are certain risks if individual accounts are immediately used for investment. To avoid such risks, Solution 2 can be adopted. First, Social Security A may pledge transferred SOE shares to the Ministry of Finance. The Ministry of Finance may take loans from the People's Bank of China or commercial banks and transfer the loan proceeds to Social Security A which will allocate the loan proceeds to each individual account based on the contributions made by enrollees. At the same time, the Ministry of Finance may issue special government bonds to individual accounts. The proceeds from the special bond issuance will be used by the Ministry of Finance to repay the loans borrowed from the People's Bank of China or commercial banks. Social Security A will use proceeds from sale of SOE shares and dividends to repay the debt of the Ministry of Finance; the cash assets already obtained by the Ministry of Finance should be used to redeem the special government bonds held by individual accounts. The individual accounts will receive proceeds from the redemption of the special government bonds. Funded individual accounts can invest in diverse assets in a market-oriented manner.

5.4 *Benefit Formula for Different Groups of Enrollees in the Transitional Period*

5.4.1 Benefit Formula for the "Old Group" and the "New Group"

There are three groups of enrollees in the basic pension system because of the 1997 reform that combines social pools and individual accounts: (i) those who entered the workforce after the reform ("new group"); (ii) those who retired before the reform ("old group"); and (iii) those who entered the workforce before the reform and retired after the reform ("in-between group"). The three-pillar reform proposal in this paper requests the government to finance deficit in individual accounts. This proposal has different impacts on the three groups of enrollees.

Because the old group retired before 1997, their pension benefits are not affected by the proposal to finance deficit in individual accounts. However, considering the situation that enrollees who retire at younger ages receive less benefit than those retiring at older ages, it is recommended that the old group should be given preferential treatment and their benefits should be raised. In the three-pillar reform, the individual accounts of new enrollees who entered the workforce after 1997 will be fully funded and their benefits will also not be affected by the reform.

5.4.2 Benefit Formula for the "in-Between Group"

Although the individual accounts of the in-between group who entered the workforce before 1997 and retire after the reform is completed would be fully funded, the benefits received by the group may not be sufficient to help them maintain a reasonable living standard due to insufficient balance in individual accounts which were established in 1997 and the decline in benefits from the public pension. To advance the reform smoothly, we believe the in-between group should be compensated for the loss of benefits in the reform. More specifically, we may set a benchmark replacement rate for the in-between group. Based on the ideas of reform proposed hereunder, 70% is a reasonable benchmark rate. The replacement rate of the public pension system and individual account of every in-between enrollee should be accessed against the benchmark rate after retirement. If the replacement rate is lower than the benchmark rate (70%), the enrollee should be compensated by the government. Given the insufficient balance in the individual accounts of the in-between group is a product of the merging of the two pension tracks, the compensation for the in-between enrollees should be borne by the government by allocating money from the government budget of the year or set aside a portion of state-owned asset as compensation fund when transferring state-owned assets to finance deficit in individual accounts.

References

Sun, B., Dong. K., and Tang. Y. (2011). Impact of the adjustment of family planning policy on the pension gap. Population and Economy, (2011) 2.

Dai, X. (2013). Collection of articles on the investment of social security funds, Beijing: China Financial Publishing House.

Wu, J. (1998). Review of China's social security reform. Economic Forum, (1998) 9.

Ma, Z., Lu, Z., and Ye, K. (2010). Labor force participation rate and labor force growth: 1982–2005. Chinese Journal of Population Science, (2010) 1.

Task force of the Institute of Economics, Chinese Academy of Social Sciences. (2009). The employment situation in the context of financial crisis. Domestic and Foreign Economic Developments, (2009) 19.

Cai, F. (2007) Problems brought by China's family planning policy. Far Eastern Economic Review, (2007) 3.

Wu, Z., Zhang, P., and Han, L. (2011). Cost and benefit estimation of enterprise annuities in the context of China's preferential policy based on specific target replacement rate. Journal of Shanghai University of Engineering Science, (2011) 10.

Davis E.P. (1998). Pension Fund reform and European financial markets[C]. LSE Financial Markets Group Special Paper, 107(10):21–35.

Davis, E.P and Steil, B. (2001) Institutional Investors [M]. MIT Press. 131–142.

Dong Keyong, professor and doctoral advisor of Renmin University of China, and Secretary-General of China Ageing Finance Forum (CAFF50). He has been granted a special allowance by the State Council, and used to be Dean of School of Labor and Human Resources and School of Public Administration and Policy at Renmin University of China, and Secretary-General of National MPA Education Steering Committee, specializing in pension policy and financing old age care.

Chapter 5
Development Path of Pillar 3 Personal Pensions in China

Keyong Dong and Bo Sun

Abstract The old age security system consists of three parts: pensions, endowment insurance and elderly care services. The pension system mainly includes public pensions (pillar 1), occupational pensions (pillar 2) and personal pensions (pillar 3). Among them, the public pensions, part of social endowment insurance, are financed on a pay-as-you-go basis and form the endowment system together with commercial endowment insurance. The occupational pensions and the personal pensions are actually designed for personal retirement savings purposes, which have no risk diversification mechanism among different enrollees, and therefore are not insurance. In China, the basic old age insurance (pillar 1) dominates the pension system, the enterprise (and occupational) annuities (pillar 2) develop slowly, and personal pensions (pillar 3) fail to come into shape. Other than that, China's pension system is faced with problems such as a severe shortage of national pension assets reserve, imbalanced development of pension system, and enormous financing pressure in the long run. Therefore, it is imminent for China to speed up the establishment of the personal pension account system. In the process of developing pillar 3, we must take China's national conditions into full consideration, put personal accounts at the core, and construct a mature system framework based on three stages of account opening, operating and cashing. At the same time, supporting mechanisms, including automatic participation, emergency withdrawal, investment consultancy, and the 2nd-pillar and 3rd-pillar account merging mechanisms, should be established to

K. Dong (✉)
Renmin University of China, Beijing, China

K. Dong
China Ageing Finance Forum (CAFF50), Beijing, China

B. Sun
Pension Management Department, China Asset Management, Beijing, China

K. Dong and Y. Yao (eds.), *Annual Report on Financing Old Age Care in China (2017)*, https://doi.org/10.1007/978-981-13-0968-7_5

complement personal pensions system. Furthermore, feasible measures should be explored to separate pension pools and individual accounts of the basic pension system, integrate personal accounts into pillar 3, rationalize and optimize the pension system structure so as to promote the sustainable development of the pension system in China.

Keywords Personal pensions · Account system · Tax deferral · Investment diversification · Separation of social pools and individual accounts

1 Definition of Pension and Related Terms

According to the UN criterion, an ageing society is defined as a country or region in which greater than ten percent of the population is over sixty years old or greater than seven percent is over the age of sixty-five. In 2000, those aged above sixty accounted for 10.2% of China's total population, marking China's entry into the ranks of ageing societies. By the end of 2015, there were 222 million people over the age of sixty in China, accounting for 16.1% of the country's total population. By 2020, China's population over the age of sixty will increase to about 255 million, 17.8% of the total population. By 2030, China's elderly population will exceed 350 million, 25% of the total population.

On the other hand, China is getting old very fast. It took the US 30 years (from 1942 to 1972) for the percentage of those aged sixty-five to grow from seven percent to ten percent of the total population. In China, this process took fourteen years (2000–2014). With respect to development trend, China and the rest of the world simultaneously entered an ageing society in 2000. By 2050, population aged sixty-five and over will reach 30.81% in China, which is close to the expected 32.03% in developed countries while the world average is expected to stand at only 19.7%. In other words, in fifty years, our country will catch up with the degree of ageing in developed countries, which is bound to pose a great challenge for China's pension system. Therefore, we must seize the time to improve the pension system when China is still able to maintain rapid economic growth and before the elderly population reaches its peak.

However, Chinese people have different understandings of old age security, pensions and endowment insurances in China. The theoretical definition of a concept is the basic premise for system design and policy making. The current misunderstandings and confusion about related concepts have affected the reforms and further development of systems related to old age security. As a result, it is necessary to define related concepts in order to lay a solid foundation for policy making.

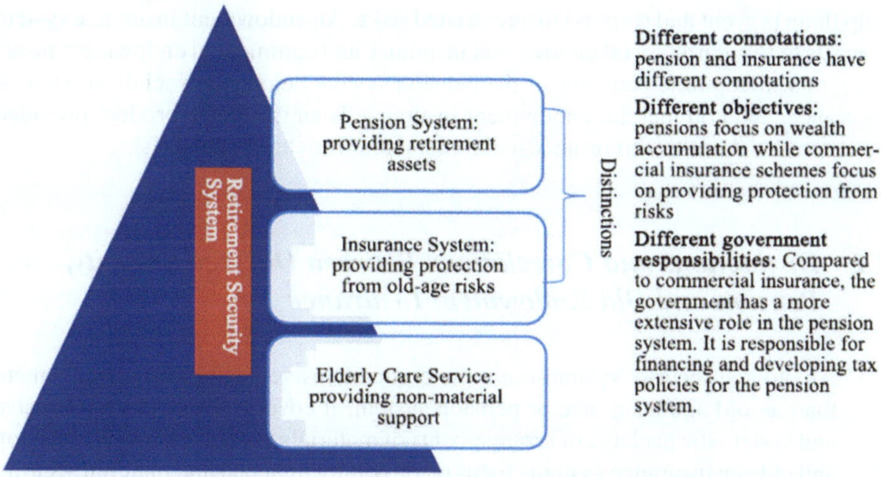

Fig. 5.1 Relationships between old age security system and related concepts

1.1 Definitions of Old Age Security, Pension and Endowment Insurance

Old age security system refers to a comprehensive institutional arrangement covering pension money saving, diversification of old age risks, elderly care and other related fields, made by an economy to meet the various pension demands of the elderly. An old age security system consists of pensions, commercial insurance and elderly care services. Among them, the pension system aims to accumulate assets for old age care, the commercial insurance is designed to help prevent long-life risks, and elderly care services are to provide non-material support to the elderly. For its framework, see Fig. 5.1.

Pension system refers to an institutional arrangement made by a state or society to provide economic support for citizens and help them maintain a reasonable standard of living after retirement through income redistribution or savings. The three-pillar system, consisting of the public pensions, occupational pensions and personal pensions, proposed by the World Bank in the 1990s has been widely adopted across the world for pension reform. In 2005, the World Bank expanded the three-pillar framework into a five-pillar framework by adding Pillar Zero which is a non-contributory, publicly financed and managed system that tackles retirement poverty and the 4th pillar of non-institutionalized solutions like informal support (family support, etc.). However, judging from the general international trend of pension development, the three pillars that assign pension responsibility to the government, employers and individuals still remain the core of modern pension systems.

Endowment insurance system Endowment insurance refers to institutional arrangements designed based on the law of large numbers and the principle of risk diversification to provide economic compensation for elderly members of a society to help them prevent and respond to age-related risks. An endowment insurance system consists of two parts: social endowment insurance and commercial endowment insurance, of which public pensions of the pension system belongs to social endowment insurance, and commercial endowment insurance is an insurance product provided by commercial entities to protect social members from age-related risks.

1.2 Distinctions and Correlations Between Old Age Security, Pension and Old Endowment Insurance

(1) An old age security system is a more comprehensive institutional arrangement than an old age insurance or pension system. It covers a more comprehensive and systematic package of arrangements of materials and services while pension and old age insurance systems focus on providing financial and material security for citizens. Improving pension and old age insurance systems can provide good economic support for the old age security system.

(2) Commercial endowment insurance serves as an important supplement to the pension system, but it is not part of the system. Firstly, the concept of pension is introduced from western countries. In English-speaking countries, a pension system (not endowment insurance system) consists of public pension, occupational pension and individual pension. Secondly, the key function of the pension system is to accumulate pension assets while that of commercial endowment insurance is risk diversification, which demonstrates the stark differences of the purposes of two systems. Thirdly, the responsibility and involvement of the government is much more prominent and deeper in the pension system. The government finance and run the pillar 1, and regulate and provide tax incentives for the pillar 2 and pillar 3. In comparison, the government's involvement in the commercial endowment insurance industry is much less since it is only responsible for regulating market behavior in the industry.

(3) Despite differences, the pension system and the old age insurance system are related. In the pension system, the public pensions are financed on a pay-as-you-go basis. They are in essence insurance that provides mutual aid to members of society, such as China's pay-as-you-go basic pension scheme for urban employees. Therefore, public pensions (pillar 1 of the pension system), together with endowment insurance, form the old age insurance system. However, the accumulative occupational pensions and personal pensions are personal retirement savings of individuals. They are part of the pension system but not insurance. For the distinctions and relationships between the pension system and the old age insurance system, see Fig. 5.2.

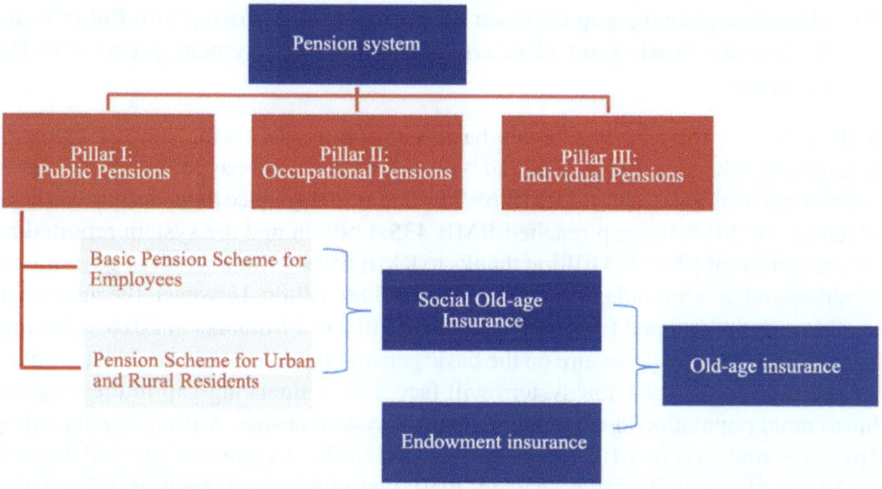

Fig. 5.2 Distinctions and relationships between the pension system and the old age insurance system

2 Urgency for Developing Pillar 3 Personal Pensions

2.1 Problems and Challenges Faced by China's Pension System

(1) China's pension reserve is severely insufficient, exerting grave challenges to provide for the aged

Globally, with the ageing population growing larger and larger, countries across the world have taken precautions and attached great importance to accumulate pension assets. Global Pension Assets Study 2017 shows that the size of global pension assets increased from USD 26.50 trillion in 2010 to USD 36.44 trillion in 2016. The growth rate of pension assets is also higher than the GDP growth rate. During 2010–2016, the global average annual growth rate of pension assets was 5.45%, while the average annual GDP growth rate was 2.39%. In comparison, by the end of 2016, the total size of China's pension assets, including basic pension, enterprise annuities and social security funds, stood at about RMB 6.8 trillion, accounting for less than 10% of China's total GDP, which was RMB 74 trillion in 2016. On the other hand, China has the world's largest population, which means the per capita pension assets are seriously insufficient and China's pension system will face great challenges in the long run.

(2) **There is a growing gap between the contributions flowing into Pillar 1 and the benefits flowing out of it, creating a massive payment pressure in the long run**

With respect to the size of China's basic pension assets, taking out the factor of government subsidies, the annual gap between revenue and payout of China's basic endowment insurance reached RMB 65.2 billion in 2014. Since then, the gap has been widening. In 2016, the gap reached RMB 435.4 billion and the system reported an annual surplus of RMB 0.3 trillion thanks to RMB 651.1 billion worth of government subsidies and an accumulated surplus of RMB 3.86 trillion. However, the number of payable months dropped from 19.7 months in 2012 to 17 months in 2016, reflecting the potential financing pressure on the basic pension fund in the future. Most scholars believe that China's pension system will face a huge financing gap in the long run due to rapid population ageing and inadequate system design. A study conducted by Boyuan Foundation in 2012 shows that, by 2033, China's pension gap will account for 38.7% of its GDP of that year; in 2050, that number will register 75% of that year's GDP.

(3) **Pillar 2 occupational pensions only cover a small number of people and their role in supplementing the pillar 2 is thus limited**

At present, occupational pensions in China include enterprise annuities for employees in urban enterprises and occupational annuities for employees from the public sector. Enterprise annuities were introduced in 2004, marked by the promulgation of *The Trial Measures for Enterprise Annuities*. An enterprise annuity is an accumulative fund contributed by an enterprise (employer) and its employees. After more than a decade of development, the pillar 2 has improved significantly but still has many problems. First of all, its size of assets remains insufficient. At present, the total amount of occupational pension funds represented more than 50% of GDP in 35 OECD member countries and less than 2% in China. Secondly, the pillar 2 only covers a small number of people. Most Chinese enterprises have not set up an enterprise annuity mechanism. That is why the aggregate size of occupational pension assets is rather small. According to the *Report on China's Enterprise Annuity Funds 2016* released by the Ministry of Human Resources and Social Security, by the end of 2016, only 76,300 enterprises in the country have set up an enterprise annuity and 23,247,500 employees were enrolled in the enterprise annuity system. Thirdly, the development of enterprise annuities is unbalanced. The development of enterprise annuities in the eastern part of China is faster than that in the central and western regions. The development of enterprise annuities among state-owned enterprises and foreign-funded enterprises with better economic returns is faster than that of private enterprises.

Occupational annuities are established for government employees to make up for the decline in the basic pension benefits after the merging of the dual tracks. Occupational annuities are accumulative pension funds contributed by employers and employees as well. The system of occupational annuities for employees of government agencies and public institutions came into force on October 1, 2014, making the sizes of it relatively small too. In the long run, occupational annuities can only cover over 30 million employees of government agencies at most, which means occupational annuities and enterprise annuities (pillar 2) will cover about 60 million people, accounting for only 17% of the population from the basic pension for urban employees in 2pillar 1. Such small coverage limited its role in supporting pillar 1.

(4) **Pillar 3 personal pensions have received wide attention but related policy has not been developed**

Early in 1991, China has proposed the idea of "gradually building an endowment insurance system consisting of basic endowment insurance, supplementary enterprise endowment insurance and personal savings." This was the first time that 2pillar 3 was brought to the public's attention in China. However, since the positioning of the pillar 3 remains unclear, no actual policy at the national level has been rolled out, only some relevant ministries and local governments have made some follow-up explorations. In 2007, Tianjin Binhai New Area attempted to carry out a program that allows up to 30% of an individual's pre-tax salary paid for premiums of commercial endowment insurance products. However, the program failed eventually due to various reasons. In 2009, Shanghai proposed a pilot project to promote for-profit products of personal tax-deferred pension. In 2015, the *Outline of the 13th Five-Year Plan* proposed to "introduce tax-deferred pension" in which the word "for-profit" was deleted. The *13th Five-Year Plan of the Ministry of Human Resources and Social Security* issued in July 2016 interpreted the concept as "the introduction to personal tax-deferred pension." During the 2017 annual parliamentary sessions of China, dubbed as "two sessions", the Ministry of Finance required that relevant departments conduct in-depth studies on policies and technical issues related to pillar 3 and rolled out relevant policy proposals.

2.2 *Significance of Establishing and Improving Personal Pension System (Pillar 3)*

China has already established a basic pension system (pillar 1) and an enterprise (and occupational) annuity system (pillar 2). However, the percentage of the pillar 1 assets to the aggregate assets in China's entire pension system is too high. As the main provider for the aged, its replacement rate has maintained at about 45%, a relatively low protection for the elderly without the support from pillar 2 and pillar 3. On the other hand, the basic pension funds in the three northeastern provinces have already failed to meet the needs of their pensioners and many more provinces are expected to face the same fate in the future. As a result, it is imperative to improve the fairness and financial sustainability of the pension system. One of the key solutions is to build the pillar 3 as soon as possible to complement and upgrade the pension system.

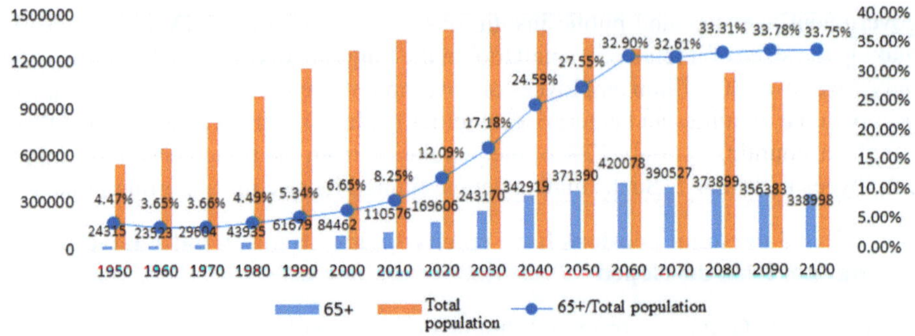

Fig. 5.3 Changes in the population aged 65 and over in china and its proportion to the total population during 1950–2100. *Source* United Nations, Department of Economic and Social Affairs, Population Division (2015). World Population Prospects: The 2015 Revision, custom data acquired via website

(1) **Pillar 1 alone is unable to deal with pension crisis brought about by population ageing**

Since China became an ageing society in 2000, its population ageing has gradually picked up pace. Judging from the trend of development, population ageing will dwell in China for a long period of time, reaching its peak around 2060 and then begin to decline. However, the total amount of elderly people will not drop with the decline of the total population, instead, the proportion of the elderly population aged 65 and above will remain relatively high (about 33%) for a considerable period till the end of the 21st century and the trend is irreversible (see Fig. 5.3).

The above demographic changes mean that the current dependency ratio of the existing pension system in our country will also continue to increase. In other words, the proportion of those who receive pension benefits will continue to increase while the proportion of those who contribute to the pension system will continue to decrease. If the existing pension system remains unchanged, China's pension system will face a huge financing gap. Based on reform experience of the developed countries, most countries that have succeeded in achieving fairness, adequacy and sustainability in pension systems have mostly implemented a multi-pillar system that provides diversified pension benefits for their citizens. Pillar 2 and pillar that assign pension responsibility to employers and individuals play an increasingly important role during the reform. Pension systems rely solely on pillar 1 such as the pension system in Greece are unsustainable and have also led to sovereign debt crisis, proving that single-pillar pension system cannot cope with multifaceted challenges posed by demographic, economic and social changes.

(2) **Pillar 3 plays a bigger role than Pillar 2 in improving the pension system**

The purpose of developing pillar 2 and pillar 3 is to perfect the pension system and split pension responsibility among the state, employers and individuals. However, after more than one decade of development, the enterprise annuities have failed to serve as an adequate supplement to the basic pension system in China. This is because pillar 2 is established by employers, and due to long-term excess of labor force, most enterprises are not motivated to establish enterprise annuities. Especially in recent years, as economic growth slows down and corporate profitability declines, the growth of enterprise annuities has been stagnant as well. By the end of 2016, only 844 new enterprise annuities were set up, up by only 1%. The number of employees enrolled in the new enterprise annuities stood at 85,300, merely up by 0.37%. Occupational annuities are designed only for over 30 million employees in government agencies. On the whole, the supplementary role of pillar 2 is very limited. In regard to pillar 3 personal tax-deferred pensions, employers' voluntary participation and initiation is not required in that the government provides direct tax incentives to encourage individual participation. Thus, it is expected to cover a wide range of people and play a great role in China's pension system by helping improving the system and reducing the financial burden on public pensions.

(3) **Pillar 3 can strengthen China's ability to provide old age security and decrease financial burden on the government**

The greatest driving force for pillar 3 is strong tax incentives provided by the government. In the United States, for example, up to about 12–15% of the average salary paid by individuals for premiums of pillar 3 can be exempted from personal income taxes. Such huge tax reduction greatly motivates individuals to accumulate pension assets during employment. Furthermore, reasonable and market-oriented investment and operation of pension funds which may last for several decades can preserve and increase their value; thus increasing the source of income for the aged and helping reduce the pressure on public pensions and the government.

(4) **Pillar 3 can help optimize the structure of the financial system and stabilize capital markets in China**

For a long time, due to the imperfect pension system and the lack of the third pillar, part of the national financial assets aimed at providing for the aged are invested in bank deposits and financing, which does not help China's financial structural adjustment that strives to "reduce indirect financing and increase direct financing." The financial system is seriously under-performing in converting savings into real investment. In the meanwhile, the government has no choice but obtaining low earnings that are below the average rate of return on investment in China. Apart from that, some pension fund assets will flow into the stock market disorderly through retail investors to capture short-term spread. These investors tend to hold winners and sell losers. As a result, the long-term attribute of pension money is not fully utilized and the flow of pension fund assets into the capital markets in this manner will also cause violent fluctuations in the capital market, which is unfavorable to the sustainability of pension funds. Setting up pillar 3 can separate the investment of pension funds from personal banking and stock investment and generate reasonable returns through specialized asset management institutions in the capital market, thus supporting the development of the real economy more effectively.

3 Positioning of Pillar 3 in China's Pension System

3.1 Improving the Structure of China's Pension System and Splitting Pension Responsibility Among the Government, Employers and Individuals

In 1991, the *Decision of the State Council on the Reform of Enterprise Pension System* proposed that China should gradually build an endowment insurance system consisting of basic endowment insurance, supplementary enterprise endowment insurance and personal savings and split pension responsibility among the government, employers and individuals. After several years of reform and practices, the government-financed basic pension system has significantly improved and the employer-financed occupational pension system has been established. However, privately-financed pillar 3 has not come into shape in China, which is not conducive to motivating citizens to save for retirement. Establishing and improving the pillar 3 is one of the important tasks in the overall strategy aimed to perfect the structure of China's pension system and roll out a system that splits pension responsibility among the government, employers and individuals.

3.2 Motivating Individuals Through Preferential Taxation to Reserve Personal Pensions to Raise the Total Amount of Pensions

The primary objective of the pillar 3 is to further expand sources of income for the elderly and improve their self-supporting ability. Personal pensions are voluntary and accumulative, and they maintain and increase value through market-oriented investment. International experience shows that the most effective incentive for voluntary pensions is tax deferral. China should also issue an effective and powerful deferred taxation policy to increase the attractiveness of personal pensions and expand the coverage of pillar 3, especially among the vast number of employees who are not covered by enterprise annuities or occupational annuities, as well as self-employed persons with certain income. Expanding the coverage of pillar 3 can increase self-protection capability of enrollees and offer another source of income for the elderly in addition to basic endowment insurance.

3.3 Creating Supplementary Pension Accounts to Protect Enrollees' Rights and Interests

So far, the transfer of basic pensions in China has been normalized. However, enrollees of pillar 2 may face pension transfer problems when they change jobs. In pillar 2, enterprise annuities are voluntarily established by corporate employers while occupational annuities, designed for employees from government institutions, are mandatory in nature. When an employee moves from an enterprise which has an occupational pension to a place without any occupational pension, the fund in his/her occupational pension account cannot be transferred, thus affecting the rights and interests of the insured. Concentrating on individuals themselves, pillar 3 opens personal pension accounts base on an individual's own will. When a participant changes jobs or retires, he/she can transfer the fund in pillar 2 to his/her personal pension account of pillar 3, which is also a common practice across the world. Using the third pillar as the centralized account for supplementary pensions can increase the convenience of supplementary pensions and better protect the rights and interests of the enrollees.

3.4 Encouraging Long-Term Retirement Savings and Following Short-Term Capital Needs of Citizens

The third pillar of personal pensions is mainly designed through institutionalized rules to encourage individuals to start early in life, according to their own circumstances, sketch pension plans and provide sufficient economic support for themselves after retirement. Such pensions are accumulative and voluntarily contributed by individuals, and the pension assets are also owned by individuals. On the other hand, enrollees of pillar 3 do not have any need for pension benefits until retirement. The fund in their personal accounts gradually accumulates during their several decades of employment. In this accumulation process, they may have emergency capital needs, such as large emergency medical expenses, first-time home purchase, and children's education. To meet the above capital needs and increase the attractiveness and flexibility of the system, Pillar 3 often allows individuals to apply for temporary withdrawal of pension assets accumulated in their personal accounts under special circumstances and repay the pensions withdrawn within a specified period. This mechanism takes into consideration both long-term pension accumulation and citizens' short-term capital needs, making it a citizens' personal pension account with comprehensive support functions.

4 Three Key Factors of the System Design for Pillar 3

Many countries in the world have established a multi-pillar pension system, among which the plan that the government provides tax incentives to encourage citizens to participate in the voluntary pillar 3 has grown rapidly and caught worldwide attention. Among them, the United States boasts the most well-developed and advanced pillar 3 in the world. As of the end of 2016, the pillar 3 assets in the United States reached USD 7.9 trillion, accounting for 30.3% of the assets in the three-pillar system, 2.8

times that of Pillar 1. Evolved after a series of reform, In the UK and Australia Pillar III has also been growing and evolving, albeit in different ways that are unique to each country. International experience shows that tax incentives, the account-based institutional framework, and investment diversification are the three key factors that affect the stability and growth of pillar 3.

4.1 Tax Deferral Is the Key Driving Force for Pillar 3 Development

(1) **The principle of designing tax deferral mechanism is that it must ensure that the tax burden in the withdrawal stage should be smaller than the sum of tax concessions in the contribution and investment stages**. Pillar 3 in most foreign countries follows the above principle. Although the tax rate of IRA withdrawals in the United States can reach as high as 20%, it is lower than the total tax burden on each individual in the contribution and investment stages. Therefore, tax incentives of Pillar 3 are attractive to most American citizens. American citizens are required to pay federal and state personal income tax during the contribution period and the minimum tax rate of federal personal income alone is as high as 15%. In the UK, the minimum tax rate of Pillar 3 is 20% during the contribution period, 25% of the pension during the withdrawal period is tax-free, and taxes will be deducted from the remaining part based on the personal income tax rate. Because the total amount of tax paid by enrollees in the withdrawal stage is significantly smaller than the sum of previous tax concessions, citizens are greatly motivated to participate in personal pension schemes.

(2) **When designing a tax incentive program, it is more effective to make pension contributions tax-free up to a specific limit rather than offering tax deduction on a pro rata basis**. Under such design, all enrollees are entitled to the same amount of tax concession regardless of the level of income. This kind of design is more suitable for pillar 3 because personal pensions, as part of the pension system, must balance incentives with fairness. If tax incentives are calculated at a specific percentage of earnings of enrollees, higher income earners will receive greater tax concessions, which will not be conducive to the income redistribution function of the social security system. As mentioned earlier, the tax deferral limit of pillar 3 in the U.S. is between USD 5500–6500 and the deferral limit of 401(k) plans is USD 17,500 per year. The aggregate deferral limit of pillar 3 and 401(k) reached over USD 25,000, which is nearly one half of the average annual salary of American people. In China, only four percent of salary contributed to enterprise annuities is exempted from personal income tax, a quite upsetting number for tax concessions, and another preferential tax policy allows citizens to pay a maximum RMB 200 a month from their pre-tax income to buy designated commercial health insurance products, which is barely satisfactory and less effective than expected too. Therefore, given the large scale of the national pension expenditure, to effectively motivate citizens, the gov-

ernment should increase tax incentives for pillar 3. Thus, it is advisable to set the upper limit of personal income tax deferral for personal pensions at RMB 1000 per month and gradually increase the deferral limit according to the level of social and economic development. In addition, greater tax incentives may be provided for adults near retirement age. For example, the government may allow those aged over 50 to defer another 20% taxable income contributed to their personal pension accounts.

(3) **The government may create a link between tax incentives for pillar 2 and pillar 3**. China has introduced a tax concession policy for enterprise annuities. However, because enterprise annuities are discretionary in nature, some companies may not have set up an enterprise annuity, thus their employees cannot contribute to enterprise annuity even if they are motivated. From the perspective of developing supplementary pensions and alleviating the pressure of public pensions, the government may offer tax incentives for setting up enterprise annuities and personal pension accounts. More specifically, the government can offer tax incentives to those who are not included in an enterprise annuity plan to increase the appeal of pillar 3 and encourage citizens to save for retirement.

(4) **Pension benefits may be taxed as regular income to encourage retirees to withdraw their pensions in installments**. Generally speaking, enrollees are not encouraged to withdraw their pensions in one lump sum after retirement because they are tempted to spend too much within a short term, leaving them short of money down the line. Therefore, in most countries, a higher tax rate is set for lump-sum withdrawal. As for withdrawals in installment, the government may tax them as regular income and set a tax-free base and progress tax rates to encourage long-term payments. This is because, for enrollees who have just crossed the tax threshold in the contribution stage, their income tax rates are lower, meaning they receive relatively less favorable tax incentives. If there is no tax-free base, their tax payment may be greater than the tax concession they have received in the contribution stage. According to related studies, if the government allows RMB 1000 from every monthly withdrawal of personal pensions to be exempted from income tax and tax the remaining amount at progress income tax rates, the tax liability due on pension withdrawals of all enrollees will be lower than their tax concessions in the contribution stage, thus creating an incentive and a positive correlation between the tax rate in the withdrawal stage and that in the contribution stage, which means the higher your income is, the higher a tax rate you pay. Under such circumstances as overall moderate tax rates, not only does this design create adequate incentives for all enrollees, increasing the participation rate, but also offers preferential tax treatment to those with lower income. Such policy transfers income from the rich to the poor and is conducive to achieve equality in financing old age care.

4.2 *Personal Accounts Are the Cornerstone of a Pillar 3 System*

As the specific foundation of pillar 3 system, personal accounts refer to special real-name accounts set up for personal tax-deferred pensions. Activities related to tax incentives and deferred levies, investment selection and right records are all carried out based on them.

(1) **The necessity to adopt personal accounts system in China**

First, a personal account system can effectively realize the value transfer of accumulated pension benefits. As we all know, the basic pension system and enterprise (occupational) annuities adopt a typical personal account system. Therefore, it is natural for personal tax-deferred pensions to adopt a personal account system. At the same time, the creation of pillar 3 personal pension accounts is subject to no restrictions while Pillar II occupational pension accounts must be created by employers. When an individual moves from an enterprise with an occupational pension scheme to an enterprise without an occupational pension scheme, his/her pension rights cannot be transferred through his/her Pillar II account. In such events, personal pension accounts can be used to collect pension rights transferred from Pillar II and improve institutional flexibility.

Secondly, a personal account system is conducive to clarifying the responsibilities of all stakeholders and increasing citizens' awareness of self-providing after retirement. Pillar 3 adopts the trust-based governance structure under the personal account system, which can help clarify pension responsibilities of the government and individuals and alleviate citizens' over-reliance on the state and their employers. At the same time, special personal pension accounts can cultivate citizen's perception of pension responsibilities and increase their awareness and participation in the pension system, strengthening their ability to provide from themselves after retirement.

Thirdly, a personal account system can make personal income more transparent and improve the taxation mechanism. Tax deferral at the account level generally requires enrollees to declare income. On the one hand, it helps the tax authorities to keep track of the real income of enrollees to further improve the personal income taxation mechanism. On the other hand, an accurate understanding of the actual income level of enrollees can also help the government determine the social insurance contribution base, promoting the accuracy in distributing social insurance contributions and payments.

(2) **Suggestions for constructing personal account system of pillar 3 in China**

First, the number of accounts. The comprehensive income taxation system is a widely adopted tax system across the world. An individual may open a personal pension account with a bank, mutual fund, insurance company or trustee. The account management agencies report citizens' taxable income to the taxation authority so it can determine whether the total tax-free amount in all personal accounts of an individual has exceeded the specified cap. However, as China still implements a schedular system of taxation, the above method cannot be used to determine a specific tax concessional limit. Therefore, the Chinese government may consider setting up personal accounts based on citizens' ID cards issued by the public security authorities. In that way, each citizen can only open a personal pension account to ensure the uniqueness of the account and facilitate tax deductions of an individual through one account.

Secondly, account custodians. To expand coverage, maximize the role of supplementary pensions, and provide a source of retirement income for citizens who are not covered by pillar 2, Pillar III personal pension accounts should allow for the voluntary participation of individuals. To this end, the account opening process should be convenient and flexible. Private pension funds may choose banks and securities agents as account custodians. On the one hand, banks and securities agents have many business outlets that can facilitate nationwide participation; on the other hand, banks and securities agents have extensive experience in account management and can handle big data efficiently.

Thirdly, the underlying account information platform. One of the key functions of a personal account system is to collect transaction information and levy personal income tax. China Securities Depository and Clearing Corporation Limited (CSDC) can serve as the underlying data recording and exchange platform for Pillar III, because the account platform of CSDC can ensure the uniqueness of personal tax-deferred pension accounts and are easy to connect the tax administration authority's information management system. CSDC also has other advantages. Firstly, as a basic service provider in the capital market, CSDC has 170 million active securities accounts and extensive experience in account management. It can not only reduce the cost for setting up a special personal tax-deferred pension but also ensure stable and efficient operation of the pension account platform. Secondly, the business network of CSDC covers the whole country and can support both pilot implementation or nationwide implementation of the personal account system. Thirdly, CSDC also enjoys natural advantage in retirement verification and identity verification, so it is more convenient to supervise accounts, search for information and conduct other services through its platform.

4.3 Pillar III Must Diversify Its Investment Portfolios

Pillar III is in essence personal savings for retirement by individuals based on their own pension needs and risk appetites and are discretionary in nature. Diversifying pension products can meet the needs of different groups of enrollees and exemplify the attractiveness and flexibility of Pillar III. **The following are some suggestions to increase the diversity of pension products in China's third pillar**:

Firstly, pension products offered by banks, funds and insurance companies to finance old age care may be included in the selection range. Pillar 3 is an accumulation system which will last for several decades. The key to its effective operation is to preserve and increase pension value through rational investment. Pillar 3 has a wide range of enrollees whose risk appetites and income levels vary considerably. For example, risk-averse enrollees may prefer bank savings, funds that generate steady yields or insurance products that provides stable support. Younger enrollees with a certain level of risk tolerance may choose equity funds to increase fund value through long-term investment and improve their ability to ensure financial security at old age. If personal investment choices are limited to a particular product category, it will undoubtedly affect the maximization of the utility of personal pension assets.

Secondly, standards should be formulated for product entry into the market. On the one hand, pillar 3 aims to meet the needs of citizens to ensure financial security at old age and the financial products they invest should match the attributes of pensions. On the other hand, there a wide range of financial products provided by banks, funds and insurance industries. In the context of an underdeveloped third-party investment advisory services industry, the lack of a market entry system may lead to a mismatch between risk appetite of enrollees and risk characteristics of products or irrational investment. Therefore, it is suggested that a market entry system for the pillar 3 should be set up by the relevant authorities. All products intended for pillar 3 should be assessed before entering the market so that enrollees are entitled to choose from regulated products freely.

Thirdly, default investment vehicles should be designated. In international communities, the pillar 2 and pillar 3 s allow individuals to choose investments for their pension contributions. However, it is difficult for some enrollees to make appropriate investment choices due to lack of financial knowledge or laziness, that is why many countries have established a default investment mechanism. For example, the United States introduced the QDIA system for 401(k) plans in its second pillar in 2006. QDIAs include target-date funds (TDFs), target-risk funds (TRFs), managed accounts and portfolios similar to balanced funds. If a participant fails to provide affirmative investment direction, his or her choice will be defaulted into a QDIA. Considering that most Chinese citizens lack financial knowledge and competent investment vision and that China's third-party investment advice services industry is underdeveloped, many default investment products should be designated in the design of individual-oriented Pillar 3. Individuals may choose default investments when opening their personal pension accounts. Then if a participant fails to decide on how to invest the money in his/her personal pension account within a specified period of time, the money will be defaulted into a qualified default investment product selected by participant. For specific default investment alternatives, we may draw experience from the United States and Hong Kong where they mainly promote target-date funds, target-risk funds and other solution-based products with distinctive attributes of financing old age care. Besides, wealth management and insurance products that are specifically designed for old age care by banks can be designated as default investments, too.

5 Framework and Supportive Mechanisms of Pillar 3

5.1 Framework of Pillar 3 Personal Pension System

Personal accounts system is the core of designing a pillar 3 personal pension system, thus an institutional framework should be created to support account opening, management and pension withdrawal.

Account Opening Stage: Citizens submit account opening information to qualified account management institutions (i.e., designated commercial banks or securities agents) to apply for an account. Account custodians exchange information with taxation authorities through the platform of CSDC and obtain approval for contribution limits from taxation authorities. Such accounts should be created with identification numbers of enrollees and each participant may only have one account. Enrollees can check their contribution, investment and other products information through this account.

Operation Stage: Securities, insurance and banking regulatory authorities should be responsible for reviewing funds, insurance, savings and wealth management products respectively, and design investment vehicles for financing old age care in a unified way. At the same time, a link should be created between designated investments and personal accounts so that enrollees may select among designated investment products based on their own risk appetites and needs. Meanwhile, a default investment vehicle system should be introduced for if enrollees fail to choose investment category on time, the money in their personal pension accounts will be defaulted into the default investment. Account custodians are responsible for submitting contribution, transaction and investment returns and other information to the system of CSDC in a timely manner. Apart from that, the information system of CSDC should be connected to the national tax information system so that taxation authorities can keep track of contributions, investment and returns of pension accounts, providing references for tax concession and deferral.

Withdrawal Stage: Based on the information from taxation authorities and CSDC's deferred personal pension account, during the withdrawal stage, enrollees withdraw pension benefits from their personal pension accounts opened in banks or securities companies while taxation authorities withhold deferred income taxes on pension withdrawals based on relevant information.

5.2 Supportive Mechanisms

(1) **Cohesive mechanism between Pillar II and Pillar 3**

Pillar 3 is based on a flexible personal account system consisting of independent personal accounts which can be easily transferred when a participant changes jobs. Occupational pensions (Pillar II) also adopt a personal account system but its establishment and function are only visible when sponsored by employers. When an employee moves from a company with an occupational pension scheme to another one without an occupational pension scheme, the pension assets in the employee's Pillar II account cannot be transferred. In this regard, China may draw from the experience of other countries and create a cohesive mechanism between pillar 2 and pillar 3. In that way, when an individual changes jobs, his/her Pillar 3 personal pension account can be used to receive pension funds transferred from Pillar II, increasing the flexibility of pension system, which is also conducive to labor mobility.

(2) **Emergency borrowing mechanism**

The purpose of personal pension accounts is to use tax deferral policies to encourage individuals to save and invest for retirement. In some special cases, personal pension accounts can also have other functions. For example, enrollees may be allowed to take an emergency loan from their personal pension accounts if the money is used to pay for health care, family education or a first-time home, which helps elevate the flexibility of pillar 3 personal pension. However, enrollees must comply with strict requirements to make emergency withdrawals and repay the borrowed money within a specified period of time. Should a participant fails to repay borrowed money in a timely manner, he/she will be subject to a penalty in addition to income tax.

(3) **Pension investment consultancy**

The funds in pension accounts of pillar 3 account are long-term capital and should be invested in a reasonable manner to preserve and increase the value of pension assets. As China's financial industry is still at an early development stage and most Chinese citizens have a relatively low level of financial literacy, professional investment consultants play an important role. Therefore, improving the general level investment advisory industry for enrollees to seek help from investment advisors when making decisions relating to investments.

(4) **Regulatory mechanism**

Pillar 3 is an important institutional arrangement concerning the standard of living of citizens after retirement. The operation of the system involves many stakeholders and therefore must be supervised and regulated by different authorities. The implementation of contribution and benefit payment policies should be developed and supervised by human resources and social security authorities. As for taxation, the Ministry of Finance should be responsible for formulating preferential taxation policies for supplementary pensions. The State Administration of Taxation is responsible for reviewing qualifications and supervising and enforcing preferential tax policies. In this stage, the role of other financial regulatory bodies should be highlighted much more, so CBRC, CSRC, CIRC and other financial regulators should fully utilize their roles and shoulder the responsibility of supervising and regulating investments of pension assets.

6 Suggestions for Transferring Individual Accounts of the Basic Pension System to Pillar 3

6.1 Necessity of Separating Social Pools and Individual Account of the Basic Old Age Insurance System

(1) **The current system that combines social pools and individual accounts fails to achieve the goals of the pension reform**

China' current basic pension system combines social pools with individual accounts. The social pooling part is operated on a pay-as-you-go basis and redistributes income through transfers of funds among citizens. Funds in individual accounts are completely accumulative, which are designed to encourage enrollees to save for financing old age care. An efficient combination of social pools and individual accounts should be able to achieve inter-generational redistribution and provide incentives, reflecting the rule of combining collective mutuality and individual responsibility. However, since there is no specific institutional design for transformation reform costs and invisible debts, when the social pooling contributions are insufficient to pay current benefits, the Chinese government has to "borrow" from individual accounts to pay the benefits promised to current retirees. This is widely called the problem of "empty accounts." This means, in reality, China's basic pension system is operated on a pay-as-you-go basis and has failed to achieve the original goals of the pension reform.

(2) **"Empty accounts" severely affects the sustainability of China's basic pension system**

Due to accelerated population ageing and the continued increase in the number of retirees, the pay-as-you-go social pooling portion of the basic pension system is under increasing pressure. In recent years, because the social pooling contributions are insufficient to pay current benefits, the overwhelming majority of contributions to individual accounts have in fact been borrowed by the Chinese government to pay the benefits promised to current retirees. Although the government has been exploring ways to finance deficit in personal accounts, shortfalls in personal pension accounts continue to increase (see Table 5.1). By the end of 2015, the amount of money "borrowed" by the Chinese government from citizens' personal basic pension accounts reached RMB 4387 billion. On the one hand, this "empty accounts" problem causes personal loss for individuals; on the other hand, the huge debt will put tremendous strain on future pension payments and become a major impediment to the sustainable development of the basic pensions system.

6.2 Rationale for Integrating Pillar 3 into the Personal Accounts of the Basic Old Age Insurance System

(1) **The ownership of both personal accounts of the basic old age insurance system and Pillar 3 vests in individuals**

The fund in personal accounts of the basic old age insurance system is entirely contributed by employees and thus owned by employees. Personal pensions of pillar 3 are also private property, making the integration of two accounts possible and feasible. Furthermore, personal accounts from the basic old age insurance system are used only for employees after retirement and are in fact mandatory personal retirement savings, while pillar 3 is also in essence voluntary personal retirement savings. Therefore, the two can be integrated.

(2) **Pillar 3 can manage personal accounts of the basic old age insurance system**

As mentioned earlier, it is imperative to separate personal accounts from the basic old age insurance system by transferring them to pillar 2 or pillar 3. Mainly sponsored by enterprises, occupational pensions can only cover a small number of people into the service of enterprise annuities and occupational annuities, about 60 million or so. Many employees are not covered by occupational pensions. Compared to pillar 2, the basic pension system has covered 380 million employees. If personal accounts of the basic old age insurance system are transferred to pillar 2, the majority of enrollees of pillar 1 will not have a pillar 2 account to receive pension benefits transferred from pillar 1 unless all companies are required to establish enterprise annuities, which is obviously unrealistic. In contrast, pillar 3 personal pensions are voluntary personal savings which are not sponsored by employers, meaning there are no institutional barriers to the transfer of personal accounts of the basic pension system from pillar 1 to pillar 3. In addition, if personal accounts of the basic pension system are merged to pillar 3 as a compulsory component, the number of enrollees covered by pillar 3 will increase by more than 300 million. The effect is similar to an automatic participation mechanism of supplementary pensions.

Table 5.1 Changes in the aggregate capital of individual accounts and pension assets of the basic urban pension scheme in 2006–2015

Year	2006	2007	2008	2009	2010	2011	2012	2013	2014	2015
Nominal value	9994	11,743	13,837	16,557	19,596	24,859	29,543	35,109	40,497	47,144
Funded portion	–	786	1100	1569	2039	2703	3396	4154	5001	3274
Shortfalls	–	10,957	12,737	14,988	17,557	22,156	26,147	30,955	35,973	43,870
Balance	5489	7391	9931	12,526	15,365	19,497	23,941	28,269	31,800	35,345

Note 1. Source: *China Pension Report 2016*, *Human Resources and Social Security Bulletins*, and *China Annual Social Security Report 2015*
2. *Unit* 100 RMB million

6.3 *Key Suggestions for Transferring Personal Accounts of the Basic Old Age Insurance System to Pillar 3*

(1) **Separate social pools with individual accounts after personal accounts are funded**

In 2016, the total shortfall of personal accounts of China's basic pension accounts exceeded RMB 4.7 trillion. If the current system of combining social pools and individual accounts remains unchanged, the shortfall will further increase. In particular, the new nominal rate formation mechanism for personal accounts introduced in 2017 links basic pension interest rates to salary growth. Under the new nominal rate mechanism, the nominal interest rate in 2016 reached as high as 8.31% while the GDP growth rate in the same year was only 6.7%. The actual rate of return on investment for corporate annuities and social security funds in 2016 was only 3.03 and 1.73% respectively. Obviously, the new mechanism will further increase the shortfall of personal accounts, putting further strain on basic pension system.

Therefore, it is necessary to fund personal accounts through various channels as soon as possible and separate the social pooling portion from individual accounts. An important way to make up the shortfall in personal accounts is to transfer state-owned assets to those personal accounts. At present, the market capitalization of Chinese state-owned companies listed in China and overseas markets exceeds RMB 20 trillion and the amount of funds required to make up the shortfall in individual accounts is less than RMB 5 trillion. In other words, this method is feasible. Moreover, transferring shares in state-owned firms to repay government debts is inherently reasonable and will not increase Chinese government's current financial burden. It should be pointed out that after separating personal accounts from pillar 1, the social pooling contributions of the basic pension system may be insufficient to pay current benefits, compelling governments at all levels to fund and invest in social pooling contributions to head off the coming payment challenge.

(2) **Merge personal accounts of the basic old age insurance system into Pillar 3 as its mandatory component**

Individual accounts separated from social pools of the basic old age insurance system may be merged into Pillar 3 as its mandatory component, whereas voluntary retirement savings serve as the voluntary component of Pillar 3. On the one hand, both personal accounts of the basic pension system and personal retirement savings of pillar 3 are private property, so it is feasible to merge accounts of the basic pension system into pillar 3 personal pension accounts. On the other hand, the transfer will quickly expand the coverage of pillar 3. Furthermore, the accumulative Pillar 3 after the merger will consist of a mandatory part and a voluntary part and the value of its assets can be preserved and increased through reasonable investment, thus increasing the ability of enrollees to ensure financial security at old age and reducing the government's financial burden.

(3) **Implement existing tax exemption policy for personal accounts of the basic old age insurance system after the transfer**

Since contributions to individual accounts of the basic old age insurance system are tax-free before the transfer, they should not take up the tax concession quota for personal retirement savings after they are incorporated into pillar 3. In addition, both pillar 2 and pillar 3 are private pensions. Pillar 2 is designed for employers with proper jobs and is generally given greater tax incentives than pillar 3. However, as indicated earlier, the number of people participating in enterprise annuities and occupational annuities in China is small. Therefore, tax concession quota of pillar 3 may be combined with tax credits of Pillar II. For those who have not participated in Pillar II or have not used up tax concession quota of Pillar II, their Pillar II tax concession quota or unused part thereof may be transferred to pillar 3 but the aggregate tax incentives not exceed the upper limit of tax incentives set for the two pillars. The purpose of such design is to encourage citizens to participate in personal pensions and promote the rapid development of Pillar 3.

References

Dong, K., and Yao, Y. (2016). *Annual Report on the Development of China's Financing Old Age Care (2016)*. Beijing: Social Sciences Academic Press (China).

Zheng, B. (2016). *China Pension Report 2016—Deepening the Annuity Reform of Pillar II*. Beijing: Economy & Management Publishing House.

The Investment Company Institute. (2017). *ICI Fact Book 2017*.

Department of the Treasury International Revenue Service: contributions to IRA & Distributions from IRA, 2015.

Keyong Dong, Professor and doctoral advisor of Renmin University of China, and Secretary-General of China Ageing Finance Forum (CAFF50). He has been granted a special allowance by the state government. Former Dean of School of Labor and Human Resources and School of Public Administration and Policy, Renmin University of China, and Secretary-General of National MPA Education Steering Committee, specializing in pension policy and financing old age care.

Bo Sun, Ph.D. in management, Postdoctoral Fellowship in Finance, invited member of CAFF50, serving in Pension Management Department of China Asset Management, specializing in financing old age.

Chapter 6
Pension Finance: Growing Total Pension Assets and Low Rates of Return

Bo Sun

Abstract China has rolled out a series of policies to promote pension reforms since 2016, including policies related to market-oriented operation of basic retirement funds, interim measures for the administration of occupational annuity funds, and tightened regulation of old age security management services, introducing the concept of retirement fund for the first time at the policy level. With the intensive introduction of policies and the vigorous advance of the market, these policies have accelerated pension reforms and created both opportunities and challenges for the pension system. In 2016, the total assets of enterprise annuities and the national social security fund exceeded RMB 1 trillion and RMB 2 trillion, respectively. However, as the rate of return in capital markets continued to decrease, the return on the assets of enterprise annuities and the national social security fund hit the lowest in the last five years. The assets of basic pensions managed by custodians designated by the government were lower than expected. Looking to the future, the pension finance will mainly focus on the expansion of the national social security fund, the investment and management of occupational annuities and the development of pillar 3 personal pensions. The size of the pension market will further increase and demonstrates the following structural characteristics: enterprise annuities will grow slowly; the assets of basic pensions managed by custodians will be less than predicted; the national social security fund and occupational annuities will witness bigger development. In addition, as macro-economic uncertainties increase, the difficulty in managing pension assets will continue to grow, and annuity councils will face the challenge of upgrading. Factors such as investment performance and comprehensive service capabilities will become main driving forces for pension management institutions.

Keywords Pension reform · Market-oriented investment of pension assets
Management of pension assets · Industrial trends

B. Sun (✉)
Pension Management Department, China Asset Management, Beijing, China

K. Dong and Y. Yao (eds.), *Annual Report on Financing Old Age Care in China (2017)*, https://doi.org/10.1007/978-981-13-0968-7_6

1 Overview of Pension Systems and Investments

1.1 Overview of Pension Systems

The development of pension systems has enjoyed a history of over one hundred years. Generally speaking, most countries adopt a multi-pillar pension system introduced and advocated by the World Bank. The multi-pillar pension system was introduced in the 1980s when western countries gradually became ageing societies and their former public pension systems financed mainly by the state had difficulty in making ends meet. Attempting to split the responsibilities for old age care among the state, enterprises and individuals, western countries began to adopt the multi-pillar pension system to help the elderly maintain a reasonable standard of living after retirement and ensure sustainability of the pension system.

So far, the three-pillar pension system is the most sophisticated and effective pension system. Pillar 1 is government-funded public pensions designed to offer minimum pension guarantees and prevent poverty in old age. Generally, pillar 1 is operated on a pay-as-you-go (PAYG) basis, which uses contributions from present employees through taxation or other means to pay the current benefits of retirees and is financed entirely by the government. Pillar 2 is occupational pensions that enjoy certain state tax incentives and are contributed by both employers and employees. Its pension funds are invested to accumulate assets and increase retirement income of employees so that they can live a better retirement life. Pillar 3 is personal tax-deferred pensions. The state grants tax concessions and individuals make contributions to pillar 3 on a voluntary basis, reflecting old age care obligations of individuals. They choose investment vehicles according to their risk appetites to achieve steady returns. The purpose of pillar 3 is to provide the elderly with more sources of retirement income.

1.2 Structure and Current Management Situation of China's Pension System

China's pension system basically follows the three-pillar pension model. Pillar 1 is the basic old age insurance system consisting of an employee's endowment insurance scheme and a pension scheme for urban and rural residents. Pillar 1 occupies the largest portion of the current pension system in China. As of the end of 2015, the assets of China's basic pension fund were RMB 3.53 trillion, most of which was invested in bank deposits and government bonds at a rate of return lower than the rate of inflation. (Public pension fund assets of Guangdong Province and Shandong Province alone stood at RMB 100 billion, respectively, excluding personal accounts in some areas entrusted to the national social security authority). By the end of 2015, the accrued assets of the pension fund for urban and rural residents reached RMB 459.2 billion, which has not been invested.

Occupational pensions (Pillar 2) in China can be divided into two categories: enterprise annuities and occupational annuities. An enterprise annuity is voluntarily set up by enterprises according to their own financial strength. Employers and employees make tax-deferred contributions to the plan. The introduction of the Trial Measures for Enterprise Annuities and the Trial Measures for the Management of Enterprise Annuity Funds, designed to standardize the development of enterprise annuities and the management and investment of annuity funds, on May 1, 2004, marking the establishment of the management and investment system of enterprise annuities. The system is ten years old now. By the end of 2015, a total of 75,500 enterprises in China has set up enterprise annuities covering 23.16 million employees. An occupational annuity is an occupational pension targeted at employees of government agencies and public institutions. The occupational annuity system is designed in reference to enterprise annuity. The *Measures for the Occupational Annuities of State Organs and Public Institutions* were promulgated in 2015. Currently, the government is conducting relevant studies and expected to roll out occupational annuity fund management and other supportive policies by the end of the year.

Pillar 3 is personal tax-deferred pensions. The 13th Five-Year Plan promulgated in 2015 clearly stated that "tax deferred pensions should be introduced"; the 13th Five-Year Plan of the Ministry of Human Resources and Social Security promulgated in July 2016 proposed the "taxes-deferred personal pensions should be introduced." However, no specific management measures have been promulgated till now. On July 4, 2017, the General Office of the State Council issued *Several Opinions on Accelerating the Development of For-profit Old Age Insurance*, stipulating that before the end of 2017, China should launch a pilot program to promote tax deferred endowment insurance.

In addition, to deal with the pension crisis that is expected to occur when China's ageing population reaches its peak, China set up the National Social Security Fund in 2000 as the state social security reserve fund. The assets under the management of the National Social Security Fund was RMB 2.04 trillion as of the end of 2016 and will continue to increase.

1.3 Operation Models and Regulation of Pensions in China

At present, China's basic pension, enterprise annuities and National Social Security Fund were all operated in a market-oriented manner. The following is brief introduction to their operation models.

1.3.1 Operation Model of Basic Pensions

In August 2015, the State Council promulgated the ***Measures for the Administration of Investment in Basic Pension Insurance Funds***, promoting the market-oriented investment and operation of basic pensions. The National Council for Social Security

Table 1 First group of basic pension custodians designated in 2016

Industrial and Commercial Bank of China Limited	Bank of Communications Limited
Bank of China Limited	China Merchants Bank Limited

Source Website of the NCSSF

Table 2 Designated equity investment managers of basic pension assets

Bosera Asset Management Co., Ltd.	China Southern Asset Management Co., Ltd.
Changjiang Pension Insurance Co., Ltd.	Penghua Fund Management Co., Ltd.
Dacheng Fund Management Co., Ltd.	Ping An Annuity Insurance Company Limited
Fullgoal Fund Management Co., Ltd.	Taikang Asset Management Co., Ltd.
ICBC Credit Suisse Asset Management Co., Ltd.	E Fund Management Co., Ltd.
GF Fund Management Co., Ltd.	Yinhua Fund Management Co., Ltd.
HFT Investment Management Co., Ltd.	China Merchants Fund Management Co., Ltd.
Huatai Asset Management Co., Ltd.	PICC Asset Management Co., Ltd.
China Asset Management Co., Ltd.	China Life Pension Company Limited
China Universal Asset Management Co., Ltd.	CITIC Securities Co., Ltd.
Harvest Fund Management Co., Ltd.	

Source Website of the NCSSF

Fund (NCSSF) is entrusted to manage and invest more pension funds on behalf of provincial authorities. The NCSSF may invest basic pension assets directly or designate an independent manager to manage the assets. Basic pension assets must be held and managed by an independent custodian, such as a professional pension manager. Although investment portfolios are different, the operation model of basic pensions is similar to that of the National Social Security Fund. In 2016, the NCSSF designated the following four pension custodians and twenty-one independent pension management institutions (Tables 1 and 2).

1.3.2 Operation Model of Enterprise Annuities

An enterprise annuity has a trustee-centered trust model involving five stakeholders. The client under an enterprise annuity contract (i.e., an employer that sponsors the enterprise annuity plan and its employees) hands over the enterprise annuity assets to a fiduciary which can be an external corporation or a self-governing council set up by the employer. To ensure the smooth management of the enterprise annuity, the fiduciary establishes a principal-agent relationship with the investment manager, the custodian and the account manager. The account manager is responsible for keeping record, checking account data and providing information when required. The investment manager is in charge of investing and managing the enterprise annuity

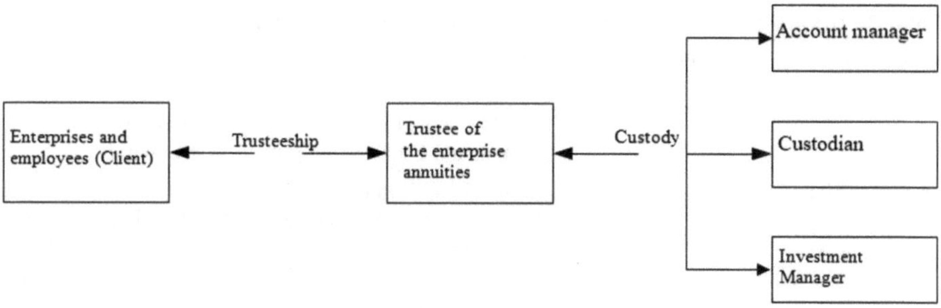

Fig. 1 Investment and management model of enterprise annuity funds

fund. The custodian is responsible for the safekeeping of enterprise annuity assets, accounting, valuation, settlement, payment and other matters. Figure 1 depicts the relationship between the above stakeholders.

Only qualified institutions can manage an enterprise annuity. In August 2005, the former Ministry of Labor and Social Security released the first batch of thirty-seven enterprise annuity fund management institutions, including fifteen investment managers (Table 3).

In November 2007, the former Ministry of Labor and Social Security released the second batch of twenty-four enterprise annuity fund management institutions, including six new investment managers (Table 4).

In November 2013, the Ministry of Human Resources and Social Security announced the qualification of Taiping Pension and Agricultural Bank of China as account manager, the transfer of CITIC Trust's account manager qualification to CITIC Bank, and the cancellation of the Shanghai International Trust's fiduciary qualification and GF Fund's investment manager qualification.

In 2015, CCB Pension Management Co., Ltd. was established and the qualifications of the fiduciary and account manager qualifications of the China Construction Bank were transferred to CCB Pension Management Co., Ltd. which also obtained the investment manager qualification.

At present, the market structure of enterprise annuity management has basically taken shape. Fiduciaries of enterprise annuities are mostly insurance companies and banks; investment managers are mainly fund management companies and insurance companies; only banks can serve as custodians; and account managers are mainly banks and insurance companies. There are relatively fewer trusts and securities companies engaging in the enterprise annuity industry.

1.3.3 Operation Model of the National Social Security Fund

The National Social Security Fund (NSSF) was established in 2000 and is a reserve pension fund of China. The assets of the NSSF come from the following sources: funds allocated from the central government's budget, capital and equity assets

Table 3 The first batch of enterprise annuity fund management institutions in 2005

Stakeholders	Number	Institutions
Fiduciary	5	Huabao Trust Co., Ltd., CITIC Trust Co., Ltd., CCT Trust Co., Ltd., Ping An Annuity Insurance Company Limited, and China Taiping Insurance Group Ltd.
Account Manager	11	Industrial and Commercial Bank of China Limited, Bank of Communications Limited, Shanghai Pudong Development Bank Co., Ltd., China Merchants Bank Limited, China Everbright Bank Co., Ltd., CITIC Trust Co., Ltd., Huabao Trust Co., Ltd., New China Life Insurance Co., Ltd., China Life Insurance Co., Ltd., China Pacific Life Insurance Co., Ltd., and Taikang Life Insurance Co., Ltd.
Fund Custodian	6	Industrial and Commercial Bank of China Limited, China Construction Bank Corporation, Bank of China Limited, Bank of Communications Limited, China Merchants Bank Limited, and China Everbright Bank Co., Ltd.
Investment Managers	15	HFT Investment Management Co., Ltd., China Asset Management Co., Ltd., China Southern Asset Management Co., Ltd., E Fund Management Co., Ltd., Harvest Fund Management Co., Ltd., China Merchants Fund Management Co., Ltd., Fullgoal Fund Management Co., Ltd., Bosera Asset Management Co., Ltd., Yinhua Fund Management Co., Ltd., China International Capital Corporation Limited, CITIC Securities Co., Ltd., China Life Insurance Assets Management Co., Ltd., Huatai Asset Management Co., Ltd., Ping An Annuity Insurance Company Limited and China Taiping Insurance Group Ltd.

Source Ministry of Human Resources and Social Security

derived from state-owned enterprise share sales, and other means approved by the State Council. It is set up to help with the looming pension crisis in the country and administered by the National Council for Social Security Fund (NCSSF). The NCSSF can either directly invest the assets of the NSSF or appoint licensed investment managers. At present, the value of assets managed by designated managers is roughly the same as that directly managed by the NCSSF.

The NCSSF have appointed eighteen domestic investment managers, including sixteen fund companies and two securities companies. No domestic insurance companies have been appointed as investment managers of the NSSF (Table 5).

Thirty-seven overseas investment managers were chosen after rounds of selection, including three domestic managers and thirty-three foreign managers (Table 6).

The NSSF has six custodian banks, including four domestic banks and two foreign banks (Table 7).

Table 4 The second batch of enterprise annuity fund management institutions in 2007

Stakeholders	Number	Institutions
Fiduciary	7	China Construction Bank Corporation, Industrial and Commercial Bank of China Limited, China Merchants Bank Limited, Shanghai International Trust Co., Ltd., Changjiang Pension Insurance Co., Ltd., China Life Pension Company Limited and Taikang Pension & Insurance Co., Ltd.
Account Manager	7	China Construction Bank, China Minsheng Bank Corporation Limited, Bank of China, Shanghai International Trust Co., Ltd., China Life Pension Company Limited, Taikang Pension & Insurance Co., Ltd., Ping An Annuity Insurance Company Limited and Changjiang Pension Insurance Co., Ltd.
Fund Custodian	4	CITIC Bank, Shanghai Pudong Development Bank Co., Ltd., Agricultural Bank of China, and China Minsheng Bank Corporation Limited
Investment Managers	6	Guotai Asset, ICBC Credit Suisse, GF Fund, Taikang Asset, PICC Asset, and Changjiang Pension

Source Ministry of Human Resources and Social Security

Table 5 List of domestic investment managers of the National Social Security Fund

No.	Company name	No.	Company name
1	China Southern Asset Management Co., Ltd.	10	China International Capital Corporation Limited
2	Bosera Asset Management Co., Ltd.	11	Dacheng Fund Management Co., Ltd.
3	China Asset Management Co., Ltd.	12	Fullgoal Fund Management Co., Ltd.
4	Penghua Fund Management Co., Ltd.	13	ICBC Credit Suisse Asset Management Co., Ltd.
5	Changsheng Fund Management Co., Ltd.	14	GF Fund Management Co., Ltd.
6	Harvest Fund Management Co., Ltd.	15	HFT Investment Management Co., Ltd.
7	E Fund Management Co., Ltd.	16	China Universal Asset Management Co., Ltd.
8	China Merchants Fund Management Co., Ltd.	17	Yinhua Fund Management Co., Ltd.
9	Guotai Asset Management Co., Ltd.	18	CITIC Securities Co., Ltd.

Source Website of the NCSSF

Table 6 List of overseas investment managers of the National Social Security Fund

No.	Company name	No.	Company name
1	AEW	20	Morgan Stanley
2	AGF	21	Neuberger Berman
3	AMP Capital	22	Newton Investment Management
4	Allianz	23	PIMCO
5	AllianceBernstein	24	Principal
6	AXA Rosenberg	25	Prudential
7	Baring	26	RBC GAM
8	Batterymarch	27	Schroders
9	BlackRock	28	Standish
10	Bosera	29	State Street Global Advisors
11	European Investors	30	Stone Harbor Investment Partners
12	Fidelity	31	T. Rowe Price
13	INVESCO	32	UBS/CICC Management Team
14	Investec	33	Wellington
15	JanusINTECH	34	Vanguard Group
16	JF Asset Management	35	Crédit Agricole
17	JP Morgan	36	Dacheng Fund and its Hong Kong-based subsidiary Dacheng International
18	Lombard Odier	37	China Universal and its subsidiary China Universal (HK)
19	Martin Currie		

Source Website of the NCSSF

Table 7 Six custodian banks of the National Social Security Fund

No.	Domestic custodian banks	No.	Foreign custodian banks
1	Bank of Communications Limited	1	Northern Trust
2	Bank of China Limited	2	Citibank
3	Industrial and Commercial Bank of China Limited		
4	Agricultural Bank of China Limited		

Source Official website of the NCSSF

2 Annual Policy Review

2.1 The National Social Security Fund Regulations

On March 10, 2016, to standardize the management and strengthen the supervision of the NSSF, the State Council promulgated the *National Social Security Fund Regulations* (hereinafter referred to as the "Regulations"). The significance of the Regulations is mainly reflected in the following aspects:

(1) **The Regulations clarify the legal status of the NSSF**. The Regulations explicitly stipulate that the National Social Security Fund is China's national social security reserve fund that is used to supplement and adjust basic pension and other social security expenditures when population ageing peaks. The NSSF is clearly defined in terms of nature, positioning, investment, supervision and legal responsibilities, with the purpose of standardizing its management and operation and strengthening its supervision. Secondly, the Regulations regulate the management and operation of social security funds throughout the country. They point out that the NCSSF is responsible for the management and operation of the NSSF fund and it should manage and operate the NSSF in a prudent manner as well as invest the NSSF according to the investment proportion approved by the State Council.

(2) **The Regulations improve the institutional arrangement of the NSSF and strengthen its supervision**. Compared with the *Provisional Regulations on the Administration of the Investments of the National Social Security Fund*, the Regulations propose that the NCSSF should formulate the asset allocation plan for the NSSF, determine major investment projects, conduct risk assessment, and discuss and decide on the institutional arrangements for the investment of the NSSF. In addition, the Regulations specify the supervisory responsibilities of regulatory authorities in relation to the NSSF and impose stricter regulations on illegal acts that may arise during the operation of the NSSF. It increases the management and supervision efficiency of the NSSF by deepening institutional arrangements, stepping up supervision and administration, and further standardizing investment and operation mechanisms of the NSSF.

(3) **The Regulations provide a legal basis for the trusteeship of NSSF assets**. Article 29 of the Supplementary Provisions of the Regulations stipulates that upon the approval of the State Council, the NCSSF may take mandate from provincial governments to manage provincial social insurance funds in accordance with the provisions of the State Council on the investment and management of social security funds. This provision means that, based on the pilot projects related to the management of basic pension funds in Guangdong and Shandong province, basic pension funds in other provinces can also be entrusted to the NCSSF. It provides a legal basis for the market-oriented operation of basic pension funds and clarifies the role of the NCSSF as pension fund trustee at the same time.

2.2 *Supportive Financial Policies for the Elderly Care Service Industry*

To further promote innovations related to financial products and services, accelerate the development of the elderly care service industry, and support the supply-side reform, the People's Bank of China, China Banking Regulatory Commission, China Securities Regulatory Commission, China Insurance Regulatory Commission and the Ministry of Civil Affairs jointly issued the *Guidelines on Financial Support for Pension Services Industry to Accelerate Development* (Y. F. No. 65 [2016], hereinafter referred to as the "Guidelines") on March 21, 2016. In respect of the pension system, the Guidelines specifically propose that measures will be taken to propel the development of the endowment insurance system. The following are guidelines related to the development of the pension system:

(1) **Improving the multi-tier old age insurance system**. The Guidelines propose that "the multi-tier, multi-pillar old age insurance system composed of basic pension, enterprise annuities, occupational annuities and for-profit insurance should be further improved" and "the coverage of employer-sponsored supplementary pensions should be expanded to SMEs." The Guidelines emphasize the importance of improving the multi-tier endowment insurance system and vigorously developing supplementary endowment insurance and the third pillar (personal tax-deferred pension).
(2) **Accelerating the innovations related to insurance products and services**. The Guidelines encourage the implementation of pilot projects related to personal tax-deferred pension and "home for care" that offers retirees an income stream to supplement their retirement income, promote the development of one-child family security plans and increase the diversity of products designed for for-profit old age insurance.
(3) **Using pension funds in a creative manner**. The Guidelines point out that China should draw on international experience in pension funds investment and promote investment of the basic pension funds, the NSSF, enterprise annuity funds and occupational annuity funds in diverse assets in accordance with investment requirements to effectively diversifying risks, preserve and increase the value of funds, and enhance the service capability.
(4) **Introducing the concept of retirement funds products for the first time**. The Guidelines point out China should actively develop differentiated products that are designed to finance old age care, provide long-term, stable returns and meet life-cycle investment needs; and vigorously promote the development of retirement funds, encourage individuals to increase their asset income through investments in various specialized financial products and enhance their ability to guarantee financial security at old age. This is the first time that the concept of retirement fund products is put forward at the policy level. Later, China

Securities Regulatory Commission (CSRC) released the *Guidelines for the Investment of Funds in Securities (No. 2)—Guidelines for the Investment of FOF*, providing a legal basis for the issuance of FOF products that highlights retirement income security, including target date funds and target risk funds.

2.3 *Interim Regulations on the Administration of Occupational Annuities*

In September 2016, the Interim Regulations on the Administration of Occupational Annuities (hereinafter referred to as the "Interim Regulations") officially rolled out. The release of the policy meant that occupational annuity funds entered the investment phase, opening a new phase of development for the annuity industry. Generally speaking, the operation model of occupational annuities is similar to that of enterprise annuities. The *Interim Regulations* include detailed provisions on the operation model of occupational annuity, functions of the stakeholders, fund investment, income distribution, information disclosure, supervision and management and other aspects. The major differences between occupational annuities and enterprise annuities are as follows:

(1) **Operation model**. An enterprise annuity can either be managed by an annuity council or an appointed corporate trustee, while an occupational annuity is managed centrally in accordance with a trusteeship agreement under which the provincial social security administrative authority, as the principal, is responsible for developing annuity plans and appointing trustees.

(2) **Stakeholders**. Enterprise annuity management qualifications also apply to occupational annuities. An enterprise annuity has a special account manager. An occupational annuity doesn't need an account manager, and an agent will be appointed instead to perform related duties. An agent refers to a provincial social insurance authority who will sign a management contract with the trustee, the custodian and the investment manager on behalf of the province. Each province has an institution appraisal committee consisting of seven, nine or eleven members who are representatives of human resources and social security departments, financial departments, other government agencies or public institutions with a large number of employees or district-level cities that report large pension assets in the province. Their duty is to choose and appoint trustees. Social security agencies are responsible for day-to-day management of the appraisal committee.

(3) **Establishment of plans. Enterprise annuities are collected by each enterprise**. An enterprise may only have one enterprise annuity plan and one rate of return. Occupational annuities are managed centrally at the provincial level. Each province may set up one or more occupational annuity plans. If multiple plans are set up, they may have one rate of return or different rates of return and the decision-making authority vests in localities.

(4) **Scope of investment**. Compared with enterprise annuities, except universal insurance, investment linked insurance and other insurance products, occupational annuity funds can invest in all products that enterprise annuities are allowed to invest in. The percentage of equity investment should not exceed 30%. Occupational annuity funds can also invest in products designed for pension funds.
(5) **Management fees**. Compared with enterprise annuities, occupational annuities don't charge account management fees while other expenses are similar to enterprise annuities: the cap of the investment management fee is 1.2% and the cap of the trusteeship and custodian fee is 0.2%. The risk reserve ratio is 20% of the investment management fee, and the total amount of risk reserve should not exceed 10% of the net portfolio value.
(6) **Responsibilities of stakeholders**. Compared with enterprise annuities, the agent and the trustee of an occupational annuity have greater authority while the custodian is subject to more restrictions. In addition to performing original responsibilities, the agent should "supervise the management of the occupational annuity plan and establish a risk control mechanism for the occupational annuity plan;" the trustee should "determine the investment proportion of large asset categories and set out risk control requirements"; investment managers should "set up portfolio risk control and periodic assessment systems and strictly control portfolio investment risks."

2.4 Stricter Regulations on Retirement Plan Products and Services

Retirement plan products and services business means that as manager, endowment insurance companies receive entrust from entities or individuals in government agencies, enterprises and public institutions, and other social organizations and provide them with retirement plan products and services and related fund management services. The market of retirement plan products and services business was firstly established in December 2009 according to the *Notice on the Pilot Project of Retirement Plan Products and Services Business* (B. J. F. No. 129 [2009]). After more than three years of exploration, the CIRC released the *Interim Measures for the Administration of Retirement Plan Products and Services Business* (B. J. F. No. 43 [2013]) in May 2013. Since then, the industry has entered a fast lane. On July 30, 2015, the CIRC issued the *Administrative Regulations on Retirement Plan Products and Services Business*, propelling the retirement plan products and services business into a new phase of development. In general, the retirement plan products and services business has the following characteristics:

Firstly, it can only be initiated by endowment insurance and pension companies. According to regulations, only the seven agencies (including Taiping Pension, Ping An Pension, China Life Pension, Changjiang Pension, Taikang Pension, Anbang

Annuity and Jianyin Pension) are qualified to manage retirement plan products and services business. In fact, the rising of the industry can be contributed to the policy support of regulatory authorities for old age insurance companies that used to have trouble in gaining profits.

Secondly, endowment insurance companies can appoint an external agency to invest and manage assets. Although retirement plan products can only be issued by endowment insurance companies, the *Administrative Regulations on Retirement Plan Products and Services Business* stipulate that pension funds can be invested and managed by endowment insurance companies or qualified investment managers. Investment managers can be securities investment fund management companies and their subsidiaries and other professional investment management agencies.

Thirdly, the governance structure can be a trusteeship, which is quite similar to publicly offered funds under which the organization or individual participate in the retirement plan is the principal, the pension insurance company is the trustee and the bank is the third-part custodian. Among them, the insurance company can manage the retirement plan by itself or appoint a financial agency to manage the plan, but they shall bear the ultimate responsibility for the management services they undertake.

Fourthly, the retirement plan products fill up an empty space in the publicly offered funds and bank financing market. The *Administrative Regulations on Retirement Plan Products and Services Business* stipulate that closed-end retirement plan products should be operated under a model similar to that of bank financing products. At present, the minimum capital requirement for a bank financing product is RMB 50,000, while the minimum capital requirement for closed-end retirement plan products for individuals is only RMB 10,000, which greatly lowers the threshold of the market. On the other hand, like publicly offered funds, open-ended retirement plan products can be designed as currency products, bonds, stocks and other financial products. However, unlike public funds, open-ended retirement plan products can invest in non-standard assets and regulations related to investment concentration, leverage ratio and information disclosure of open-ended retirement plan products are relatively lenient. Thus, on the one hand, retirement plan products lower the threshold of bank financing, which enables them to gain a piece of pie from the bank financing market. On the other hand, endowment insurance companies can establish a public fund product line through endowment insurance products. To sum up, management of the retirement plan products and services business will exert a certain impact on bank financing and public funds.

On November 15, 2016, the CIRC released the *Notice on Further Strengthening the Supervision of Retirement Plan Products and Services Business Management* (B. J. S. X. No. 230 [2016]), strengthening the supervision of retirement plan product management to fight systematic arbitrage. The following are major changes stipulated by the new regulations.

(1) **Raising the access threshold of retirement plan products to the market**. Document No. 73 stipulates that endowment insurance companies can engage in old age security business activities, but it does not set out any requirements about registered capital and net assets. Document No. 230 stipulates that the

Table 8 Provisions of document 230 on the percentage of non-standard investments of open-ended retirement plan products

Dealing frequency	<30d	30–180d	180–360d	>360d
Investment ratio (%)	20	30	40	75

registered capital and net assets of a retirement plan management business must be higher than 500 million. In addition, Document No. 73 provides in the Supplementary Provisions that "pension management companies shall comply with the provisions of this policy when engaging in retirement plan product management business." Document No. 230 specifically points out that institutions that are allowed to engage in retirement plan management include endowment insurance companies and pension management companies. At present, the average registered capital of endowment insurance companies and pension management companies is over RMB 2 billion, and the new regulations have no real impact on them. However, certain barriers to entry have set up for potential agencies which wish to enter this market.

(2) **Setting limits for bond leverage and alternative investment ratios**. First of all, the extent of leverage incorporated in a portfolio is restricted. Document No. 73 does not limit the extent of leverage employed in a portfolio, but Document No. 230 stipulates the fund balance for repurchase of a closed-end bond portfolio shall not exceed 100% of the net asset value of the portfolio while that of an open-ended bond portfolio shall not exceed 35%. Secondly, detailed percentage requirements are set out for alternative investments. Document No. 230 has amended the provision that "the balance of investments in infrastructure investment plans, real estate related financial products and other financial assets shall not exceed 75% of the value of the portfolio, of which the investment balance of any single project shall not exceed 50% of the value of the portfolio" and set out detailed percentage requirements for alternative investments (see Table 8). This will exert a negative impact on the return on investment of retirement plan products, especially open-ended portfolios. The percentage of non-standard assets in T+1 open-ended currency products in the current market shall be reduced to less than 20%.

(3) **Stepping up liquidity regulation**. Document No. 230 contains a restriction on a large-amount withdrawal of benefits from retirement plan products, which reduces the liquidity risk of retirement plan management. In addition, in order to standardize the management of product liquidity and reflect the real condition of products, the new regulations require that issuers should not prefund withdrawals. Therefore, most retirement plan products, especially open-end currency products, don't offer rapid redemption at T+0.

(4) **Expanding the scope of investment and increasing investment flexibility**. Document No. 230 has changed the "listed equity assets" in the scope of investment of retirement plan management into "equity assets" and extended the scope

of investment to include equity. It also adds stock index futures into the scope, but such investments are only allowed for hedging or risk aversion purposes. Furthermore, to increase the flexibility of asset conversion, Document No. 230 stipulates that "with the consent of the principal or beneficiary, assets within an asset account of a retirement plan product can be traded with other asset accounts managed by the manager at the market price." On the one hand, this provision helps reduce the cost of investment matching. On the other hand, it tends to increase the likelihood of moral hazard for investment managers.

Overall, considering the institutional advantages of products, there is ample market space for retirement plan management business. Compared to enterprise annuities, group products are more flexible and thus more attractive. Compared to public funds and wealth management products, personal products can invest in a broader range of assets and face a lower barrier to the market. If the retirement plan products can enjoy tax deferral treatment in the future, they will benefit hugely from the tax deferral policy, boasting great development prospects.

3 Annual Industry Review

3.1 The Assets of Enterprise Annuities Exceeded RMB 1 Trillion but the Growth Rate Continues to Drop

As of the end of 2016, the assets of enterprise annuities exceeded RMB 1 trillion for the first time and the number of investment portfolios reached 3207. The annual growth of enterprise annuity assets stood at RMB 149.6 billion, representing an increase of more than RMB 100 billion for the fifth consecutive year. However, affected by the increase in the contribution rate and benefit payouts, the annual growth rate of enterprise annuities dropped from 63.2% in 2009 to only 16.2% in 2016 (Fig. 2).

3.2 The Assets of the NSSF Increased to RMB 2 Trillion

After fifteen years of development, by the end of 2016, the total assets of the NSSF were RMB 2023.228 billion. Among them, equity assets stood at RMB 1948.807 billion, among which, the equity assets of the NSSF were RMB 1604.258 billion, the equity assets of personal accounts were RMB 118.151 billion, and the equity assets of local social security funds were RMB 226.398 billion. This is the first time that the assets of the NSSF exceed RMB 2 trillion, a great step towards addressing the looming pension crisis caused by the deteriorating demographics (Fig. 3).

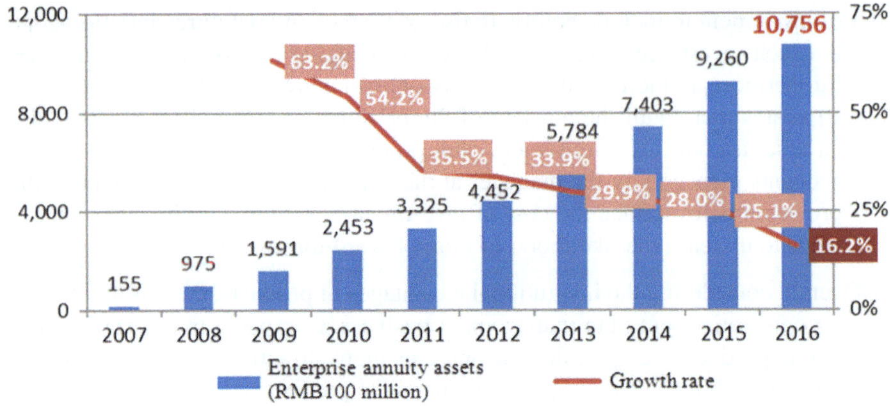

Fig. 2 Assets and growth rate of enterprise annuities by year. *Source* The Ministry of Human Resources and Social Security

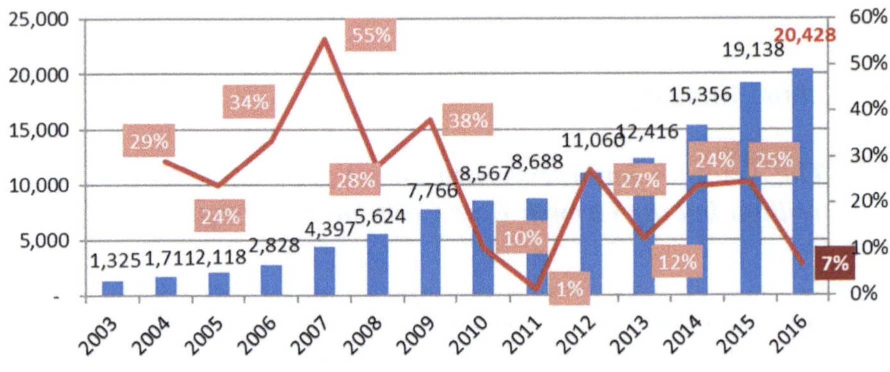

Fig. 3 Assets of the NSSF by year. *Source* The NCSSF

3.3 *The Regulatory Framework of Occupational Annuities Continues to Improve*

In September 2016, the Ministry of Human Resources and Social Security and the Ministry of Finance jointly issued the *Interim Regulations on the Administration of Occupational Annuities*, marking the official introduction of occupation annuities, which are a useful supplement to basic endowment insurance. Later, to improve the top-level design of occupational annuity plans and refine the implementation plan, the CSRC promulgated the a series of documents such as the *Notice on Relevant Issues concerning the Filing and Encoding Rules of Occupational Annuity Plans*, the *Notice on Issuing the Guidance for Occupational Annuity Plan Management Contracts*, the *Notice on Issuing the Professional Annuity Fund Management Code*, and the *Notice on Issuing the Professional Annuity Fund Data Exchange Regulations*.

These documents standardize the encoding, contract-signing, operation procedures and data exchange of occupational annuity funds.

However, except the top-level design, policymaking in relation to the establishment of occupational annuity trust plans, screening of regulatory agencies, fund management, plan supervision and management, establishment of related information systems and other details is still in progress. The investment of occupational annuity funds remains in the preparation stage.

3.4 Basic Pension Management Agencies Have Been Appointed

On March 10, 2016, the *National Social Security Fund Regulations* was issued. Article 29 of the Supplementary Provisions of the policy stipulates that "upon the approval of the State Council, the NCSSF may take mandate from provincial governments to manage provincial social insurance funds in accordance with the provisions of the State Council on the investment and management of social security funds." This provision has provided a legal basis for the market-oriented operation of basic retirement funds. It further clarifies the role of the trustee of the basic pension defined by the *Guidelines for the Investment Management of Basic Endowment Insurance Funds* and stipulates that the NCSSF shall serve as the trustee of the basic pension fund.

To manage the above fund, the NCSSF needs to set up a pension management department and a pension accounting department. The pension management department is mainly responsible for the comprehensive management of pension funds, develop asset allocation plans and sponsor studies related to pension investment policies and capital markets; and the pension accounting department is mainly responsible for, among others, the management and independent accounting of pension fund assets and accounts, and custody services related to pension fund assets.

On the basis of the above efforts, in November and December 2016, the National Council for Social Security Fund selected and approved four basic pension fund custodians and twenty basic pension fund securities investment management agencies according to the *Guidelines for the Investment Management of Basic Endowment Insurance Funds* (G. F. No. 48 [2015]) and related review regulations. So far, the bidding round of basic endowment insurance fund managers has been completed. The market-oriented management of the basic endowment insurance fund has officially entered the countdown stage.

3.5 Endowment Insurance Companies Grew Rapidly, New China Pension Opened for Business and the Insurance Regulator Approved the Establishment of PICC Pension Insurance

In September 2016, New China Pension Insurance Co., Ltd. (New China Pension) was formally established, becoming the seventh endowment insurance company in China.[1] With a registered capital of RMB 500 million, New China Pension is a joint venture between New China Life and New China Assets, in which New China Life holds 99% of the stake, making it the controlling shareholder of New China Pension. On January 5, 2017, the CIRC approved the establishment of PICC Pension Insurance with a registered capital of RMB 4 billion, making it the eighth endowment insurance company in China.

According to the scope of business, pension insurance companies can be divided into three categories. The first category consists of only Anbang Annuity because it has no annuity or basic pension qualification and is mainly engaged in traditional for-profit insurance and retirement plan business. The second category consists of China Life Pension and Changjiang Pension, which have annuity and basic pension qualifications but specializes in pension and retirement plan business only. Such companies are positioned as pension asset management companies. The third category consists of Ping An Pension, Taikang Pension, Taiping Pension and Anbang Annuity. They engage in diverse business activities, including for-profit insurance, pension asset management, and retirement plan business.

New China Pension mainly engages in annuity, life insurance and health insurance business, while the scope of pension business of China Life Pension is rather smaller, including group endowment insurance, personal endowment insurance, and annuity but no health insurance business. Clearly, the above two endowment insurance companies will learn from Ping An's retirement plan business model and expand business scope to encompass traditional insurance, annuity asset management and retirement plan products. This model is highly adoptable because a company must be qualified to enter the annuity market, and traditional commercial insurance business can help support the development of the company in the initial stage when retirement plan products are still in the infancy stage.

3.6 Assets of Retirement Plan Products Exceed RMB 100 Billion

So far, seven companies are qualified to manage retirement plan assets, including six endowment insurance companies and CCB Pension. The CIRC has not disclosed the relevant information of retirement plan management companies. Based on the

[1] The first six endowment insurance companies are China Life Pension, Ping An Pension, Changjiang Pension, Taiping Pension, Taikang Pension, and Anbang Annuity.

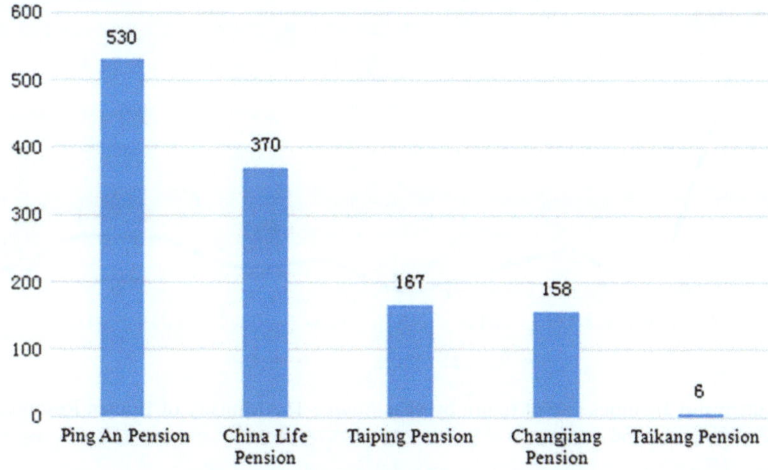

Fig. 4 Scale of retirement plan products management at the end of 2016. *Source* Official websites of endowment insurance companies (as of the end of 2016)

annual disclosure reports of management companies, as of the end of 2016, the total assets of retirement plan products exceeded RMB 120 billion. Specifically speaking, Ping An Annuity Company Limited reported the largest assets in that it took advantage of its existing product portfolios and distribution network, and the assets under its management reached more than RMB 53 billion, representing an increase of RMB 14 billion over 2015. China Life Pension Company Limited reported the second largest retirement security assets, which were RMB 37 billion. Due to first mover advantage and a rate of return that is slightly higher than currency funds, the sale of Guotai Jianian, a currency pension security product jointly launched by China Life Pension and WeChat Wealth, has risen rapidly, accounting for a large proportion of China Life Pension's retirement security assets. As latecomers, both the assets under the management of Taiping Pension and Changjiang Pension stood at RMB 16 billion. The retirement plan assets under the management of Taikang Pension totaled only RMB 600 million, far lower than other companies (Fig. 4).

4 Asset Management

4.1 The Investment Return of Enterprise Annuities and the NSSF Hit a Record Low

In regard to enterprise annuities, the average annual rate of return on enterprise annuities in 2016 was 3.03%, of which the weighted return on portfolios with embedded

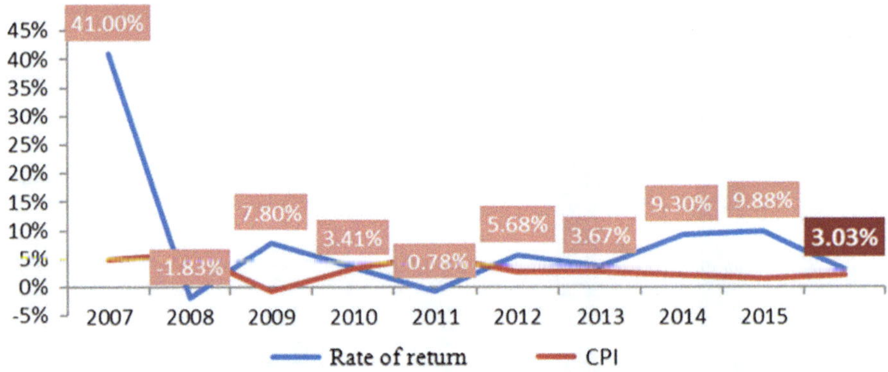

Fig. 5 Enterprise annuities rate of return by year. *Source* The Ministry of Human Resources and Social Security and Wind

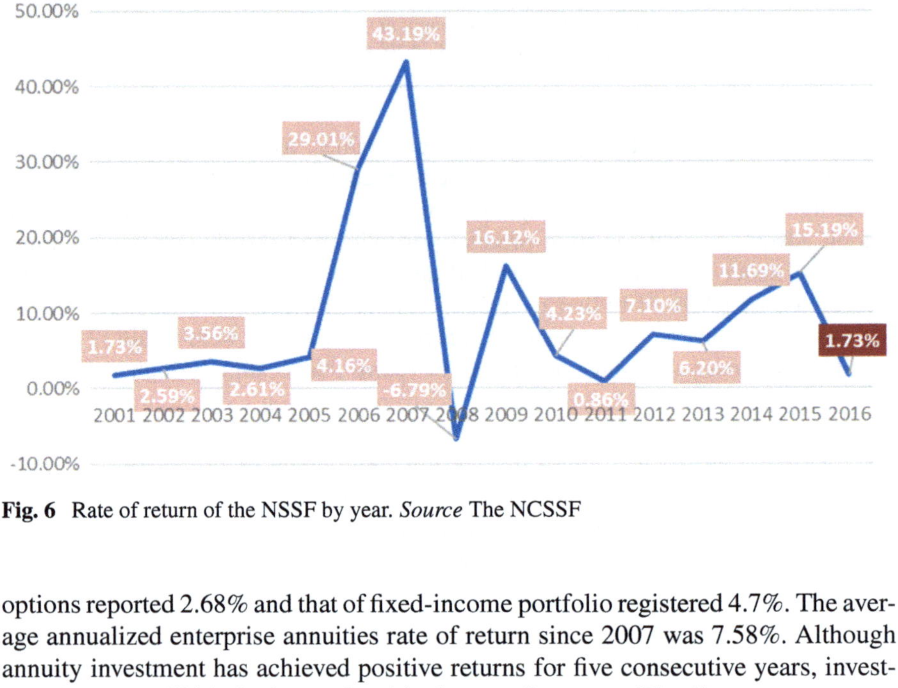

Fig. 6 Rate of return of the NSSF by year. *Source* The NCSSF

options reported 2.68% and that of fixed-income portfolio registered 4.7%. The average annualized enterprise annuities rate of return since 2007 was 7.58%. Although annuity investment has achieved positive returns for five consecutive years, investment income still hit the lowest level in the past five years (Fig. 5).

In 2016, the total investment income of the NSSF reached RMB 31.318 billion and its rate of return reached 1.73%, which was the third lowest annual rate of return since 2001, only higher than −6.79% in 2008 and 0.86% in 2011. Compared to the 15.19% return on investment in 2015, the rate of return of the NSSF dropped sharply in 2016 (Fig. 6).

The main reason for the decline in the investment income of enterprise annuities and the NSSF is that both the equity and fixed income markets were gloomy in 2016.

In the equity markets, China's Shanghai Composite Index dropped 12.31% in 2016, down 435.54 points from the highest record in the year and closed up at 3103.64 points, the worst performance among major global stock markets. In 2016, the three major US stock indexes rose across the board with the Dow Jones Industrial Average up 13.74%, the S&P 500 up 10.05% and the Nasdaq up 8.48%. Among the three major European indexes, Britain's FTSE 100 index rose 14.06%, Germany's DAX 30 Index rose 6.59% and France's CAC40 Index gained 4.34%. In Asian markets, Hong Kong's Hang Seng Index and the Nikkei 225 Index were basically the same.

In the bond market, the stated interest rate of the bond issued by China Development Bank at the beginning of 2016 hit 3%. Then the China Bond Aggregate Index fell by 80 bp in April as the rate of investment of bonds rallied in April due to frequent credit events. Towards the end of the year, under the background of tightened control, overruled demand and oversubscribed demand led to liquidity tensions in the bond market. The China Bond Index fell 2.4% in November and December, and closed at the annualized rate of return of 1.31%. Although the performance of China's bond market in 2016 is not the worst compared with that of the United States, Canada and the EU, it still hit a three-year low compared with 11.23 and 8.03% in 2014 and 2015.

It should be pointed out that the reason why the rate of return on enterprise annuities was higher than that of the NSSF is that the asset allocation of enterprise annuities was more stable. Equity assets accounted less than 10% of enterprise annuities and about 30% of the NSSF. In the long run, different asset allocation structures will lead to different final returns. In general, the investment in annuities had smaller fluctuations with a lower average return, with the highest rate of return in 2007 at 41%, the lowest rate of return in 2008 at 1.83% and the average annualized return rate of return in 2007–2016 at 7.57% respectively. The NSSF reported higher volatility, with the highest rate of return of the NSSF in 2007 standing at 43.19%, the lowest rate of return in 2008 at −6.79%, and The average annualized rate of return of the NSSF from 2001 to 2016 was 8.37%.

4.2 *The Market Share of Insurance Companies in the Enterprise Annuity Management Market Continued to Rise*

At the early stage of development of enterprise annuities, the market shares of fund companies and insurance companies were basically equal. The market share of insurance companies has been on the rise since 2010 and exceeded 50% in 2014, accounting for nearly 54% of the total enterprise annuity assets. In comparison, the market share of fund companies dropped to 38% and that of securities agents dropped slightly from 8.9 to 8.27%. The steady rise in the market share of insurance companies is mainly due to the fiduciary role, the development of investment management and

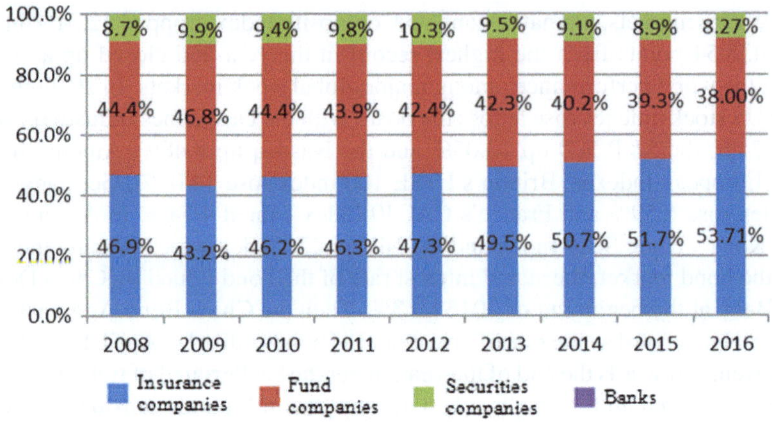

Fig. 7 Market shares of insurance, fund and securities companies in the enterprise annuity market. *Source* The Ministry of Human Resources and Social Security

account management qualifications, higher business coordination and more adequate staffing of insurance companies (Fig. 7).

4.3 The Proportion of Assets Managed by Corporate Trustees Increased and the Level of Concentration Continued to Rise in the Industry

The market concentration of trusteeship management services for enterprise annuity plans is on the rise, as reflected primarily in the following two aspects. (i) The aggregate market share of corporate trustees increased from 57% in 2009 to 64.9% in 2016, reaching its highest level in recent years. There are two crucial reasons why the market share of corporate trustees has increased. First, since the introduction of enterprise annuity policy a decade ago, enterprises owned by the central government and other state-owned enterprises, foreign-funded enterprises and well-run private-owned enterprises which have the capability to sponsor enterprise annuity plans have set up annuity councils, while enterprises which have just set up enterprise annuities tend to be small in size and unable to set up an independent annuity council. In contrast, corporate trusteeship can help SMEs to establish enterprise annuity plans, benefit from the economies' scale effect, boost profits and save costs. Secondly, as assets under management increases, corporate trustees will accumulate more management experience and gain more professional skills. Compared with a council that manages a single plan, corporate trustees have more advantages in terms of management structure, staff reserve and talent pipeline structure. In addition, as enterprise annuities grow, some small annuity councils have transferred into corporate trustees.

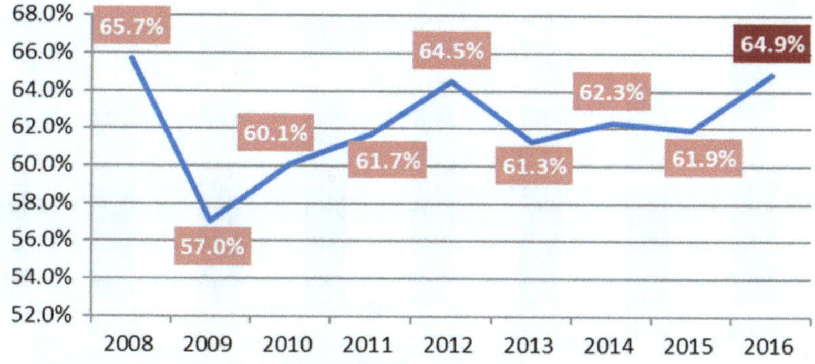

Fig. 8 Percentage of enterprise annuity assets managed by corporate trustees. *Source* The Ministry of Human Resources and Social Security

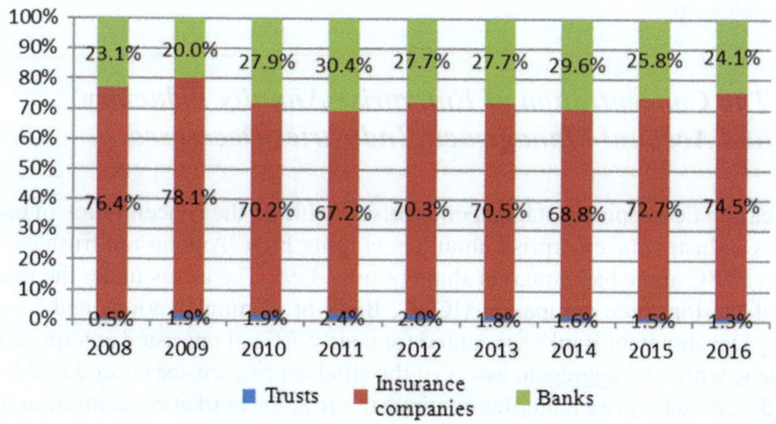

Fig. 9 Market shares of corporate trustees. *Source* The Ministry of Human Resources and Social Security

From 2012 to 2016, the number of councils decreased by 26% from 242 to 178 (Fig. 8).

Second, the market concentration among corporate trustees has also further grown. At the industry level, insurers and banks have a majority market share (74.5 and 24.1% respectively), and the market share held by trusts has dropped to only 1.3%. At the institutional level, the top three corporate trustees are China Life Insurance, Ping An Pension and ICBC with a market share of 30.86, 23.9 and 13.33% respectively. In recent years, the market share of the three has been steadily increasing. At the end of 2016, the total share even reached more than 68%, which was its highest level in the past five years. The market shares of corporate trustees in the corporate annuity market by year (since 2008) are as shown (Fig. 9).

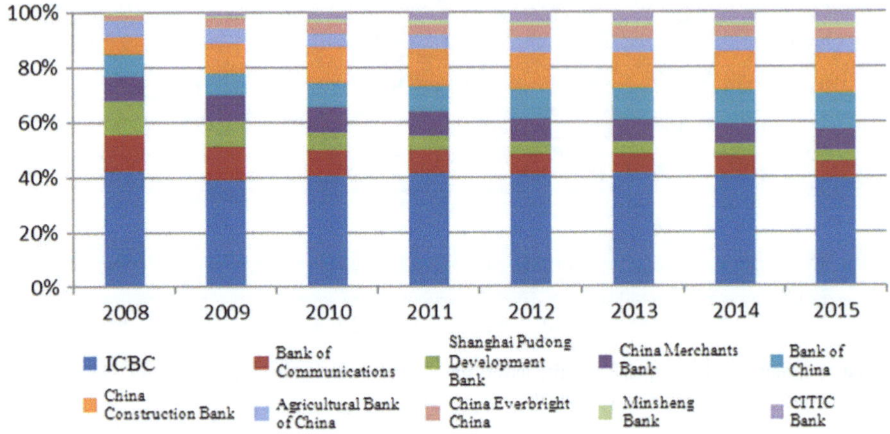

Fig. 10 Market shares of enterprise annuity custodians. *Source* The Ministry of Human Resources and Social Security

4.4 The Concentration of Enterprise Annuity Fiduciary and Account Management Industries Decreased

In the earlier development stage of enterprise annuities, the concentration of custody services industry for enterprise annuities is quite high. Among ten trustees in the market, ICBC alone had a market share of over 42%. The assets under the management of the top three companies (ICBC, Bank of Communications and Shanghai Pudong Development Bank) accounted for nearly 70% of entrusted enterprise annuity assets, while the aggregate assets of the smallest five trustees accounted for less than 15%. As enterprise annuities continue to grow, the market concentration of custody business declines. The market shares of the Bank of China, China Construction Bank, CITIC Bank and China Everbright Bank have all risen significantly. However, the aggregate market share of ICBC, Bank of Communications and Shanghai Pudong Development Bank dropped from nearly 70% in 2008 to less than 50% in 2016. Nevertheless, considering the overall structure and threshold of the industry, the concentration of the enterprise annuity management industry will remain high (Fig. 10).

The enterprise annuity account management section also shows a high degree of concentration at the beginning. In 2008, ICBC managed 9.38 million individual accounts, accounting for 48.83% of the total individual accounts, followed by Changjiang Pension, China Merchants Bank, Bank of Communications and China Everbright Bank. The top five account managers take up nearly 90% of the market and the remaining fourteen account managers together account for less than 10% of the

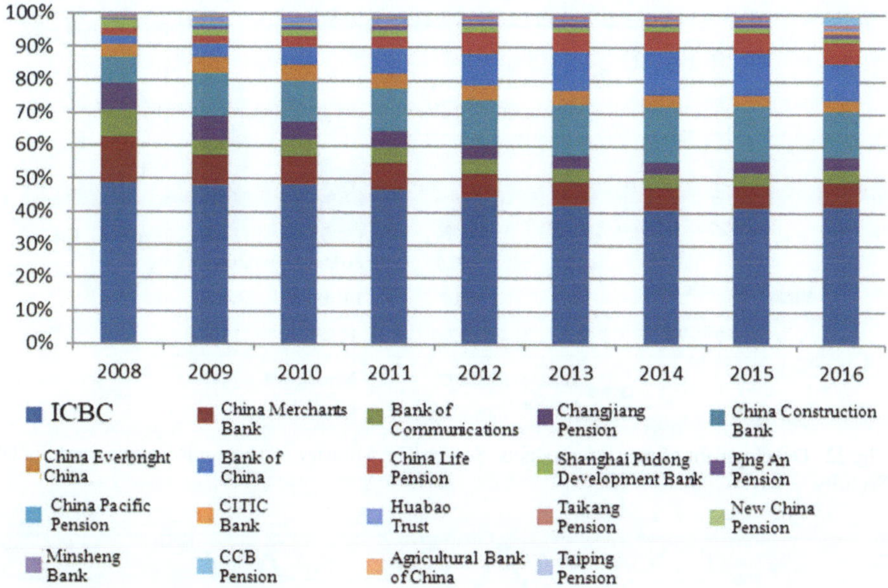

Fig. 11 Market shares of enterprise annuity account managers. *Source* The Ministry of Human Resources and Social Security

market. By 2016, the concentration of the account management section has slightly declined because the market shares of China Life Pension, Bank of China and China Construction Bank have continuously increased. However, the total market share of the top five account managers in 2008 decreased from 87% in 2008 by 16–71% in 2016, reflecting that the market competition has gradually increased (Fig. 11).

4.5 Pension Products: The Size of Pension Assets Continue to Rise with Competitive Rates of Return

As the growth of enterprise annuity market slows down, asset allocation is becoming more and more important. As an important tool for attracting inflows and realizing asset allocation, pension products are gaining more and more attention from investment managers, corporate trustees, boards of directors and principals. By the end of 2016, there were 179 pension products in operation in the whole industry, up by 51.69% over the previous year; their assets amounted to RMB 221.4 billion, which was an increase of 85.15% over the previous year.

In contrast to enterprise annuity funds which is slowing down, pension products still grow at a fast pace. Benefiting from the regulations on the investment of occupational annuity and the basic retirement fund, the development of pension products does not depend solely on enterprise annuities, which means that the market size

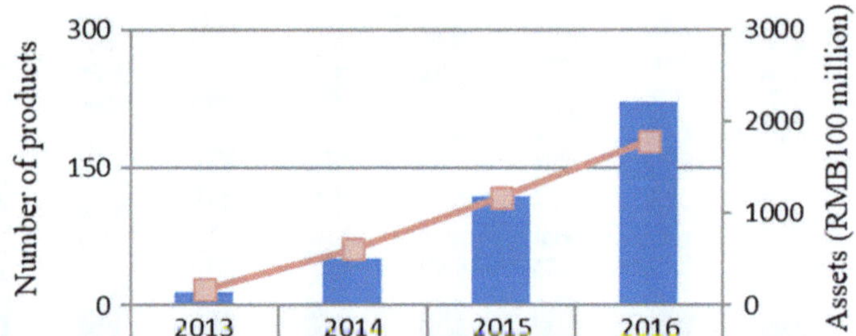

	2013	2014	2015	2016
Assets (RMB100 million)	149	514	1196	2214
Number of products	17	62	118	179

Fig. 12 Development of pension products. *Source* The Ministry of Human Resources and Social Security

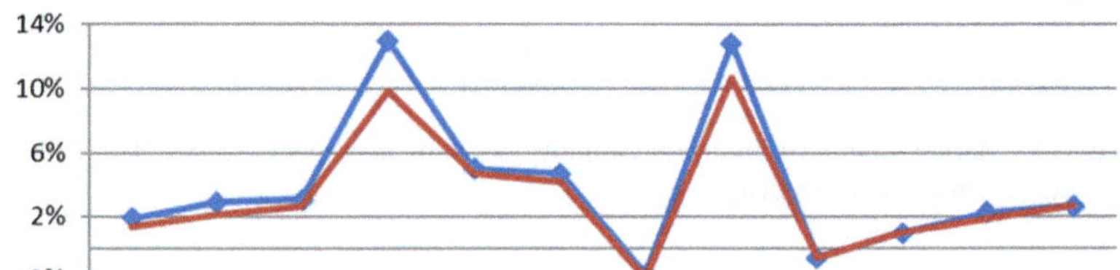

	2014 Q1	2014 Q2	2014 Q3	2014 Q4	2015 Q1	2015 Q2	2015 Q3	2015 Q4	2016 Q1	2016 Q2	2016 Q3	2016 Q4
Hybrid pension products	1.92%	2.92%	3.11%	13.00%	4.97%	4.66%	-1.62%	12.82%	-0.60%	0.99%	2.25%	2.65%
Enterprise annuity equity products	1.32%	2.14%	2.66%	9.88%	4.66%	4.19%	-1.92%	10.60%	-0.58%	1.05%	1.85%	2.68%

Fig. 13 Investment income of hybrid pension products and annuity portfolios. *Source* The Ministry of Human Resources and Social Security

and development potential for pension products will be even greater in the future (Fig. 12).

With respect to investment income of products, the average return on investment of pension products in 2016 reported 3.49%, of which fixed-income products was 4.83%, currency products 3.28%, hybrid products 2.65% and equity products 0.32%. The asset structure of hybrid pension products is similar to that of ordinary annuity portfolios and their rates of return are similar. Overall, since 2014, the investment performance of hybrid pension products has been higher than the average industry-weighted portfolios for most of the time, reflecting the notable improvement in management efficiency and investment returns (Fig. 13).

The following are the reasons for the high rates of return for hybrid pension products. First, they can enhance the ability to obtain resources, especially for small account annuity funds since pension products can participate in the trading of interbank bond varieties and over-the-counter transactions through economy of scale and effectively reduce the investment threshold of small accounts and increase the sources of revenue. Secondly, they can quickly start the investment process and thus increase investment efficiency. If an enterprise annuity plan is operated as a portfolio, the trustee and the investment manager need to sign an investment management contract and open accounts for annuity assets and asset allocation, which will last for three months. The preparation period for investment is very long. With pension products, there is no accounting opening or asset allocation period, thus increasing investment efficiency and returns. Thirdly, they can diversify investment and reduce fluctuations in performance caused by high concentration. Small annuity portfolios are unable to achieve sufficient diversification, but pension products can invest in a wider range of asset categories and classes; thus achieving a high level of diversification. Fourthly, they can share the best research and development resources in the market. Strict disclosure requirements of pension products make the market highly transparent. Investment managers attach great importance to investment performance and often hire the best investment managers to manage pension products. But as experienced investment managers are in shortage and there are too many annuity portfolios, pension products are another convenient way to enjoy high-quality research and development resources.

4.6 Third-Party Agents Are Allowed to Invest in Basic Pension Assets

In 2016, in addition to the appointment of third-party custodians and third-party managers, the NCSSF also signed basic pension trustee service contract with local governments and hired third-party investment managers to invest basic pension funds. As of the end of the first quarter of 2017, seven provinces, including Beijing, Shanghai, Henan, Hubei, Guangxi, Yunnan and Shaanxi, have signed a trustee service contract with the NCSSF involving a total asset value of RMB 360 billion and the value of assets that are held by the NCSSF in trust amounted to RMB 137 billion. Other funds will be in place in installments in accordance with agreed terms too. However, among the three provinces where basic pension fund asset exceeds RMB 300 billion (Guangdong, Jiangsu and Zhejiang), except Guangdong entrusted the NCSSF to manage RMB 100 billion worth of basic pension fund assets in 2012, Jiangsu (with a balance of RMB 311.4 billion at the end of 2016) and Zhejiang (with a balance of RMB 300.9 billion at the end of 2016) has not yet signed a trustee service contract with the NCSSF. With respect to the rate of return, since the basic pension trust service contracts receive trusts from local governments and enrollees have short-term payment needs, the volatility and the rate of return of the basic pension is relatively low. In fact, the NCSSF requires that the probability of loss for entrusted basic retirement funds should not exceed 95%, so the proportion of stock investment in asset allocation of basic pension funds is also lower than that of social security funds.

5 Existing Problems and Challenges

5.1 The Financing Pressure of the Basic Pension Continues to Increase

With the acceleration of population ageing in our country, the proportion of retired population keeps rising while the proportion of working population declines. In the past ten years, the growth rate of basic pension contributions has been less than the growth rate of the expenditure. Judging from the size of the basic pension, if only considering contributions and expenditures (assuming there is no government subsidy), the annual financing gap would reach RMB 652 billion in 2014 and has been expanding ever since. In 2016, the gap between the income and expenditure reached RMB 435.4 billion. Only with the current financial assistance of RMB 651.1 billion at that time, a surplus of RMB 0.3 trillion for the year and a cumulative surplus of RMB 3.86 trillion were reported. Even with the annual financial subsidies, after peaking in 2012, the balance of the basic pension has been declining for four consecutive years. In particular, since 2016, in order to cope with the economic downturn, the central government has introduced a temporary policy to reduce social security contributions and the rate of contributions by employers. Although the policy helps enterprises reduce their costs and financial burdens, it generates a negative impact on the financial sustainability of the basic pension.[2] According to the current trends related to the number of enrollees, contributions and the number of retirees, the financing gap of the basic pension will continue to increase, putting the government under greater pressure (Table 9).

5.2 Local Governments Are Unwilling to Give up the Authority of Managing Basic Pension Funds

As of the end of March 2017, the funds entrusted by local governments to the NCSSF amounted to RMB 137 billion, accounting for 3.5% of the basic pension fund balance (RMB 3.86 trillion) by the end of 2016. The remaining basic pension fund assets of each province have not been entrusted to the NCSSF. Overall, the progress in the

[2]The State Council required that, within two years starting from May 1, 2016, employer contribution rate shall be reduced to 20% in provinces where the previous rate is above 20%; employer contribution rate shall be reduced to 19% in provinces where the previous rate is 20% and the cumulative balance of the basic pension insurance fund for enterprise employees by the end of 2015 is sufficient to pay for more than nine months of such contributions.

Table 9 Income and expenditure of basic pension by year

	2008	2009	2010	2011	2012	2013	2014	2015	2016
Number of enrollees	21,891	23,550	25,707	28,391	30,427	32,212	34,115	35,361	37,930
Revenue from contributions	8016	9534	11,110	13,956	16,467	19,270	21,100	23,717	27,500
Growth rate (%)		18.94	16.53	25.62	17.99	17.02	9.50%	12.40	15.95
Fund revenue	9740	11,491	13,420	16,895	20,001	22,484	25,252	29,250	35,058
Growth rate (%)		17.98	16.79	25.89	18.38	12.41	12.31	15.83	18.06
Fund expenditure	7390	8894	10,555	12,765	15,562	18,417	21,752	25,799	31,854
Growth rate (%)		20.35	18.68	20.94	21.91	18.34	18.11	18.60	22.39
Annual balance	2350	2597	2865	4130	4439	4067	3500	3452	2104

Note 1. *Source* The Ministry of Human Resources and Social Security
2. *Unit* Number of enrollees (100 million); asset value (RMB 100 million)

investment and operation of basic pension assets is slow, and the incentives for local governments to entrust basic pension assets are not strong. The main reasons are as follows:

First of all, with respect to fund security, as the basic pension fund is the main source of retirement income for Chinese citizens, fund security is of the utmost importance. Therefore, basic pension assets must be invested in a prudent manner under market-oriented operation. At the same time, with the growth of the real economy slowing down and the return on assets dropping and facing fluctuations, some local governments have taken a wait-and-see attitude. Poor performance of earlier investment may discourage local government to sign trustee service contracts as well. Secondly, for local governments, because of local economic downturn and the difficulty in increasing financial revenue, the willingness to retain administration authority over basic pension funds may be more intense than that of entrusting basic pension funds to the NCSSF. Although trustee services can bring certain investment income, it also means net outflows of capital for local governments. On the contrary, if this huge amount of money remains in the local financial system, it can support local social and economic development through channels such as banks. Furthermore, in terms of the level of social pooling, the *Guidelines for the Investment Management of Basic Pension Insurance Funds* stipulate that the trustee should formulate pension fund pooling plan and pool social security funds into provincial financial accounts. However, few provinces have truly achieved provincial social pooling and most local pension funds are still pooled at the district level. The fragmentation of the pension system is also an important factor that affects the progress of trustee management of basic pension funds.

5.3 Pension Funds Fail to Play to Their Strengths in Funding

Unlike public funds which are vulnerable to changes in market conditions, pension funds can remain stable over long periods of time and is more risk-resilient because their income, expenditure and assets tend to see little fluctuation and low incidence of unexpected withdrawals. Therefore, unlike short-term investments that usually adopt pro-cyclical investment strategies, investments of pension funds can be counter-cyclical. For equity assets, to share the long-term growth value of enterprises, counter-cyclical investments focus more on long-term profitability of enterprises rather than short-term price fluctuations. For fixed-income assets, pension funds can get a higher return on investment by investing in major national projects such as infrastructure projects with a long investment cycle. In a nutshell, the long-term nature of pension funds trade time with space, allowing them to capture long-term risk premium and avoid short-term asset volatility and low liquidity risks.

In foreign countries, pension funds typically tends to focus on longer time term, invest a high proportion of their portfolio in equity and attach great importance to asset allocation in a global context. For example, the percentage of equity assets in the portfolio of Canada Pension Plan Investment Board (CPPIB) has been kept over

50% for a long period of time and the proportion of overseas asset allocation has been maintained at about 50%. The average annualized rate of return of CPPIB since 1999 is 7.3%.[3] As the second pillar of America's retirement system, 401(k) also invested 60% of its assets in equity assets, achieving an average annualized rate of return of above 7% over the past 10 years.

However, in China's case, many factors have led to the failure of pension funds to benefit from their long-term nature. Take enterprise annuities for example. First of all, individuals are not allowed to make investment decisions in relation to enterprise annuities and the overall investment style tends to be conservative. The proportion of equity assets fluctuates around 10%, far below the stipulated ceiling of 30%. Secondly, the contract term of an enterprise annuity is typically three years and assessed on an annual basis. Some principals may change investment managers based on annual assessment results, forcing investment managers to focus only on short-term performance. Thirdly, some principals lack a scientific manager evaluation system which also lacks openness, transparency and regulation. It may also motivate investment managers to choose short-term investments. Fourthly, enterprise annuities and the basic pension are not allowed to invest in overseas assets, which also restricts the allocation of pension assets and hinders diversification and profit maximization. The NSSF, as a reserve pension, does not have short-term liabilities; thus can invest a high proportion of its portfolio in equity assets. However, in reality, equity assets only account for about 20–30% of its portfolio, far below the 40% ceiling set by the related policy.

5.4 *The Growth in the Assets of the NSSF Is Slower Than Expected*

The assets of the NSSF by the end of 2016, net of basic pension assets entrusted by Guangdong and Shandong as well as individual accounts entrusted by the three provinces in Northeast China, were RMB 1,604.258 billion. According to the forecasts made by the NCSSF in 2009, the assets of the NSSF were RMB 1 trillion in 2010, RMB 2 trillion in 2015, RMB 3 trillion in 2020 and RMB 6 trillion in 2030 (Dai 2013). Based on that forecast, the current growth of the NSSF is relatively slower.

On the other hand, the population in our country is ageing at an extremely fast pace. The length of time taken by the percentage of population aged sixty-five to grow from seven percent to ten percent is thirty years (1942–1972) in the United States and fourteen years (2000–2014) in China. China and the rest of the world simultaneously entered an ageing society in 2000. By 2050, population aged sixty-five and over will reach 30.81% in China, which is close to the expected 32.03% in developed countries. In comparison, the world average is expected to stand at only 19.7% in 2050. China is going to grow old before it gets rich. In this context, the

[3]Data current as of April 30, 2016.

national pension system is under tremendous pressure. According to Gao Peiyong, Cao Yuanzheng and Ma Jun, China's pension gap will exceed RMB 10 trillion in the future. Therefore, as a reserve pension fund, the NSSF is still too small and should be expanded through various channels as soon as possible.

5.5 The Growth of Enterprise Annuities Almost Stops

Enterprise annuities have over the past more than ten years grown more mature. As of the end of 2016, the assets of enterprise annuities exceeded RMB 1 trillion, but the growth rate decreased from 64% in 2009 to 15% in 2016. From the perspective of system design, enterprise annuities are supplementary pensions voluntarily sponsored by enterprises. Enterprises which sponsor an enterprise annuity are required to contribute to the basic pension plan according to the law, develop corresponding financial strength and establish a collective consultation mechanism. According to the data from the Bureau of Statistics, in 2015, the number of corporation in our country exceeded 12.95 million, most of which were SMEs. Currently, 76,298 enterprises have established annuity plans, most of which are large and medium enterprises. Affected by weaker economic fundamentals and the drop in the growth of real economy, the likelihood to sponsor an enterprise annuity is small for most SMEs. Therefore, the overall coverage of the enterprise annuity system is low and is obviously very difficult to change.

By the end of 2016, the annual increase in the number of enterprises sponsoring an enterprise annuity plan was only 844 (about 1%), which was the lowest since 2010. Affected by this, the number of employees participating in enterprise annuity plans remained at twenty-three million and the growth rate dropped by 0.4%. It is estimated that the growth in the number of new enterprise annuity plans and employees participating in enterprise annuity plans will further slow down in the next few years (Figs. 14 and 15).

In addition, against the background of economic downturn, the declining profitability of enterprises has led to a decline in their contribution ability. Some enterprises in some industries that have suffered heavy losses have even stopped contribution. With the increase in the number of retirees, the outflow of enterprise annuity funds has been on the rise. The inflow into enterprise annuity funds gradually decreases or even ceases, while the number of retirees making withdrawals is rising steadily, placing enterprise annuity funds under tremendous pressure. Enterprise annuity development will soon bid farewell to the rapid development period and enter the era of low growth.

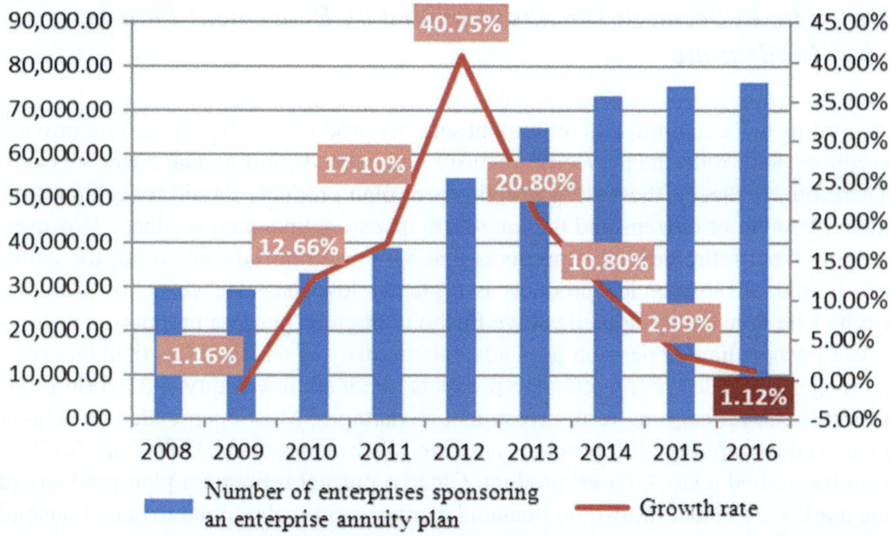

Fig. 14 Number of enterprises that have established enterprise annuities and its growth (*Unit* RMB 100 million). *Source* The Ministry of Human Resources and Social Securities

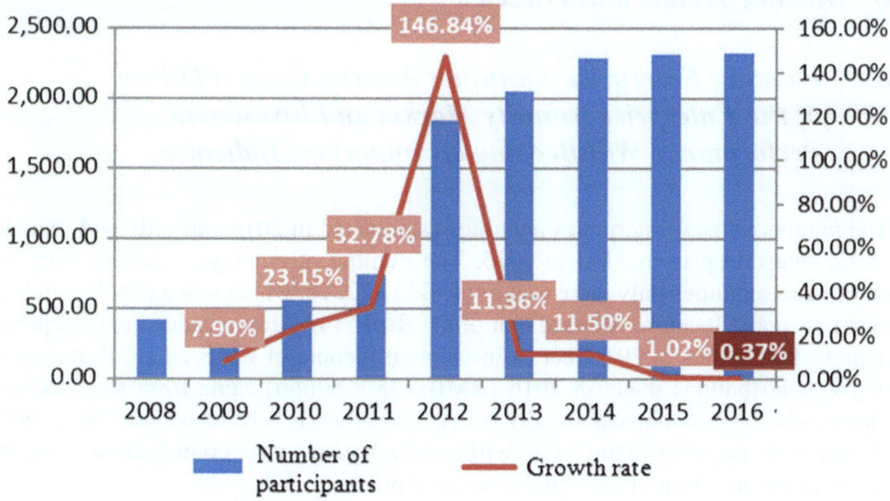

Fig. 15 Number of enrollees in enterprise annuities and its growth. *Source* The Ministry of Human Resources and Social Security

5.6 *The Retirement Income Provided by Retirement Plan Is Inadequate*

According to the definition of retirement security products, their purpose is to provide enrollees with retirement income security and related fund management services. Therefore, in theory, the design of retirement plan products should focus on retirement planning of citizens and the long-term investing financing products. However, judging from retirement plan products that have been introduced so far, the maturity period of close-ended products is typically less than one year. For example, China Life Pension has issued twelve Fushou Fengnian pension products and sixty-seven Fushou Jianian pension products, the maturity of which is less than one year. Among open-ended retirement plan products, there are few equity and hybrid products that can reflect long-term investment advantages. Most open-ended retirement plan products are liquidity products and fixed-income products. Only Ping An Pension has issued a stock-based product. Clearly, current retirement plan products in the market are in fact short-term financial management tools similar to bank financial management products and have little to do with old age income security, failing to serve the institutional objective of guarantying income security in old age (p. 152).

6 Market Trends and Forecast

6.1 *Existing Enterprise Annuities Are the Largest Driver of the Enterprise Annuity Market and Investment Performance Will Become an Important Indicator*

The number of new enterprises annuities established in 2016 was only 844, which was a sharp drop from 2193 in 2015. The number of employees participating in enterprises annuities only increased by 86,000 in 2016, which was a new low in the past five years. It can be inferred that of the RMB 149.9 billion added to enterprise annuity fund assets in 2016, net of investment income of RMB 28.1 billion, most of the contributions made in 2016 (RMB 125.1 billion) came from the existing clients who had established annuity plans. Therefore, it is believed that the growth of enterprise annuities in the future will mainly depend on the contributions made to and investment return of the existing annuity plans.

Under this background, as the principals of the existing enterprise annuity plans have gradually matured, the focus of the review of investment managers will shift further to investment performance and customer services. In 2016, among the twenty-one investment managers in the market, seven reported an increase in market share, and the other fourteen managers reported a decline in market share, which means the market concentration increased. The main reason for the additional funding of the seven companies that gained market share was their good performance in recent years. Thus, we believe the Matthew effect will become more obvious in the annuity market, the growth of which depends largely on the existing annuities and good investment performance will become a core competency of investment managers of enterprise annuities. Therefore, to promote the growth of the annuity market, all investment managers should pay more attention to investment capacity-building and make greater efforts to enhance and stabilize the investment performance.

6.2 The National Social Security Fund Will Increase Rapidly

As mentioned earlier, although the national social security fund reached RMB 2 trillion in 2015, it still does not reach the expected target. This is also a key concern for policymakers. The report of the Third Plenary Session of the 18th CPC Central Committee put forward a proposal to "transfer some state-owned capital to the social security fund." The idea was also mentioned at the Fifth Plenary Session of the 18th CPC Central Committee and in the 2016 Government Work Report. The National Social Security Fund Regulations (hereinafter referred to as the "Regulations") promulgated by the State Council in March 2016 also clearly stipulates that the transfer of state-owned capital is one of the funding sources of the national social security fund. In May 2017, Lou Jiwei also pointed out at the first meeting of the sixth National Social Security Fund Council that it would pick up its pace to increase the assets of the national social security fund by, among others, improving and implementing the plan for transferring state-owned capital to the national social security fund as soon as possible, exploring efficient ways to manage transferred state-owned capital, facilitating government transfer (central government), lottery revenue and state-owned capital to the national social security fund, and actively searching for new funding sources.

Generally speaking, under the background of population ageing, public pensions are facing increasing financial pressure. As the national pension reserve fund, the National Social Security Fund is in urgent need for expansion. With the introduction of a series of policies within a short time, relevant authorities have steadily push forward the transfer of state-owned assets into and accelerate the expansion of the national social security fund. It is expected that the national social security fund will increase at a significantly faster pace.

6.3 Pension Products Will Continue to Grow at a Fast Pace

At earlier stages, the goal of promoting pension products is to solve the problems in the multiple account system of enterprise annuities and improve the efficiency of investment of enterprise annuity funds through back-end integration. However, as the integration of SME annuity portfolio is progressively carried out, the role of pension products will gradually shift from back-end integrator to an asset allocation tool for corporate annuities, basic pensions and possibly even occupational annuities in the future and will continue to grow rapidly mainly due to the following reasons:

From the clients' point of view, first of all, compared to ordinary portfolios, they perform better and thus are more attractive. From 2014 to 2016, the average annualized yield of hybrid pension products reached 8.66%, significantly higher than 7.65% of the single-plan option portfolio. By the same token, the average annualized return on fixed-income ordinary pension products in the past three years was 7.59%, much higher than the 5.96% of single-plan fixed income portfolios. Secondly, they have an asset allocation function. Under the original operation model, one plan may be managed by multiple investment managers, but all managers must adopt similar asset allocation strategies due to policy restrictions and thus cannot play to their respective strengths. However, since there are a great variety of pension products in the market and investment managers are willing to play to their own strengths, annuity plans can allocate large assets according to the needs of beneficiaries so that they can choose well-performing pension products.

From the perspective of investment managers, first of all, pension products can help them integrate small accounts in their custody. As enterprise annuities grow, the number of annuity portfolios has increased from 586 in 2008 to 3,207 in 2016. This means that the average number of annuity portfolios managed by one investment manager was 152 at the end of 2016, which put a lot of management and service pressure on investment managers, especially when the small-account trend after the achievement of universal coverage among SMEs leads to a sharp increase in their workload related to investment management, valuation and information disclosure. Pension products can effectively converge small accounts through back-end integration and improve the investment efficiency of annuity portfolios. Secondly, pension products are a tool to increase capital. As the enterprise annuity market matures, the number of new plans drops and the size of enterprises establishing enterprise annuity become smaller. The main driving force for the growth of the annuity market is the existing annuity customers and annuity customers' knowledge and acceptance of pension products will continue to grow. As a result, pension products have become investment vehicles for investment managers to increase capital under the original system. In addition, the regular disclosure system of pension products has increased the transparency of product information and investment performance, which makes sure pension products can be fully and effectively understood. As a result, it also poses higher challenges for investment managers and propels them to pay more attention to the investment of the pension products.

Meanwhile, it should also be noted there will be more customized pension products in the market as the pension products develop more rapidly. Among the 179 pensions that have been in operation by the end of 2016, nineteen were held by the same holder and they can be basically defined as customized pension products. However, if the number of customized products increases sharply, the significance of the back-end integration function of pension products will be weakened. In the long run, there may also be a trend of multi-account management of similar portfolios, which may increase the number of portfolios corresponding to each annuity plan.

6.4 *What Is at the Core of a Tax Deferred Pension: The Product or the Accounts?*

Pillar 3 has drawn wide attention in recent years. During the 2017 annual parliamentary sessions of China, the Ministry of Finance announced that the relevant departments had conducted in-depth studies on policy-related and technical issues of pillar 3 and the relevant policy proposals had been put forward. China's pillar 3, which consists of personal tax-deferred pensions, is in a critical policy formation stage. All stakeholders have reached consensus on the preferential tax treatment, which has laid a solid foundation for the establishment of pillar 3. However, opinions on whether pillar 3 should be product-based or account-based remain varied. Under an account-based system, personal accounts are set up, tax incentives are offered, and deferred levies are conducted on an account-by-account basis. Under a product-based system, tax incentives are designed based on specific investment products. According to the experience of foreign countries, an account-based system is more conducive to the long-term development of pillar 3.

First, an account system can make the integration of personal tax-deferred pensions, basic pensions and occupational pensions easier. In 2015, the Outline of the 13th Five-Year Plan proposed to "introduce tax-deferred pension." In 2016, the 13th Five-Year Plan of the Ministry of Human Resources and Social Security again stressed the "taxes-deferred personal pensions should be introduced" and place it on the same priority level of basic pensions, enterprise annuities and occupational annuities. As we all know, China's first pillar (the basic pension for employees) and second pillar (enterprise and occupation annuities) are operated under an account system. Therefore, it is only natural for personal tax-deferred pensions to adopt a personal account system.

Secondly, most foreign countries, including the United States, Australia, the UK, Chile and other countries which have an advanced third pillar, have all adopted an account system for their pillar 3. In the United States and Australia, pillar 3 is directly referred to as individual retirement accounts. There are many reasons for why so many countries adopt an account system. Firstly, an account system can accurately reflect contributions and investment income of individuals, and income tax on withdrawals can be calculated more accurately on an account-by-account basis. Secondly, individuals can transfer their retirement savings in pillar II to pillar 3 or vice versa without restarting the vesting clock, thus increasing the mobility in the labor market.

Thirdly, an account system has many positive externalities: (1) Personal pension accounts can raise citizens' awareness of personal pension responsibilities and involvement in the pension system; thus enhancing the ability of citizens to provide for themselves at old age; (2) the overall arrangement of the tax deferral system at the account level helps increase the income transparency of enrollees, consolidate the payment base of social insurance, and increases accuracy of social insurance contributions and benefit payments; (3) it also helps tax authorities keep track of enrollees' income and thus improves the personal income tax collection mechanism.

In contrast, there are some inherent drawbacks of a product-based system:

First, it will be more difficult to achieve the diversification of investments under a product-based system. Let's take a look at international practice in this regard. Most countries that have set up an account system for pillar 3 do not impose excessive restrictions on the funding of personal pension accounts and encourage individuals to make choices among a great variety of pension financial products. For example, in 2016, of the total assets in personal retirement accounts in the United States, mutual funds accounted for 46.8%, stocks and bonds accounted for 40.5%, bank deposits accounted for 7.6%, and commercial insurance products accounted for 5.1%, showing great diversity of products. The logic is that personal pension accounts are owned by individuals and enrollees may choose underlying investments according to their own risk appetites under reasonable supervision of the state. Conversely, if it is stipulated that enrollees in pillar 3 can only choose one type of product, such restriction will prevent pillar 3 from effectively performing its functions.

Secondly, policy flexibility is significantly reduced if products of low liquidity are selected. Take the third pillar of the United States for example. Among the investments of the IRA, standardized negotiable securities such as mutual funds, stocks and bonds take up 90%. The advantage of this is that if the enrollees consider the investments unattractive, they can sell them and select other products on the open market at any time. However, if the tax deferral policy for the third pillar only works for a certain type of products, such products may increase transaction costs for enrollees if the transaction is not convenient or not tradable. For instance, if a participant who bought a commercial annuity product (Product A) ten years ago finds another product (Product B) more attractive and wishes to switch to Product B, he/she will face a high surrender charge. On the other hand, in order to encourage participation in the third pillar, many countries have allowed personal pension accounts to be used for multiple purposes. For example, the IRA program in the United States provides for hardship withdrawals (for housing, education, health care, and so forth) and allows enrollees to borrow from their individual retirement accounts. The above arrangement increases the flexibility and practicability of the third pillar, especially for young people. It takes into consideration enrollees' old age and housing, education and other needs in the nearer term, thus increasing its attractiveness among young people. If the third pillar only consists of non-tradable products, enrollees will face severe illiquidity which prevents them from withdrawing money in case of emergency.

Therefore, it is clear that, to establish a personal tax-deferred pension system that works for China, the government should put the account-based system at the core of Pillar 3 as it deliberates policies.

6.5 Annuity Councils Need a New Model

Recent years have witnessed a continual drop in the number of annuity councils and the percentage of entrusted assets (from 21 to 13%) in the enterprise annuity market. In the meantime, under the market-oriented investment strategy of occupa-

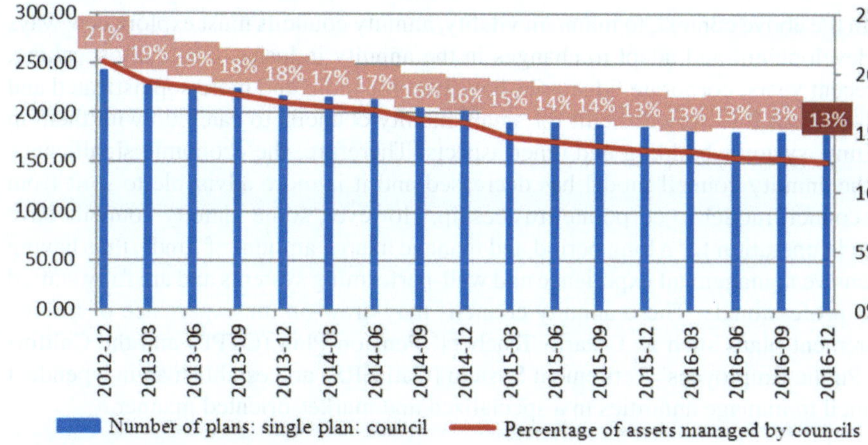

Fig. 16 Number and percentage of single-enterprise annuity plans managed by an annuity council. *Source* The Ministry of Human Resources and Social Security

tional annuities, legal person fiduciaries are chosen instead of annuity councils in other words, the council model has encountered difficulties in its development and new ways need to be explored to promote the development of enterprise annuities (Fig. 16).

Let's take a look at the efficiency of an annuity council from the perspective of its internal working mechanism. First of all, an annuity council is composed of representatives from the enterprise, staff representatives and a handful of third-party professionals. The level of professionalism of the council is relatively low. Secondly, the council model does not have the effect of economies of scale because only one annuity fund of an enterprise is entrusted to the council, which leads to low efficiency. Thirdly, the council is sponsored by the enterprise and thus not independent. Subject to intervention by the enterprise, it may make irrational investment decisions. Fourthly, the trusteeship, investment supervision, risk monitoring and other working systems of annuity councils are inadequate. Fifthly, the responsibility of annuity councils is in essence asset management which is capital-intensive and highly market-oriented, making it difficult for annuity councils to attract financial professionals.

From market-related aspects, (i) the increase in annuity assets and the expansion of investment scope poses new challenges to asset allocation and makes it more difficult for an annuity council to manage and supervise the investment of an annuity fund when it does not have sufficient professionals; (ii) with the slowdown of the real economy and the drop in asset returns, credit risks have soared, posing new risk control and challenges for annuity asset management; and (iii) the rapid development of pension products has provided the possibility for annuity councils to realize asset allocation in larger categories. However, annuity councils themselves lack the capability to evaluate and select pension products and managers.

In the above context, to maintain vitality, annuity councils must explore new ways of development and adapt to changes in the annuity industry. Generally speaking, in recent years, corporate fiduciaries have become more and more sophisticated and full-fledged. It is very difficult for small annuity councils to catch up with them in staffing, systems building and other aspects. Therefore, the economic significance of the annuity council model has decreased and it is more advisable to shift from the council model to corporate trusteeship. However, some annuity councils have been in operation for a long period and manage a large amount of funds, thus having extensive management experience and well-performing systems and are fully staffed with professionals. These annuity councils may draw on the experience of foreign retirement plans such as Ontario Teachers' Pension Plan (OTPP) and the California Public Employees' Retirement System (CalPERS) and establish an independent council to manage annuities in a specialized and market-oriented manner.

6.6 Occupational Annuities Create New Opportunities for the Annuity Industry

Under the background of low enterprise annuities growth and sluggish development of the annuity industry, the market-oriented management of occupational annuities will become the new growth point for the annuity industry. First of all, since enterprise annuities are established on a voluntary basis and most companies in China are SMEs, the development of enterprise annuities has been slow and only twenty-three million workers were covered by enterprise annuities by 2016. In contrast, as occupational annuities are mandatory and cover about thirty million employees of public institutions and more than seven million employees of government agencies, its coverage is significantly larger than enterprise annuities. Furthermore, the contribution rate of occupational annuities is 12%, while enterprise annuities enjoy 9% tax concession, a quite larger tax incentive. Thirdly, the average annual salary of non-private businesses in urban areas in 2016 was RMB 67,569 (including state-owned enterprises, government agencies and public institutions, of which the salaries of employees of government agencies and public institutions are lower). Suppose the average annual salary of government agencies and public institutions is RMB 60,000, the contribution ratio of public institutions is 12% and the contribution ratio of government agencies is 4% (in fact, 8% of the government-financed public organizations may adopt the accrual-basis accounting, but some provinces and cities may use the accrual-basis accounting method), the total annual contributions to occupational annuities will be between RMB 150 billion and RMB 200 billion. Taking into account investment returns, the assets of occupational annuities will grow at a fast pace. On the other hand, considering the drop in the growth rate of annuity enrollees and the increase in the number of pensioners collecting benefits, the growth of enterprise annuities will slow down. It is believed that occupational annuities will likely catch up with enterprise annuities in terms of total assets in the next five years.

6.7 *The Difficulty of Pension Fund Asset Management Will Continue to Increase as the Chinese Economy Enters the New Normal*

The average annualized rate of return of enterprise annuities from 2007 to 2016 was 7.58% and that of the National Social Security Fund since its establishment in 2016 was 8.36%. However, the return on investment of pension assets drastically dropped in 2016, with the rate of return of enterprise annuities being 3.03% and the national social security fund only 1.73%. Considering the macroeconomic situation and the capital market environment in the future, we believe the difficulty of pension asset management will continue to increase. The reasons are: (1) with annuity investment included into the primary market and alternative products, the possibility of investment in overseas assets will demand higher asset allocation and risk management abilities of investment managers; (2) As the economic growth gradually slows down and the risk-free rate of return goes down, the yield of pension investment will also drop. To maintain or increase pension assets, the proportion of equity assets will be increased passively, and the risk and volatility of annuity investment will also grow. (3) As the scale of pension assets continues to grow, the proportion of investment in capital market will gradually increase and the difficulty of obtaining abnormal returns will also increase. To achieve profitability and control volatility simultaneously, more diversified and refined asset allocation and investment management will be required, posing new challenges that will test the ability of fiduciaries and custodians.

Acknowledgements We are grateful to Mr. Liu Yi, Deputy General Manager of China Asset Management Fund, and Dr. Zheng Jian, Director of Corporate Business Department, for their guidance.

Reference

Dai, X. (2013). *Collection of Dai Xianglong on social security fund investment*. Beijing: China Financial Publishing House.

Bo Sun doctor of management, postdoctoral fellowship in finance, senior vice president of Pension Department, China Asset Management, invited member of CAFF50, specializing in financing old age care.

Chapter 7
The Financing of Elderly Care: Cross-Industry Diversification

Lei Yue

Abstract Financial service for the elderly refers to the financial activities carried out by financial institutions to meet consumption, investment and derivative needs of social members in relation to retirement, with the objective of "providing care for the elderly", with a focus on "services" through "financial means". It involves a wide range of areas and has inclusiveness, long-term nature, stability, security and other characteristics. In recent years, as population ageing accelerates, a series of policies on financial service for the elderly have been introduced and financial institutions have also made several explorations in this field which is faced with problems such as homogeneous products and insufficient supply. In order to get out the predicaments faced by the development of the industry, we still need to improve the supportive policies, promote pension reforms, and clarify the regulatory framework. In the long run, driven by population aging, financial reforms, product innovation and the development of financial technology, the financial service for the elderly will unleash its great potential.

Keywords Financial service for the elderly · Population aging
Financial innovation · Financial regulation · Financial technology

1 Overview of Financial Services for the Elderly

1.1 Definition of Financial Services for the Elderly

Financial service for the elderly refers to financial service activities carried out by financial institutions to meet consumption, investment and derivative needs of social

The views expressed here are solely those of the author and do not in any way represent the views of the employer of the author.

L. Yue (✉)
China Merchants Fund Management Co., Ltd, Shenzhen, China

K. Dong and Y. Yao (eds.), *Annual Report on Financing Old Age Care in China (2017)*, https://doi.org/10.1007/978-981-13-0968-7_7

members in relation to retirement, with the objective of "providing care for the elderly", with a focus on "services" through "financial means".

Financial services for the elderly are related to human capital over the life cycle. Life cycle consumption theory holds that people are faced by different economic conditions and have different disposable income in different stages of their life cycle. In order to maximize personal and household utility across their lifetime, they need to make optimal consumption and saving arrangements. For individuals, they should allocate assets to support consumption across the life-cycle and a reasonable standard of living in old age.

Financial service for the elderly will be an important choice for individuals or families from different background in China. Household financial resources involved in retirement financial services generally include financial assets, real assets and real estate. The objective of financial services for the elderly are to allocate household financial resources among different investment products and plan for retirement by taking into consideration the circumstances of individuals throughout their life cycle. At present, investment products that can be selected for household asset allocation include bank deposits, bank's wealth investment products, stocks, government bonds, funds, trusts, commercial insurances, real estate, and collections such as antiques and paintings.

As of the end of 2016, China's total population reached 1.383 billion; population of those aged 60 and over exceeded 230 million, accounting for 16.7% of the total population[1]; more than 150 million people were aged 65 and over, accounting for 10.8% of the total population. The rapid growth of the elderly population and accelerated population aging will lead to a huge demands for retirement related products, and financial services will be the key to meeting those demands.

1.2 Understanding Financial Services for the Elderly

Financial services for the elderly aim to meet consumption, investment and derivative needs of members of the community in relation to retirement and involves a wide range of areas and financial products. In March 2016, five industry regulators, including the People's Bank of China, jointly released the *Guidelines on Financial Support for Pension Services Industry to Accelerate Development*, which clearly defines and makes a plan for financial services for the elderly at the national level for the first time.

[1]Source: Statistical Communiqué of the People's Republic of China on National Economic and Social Development (2016), official website of the National Statistics Bureau. Available at http://www.stats.gov.cn/tjsj/zxfb./201702/t20170228_1467424.html (accessed February 28, 2017).

1.2.1 Specialized the Financing of Elderly Care Products

The state encourages financial institutions such as commercial banks, securities companies, trust companies, fund companies and insurance companies to increase their innovation efforts and support and actively develop differentiated retirement financial products that can provide long-term and stable returns and are in line with demand over the life cycle to meet the needs of retirement income security for people of different ages and groups. Such products mainly include:

(1) Banking sector: products such as old age savings, wealth management products designed to finance old age care, and "home for care" loans; and non-cash payment instruments such as bank cards that provide specific services to the elderly.
(2) Insurance sector: for-profit old age insurance for individuals and groups, "home for care" pension for the elderly, etc.; research and development of long-term care insurance, health insurance, accidental injury insurance and other insurance products in line with the needs of the elderly; and retirement asset management business.
(3) Trust sector: retirement-linked trust products, and trust products linked to senior housing, geriatric health care, senior fitness, senior tourism and other retirement-related industries.
(4) Fund sector: retirement fund products, including life-cycle funds and target risk funds.

1.2.2 Convenient Financial Services

(1) Improving the availability and convenience of financial services for the elderly: for example, financial institutions should optimize the layout of their branches, improve their branches and service facilities for the elderly and provide senior citizens with special services such as designated service windows and green channels.
(2) Financial institutions should optimize service processes for senior citizens. For example, banks should provide online banking and mobile banking services that meet the needs of the elderly; the insurance industry should provide insurance claim processing services tailored to the elderly.
(3) Financial institutions should provide comprehensive financial services that integrate financial products closely to life in old age and make life more convenient for the elderly.

1.2.3 Basic Financial Services and Protection of Rights

(1) Financial institutions should actively get involved in businesses such as social security, enterprise annuities, occupational annuities and employee benefit

plans, ensure basic services such as settlement, account management, custody and investment, and provide basic financial support to help citizens maintain a reasonable standard of living at old age.

(2) Financial institutions should step up education and protection of elderly consumers. For example, they may set special requirements on large-amount fund transfer, prohibit staff members from providing any misleading or false information to the elderly, and protect the elderly from financial fraud and exploitation.

1.3 Characteristics of Financial Service for the Elderly

1.3.1 Inclusiveness

Financial service for the elderly has a high degree of inclusiveness, that is, it can enhance social welfare and social security through financial means and provide ordinary residents with better, more secure, more convenient financial services at a lower cost. On the one hand, in the context of inadequate old age insurance system and declining replacement rate in China, the demand for financial service for the elderly of Chinese citizens is rising and becoming a universal demand. On the other hand, elderly care is something that every member of the society will eventually face, and the planning for old age is best done early in life.

1.3.2 Long-Term Stability

The objective of financial services for the elderly are to allocate household financial resources on different investment products and plan for retirement by taking into consideration the circumstances of individuals throughout their life cycle. The service process of a retirement financial product may last for decades. At the same time, retirement financial products provided by various financial institutions have high conversion cost and high stability.

Take old age "home for care" insurance for example. After a senior citizen subscribes for a "home for care" program which is a long-term investment, they receive monthly payments. After the policy has taken effect, if the policyholder surrenders the policy, the policyholder will face a surrender fee and other fees. In addition to high financial loss, the policyholder will also need to go through a cumbersome process.

1.3.3 Financial Security

The financial security requirement of financial services for the elderly are reflected in two aspects:

First, funds for the financing of elderly care are related to retirement income security and have low risk tolerance and invested prudently in a method meant to ensure that retirees receive promised benefits.

Secondly, clients of the financing of elderly care are typically middle-aged and elderly people who will withdraw or have withdrawn from the labor market and whose main source of income are or will be old age assets. If they do not attach importance to financial security, they may face an uncertain future in their old age. In addition, Chinese senior citizens' attitude towards investment is relatively conservative. They also lack financial knowledge and can be easily misled or tend to make irrational investment decisions. Therefore, regulators and financial institutions at all levels should attach great importance to financial security and risk mitigation.

2 Development Status of the Financing of Elderly Care

In China, rapid economic and social development has led to a substantial increase in wealth of citizens and the income of the elderly, and their demand for the financing of elderly care is on the rise. In recent years, a series of policies on the financing of elderly care have been introduced, drawing a clear development path for the industry. Various financial institutions are also actively exploring ways to promoting the development of the industry.

2.1 A Series of Policies on the Financing of Elderly Care Have Been Introduced

In recent years, the government has gradually increased support for the retirement service industry. As an important part of the elderly service industry, the financing of elderly care has also drawn increasing attention and a series of related policies have been introduced.

It was not until 2016 did China define financial service for the elderly within a policy. Before 2016, only related content was mentioned in elderly care policies and plans, including the *Plan for the Social Elderly Care Service System (2011–2015)* issued by the State Council in 2011, the *Guidelines on Accelerating the Development of the Elderly Care Industry* issued by the State Council in 2013, and the *Guidelines on the Participation of the Private Sector in the Elderly Care Industry* issued by ten ministries and government agencies (including the Ministry of Civil Affairs), meant to encourage and provide relevant guidance for financial institutions to actively participate in and support the elderly care industry and speed up the innovation of financial products and services. However, there was no specific definition or plan for financial service for the elderly at the time.

It was until March 2016 that five industry regulators, including the People's Bank of China, jointly released the *Guidelines on Financial Support for Pension Services Industry to Accelerate Development*, which clearly defines and makes a plan for financial service for the elderly at the national level for the first time and develops a systematic design for how financial industries should engage in retirement services and how to set up a multi-level retirement financial system (Table 1).

2.2 Products Designed to Finance Elderly Care Are Becoming More Diversified

Thanks to supportive policies, financial institutions have accelerated exploration and innovation in the field of the financing of elderly care and related products and services provided by banks, insurance companies, trusts, funds and other financial institutions have become more diversified.

2.2.1 Diverse Specialized Products Designed to Finance Old Age Care

(1) **Banking Sector**

Banks have the most extensive customer base and are also the most trusted financial institutions in the field of the financing of elderly care. Retirement financial products provided by the banking industry include:

a. Retirement savings, that is, deposits for the purpose of supporting life at old age. With low risk, stable return and convenient process, retirement savings are the most common form of wealth management for the financing of elderly care among Chinese residents. The *2016 China Retirement Preparation Index Research Report* published by Tsinghua University and Tongfang Life Insurance points out that more than 60% of respondents listed bank deposits as the main source of retirement income. According to the data of the National Statistics Bureau of China, China has a high national saving rate which reached 50.9% in 2010 and dropped to 47.9% in 2015 (Fig. 1).

b. Pension wealth management products, that is, long-term products designed and sold by commercial banks. These products are designed to generate long-term steady return. As of the end of 2015, cumulative sales of retirement financial products issued by commercial banks, including Bank of Shanghai, China Construction Bank, Bank of Communications, Industrial Bank, China Everbright Bank and some city commercial banks, exceeded RMB 100 billion (Zhang 2016).

Products designed to finance old age care by banks can be divided into three categories: (i) those targeting specific customer groups, such as deposit cards for elderly customers and exclusive financial products for enrollees of enterprise annuities and

Table 1 Policies Designed to Support The financing of elderly care

Date	Issued by	Name of policy	Content related to the financing of elderly care
2011	State Council	*Plan for the Social Elderly Care Service System (2011–2011)*	Encourage financial institutions to innovate financial products and service methods and improve financial services for the social elderly care industry and provide relate guidelines
2013	State Council	*Guidelines on Accelerating the Development of the Elderly Care Industry*	Include the financing of elderly care into the elderly care industry, encourage financial institutions to develop wealth management, credit, insurance and other financial products suitable for the elderly and set out relevant guidelines and regulatory requirements
2014	CIRC	*Guidelines for Pilot Project of the "Home for Care" "Home for Care" for Seniors*	Launch the Pilot Project of "Home for Care" "Home for Care" for Seniors in Beijing, Shanghai, Guangzhou and Wuhan
2015	Ministry of Civil Affairs	*Guidelines on the Participation of Development Finance Institutions in the Social Elderly Care Industry*	Allow China Development Bank to provide financial support for the social elderly care industry
2015	10 ministries and commissions (including the Ministry of Civil Affairs)	*Guidelines on the Participation of the Private Sector in the Elderly Care Industry*	Improve policies related to financing for the elderly care industry, introduce incentive measures and support financial institutions in accelerating innovation.
2016	Five ministries and commissions (including the People's Bank of China)	*Guidelines on Financial Support for Pension Services Industry to Accelerate Development*	Development a national top-level design for the involvement of financial industries in the elderly care industry
2016	CIRC	*Notice on Extending the Term and Expanding the Scope of the "Home for Care" "Home for Care" for Seniors Pilot Project*	Extend the term and expand the regional scope of the "home for care" pilot project

Source Official websites of the Chinese government, CIRC and other agencies pension schemes; (ii) fund management products related to enterprise annuities and other pension schemes, compensation schemes, and group insurance policies; and (iii) ordinary banking products labeled as old age-related, suitable for all types of customers.

c. Reverse mortgage. A reverse mortgage is a type of loan which a homeowner can borrow money against the value of his or her home. It is designed to meet financing needs of senior citizens. At present, there are only a few Chinese commercial banks providing reverse mortgage loans, including CITIC Bank which launched a reserve mortgage product in Beijing and Shanghai in 2011, Industrial Bank which launched a reserve mortgage product in 2013 following Anyu Rensheng, and Bank of Shanghai which also launched its reverse mortgage product in 2013.

A reserve mortgage works the opposite way to a traditional mortgage loan. Under a reverse mortgage, a borrower obtains a loan from a bank and no repayment of the mortgage is required until the borrower dies. The borrower, who should be a senior homeowner, uses a house's equity as collateral. The amount of money the borrower can receive is determined by the current value of the house, future appreciation or depreciation of the house, the health condition and life expectancy of the senior homeowner and other information. The loan proceeds are paid in annual or monthly installments. However, reverse mortgages provided by domestic banks are not reverse mortgages in the true sense of the concept. They have a fixed term which ends before the death of the borrower who is required to pay the principal and interest when they are due. For example, the term of a retirement mortgage loan offered by CITIC Bank does not exceed ten years and the borrower must pay off the principal and interest when it is due; otherwise, the bank will dispose of the property. In terms of business

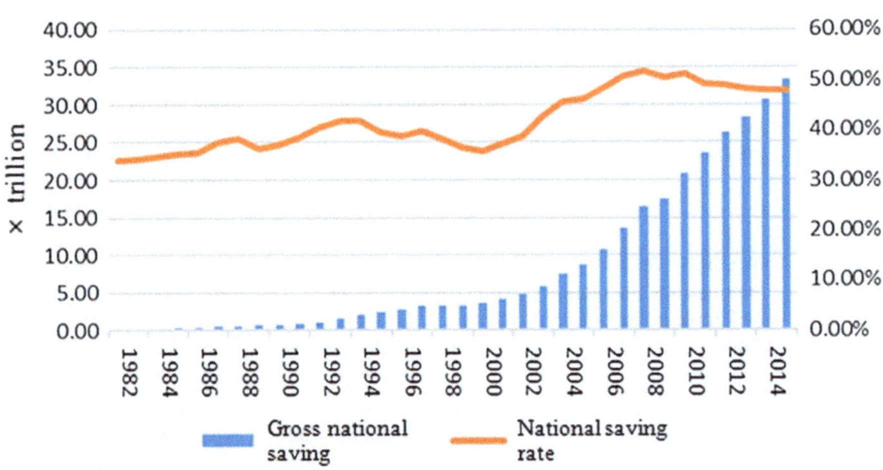

Fig. 1 China's Gross National Saving and National Saving Rate (1982–2014) *Source* National Statistics Bureau and WIND

performance, due to heavy regulations, lack of policy support and fast growth of housing prices, the sale of reverse mortgages is very small.

d. Bank cards with old age care functions, which can be divided into two categories: (i) cards issued by banks to holders of social security cards in accordance with the *Notice on Adding Financial Functions to Social Security Cards* issued by the Ministry of Human Resources and Social Security in 2011. In addition to information recording, information inquiry, business processing and other functions of old social security cards, they also have cash deposit and withdrawal, transfer, payment and other financial functions. (ii) Bank cards provided by banks to senior citizens, such as "Evergreen" Debit Card issued by the Bank of China and the "Better Life" Card issued by Bank of Shanghai. Holders of the above two types of cards generally enjoy favorable treatment, including relief from account opening fee, annual fee, small account management fee and other related costs.

(2) **Insurance Sector**

In August 2014, the State Council issued *Several Opinions on Accelerating the Development of Modern Insurance Services*, specifying the important position of the insurance industry in the multi-level social security system and its role in innovating old age care products and services. For a long time, the insurance industry has been exploring ways to develop the financing of elderly care.

a. For-profit insurance, which refers to insurance products and services provided by commercial insurance companies, with old age risk insurance and retirement fund management as the main components, and is an important part of the retirement income security system. As the government-sponsored basic pension is the major source of retirement income of Chinese citizens and there is a lack of tax incentives, Chinese citizens are seriously under-invested in for-profit personal insurance. *China Pensions Report 2015: Top-Level Design of the Third Pillar Endowment Pensions* (Zheng, 2016) estimates that China's endowment insurance accounted for only 2.6% of GDP in 2014 with an insurance density of RMB 185 per capita, compared to the 42.5% and USD 1258 per capita in the United States.

However, in recent years, for-profit insurance represented by annuities has maintained steady growth, but the overall market size is still small. According to CIRC, premiums paid for life insurance policies that provide a source of income security throughout enrollees' old age (mainly annuities) in 2016 were RMB 860 billion, accounting for only 25% of the total premiums paid for life insurance policies. However, premiums paid for endowment insurance policies in the true sense (which provide retirement benefits in installments) were RMB 150 billion, accounting for only 4.4%. There were only 13.48 million valid policies and 17.07 million valid insurers. In contrast, global premiums paid for life insurance policies that provide a source of income security throughout enrollees' old age accounted for about 50% of the total premiums paid for life insurance policies; premiums for annuities alone accounted for more than 35% of the total premiums for life insurance. Clearly, the development of China's endowment insurance is still lagging behind.

In June 2017, the *Several Opinions on Accelerating the Development of Private Pensions* was released, introducing various measures to encourage the development of for-profit insurance, such as encouraging commercial insurance institutions to innovate for-profit insurance products and services, invest in and promote the development of the old age care industry, facilitate the safe and steady operation of for-profit insurance funds and improve the quality of management services.

b. Reverse mortgage insurance, which provides a source of income for senior homeowners who don't have sufficient retirement income. Similar to reverse mortgage loans provided by banks, a reverse mortgage insurance policy also increased the number of financing options of the elderly to meet their needs of in-home care and increasing retirement income. Reserve mortgage insurance is especially suitable for low-income families, seniors with no children or living further from children and single elderly people.

In June 2014, CIRC released the *Guidelines for the Reverse Mortgage Insurance Pilot Program*, announcing that a reverse mortgage insurance pilot program would be carried out in four cities (including Beijing) in two years commencing on July 1, 2014. On March 25, 2015, Happy Life's reverse mortgage insurance program ("Fanglaiba") was approved as the first version of reverse mortgage products in the insurance industry. Although reverse mortgages are an innovative source of retirement income for seniors, as a niche business, the reverse mortgage industry has encountered challenges in relation to the traditional concept of old age insurance, the policy environment and the market environment. Therefore, the pilot results have not been satisfactory. According to Beijing Times, as of June 2016, 60 households (78 senior citizens) in Beijing, Shanghai, Guangzhou and Wuhan took out a reverse mortgage "home for care" insurance.[2]

c. Old age assets management products. According to the CIRC regulations, a old age assets management product refers to a program sponsored by an old age insurer or pension management company, under which the old age insurer or pension management company takes a mandate from a government agency, enterprise, institution or other corporate client to design a retirement plan, manage accounts and investments, and offer payment services and other services.

The concept of old age assets management business was introduced in China as early as 2009. At that time, there were only group old age assets management programs in the market. They were initially positioned as an alternative or supplement to enterprise annuity plans, with properties similar to annuities. In May 2013, the *Interim Measures for the Administration of Old Age Assets Management Services* was promulgated, allowing old age assets management products to be sold to individuals, drawing market-wide attention. In 2015, the *Measures for the Administration of Old Age Assets Management Services* was released, requiring that the annual increase in old age assets held in trust by an old age insurer for a term of three

[2]Source: Official website of Beijing Times, http://epaper.jinghua.cn/html/2016-07/11/content_317946.htm.

years or less under a closed-end old age assets management program should match the capital strength of the insurer, and allowing pension management companies to engage in the old age assets management industry. In November 2016, the *Notice on Further Strengthening the Supervision of Old Age Assets Management Services* further raised the market entry threshold for old age assets management products, and put forward the requirements of strengthening investment management and product filing. In June 2017, *Several Opinions on Accelerating the Development of Private Pensions* set forth new requirements for the development of individual old age assets management business. The document requires that, in addition to compliance with laws and regulations, an individual old age assets management program should have a function concerned with long-term wealth building to supplement retirement income and should adopt the life-cycle approach.

So far, seven companies have been qualified to manage old age assets, including six retirement insurance companies and CCB Pension. The CIRC has not disclosed the relevant information of old age assets management companies. Based on the annual disclosure reports of management companies, as of the end of 2016, the total old age assets held in trust exceeded RMB 120 billion.

(3) **Trust Sector**

Trust companies are late comers in the financing of elderly care. Only a few trust companies provide trust services to old age assets. Trusts have a lot of advantages in relation to old age assets that other sectors do not have. For example, a retirement plan trust can ensure the isolation of assets, achieve a specific retirement saving purpose and have a wide range of investment options.

A retirement trust can be seen as the application of the trust mechanism in the retirement asset management industry. It is a legal relationship created when the settlor places old age assets under the control of the trustee (typically a trust company in China) for the benefit of the beneficiary. It aims to ensure a financial security for the beneficiary at old age, provide elderly care for the beneficiary, or manage and invest old age assets. The concept of retirement trusts is relatively broad. From the perspective of demand, retirement trusts involve management of old age assets and senior consumer services and can be divided into retirement financial trusts, senior consumer service trusts, etc. From the perspective of supply, retirement trusts involve health care supply, construction of retirement communities or facilities and other services and can be divided into senior housing trusts, retirement infrastructure trusts, etc.

At present, China's retirement trust industry remains in its infancy stage, and the supply of related products in the market is relatively small, with only a few products from CITIC Trust, China Foreign Economy and Trade Trust Co., Ltd. (FOTIC) and other trust companies. The in-home elderly care trust product offered by CITIC Trust has a low minimum investment requirement. The products pay for health data management, emergency services and other in-home elderly care services for a term of only one year. It has three versions which require an investment of RMB 10,000, RMB 20,000 and RMB 30,000 respectively and beneficiaries can enjoy differentiated services corresponding to the level of investment. FOTIC and Industrial Bank jointly launched a retirement financial trust ("Happy Life") requiring a minimum investment of RMB 6 million. The target customer base of the Happy Life Trust is the high-net-worth private banking customers and only senior citizens can be named as beneficiaries. It aims to ensure retirement income security and smooth transfer of an inheritance through a fiduciary arrangement.

(4) **Fund Sector**

In recent years, the fund industry has also actively participated in the elderly care industry. In 2006, HSBC Jinxin issued China's first hybrid target-date fund that provides retirement income. Later, Dacheng Fund and ICBC Credit Suisse also issued hybrid target-date funds and target-date bond funds. On the other hand, in 2012, Tianhong Asset Management Co., Ltd. launched the first retirement fund in China - Tianhong Ankang Retirement Hybrid Fund. As the retirement plan market continues to heat up, more and more retirement funds have been issued. As of the end of 2016, there were thirteen retirement mutual funds in the market, issued by nine fund companies. The total net asset value of the funds reached RMB 14.299 billion.

In March 2016, the *Guidelines on Financial Support for Pension Services Industry to Accelerate Development* proposed for the first time that China should vigorously promote the development of retirement fund products, encourage individuals to increase their asset income through investments in various specialized financial products and enhance their ability to guarantee financial security at old age. This is the first time that the concept of retirement funds is mentioned under a national policy. Since then, the fund industry and related regulators have been actively exploring ways to allow fund companies to participate in the elderly care service industry. In May 2017, the *Guidelines for Public Offering of Pension Securities Investment Funds (Trial)* was issued to solicit public opinions, paving the way for the introduction of real pension funds. A pension fund refers to a securities investment fund that can properly control portfolio risks in accordance with a mature asset allocation strategy, with the objective of providing long-term steady returns on old age assets. Investors are encouraged to hold on to a pension fund for a long period.

The draft guidelines for retirement funds set forth detailed guidelines for the legislative basis, product definition, product types, investment strategies, investment ratio, sub-fund requirements, fund managers, fund manager eligibility, model of operation and cost, fund sales applicability, change in existing products and other aspects of retirement funds. The document remains in draft form to solicit public comments and may be improved in the future.

At present, the number and assets of pension funds provided by the fund sector, which can be divided into life-cycle funds and retirement-themed funds, remain small. If the investment, risk control or other operation activities of a mutual fund whose name contains the word "retirement" does not meet the requirements set forth in the Guidelines, the fund manager shall modify the fund name in accordance with the related procedure; existing funds that meet the review requirements may be renamed as retirement funds in accordance with the related procedure.

2.2.2 Convenient Financial Services

(1) **Optimization and Remodeling of the Branch Network of Financial Institutions**

Middle-aged and senior clients generally have varying limitations in physical mobility and sources of income, prefer low-risk savings and lack financial literacy. Financial institutions such as banks have taken the lead in optimizing the layout of business service centers, opening bank branches and pension-themed branches in neighborhoods with a high concentration of middle-aged and elderly population. Some banks have remodeled branches or community service centers with senior clients in mind, made counters, seats and convenience facilities more senior-friendly, and optimized services processes for senior clients. For example, Industrial Bank has taken the needs of elderly customers into consideration and tailored the counters and seats of its community-based branches for senior citizens.

(2) **Convenient Online Banking and Mobile Payment Services**

With the advent of the Internet Plus era, the number of elderly customers using mobile phones is increasing and their preference related to financial service channels is gradually shifting from offline to online. The percentage of senior citizens using mobile payment is also on the rise.

Taking into consideration the actual needs of elderly customers, Bank of Shanghai launched the "Better Life" mobile banking app tailored to the needs of the elderly in August 2016. Compared with its regular mobile banking app, the "Better Life" mobile banking app has four major features: safer money transfer, senior-friendly interfaces, larger font and services tailored to the needs of the elderly. The app effectively addresses safety, simplicity and convenience issues that have kept senior citizens away from mobile banking.

(3) **Integrated Retirement Financial Services**

Commercial banks have made a further step in innovation in the financing of elderly care by integrating financial products involving personal retirement services to create an integrated retirement financial plan and expand the scope of the financing of elderly care. Banks can integrate internal resources to develop bank cards, wealth management products, for-profit insurance and other financial products tailored to the needs of the elderly, and cooperate with elderly care companies to expand the scope of value-added services provided to senior clients and create an integrated elderly care platform that offer payment services, health management, tourism and leisure, medical registration and other related services.

Industrial Bank launched in 2012 an integrated financial services program (Happy Life program) which takes into consideration the safety and convenience concerns of senior clients regarding financial services. The program provides specialized wealth management, savings account, convenient settlement, fee exemption and other services. Value-added services offered by the program include old age insurance, health management, leisure, elderly care and productive ageing. For example, in addition to 24-h legal advisory and insurance services, to meet the diverse healthcare needs of the elderly, the program also provides health expert appointment scheduling services, whole-process medical guide services, physical examination and other health services.

2.2.3 Basic Financial Services

(1) **Involvement in Social Insurance, Enterprise Annuities and Other Related Business and Construction of Infrastructure for the Financing of Elderly Care**

Most domestic financial institutions' engagement in the financing of elderly care is limited to social old age insurance, enterprise annuities and NSSF management at first and later gradually expand the scope of business activities to other related fields. Take commercial banks for example. A commercial bank usually starts from providing collection, payment, deposit and pooling services for public pension schemes as well as pension benefit payment services to tens of millions of retirees and then expands its business scope to old age savings, old age assets management and other retirement financial services.

Financial institutions have extensive experience in social security fund management, enterprise annuity management and other related fields. They have invested heavily in account management, capital management, investment management, payment and settlement and other specialized systems and usually have a sound service platform. Take enterprise annuities for example. Financial institutions, especially commercial banks, ensure the safe and efficient operation of enterprise annuities and achieve asset preservation and appreciation in annuities through trust service, account management and custody service systems. At the same time, they also provide multi-channel account inquiry, annuity withdrawal and other services.

(2) **Financial Literacy and Protection of Senior Clients**

Financial institutions have spared no effort in promoting financial literacy and protecting consumers. Elderly customers are the key focus of such efforts. Take banks for example. Banks have been using their branches, the Internet and WeChat accounts to educate the public about wealth management products and other new financial products. To prevent financial abuse of the elderly, according to the Notice on Preventing and Combating Cyber Crime, as of December 1, 2016, funds transferred by an individual through ATMs to an account under another name will require a 24-h holding period.

2.3 *Insufficient Supply and Homogeneous Products*

Despite a low profit margin, financial services tailored to the elderly and the elderly care industry faced the same risks as other financial services provided by financial institutions, making it difficult for financial institutions to strike a balance between development of financial service for the elderly and their own commercial sustainability. The financial sector is still exploring efficient ways to participate in the elderly care industry. The number of financial institutions providing retirement financial services is small. Therefore, the financial service for the elderly faces two major problems:

First, homogeneous products. Take wealth management products designed to finance old age care for example. The level of differentiation between products provided by each industry is low. Such products provided by banks are mostly income-based products and there is no substantive difference in term, return, investment orientation and other aspects between wealth management products designed to finance old age care and other wealth management products provided by banks. The wealth management products provided by the insurance industry to finance old age care are also mostly short-term products. Old age insurance companies mainly provide open-end currency and closed-end fixed-income products.

Secondly, insufficient supply. Population ageing has led to an increase in the financial demand of older people, but the supply of corresponding financial products is seriously insufficient. For example, older people prefer traditional outlets and community-based banking services, but only a small percentage of banks have carried out senior-friendly remodeling and provide services tailored to senior clients. Most wealth management products provided by financial institutions to finance old age care are short-term or medium-term products which fail to meet the long-term income needs of customers. At the same time, the number of products and assets under management are small and does not match the huge market demand. For example, the trust industry currently only offers one or two types of retirement trust products. The retirement funds provided by the fund industry in the true sense of the term are still under discussion. There are only dozens of retirement-themed funds in the market.

3 Predicaments of Financial Services for the Elderly

3.1 *Insufficient National Net Wealth and Weak Financial Base for the Financing of Elderly Care*

An important precondition for the development of the financing of elderly care is sufficient wealth accumulation. However, China is going old before it gets rich and the national net wealth is insufficient. In other words, the financial base for the financing of elderly care in China is weak.

3.1.1 Due to Rapid Population Aging, China Is Getting Old Before Getting Rich

In 2000, population aged 60 and over accounted for more than 10% of the total population in China, and 7% of the population were aged 65 and over. According to the UN statistical standards, China has become an ageing society.[3] China is ageing more rapidly than many developed countries. For example, the length of time taken by the percentage of population aged 65 and over to grow from 7 percent to 10 percent is 30 years (1942–1972) in the United States and fourteen years (2000–2014) in China. Most developed countries become an ageing society after their national wealth reaches a relatively high level, but China is getting old before getting rich. In 2000, China's GDP per capita was RMB 7912, equivalent to about USD 955.8 at the prevailing exchange rate. In comparison with China, when the United States became an ageing society in 1942, its GDP per capita reached USD 13,138 at constant prices.

Furthermore, the poverty rate in the elderly population in China also high and there is a large gap in poverty rate among older persons between rural and urban areas, According to the 2013 China Health and Retirement Longitudinal Study (CHARLS),[4] 42.4 million people over the age of 60 in China lived below the poverty line, accounting for about 22.9% of the population aged over 60; the rural elderly population has a poverty rate of 28.9%, much higher than that of their urban counterpart (9.5%). *Disparities among Older Persons in China*,[5] a report released by the UN Entities in China, also points out that China ranks lowest in the income security domain (75th) due to high old age poverty rate.

3.1.2 The Proportion of Financial Assets in Household Asset Is Low

Chinese households hold most of their assets in real property and the proportion of financial assets is very small. Financial assets held by households show a trend of polarization in relation to risk exposure, and the assets set aside specifically to provide for old age care are seriously insufficient. According to the *Risk Report on Household Financial Assets Allocation in China* released by the Survey and Research Center for China Household Finance, average assets per Chinese household were RMB 1.034 million in 2016, mainly in real estate (68.8%). In 2013, real estate accounted for only 15.5% of assets held by U.S. households. Financial assets accounted for

---

[3] According to the criteria set by the United Nations in *The Aging of Populations and its Economic and Social Implications* published in 1956, if people aged 65 and over in a country or region accounts for more than 7% of the total population, it means the country or region has become an aging society. In 1982, the World Assembly on Aging in Vienna determined that if people aged 60 and over accounted for more than 10% of the total population of a country or region, it means the country or region has become a super-aging society.

[4] Source: China Health and Retirement Longitudinal Study. Available at: http://charls.pku.edu.cn/zh-CN.

[5] Source: Report: High poverty rate and low relative welfare among older persons in China. ThePaper.cn. Available at http://www.thepaper.cn/newsDetail_forward_1573529.

11.5% of the total assets held by Chinese households, of which deposits accounted for 45.8%, far higher than the 34.4% of the EU and 13.6% of the United States. On the other hand, there is also a lack of rationality in the allocation of financial assets. Chinese families either hold no assets in stocks or invest heavily in stocks, causing polarization in terms of risk exposure.

3.1.3 Senior Citizens Lack Diverse Sources of Income but Their Consumption Spending Continues to Increase

China's elderly people generally lack diverse sources of income. According to the *Fourth Sampling Survey on the Living Conditions of the Elderly in Urban and Rural Areas of China*,[6] in 2014, the proportion of social security benefits accounted for 79.4% of the total income of senior people in urban areas and 36% in the total income of their rural counterparts, and other sources of income of Chinese senior citizens included operating income, property income, and family transfers. Pension benefits are the main source of income for the urban elderly population and the level of pension benefits is high. However, the elderly people in rural areas still need to earn income through work or rely on their children. Both urban and rural elderly people lack diverse sources of income. There is also a big income gap between urban and rural elderly population. In 2014, the per capita income of urban seniors was RMB 23,930, which was 3.1 times that of rural senior citizens (RMB 7621).

The consumption spending of Chinese senior citizens is also increasing dramatically. Due to ageing and declining health, the elderly population's spending on routine care, old age supplies, medical spending and other items increase dramatically. In 2014, the per capita consumption expenditure of urban and rural seniors in China was RMB 14,764, of which daily expenses, non-recurring expenses and medical expenses accounted for 56.5, 17.3 and 12.9%, respectively, and 86.7% in total.

3.2 Due to Low Levels of Financial Literacy, the Majority of Chinese Citizens Don't Know How to Use Financial Instruments to Prepare for Retirement

The majority of Chinese citizens lack knowledge about financing old age care, leading to insufficient old age provision. According to *China Retirement Readiness Insight Report* released by Citibank and AIA in November 2015, the understandings of the majority of Chinese citizens about financial products designed to finance old age care were insufficient and preferred low-risk and high-yield financial products. While evaluating retirement financial products, the respondents pay attention to safety and

[6]Source: Official website of the Ministry of Civil Affairs. Report of the Fourth Sampling Survey on the Living Conditions of the Elderly in Urban and Rural Areas of China. October 9, 2016, http://www.mca.gov.cn/article/zwgk/mzyw/201610/20161000001974.shtml.

sustainability, guaranteed returns and reputation and credibility of financial institutions and their expected rate of return of products designed to finance old age care reached 7.9%.

Low levels of financial literacy are particularly notable among seniors. On the one hand, senior people generally are more conservative about financial matters, especially about planning for wealth management at old age. They have a high propensity to save and attach great importance to the safety and stability of investment and wealth management. After retiring, most retirees prefer bank deposits over financial products such as bank financing, insurance for wealth management and Internet finance. On the other hand, the average education level of the elderly population is low. Most senior people lack financial knowledge and risk awareness. They are not fully aware of the distinction between investment and wealth management and their understandings about the complicated financial investment vehicles in the market are insufficient. In addition, investor education provided by the financial sector do not tend to benefit the elderly population. For these reasons, most Chinese senior citizens are poorly prepared to make full use of financial instruments, further hampering the development of the financing of old age care.

3.3 Deficient Regulation of Wealth Management Products Designed to Finance Old Age Care Leads to a Failure of Market Discipline

Due to the imperfect market mechanisms and narrow channels for private investment and financing, the private lending market have been very active in recent years. The deficient regulation of the private lending market, together with the lack of wealth management knowledge and risk awareness among the elderly and the lack of relevant regulatory mechanisms for financial services for the elderly, has left many elderly citizens vulnerable to exploitation.

The *Risk Investigation Report on Financial Crimes against the Elderly* released by Beijing Senior Protection Office of Zhicheng Public Interest Lawyers in October 2016 revealed that about 21% of the cases involving senior citizens were related to financial crimes against the public. Some senior citizens lost up to RMB 3 million to fraud and 52% of senior citizens were reluctant to tell their children about such incidents because of fear of being blamed. One of the common characteristics of financial crimes against the public involving corporations, wealth management, retirement plans, works of art and other investments is the purported high returns which are meant to lure older people into financial traps.

In response to inadequate regulation of the financing of elderly care, a series of policies in this regard have been introduced in recent years. However, most of them are macro-level polices and fail to provide detailed operational guidelines and implementation details. Therefore, the efficiency of regulation remains low. Furthermore, most regulations related to the financing of elderly care are scattered in policies for the elderly care industry and the insurance industry. Only the *Guidelines on Financial Support for Pension Services Industry to Accelerate Development* is a systematic and complete document. Currently, there are no specific laws and regulations on the financing of elderly care in China, nor are there any special guidelines issued by regulators to define and standardize the scope of business, activities of institutions, services and business processes, leading to inadequate regulation of the industry.

3.4 The Market of Financing Old Age Care Needs a Reasonable Entry Threshold and an Effective Business Model

Although financing old age care is regarded as the "new blue sea" of the future financial industry and will create new business opportunities and sources of income for the financial industry, a reasonable entry threshold for the market of the financing of elderly care is yet to be set up. In the meanwhile, the profitability of the industry remains undesirable and the industry is still searching for a sustainable business model.

3.4.1 The Approval and Licensing System of the Financing of Elderly Care Has Limited the Ability of Financial Institutions to Enter the Market

The financing of elderly care can create significant synergies between pension, services for financing old age care and elderly care industries. Financial institutions generally promote financial service for the elderly as a whole. However, the pension industry has strict entry requirements. Take enterprise annuities as an example. The enterprise annuity industry has four business qualifications (i.e., trustee, account manager, custodian and investment manager qualifications). So far, only 35 institutions are qualified to manage enterprise annuities (57 enterprise annuity management licenses in total). The regulator appointed two groups of enterprise annuity managers in 2005 and 2007. Since then, more than a decade has passed and no additional managers have been appointed. The lack of a business licenses has significantly hindered the business and product layout of financial institutions in the financing of elderly care, making it difficult for financial institutions to generate synergies and provide integrated retirement financial products. Furthermore, some financial products designed for old age care are also subject to approval of regulators and certain restrictions. For example, only old age insurance companies and pension management companies are allowed to engage in old age assets management activities.

3.4.2 The Financial Service for the Elderly Lacks Efficient Business Formats

Various financial institutions have been experimenting in the field of the financing of elderly care. At present, retirement financial products provided by financial institutions can be divided into two categories: (i) extended pension asset management services or integrated traditional banking services, which may deviate from the actual needs of the elderly population, resulting in the slow development of many retirement financial products and limited contribution to the profits of financial institutions; and (ii) diverse retirement financial products developed by financial institutions, including retirement products provided by bankers, retirement trusts, old age assets management products and credit cards tailored for senior clients. However, both categories have been growing slowly and financial institutions are still searching for efficient business model in their attempt to establish a sustainable business ecosystem.

4 Policy Recommendations for the Financing of Elderly Care

4.1 Improve Policies to Support the Development of the Financing of Elderly Care

The financing of elderly care has significant social and economic implications and requires the involvement of both the government and the private sector. Therefore, we should first define the roles of the government and the private sector and the scope of their respective functions. For example, the government should finance and administer basic pension schemes and regulate the middle and high-end markets. The private sector should provide products to supplement basic pension schemes. Therefore, to promote the development of the financing of elderly care, the government needs to develop relevant top-level system designs and supporting policies.

In China's case, the central government has developed top-level designs through the *Guidelines on Accelerating the Development of the Elderly Care Industry*, the *Guidelines on Financial Support for Pension Services Industry to Accelerate Development* and other policies. The next step should be to improve and introduce more guidelines and supporting rules to encourage more financial institutions to engage in the financing of elderly care. On the basis of a solid regulatory framework, the government and the private sector should work together to create the system of the financing of elderly care. In particular, regulatory authorities should issue rules and regulations on financial support for elderly care as soon as possible. Furthermore, local governments should introduce supporting policies and create a favorable regulatory environment for the development of the financing of elderly care through tools such as discount rates, special subsidies and government-led funds.

4.2 *Improve the Pension System and Increase the Sources of Retirement Income*

With the advance of reform programs of China's basic pension system for urban employees, a multi-pillar system is gradually taking shape in the country. However, there is a notable imbalance in the system structure. The amount of assets of the Pillar I accounts for 70% of the total pension assets, enterprise annuities of the Pillar II grow at a snail's pace, while Pillar 3 system (individual pensions) is yet to be established. As a result, current retirees mainly rely on the basic pension system. Although the average basic pension benefit per capita was RMB 2362 in 2016,[7] the replacement rate was only around 42%, which was in the neighborhood of the minimum replacement rate (40–50%) set forth by the World Labor Organization. In general, a replacement rate of 80% is required to maintain the pre-retirement standard of living. In countries which adopt the three-pillar pension system, including the United States and Australia, the average national replacement rate can reach 60%. Pension benefits for urban and rural residents are even more inadequate.[8] At present, over 500 million enrollees are covered by the basic pension scheme for urban and rural residents and the number of people receiving benefits surpasses 150 million. The pension benefits per capital provided by the basic pension scheme for urban and rural residents was only RMB 117 in 2016.

Therefore, China still needs to improve its pension system, increase the sources of income for the elderly, provide financial support for elderly care and increase the purchasing power of senior citizens. It should further expand the coverage of basic pension schemes, raise the social pooling level of the basic pension system, speed up the market-oriented operation of pension funds and improve the individual account system; expand the coverage and increase investment options of enterprise annuities, allow individuals to make investment decisions, increase the participation rate of enterprises and individuals; set up a regulatory framework for the third pillar (personal tax-deferred pensions) as soon as possible and encourage individuals to plan for their own retirement. All stakeholders should make concerted efforts to establish a sound multi-pillar pension system and pave the way for the development of the market of the financing of elderly care.

---

[7]Source: Official website of Ministry of Human Resources and Social Security of the People's Republic of China, http://www.mohrss.gov.cn/SYrlzyhshbzb/dongtaixinwen/buneiyaowen/201705/t20170525_271399.html.

[8]Ibid.

4.3 Improve the Legal and Taxation Systems to Support the Development of the Market of the Financing of Elderly Care

Fragmented and decentralized regulation undermines the development of the financing of elderly care in China. The industry is in urgent need for specialized and authoritative laws and regulations.

Policymakers should improve the regulatory system of the industry and provide a legal basis for pension asset management, reversed mortgages and retirement investment and financing and other retirement-related financial activities to ensure the safety of pension assets and sustainability of the market of the financing of elderly care. For example, reserve mortgage policies and relevant tax laws should clearly set forth terms and conditions related to the renewal and disposal of land use rights. The legislature should improve related property tax, inheritance tax and property tax laws and regulations and protect financial institutions against legal risks in the disposal of real estate; and amend the regulations on the transfer of rural housing land use right to facilitate the use of "home for care" in rural areas and increase sources of income of rural elderly population.

Secondly, it should improve tax policies related to retirement-related industries and promote the development of the market of the financing of elderly care. The first step is to improve tax incentives for the pension system. For enterprise annuities, the Chinese government should consider raising the level of tax incentivization to encourage more enterprises and employees to participate in enterprise annuities. For individual pensions, preferential taxation policies should be introduced and the personal tax-deferred account pilot program should be rolled out as soon as possible; a favorable environment should be established to allow financial products to compete fairly and contribute to the development of pillar 3. Market players in the market of the financing of elderly care may enjoy tax reduction for certain revenue generated by investment in elderly care infrastructure, retirement financial products and related business activities to incentivize participation in the financing of elderly care.

4.4 Strengthen the Regulatory Framework to Promote the Sustainable Development of the Industry

China has a fragmented financial regulatory structure under which there are different regulatory authorities for different types of financial products and services. For example, traditional banking, securities, and insurance industries are regulated by China Banking Regulatory Commission (CBRC), China Securities Regulatory Commission (CSRC), and China Insurance Regulatory Commission (CIRC), respectively.

However, market players engaged in retirement financial activities come from many industries. Therefore, the regulatory responsibilities of the financing of elderly care are fragmented among multiple market regulators and government agencies, including CBRC, CSRC, CIRC, the Ministry of Human Resources and Social Security and the Ministry of Civil Affairs. China's the financing of elderly care remains in the infancy stage, and relevant regulators are groping their way towards more effective regulation. Therefore, a clearly defined regulatory framework will be the key to the healthy and orderly development of the industry. To this end, relevant regulators should make concerted efforts to establish a regulatory framework suitable for financial service for the elderly, strengthen market and industry regulation, and introduce industry standards, service processes and risk monitoring mechanisms for the industry. For example, in response to the frequent occurrence of financial frauds and scams targeting seniors, China should crack down further on illegal financial and fund-raising activities and create a safe and reliable investment environment for the elderly. In addition, financial institutions engaging in the financing of elderly care should be required to improve their internal risk control systems and procedures, design and information disclosure system, reduce the risk of moral hazard of internal institutions and employees, and protect the legitimate rights and interests of customers.

4.5 Provide Guidance on Retirement Planning and Step up Financial Education

Chinese citizens' low retirement planning awareness and lack of financial literacy has hindered the development of the financing of elderly care. The government, financial institutions and individuals should make concerted efforts to address this issue.

First, the government should step up the provision of guidance on retirement planning and raise residents' awareness of provision for old age security. For example, the Chinese government should step up public education about retirement planning. Local government agencies should formulate financial training programs tailored to the elderly population in their respective regions to raise their awareness and financial literacy.

Secondly, financial institutions should consolidate industry resources and exert industry influence through trade associations and other organizations, step up public education about retirement income security, increase the influence of the financial service for the elderly, and enhance public awareness in this regard.

Thirdly, citizens should also take the initiative to understand the population ageing trend in China, improve financial knowledge, learn their own financial conditions and household demographic structure, raise awareness about retirement planning and start retirement planning as early as possible. Most importantly, citizens should not engage in any illegal financial or fund-raising activity and protect themselves against fraud.

5 Major Trends for the Financing of Elderly Care

5.1 Population Ageing Will Cause a Significant Increase in the Demand for Retirement Financial Services

The acceleration of population ageing has presents tremendous challenges in China. According to the *13th Five-year Plan for the Development of the Elderly Care Industry and the Old Age Care System*, the number of older persons aged 60 years or over has risen to around 255 million, representing an increase of 24 million from 2016; the proportion of older persons in the total population has risen from 16.7 to 17.8%; the number of seniors living alone continues to increase, and the ageing trend will persist. Changes in the family, including decline in family size, ageing members, empty nesters, and loss of functions, have presented challenges to the traditional family caregiving of senior people and the demand for other elderly care services is on the rise. As the process of urbanization picks up the pace, migration and residential mobility has led to the gradual dissolution of the traditional Chinese family structure and the declining of family size. Other forms of old age security are needed to replace the traditional practice of "raising children as a protection against old age." Increasing importance has been attached to the development of a centralized pension system at the national level. The elderly care industry has become the focus of future development and is even regarded as an important engine for the Chinese economy.

On the other hand, Chinese citizens have benefited greatly from the rapid economic growth for the past three decades. The accumulation of national wealth has paved the way for the development of financial service for the elderly. According to the data from the National Office on Ageing, the potential consumer spending of China's elderly population is expected to grow from about RMB 4 trillion (8% of GDP) in 2014 to about RMB 106 trillion (33% of GDP) in 2050, which will certainly drive the development of the elderly care industry. The elderly care industry involves all sectors of the society, including basic necessities of life, care services, manufacturing, health care, culture, fitness and entertainment. Virtually every sector needs financial services. Financial needs of the elderly care industry are expected to skyrocket.

5.2 Financial Reforms and the Financing of Elderly Care Have Become a New Impetus for Economic Development

The 2017 National Economic Reform Conference proposed that China should deepen the reforms of "financial institutions and the financial regulatory system, improve the multi-level capital market and create a favorable environment for the development of the real economy." Deepening financial reforms and the marketization, globalization and diversification of the finance market have presented tremendous challenges to traditional businesses and development models of financial institutions. The financial industry has entered a crucial transformation and upgrading stage.

Development of the financing of elderly care will create new opportunities and new room for the reforms and development of financial institutions. On the one hand, the financing of elderly care, as the "new blue sea" for financial institutions, will bring long-term sustainable sources of income and unlock new sources of profitable growth for financial institutions. On the other hand, the financing of elderly care will become a "booster" for the transformation and upgrading of financial institutions and push financial institutions to develop innovative service models and products.

For example, the financing of elderly care will bring new impetus to the development of commercial banks. First of all, compared with traditional banking activities, long-term assets, stability, economies of scale and other attributes of the financing of elderly care will generate long-term stable income for commercial banks. Secondly, the financing of elderly care complements the traditional banking business and can help the banking sector expand the customer base. Senior clients can also provide long-term, stable funding sources for commercial banks through bank deposits and wealth management products. Thirdly, most retirement financial services are innovative and integrated services spanning multiple businesses and divisions within the banking sector and may even involve securities, insurance and funds. Therefore, development of the financing of elderly care can help promote the cooperation between corporate banking, personal finance, financial markets, investment banking and other sectors as well as internal resource integration between subsidiaries within a bank group. Fourthly, in addition to the financing of elderly care, commercial banks can engage in management of pension fund assets such as basic pension funds, enterprise annuities and occupational annuities, which will drive the development of the asset management business of the banking sector and help the banking sector unlock new sources of revenue and profit.

Development of the financing of elderly care has similar implications for insurance companies, securities companies, fund companies, trust companies and other financial institutions. More and more financial institutions will regard the financing of elderly care as a key component in their development strategy, strive to improve their financial services by integrating internal and external resources and innovating their organizational structure, and take advantage of opportunities presented by the financing of elderly care to achieve their own upgrading.

5.3 *Product Innovation and Integration Will Help Expand the Financial Service for the Elderly*

The core objective of innovation in financial products is to provide financial services that truly meet the needs of residents to prepare for retirement and contribute to the establishment of a sound retirement financial system and expand the fields of financial service for the elderly over the long run. We believe innovation related to retirement financial products will be achieved through the following means:

First, introduction of products tailored to specific needs of clients in relation to retirement. Financial institutions will design personalized, differentiated and multi-level pension services tailored to the needs of different customer groups divided by age, region, economic status, investment experience and risk appetite based on the results of in-depth investigation and analysis.

Second, the integration of different formats, especially the integration of the financing of elderly care and the elderly care industries. The elderly care industry has a huge demand for long-term financing. Financial institutions can develop innovative solutions that integrate insurance, wealth management and fund functions to match the demand of the elderly care industry. In this way, not only can the elderly care industry gain access to long-term sources of funds but also these innovative solutions will provide residents with long-term and stable return on their investments and retirement planning and elderly care services, which is a win-win situation.

Third, shifting from traditional financial products that have typically been designed around single financial functions to "integrated" and "hybrid" financial solutions. Such hybrid financial solutions (i) integrate multiple financial functions (property management, insurance, funds) to meet family asset allocation, retirement planning, post-retirement wealth management and other needs of clients of different ages and incomes across their life cycle; and (ii) integrate financial services and elderly care services, including daily elderly care, elderly care community program, leisure and entertainment, education and consultation, legal advice and other value-added services. There are only a few financial institutions that currently have the capacity to provide integrated solutions to the financing of elderly care which will become a major trend in the future because, for financial institutions, the provision of integrated solutions not only can improve customer experience and customer loyalty but also can generate more revenue.

5.4 *Financial Technology Will Boost the Rapid Development of Financial Service for the Elderly*

Technology-driven financial innovation related to business models, applications, processes and products has a significant impact on the financial market, financial institutions and the way financial services are delivered. It is foreseeable that the rapid development of financial technology will spur the development (possibly "leapfrog" development) of financial service for the elderly in the following fields:

(1) **Widespread Use of the Internet and Mobile Payment Technology Can Provide Convenient Access to Financial Services for People from Middle Age to Old Age**

According to the *2017 Statistical Report on Internet Development in China*, as of December 2016, the number of Chinese Internet users reached 731 million and the

Internet penetration rate reached 53.2%. Mobile Internet users accounted for 95.1% of the total Chinese Internet users and the proportion of Chinese Internet users making mobile online payment increased to 67.5%. The number of Internet users from middle age to old age is also growing, so is the number of people from middle age to old age using online payment and mobile payment.

The development of the Internet and the widespread use of smartphones have provided middle-aged and elderly people with much more convenient access to financial services. Financial institutions can provide diversified financial products to people from middle age to old age and improve their financial literacy through Internet platforms such as official websites, online banking, mobile APPs and third-party platforms. The Internet has also shortened the spatial distance between service providers and clients. Financial institutions can provide financial services for elderly people in rural areas through online platforms which reduce the cost of financial institutions, further expand their customer base and embody the spirit of inclusiveness in the financing of elderly care.

(2) **Intelligent Technology-Enabled Investment Consulting Services Will Help Improve the Performance of Pension Fund Investments**

Personalized, diverse intelligent investment consulting services enabled by big data technology, quantitative financial models and intelligent algorithms shall be provided, taking into consideration various factors such as investor's risk tolerance, financial status, expected profit target and risk preference. In the United States, as a new technology-enabled financial instrument, intelligent investment consulting services have developed rapidly and changed the traditional wealth management industry. By the end of 2015, assets under management in this niche market reached USD100 billion. Characterized by low cost and risk diversification, intelligent investment consulting services provide innovative ideas for the traditional pension management business and help individuals make rational investment decisions. According to the theory of behavioral economics, individual investors are plagued with a variety of behavioral biases such as, among others, overconfidence, self-serving bias, and loss aversion. Intelligent investment consulting services help create customized asset allocation portfolios through big data and artificial intelligence analysis of personal investment preferences and long-term investment goals, develop an automated portfolio rebalancing strategy to control investment risks and reduce irrational transactions, help investors stick to long-term investment targets and achieve the goal of capital preservation or appreciation.

(3) **Blockchain Technology Will Improve Operational Efficiency and Security of the Financing of Elderly Care**

Blockchain is a new application model of computer technologies such as distributed data storage, point-to-point transmission, consensus mechanism, and encryption algorithm. It is recognized as a fundamental and disruptive technology in financial fields. With its decentralization, openness, autonomy, anonymity and other characteristics, blockchain can ensure that the data in any given block cannot be altered.

Blockchain technology is expected to be applied in the field of the financing of elderly care. For example, blockchain technology can integrate big data at all levels and classify and analyze behavior, investment preferences, wealth inheritance, and health status of individuals. Financial institutions can use blockchain to develop personalized products to meet retirement planning and elderly care needs of customers. Furthermore, with its decentralization, ledger design and data immutability, blockchain technology can improve the security of the financing of elderly care.

References

Sun, B. (2016). Financial Service for the Elderly in the Context of an Ageing Society. *Tsinghua Financial Review*, 2016(2).

Yue, L. (2016). Policies on Financial Service for the Elderly. *Financial View (Wealth)*, 2016 (12).

Yue, L. (2016). Supply-Side Layout of the Financial Service for the Elderly. *The Chinese Banker*, 2016(5).

Yue, L. (2016). Four Major Challenges Faced by Commercial Banks in the Financial Service for the Elderly. *China Banking*, 2016(1).

Zhang, L., and Chen, D. (2016). Current Situation and Development Trend of Retirement Financial Services Provided by Commercial Banks. *China Financialyst*, 2016(9).

Meng, D. (2016). Innovation and Review of Personal Retirement Financial Products Provided by Commercial Banks. *Qinghai Finance*, 2016(7).

Zheng, B. (2016). China Pension Development Report 2015. Economy & Management Publishing House, 2016.

Yue, L. and He, L. (2016). Predicaments of Reserve Mortgages. *Financial View (Wealth)*, 2016(7).

Yue, L. and Li, M. (2017). The Spring for the Old Age Assets Management Industry. *Financial View (Wealth)*, 2017(1).

Wu, Y. and Lv, Y. (2016). Retirement Planning Research. *Modern Marketing*, 2016(12).

Wu, Y. and Dang, J. (2014). Blue Book on Population Ageing: Report on the Development of China's Elderly Care Industry (2014). Beijing: Social Sciences Academic Press, 2014.

Lin, T. (2015). How Can Commercial Banks Make Breakthroughs in Financial service for the elderly? *China Rural Finance*, 2015(9).

Tian, X. (2016). Development Path and Policy Review of Consumption Financing of the Elderly. *Theory Monthly*, 2016(12).

Chen, Y. (2016). Blockchain Financial Market, Retirement Financing and "Retirement Points". Available at: http://zhuanti.cebnet.com.cn/20160728/ 101919250.html (accessed on July 28, 2016).

Lei Yue, CFA, Chinese actuary, Senior Manager of Pension Department of China Merchants Fund Management Co., Ltd., Pensions Business, Invited Research Fellow of COACFF50, specializing in retirement financial services.

Chapter 8
Finance for the Elderly Care Industry: Business Mergers and Development Diversity

Zhuojun Cao and Qin Jing

Abstract With the further development of industrialization and urbanization, the traditional elderly care has been on the decline while the community care becomes popular. The elderly care industry, a new industrial form, emerges and is under constant improvement. Since the elderly care industry is marked by huge investment and long return cycle that requires strong supports of the financial sector, finance for the elderly care industry is thus developed. In recent years, under the joint efforts of the government and the market, finance for the elderly care industry in China has seen a series of achievements and is gradually moving toward industrialization and marketization. However, at present, China's elderly care industry is still young and facing a series of challenges such as the implementation of macro-policies and the rigid financing channels for enterprises. With the increasing ageing population, the demand for elderly care industry will grow exponentially. It can be predicted that with the joint efforts of the government and the market, there will be tremendous room for the development of elderly care industry financing.

Keywords Finance for the elderly care industry
Pension funds and capital markets · PPP international mergers and acquisitions

1 Elderly Care Industry: History and Current Situation

1.1 The Emergence of Elderly Care Industry in a New Age

At present, the definition, implication and application of the term "elderly care industry" are not uniform. According to Dr. Dang Junwu (2015), deputy director of the China Research Centre on Ageing, the elderly care industry can be regarded as "the industry for the ageing population," including various industries that provide related products and services provided for all senior citizens. How-

Z. Cao · Q. Jing (✉)
Hejun Consulting Group, Beijing, China

K. Dong and Y. Yao (eds.), *Annual Report on Financing Old Age Care in China (2017)*, https://doi.org/10.1007/978-981-13-0968-7_8

ever, the OLDAGE puts forward that the elderly care industry is an individual-oriented life security industry and is developed in accordance with geographical environment, social environment, and the development level of respective society and economy. Yan Xiaohui (2008) believes that the elderly care industry is an industry that provides products and services especially for the elderly. On this basis, the elderly care industry can be defined in a more general term or a more specific term. The former refers to a system composed of the government, enterprises and social organizations to address the material and spiritual needs of the elderly. The latter refers to three key service providers: institutions, communities and private residences, which provide products and services for the seniors, including daily care, health care, rehabilitation, mental and spiritual support, and funeral services. As used herein, "elderly care industry" adopts the general definition.

The development of China's elderly care industry is closely related to the growth rate of ageing population. In 2000, when the people over the age of 65 accounted for more than 7% of the total population, China became an ageing society. At that time, the Central Committee and the State Council successively issued a series of major policies concerning the elderly care industry, such as the *Decision of the CPC Central Committee and the State Council on Strengthening the Work on Ageing*, and the *Outline of the Tenth Five-year Plan for the Development of Industries for the Old Age (2001–2005)*, suggesting the initial development of elderly care industry in China. At this stage, the elderly care industry was mainly led by the government with insufficient participation from the society. With the increasing ageing population, it is difficult to meet the diverse needs of the elderly by relying solely on the government-run institutions (Fig. 1).

1.2 Initial Stage of Unrestrained Growth (After 2013)

In 2012, when China's population over the age of 65 exceeded 120 million, the government began to actively introduce the social capitals in building the elderly care industry, promulgated the *Ministry of Civil Affairs on Encouraging and Introducing Private Capital into the Field of Retirement Services*, and *Ministry of Civil Affairs Opinions on the Open Bank on Implementing the Cooperation Agreement for Supporting the Construction and Planning of Social Pension Services System to Promote the Construction of Social Retirement Services*. By 2013, the State Council promulgated the *Opinions of the State Council on Accelerating the Development of the Old Age Care Services*, that is, the "Circular No. 35" at the initial stage of the elderly care industry. The government thus fosters development of the elderly care industry with supporting policies in the following six aspects: investment and financing, land supply, preferential tax break, subsidies, talent training and employment, and charity organizations.

From the industrial economics perspectives, the industrial evolution is divided into four stages: startup, scale-up, agglomeration, and balance/alliance. Compared

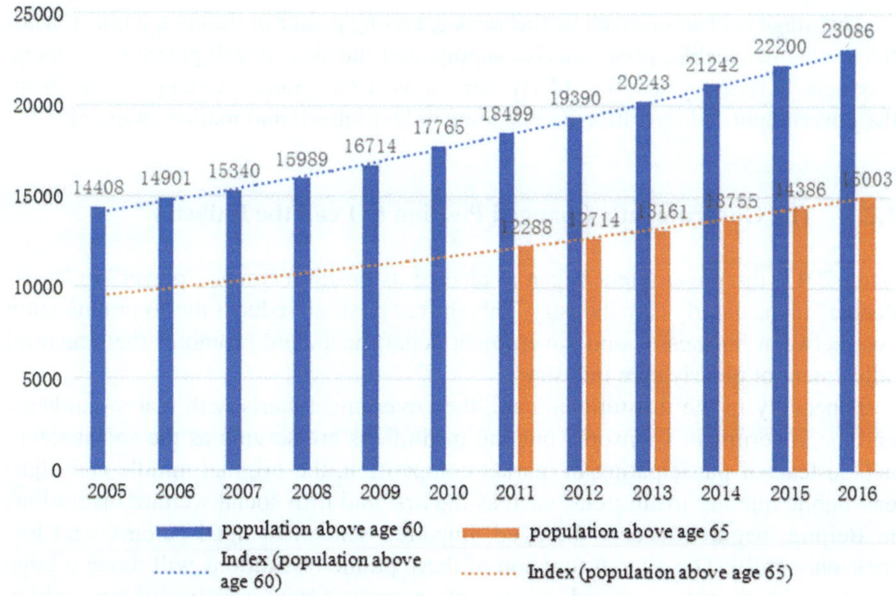

Fig. 1 China's Ageing Population 2005–2016 (*Source* 2005–2016 statistical bulletin on national economic and social development, National Bureau of Statistics)

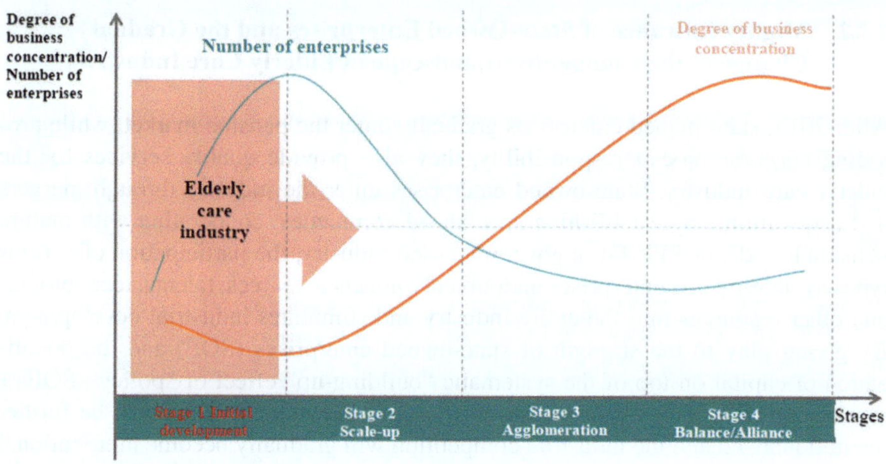

Fig. 2 The development of the elderly care industry

with other social service industries, a plethora of businesses with extremely low concentration keep the elderly care industry in the early stages of industrial development. At this stage, although the central and local governments keep promulgating relevant policies, the industrial enrollees have not yet discovered a mature business model and the industry as a whole is still in the initial stage of development (Fig. 2).

This stage is characterized by the weak spending power of the customers, a "scattered, chaotic, feeble, poor" market supply, and the slow development of financial products. In recent years, the elderly care industry has gradually stepped away from the government-led operation and become industrialized and market-oriented.

1.2.1 The Government's Changed Position to Lead the Industry

After 2013, the government began to change its position from a "player" to "goalkeeper" in the elderly care industry. This shift of position reduces the communication cost between businesses and government departments and promotes the structural adjustment of elderly care industry.

Especially in the institutional care, the government starts with macro-guidance and the government-sponsored nursing institutions are serving as the social safety net. Instead of participating in market competition, the original middle and high-end public nursing institutions, such as the first and fifth social welfare institutions in Beijing, begin to accept the aged, impaired seniors or aged parents who lost their only child. The altered function of these public institutions will direct a large number of high-net-worth individuals into private elderly care institutions, which will undoubtedly gain a larger market share in the industry.

1.2.2 Mighty Entrance of State-Owned Enterprises and the Gradual Change of the Competitive Landscape of Elderly Care Industries

After 2013, state-owned enterprises gradually enter the pension market; while providing corporate social responsibility, they also provide quality services for the elderly care industry. State-owned enterprises enter the industry through mergers and acquisitions, by establishing specialized companies, cooperating with mature pension brands, or PPP. For a government-led industry, the participation of various types of state-owned enterprises undoubtedly injects resources, talents, technologies and other resources into the entire industry and stimulates industrial development. By giving play to the strength of state-owned enterprises (SOE) and the privatization of capital on top of the systematic "building-up" effect of "policy + SOEs + implementing agencies", the entire elderly care industry in China will be further institutionalized and the industrial competition will gradually become more rational and orderly. However, from another point of view, the involvement of state-owned capital has drastically reduced the market share for private-owned enterprises. The elderly care industry itself is an industry dominated by "big capital" enterprises. The chance for small enterprises to survive is inherently small. The successive entry of state-owned enterprises and large capitalized enterprise groups will undoubtedly force a large number of small and medium-sized companies to adopt strategic shifts or even back out of the industry competition. This will promote the scale-up of the elderly care industry.

1.2.3 Home or Community Care Service System with Institutional and Healthcare Support Gradually Established

The traditional concept of elderly care in China is "home-based retirement", in which the elderly can spend their old age in their own familiar environment (family or community) independently and enjoy the basic living services and basic medical services provided by the community. With the introduction of a series of policies and the continuing market exploration, home and community care service has gradually become the focus of the market. The combination of home care and medical care has gradually become the new agenda in policy making and the new battleground for the market, which are crucial market factors in old age services sector. At the same time, the position and function of institutional pension in the old age service system have gone through the process of "supplement-support-supplement". This change marks that the old age service system in China will be much improved in the dual readjustment of policies and markets.

1.2.4 Market for Financing Old Age Care to Be Improved

Overall, the products designed to finance old age care are not diverse enough in China, where the ageing financing market needs to be further developed. On the one hand, due to their limited spending power, the elderly have lower risk-bearing capacity toward financial products and mostly keep their pension in bank saving accounts. On the other hand, in terms of product supply, such as savings, insurance, and trusts, are in small numbers and of similar types, limiting the development of China's financial service for the elderly.

2 Financing Tools and Measures for Elderly Care Industry

2.1 Policy Measures: Government Guidance and Incentive

2.1.1 Prevalence of PPP Projects, Government Credit and Social Capital Work Together to Promote the Development of Old Industries

The PPP is an abbreviation for Public-Private-Partnership. It refers to the partnership between government and private sector to carry out urban infrastructure projects; or to provide certain public goods and services, a partnership is formed by signing a concession agreement that clarifies the rights and obligations of both parties to ensure the successful completion of cooperation, and ultimately to achieve more favorable results through the cooperation rather than separate action.

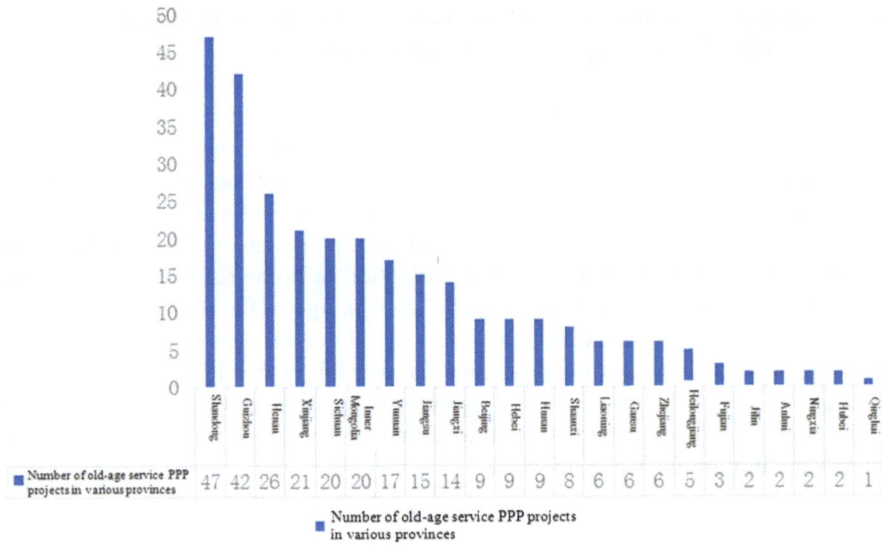

Fig. 3 Distribution of PPP projects in China (*Source* China Public Private Partnerships Centre)

To match the elderly care industry with PPP projects is feasible and necessary. First of all, the state has promulgated policies to encourage the old age service industries to adopt the PPP model. For example, the strategic policies include relaxing market access and actively encouraging social capital to invest in elderly health care service projects; giving social capital the priority when adding health care and pension services; encouraging social capital to adopt PPP through various channels in areas with rich public resources to participate in medical care, elderly care community, fitness facilities and public institution reform.

As of April 2017, according to the China Public Private Partnerships Centre, the number of elderly care-related PPP projects totaled 292; in eastern China, Shandong Province, Jiangsu Province and Beijing Municipality, are three administrative units with the highest number of projects, with 47, 15, and 9, respectively; in the central region, the top three regions are Henan Province, Jiangxi Province, and Hunan Province with 26, 14, and 9 PPP projects, respectively; in western China, the top three regions are Guizhou Province, 42; Xinjiang Uygur Autonomous Region, 21; Sichuan Province and Inner Mongolia Autonomous Region tied for third place with 20 PPP projects. Overall speaking, PPP projects in Shandong, Guizhou and Henan Provinces add up to 115, accounting for 39.4% of the total number of old age service PPP projects in China (Fig. 3).

China's current PPP elderly care projects display the following features: first, these projects are mostly concentrated in the area that combines elderly care and healthcare services, with only a few projects distributed in other areas. The current trend of old age service industry is moving toward comprehensive development. In addition to the traditional daily care, rehabilitation, and special products development, the industry covers many fields catering for the senior population including food, daily products, healthcare, insurance, tourism, culture and education. Therefore, the government should pool the capital from various sectors, encourage the establishment of large-scale old age care agencies, and organize resources and professionals to form an integrated industrial park for retired seniors. Second, the existing PPP projects are mainly operated in BOO or BOT schemes. Old age care and service providers should choose a reasonable profit model to maximize both economic and social benefits according to the actual conditions. In addition, due to the large amount of initial investment and the long time required for benefit return, such PPP projects should start with many fronts and focus on the project's risk management.

2.1.2 Local Governments Have Set up Investment Fund for Elderly Care Industry

The government's introductory fund for the elderly care industry is usually a policy fund set up by local governments and operated in a market-oriented manner. It is also a common way for the government to cooperate with social capital, which expands the government's financial support for the elderly care industry. The fund is set up by local governments and endorsed by the government's credit to raise funds from social capital, to dive the social forces and to develop the elderly care industry. While providing a direction for the new entrants to the pension industry, the guiding fund also provides financial support for growing companies that have well-defined operation model. At the same time, this guiding fund, through market-oriented operation, serves as screening of pension-related enterprises in the market and thus accelerates industrial consolidation. In the end, the fund will introduce leading enterprises in each segment and liberalize elderly care-related industries.

In 2014, the Ministry of Finance and the Ministry of Commerce jointly launched a pilot program on market-based old age care. The two departments issued a document noting that the central government would allocate an annual special fund of RMB 2.4 billion to the local government in 8 provinces, namely, Jilin, Shandong, Anhui, Jiangxi, Hunan, Hubei, Gansu and Inner Mongolia and autonomous regions from 2014 to 2016. Each year, the central government allocated RMB 300 million to these provinces, and then the local banks or social capital matched the funds at a ratio of no less than 1:4 with RMB 1.2 billion or more to set up an annual old age service investment fund of RMB 15 billion. The duration of the fund was generally in the format of 7 + 2, or 7 + 3 and the return rate and cycle were guarded by fund management, bank custody, and professional team operation. And after the fund was matured and the withdrawal of the financing funding, the government continued to support industry by providing a safety net, while passed the commercial portion to the market, which was to fulfill the middle and high-end needs of the elderly and drive the development of the industry.

After the three-year trial was completed, these eight provinces already established the introductory fund that sped up the liberalization of the local elderly care industry. Under the influence of the pilot cities, other provinces and cities across the country, such as Beijing, Jiangsu and Fujian, have also set up investment funds for the elderly care industry, attracting a large amount of social capital into the industry (Table 1).

2.1.3 City Investment Corporations Led the Issue of Bonds Specific to the Elderly Care Industry

After the National Development and Reform Commission released the *Guidance on Issuance of Special Bonds to the Elderly Care Industry* in 2015, all the investment companies in cities and towns prepared to issue while local governments began to issue the bonds specific to the elderly care industry. first, these special debts are categorized as SASAC projects requiring expedited and simplified audit; second, the city investment company that issues the bonds is not subject to national issuance targets; third, companies are allowed to use up to 50% of the proceeds to repay bank loans and replenish operational cost; fourth, the land obtained through the transfer method and used for old age services can be included in the assets of the enterprise that issues the bonds. Therefore, when the central government is restricting the local governments' scale of the debt expansion, the special bond has become the ideal way for local governments to raise funding for the development of the elderly care industry. At present, the policy has just implemented, and the implementing entities are still exploring reasonable and compliant operating modes. Therefore, only some cities in five provinces of Hunan, Zhejiang, Liaoning, Guizhou and Sichuan have issued the specific bonds and the investment targets are mostly local services agencies that provide living care, rehabilitation and nursing care, among others, for the elderly (Table 2).

When the specific bonds was launched, it was an immediate hit among investors, the first special bonds worth of RMB 800 million issued by Chenzhou Baifu Investment Group Co., Ltd. had 2.18 times the subscription; in September, the elderly care industry special bonds issued by Xingyi Construction Investment Co., Ltd. in Yizhang County, Hunan Province also had 1.71 times the subscription. These bonds have brought plenty of low-cost cash flow for the development of local elderly care industry. The local special bonds are so popular because that when compared to other financial products, the small volume of bond issuance is far less than demand. On the other hand, the state strongly supports the development of the elderly care industry, which leaves investors an impression of the elderly care industry as an investment opportunity in the future; coupled by the local government's endorsement, the subscription ratio of the special bond for the elderly care industry is relatively high.

At such a high investor subscription, raising funds is no longer a problem. The problem for local city investment company's is how to use the funds to invest in growing pension projects. Given the current dilemma of the senior's outdated consumption concept and low spending power, how to make the return rate of funds raised outperform the rate of inflation and obtain the return on investment within

Table 1 Introductory fund for elderly care industry in eight pilot cities

Title	Time of establishment	Size (Billion)	Major investment areas
Hunan Province Healthy retirement investment fund	2015.08.14	0.4	The old age service industry for the general public with focuses on the construction of information databases on the elders in community, community mutual assistance and aged care centers, and family-based support network for the elderly, and the development of public elderly care services
Gansu Province Retirement services industry development fund	2015.08.21	0.7	Medical and nursing care, home care, community care center, and other old age care services
Jiangxi province Retirement services industry development fund	2015.12.28	6	Home care, community-based comprehensive services, public and community care, and other public elderly care industry projects
Yantai City, Shandong Province Elderly care industry introductory fund	2017.06.02	1.35	Congregated old age care, "medical and nursing care" combined with rehabilitation center, hospice care, medical rehabilitation and other equipment development, mobile services for the old age, nursing care training, elderly cultural activities and other services for the public elderly care industry

(continued)

Table 1 (continued)

Title	Time of establishment	Size (Billion)	Major investment areas
Anhui Province HealthCare industry investment fund	2016.01.15	4.5	To support the construction of home and community care for the elderly, to cultivate a competitive branded service for the elderly, to develop viable middle-and-small enterprises to provide old age services, to develop old age service products, and to promote integration of old age care services with domestic services and medical services
Hubei Province Elderly care services development guidance fund	2016.04.26	0.6	Community-based home care service system, medical care-supported elderly care service provider, and online care information service network
Jilin Province Elderly care industry equity investment fund	2016.10.21	1	To build a comprehensive service center that include hospital and fitness center for the seniors, as well as projects related to the industry to create a comprehensive elderly care complex
Inner Mongolia Autonomous Region	Interim Measures for the Administration of Government-Guided Funds for the Elderly Services Industry in the Inner Mongolia Autonomous Region, issued in March 2016		

Sources Official websites of provincial governments

Table 2 Bonds specific to the elderly care industry issued in various regions

Bond title	Date of issue (not approval)	Amount (billion)	Term (years)	Purpose
2016 bonds specific to the elderly care industry issued by Baifu Investment Group Co., Ltd. of Chenzhou City	2016.03.22	1.49	10	RMB 1.2 billion for the integrated old age service industry project in Bozhou City, and RMB 290 million for replenishing liquidity
2016 bonds specific to the elderly care industry and urban parking lot construction issued by Hunan Shaoyang Duliang Investment Development Co., Ltd.	2016.04.13	1.11	7	RMB 5.1 billion for Wugang Comprehensive elderly care industry Project of Shaoyang City, RMB 300 million for the Wugang City Parking Lot Construction Project in Shaoyang City and RMB 300 million for the replenishing working capital
2016 bonds specific to the elderly care industry issued by Kaihong Asset Management Co., Ltd. of Qiandongnan Prefecture, Guizhou	2016.04.29	1.4	10	Qiandong Nanzhou Healthy Elderly Care Industry and Supporting Facilities Construction Project
2016 pension project specific bonds issued by Ningxiang County Urban Construction Investment Group Co., Ltd., Hunan	2016.06.02	1.03	10	Ningxiang Sunshine Elderly Care Community Project

(continued)

Table 2 (continued)

Bond title	Date of issue (not approval)	Amount (billion)	Term (years)	Purpose
2016 bonds specific to the elderly care industry issued by Xingyi Construction Investment Co., Ltd. in Yizhang County, Hunan	2016.09.02	0.8	8	RMB 600 million for Yizhang County Comprehensive Elderly Care Industry Construction Project, with the remaining RMB200 million used to supplement working capital
2016 bonds specific to the elderly care industry issued by Dawa County Lingang Ecological New Town Investment, Construction and Development Co., Ltd.	2016.10.19	1.47	8	RMB 1.16 billion for the comprehensive development and construction of the Honghaitan Hot Springs Wetland elderly care industry Base in Dawa County, and RMB310 million to supplement liquidity.
2016 bonds specific to the elderly care industry issued by Xin'anjiang Development Corporation of Chun'an County, Zhejiang	2016.11.04	0.69	7	RMB 540 million for Qiandao Lake Ecological Elderly Care Park Project, and RMB150 million to supplement the issuer's liquidity
2017 bonds specific to the elderly care industry issued by Tiantai Industrial Co., Ltd. of Suining City, Sichuan	2017.03.20	1	7	RMB 700 million investment for project in Sichuan retirement and recreation center project, RMB 300 million to supplement working capital

Source China Bond Information Network

10 years is the next question to be considered by local city investment companies. And different from the government's introductory fund, the special bond for elderly care industry is managed by the local city investment companies, which required the companies to have higher cost management capabilities and projects profitability. Therefore, the next task for the city investment companies is to shore up the weak links; to strengthen the capacity of in-house investment team when recruiting talents in the industry; to maintain a long-term perspective investment instead of chasing the short-term returns; and to promote the development of local elderly care industry when there are extra earnings.

2.1.4 Policy Bank's Special Loans for Pension Project

Policy banks refer to the institutions initiated and funded by the government to carry out financing and credit activities for implementing and coordinating with government's specific economic policies and plans. There are three major policy banks in China: China Development Bank (CDB), the Export-import Bank of China and Agricultural Development Bank of China. At this stage, only China Development Bank has launched a special loan for late adulthood service programs. This provides financial support for building an institutional mechanism to develop social services that is "led by government, supported by funds, participated by the general public and operated by market."

Different from working capital loans of commercial banks, China Development Bank screens and issues loans for old age service projects on the basis of *Ministry of Civil Affair Opinions on the China Development Bank's Financial Support for Implementing Social Pension Services*. This announcement details the key areas of service projects and loan conditions supported by CDB as well as the functions and responsibilities of civil affairs departments.

China Development Bank loans feature low interest rates and longer lending periods, and are mainly to support uncharted areas of the startups that commercial banks are unwilling to support. CDB's current round of special loans made to the old age pension project has a term of up to 15 years and may be granted a grace period of 3 years, which is regarded a long-term funds by the institutions in elderly care industry. The other supportive policies, such as capital requirements of the borrower's own fund is set at 20% and the project needs the recommendation of the local civil affairs departments, provide long-term, low-cost sources of funding for local mid- to large-size old age care businesses and will boost local elderly care industry.

2.2 *Market Measures: The Help for Capital Markets*

2.2.1 Pension Real Estate Financial Innovation Model: REITs

REITs stand for real estate investment trusts. It is a financial product derived from the thriving real estate and an important means of asset securitization. Through the REITs, the less liquid, non-securities real estate investments can be directly converted into liquid securities assets in the capital markets.

Judged by the transformation and development of China's large-scale senior housing, whether it is Wanda to enter the medical care sector or real estate giants such as Vanke and Huaxia Happy to lay out their plan in elderly care industry, the corporate idea in developing elderly care housing is moving from "selling houses" to "selling services;" from the original concept of real estate operation to the emphasis on the "retirement + real estate" model; from the location as the prime factor to the duel incentives of location and services. The shift of focus shows that retirement real estate industry is shaking off the traditional operation ideas and moving toward consumer-oriented service businesses. However, senior housing also faces operating difficulties. If solely relying on the retirement services provided, it will be difficult for the real estate company to cover the initial cost of land acquisition and construction. Meanwhile, the marginal profit of old age services will prolong the payback period of real estate projects. This will occupy the initial investment funds for a long time. Therefore, to secure long-term stable investment funds becomes the key factor concerning the early stage of construction, and REITs are the good solution to meet the long-term funding demand.

So far, China's senior housing has no listed REITs. The reason is that on the one hand, to list in China will face the issue of dual taxation, that is, to pay both business tax and enterprise income tax. On the other hand, the elderly care real estate in China has not yet reached the bottleneck of industrial development. In order to speed up the growth of REITs, the elderly care real estate needs to mature first in addition to addressing the issue of double taxation.

2.2.2 A Surging New Market: The New Third Board

The National Equities Exchange And Quotations Co., Ltd. (commonly known as the new third board) drew much attention in 2016 Capital markets. Regarded as the future Nasdaq of China, the New Third Board attracts a lot of start-up companies needing financing with lower listing requirements. As of the end of April 2017, the new three-board had listed 11,070 companies, exceeding the number of companies on Main Board, SME board and GEB (Second Board). Among these companies, 26 enterprises are related to elderly care industry in such areas as pension services, home care, medical care, travel, healthcare products, information system design for retirement service agencies, and so on. Most of the enterprises on the New Third Board adjusted their targeted consumer groups to include the elderly population and old age care institutions based on the original consumer structure. Their major business is usually not the core business of the elderly care industry. However, three listed retirement service operators: Yada Group, LangGao Pension Co., Ltd. and Ainong Pension Co., Ltd. catch the investor's attention. With the listing of the new third board, they increase the company's credit and with the endowment of the capital market, they obtain equity investment to pursue chain-oriented scale-up, which in turn, increases the company's valuation in the capital market. Through several rounds of interaction between industry and finance, they become the leader of the industry.

In general, most of the listed elderly care companies on the New Three Board focus on the "smart living" of retirement, only few companies are devoted to the essential areas of the industry, such as rehabilitation, physiotherapy, and caregiver training. This is due to the fact that China is aged before getting rich. In view of the low consumption power of the seniors that leads to the low profitability to most elder service providers, the company is financially not able to afford the costs of share reform and the due diligence conducted by third-party agencies before listing on the new three boards. Furthermore, equity transfer system establishes invisible listing by negative lists and has some current and future profitability requirements for listed companies, which causes some old age care operators fail in their attempted listing. However, the success of Yada Senior Living Group, LangGao Elderly Service and Ainong Senior Care rejuvenate the retirement service industry. These operators are valued in the New Third Board market with their clear business model, competence of profitability, multiple local branches, and rapid development through chain-like business duplication.

2.2.3 Listed Companies' Strategic Entry to the Main Board Market

In the A-share market, a total of 58 enterprises have prepared or entered the elderly care industry, of which six are more involved in the field of information system, seven in intelligent retirement, eleven in senior housing, eleven in pension services, nine in medical services, five in old age care equipment, five in medical and healthcare, two in the financial investment and two in medical examination.

After many listed companies rushed into the pension market, the industry is now becoming more rational and cautious towards a diversified expansion. For example, a listed company that has entered the elderly care industry featuring virtual nursing home closed its virtual old age center in some areas and only retained the ones in the core areas. Starting with the business with radio communication equipment, this company entered the market with diverse yet irrelevant businesses. After its initial expansion period, the company is now gradually closing down those virtual centers that suffer severe losses, difficulty to attract consumers, or low customer flows. Instead of expansion, the company now focuses on existing and well-run senior care centers. This fully reflects the listed companies are more prudent and pragmatic in managing business of the elderly care industry.

The fields that listed companies are involved in include information system, smart retirement, elderly care housing, financing and investment, medicine, healthcare products, elderly care equipment, medical examination, old age services and old age insurance, covering almost the entire business chain of the industry. Judged by the major operation of these listed companies, the companies that transition into the elderly care industry are mainly distributed in four sectors: information system, real estate, insurance and medicine. On the one hand, these enterprises have accumulated some capital in the early stages of their respective original industries and obtained excess profits in those industries. As a result, they have industrial capitals to diversify their business. On the other hand, these businesses are inherently coherent with elderly care industries, and their corporate resources can be used directly in developing old age care businesses without making a fresh start. However, many listed companies have attached great importance to old age care business. Since the elderly care industry is still in the early stage of development, the profit-making model is not yet mature. Except Yihua Health Care, which is completely transformed from the real estate business into the elderly care living business, most listed companies are carefully stepping into the industry. More often, the listed company will set up a special subsidiary devoted to old age service business instead of loading the business into the listed company so as to prevent the profit rate of the listed company from decreasing.

In our opinion, the elderly care industry will gradually pass the initial development through the capital help. When providing services, the elder care institutions should pay attention to the development of listed companies, keep the mentality of mutual benefit and solve the current problems concerning capital and customer flow through merger into the stable listed companies; as the industry deepened, scale increased and strength enhanced, the service providers will be able to serve more elderly people and to provide quality care. As for the listed companies, it is unwise to invest heavily on building an elderly care institution or service provider from the very beginning in order to share the huge pension market. The most sensible approach is to cut into the industry through mergers and acquisitions, start the planning in the early stages of development, and glean profits when the industry flourishes.

3 Major Financial Events of the Year in the Elderly Care Industry

3.1 Frequent M&As

Following the acquisition of Ankangtong by Sanbest in early 2016, capital rushed into the elderly care industry and many elderly care institutions that have taken root in tier-1 cities were acquired one after another. Here is a brief introduction to the four major M&A cases of 2016 in the industry.

3.1.1 Yihua's Acquisition of Cherish-Yearn

On January 18, 2016, Yihua Group announced that it acquired 58.33% of the equities of Cherish-Yearn with a total of RMB 408 million, becoming the controlling shareholder. As a major move of Yihua into the elderly care industry, the acquisition allows Yihua to make use of the good operation model, experience, and brand value that Cherish-Yearn has accumulated over the years to lay solid foundation for its further deployment in the industry. Yihua's stock price dropped after the announcement, showing that the market was not optimistic towards this move in the short run, but after nearly a year, we see Yihua maintains sound profitability despite selling out its real estate business, and the market is now turning confident. By November 5, 2016, its stock price was back to the level of early that year.

As Yihua's stock perked up, we have reasons to believe that the approach for an enterprise to march into the health and elderly care industry has shifted from acquiring non-performing institutions and reforming them to acquiring established and well-performing institutions already in the industry. Years of accumulation of these acquired institutions helped their parent companies grow and expand. The purpose of such acquisitions is not to gain profit soon but to secure market share and prepare for long-term growth.

As for Cherish-Yearn which was established with an investment of nearly RMB 600 million, ten years of efforts and an occupation rate up to 95% gave it a market value of merely RMB 700 million. This has clearly revealed the fact that enterprises in the health and elderly care industry have tight cash flow and low market value. Cherish-Yearn had long been trying to go public on the NEEQ before the acquisition, but did not succeed. Therefore, the acquisition surely solved the cash flow problem that the company had suffered for quite a while and helped it maintain positive business momentum.

3.1.2 Everbright's Acquisition of Huichen

Beijing Huichen Elderly Care Institution Management Co., Ltd., founded in 2007, focuses on elderly care institutions, medical care for the old, and community-based service delivery, with an aim to build a four-pronged elderly service system covering care, nursing, medical services, and rehabilitation. By October 2016, Huichen had established six elderly care communities and one day care center in Beijing plus one elderly care community in Weihai. As private NPO, Huichen is mainly engaged in running medium-sized community-based elderly care institutions. It rents venues to form a chain of such institutions and focuses on the management and operation of them rather than assets. China Everbright Holdings, established in Hong Kong in 1997, is a financial subsidiary of China Everbright. Upholding the concept of broad assets management, it runs assets management and investment projects across a wide variety of industries. It started to consider entering the elderly care industry in 2015, and decided to invest in Huichen after studying a number of similar institutions.

On May 13, 2016, Everbright Holdings announced the acquisition of 67.27% of Huichen's equities and the estimated value was about RMB 400 million. With this acquisition completed, Everbright Holdings strengthened its health care division and put Huichen in good coordination with its financial leasing and insurance subsidiaries, forming an alliance of "real economy + finance". According to the amount of fund involved and the proportion of equities transferred, this acquisition is believed not to be a short-term investment, rather, it is major strategic move for a better future in the health industry.

Huichen, after nearly ten years of strenuous effort, has come through the early period when survival was a big concern with an operational model that attaches little importance to property ownership. It has achieved an annual profit margin of 10% but its expansion has been slow for the elderly care industry on the whole is not very lucrative. As Everbright infused capital, Huichen became financially much stronger. While improving its operation and services, it will expand into a franchise with a faster pace in the next three to five years, first in tier-1 cities such as Beijing, Shanghai, Guangzhou and Shenzhen, and then moving fast into tier-2 cities. With its strengths in running elderly care institutions as core competence, Huichen will serve both local elderlies and migrant elderlies by building itself into a conglomerate.

3.1.3 CCIG Ruihua's Acquisition of Joyway

CCIG Ruihua (Shanghai) Health Care Industry Investment Co., Ltd. acquired 60% of the equities of Joyway Senior Care Service and became the largest shareholder of Joyway. Founded in September 2014, CCIG Ruihua is a major move of CCIG into the elderly care industry. The company has been making active moves according to CCIG's strategic deployment since its inauguration and it now has built, acquired, or commissioned 12 elderly care institutions in Shanghai, Ningbo, Nantong, and other cities. Centered on these institutions, it also provide home-based elderly care services, train elderly care professionals, develop smart elderly care service platforms, and run of elderly care institutions on, building the brand of Brightown.

Joyway Senior Care Service was founded in 2011. It provides home-based elderly care services in Shanghai. Over the past five years, it has established 12 service outlets and four service stations, and delivers relevant services to homes all over Shanghai. Based on the different health conditions and service demands, Joyway provides family nurses, traditional Chinese medicine consultation at home, nutritionist consultation at home, household services, etc., mainly to elderlies who are able to take care of themselves, post-op elderlies, and other people with special needs.

This acquisition allowed Joyway to explore its market potentials by integrating its services into CCIG Ruihua's health and elderly care service system, reach out from Shanghai to the entire east China region and serving more people by making use of Ruihua's established service network. This will help Joyway focus more on improving its service quality as the relevant marketing task is shifted to CCIG Ruihua. Joyway will thus make itself more professional and dedicated and grow into a specialized elderly care service provider in East China. For CCIG Ruihua, the acquisition enriched its elderly care industry system, helped it combine institution-based with home-based care to form a closed cycle. Joyway's ability to deliver services to homes allows it to provide even better services to people living in its elderly care institutions. As the two combined their strengths, a franchise system was created and a whole service chain was formed in the elderly care industry in East China.

3.1.4 Establishment of Shokai Cuncao Elderly Care Service Co., Ltd

On July 15, 2016, Beijing Capital Development Holding (Group) Co., Ltd. and Beijing Cuncao Care and Consulting Co., Ltd. joined hands to establish Beijing Shokai Cuncao Elderly Care Service Co., Ltd.

Beijing Capital Development Holding (Group) Co., Ltd., founded on December 10, 2005, is a large municipal-level conglomerate of Beijing, mainly engaged in real estate development. As a number of state-owned enterprises move into the elderly care industry this year, it also speed up its progress in this regard. As a listed company with strong capacities in the real estate and property management industries and sound capital operation abilities, it joined hands with a private elderly care institution to move into the industry in response to national policies calling for support for the industry.

Beijing Cuncao Care and Consulting Co., Ltd., founded in 2011, is a professional nursing institution for elderlies in need of assisted living and memory care. Over the past five years, its services and professional quality has improved continuously, and nursing beds here have fallen short of demand. However, as land price is high, the company does not have the capital to acquire more land plots and build more facilities, and thus was not able to grow into a franchise. While running elderly care institutions, Cuncao also undertook the elderly catering program funded by the government and worked on the formulation of relevant standards, striving to set a good example and become the leader in the field of nursing services for elderly people in need of assisted living and memory care. By joining hands with Shokai, Cuncao benefits from its strengths in real estate development and property management and gets access to capital for its expansion into a franchise. Meanwhile, it will also spread the standards of professional nursing services and operation is has created so as to establish itself as a benchmark in the industry.

3.1.5 Summary

Judging from the change of attitude towards elderly care projects on the capital market, we can see that capital was hesitating in 2015, but in 2016, a tide rose following Yihua's acquisition of Cherish-Yearn and capital owners rushed to purchase quality elderly care institutions. In 2016, mature elderly care institutions in Beijing, Shanghai and other tier-1 cities were acquired and even competed for one after another.

Generally, the institutions that were acquired showed the following three characteristics:

First, they adopt an operation model that does not emphasize property. As we can see in the major acquisition cases of 2016, capital was no longer attracted to elderly care institutions that purchase their own properties. Instead, they turned to those who rent facilities or deliver services to homes. In the elderly care industry, it takes a relatively long time for investment to get returns and profit comes from how satisfied people are for the services they receive, not what kind of equipment they use. Therefore, only those elderly care institutions that focus on services can stay profitable and viable over the long run despite the overall sluggishness of the elderly care industry as a whole.

Second, they have mature business models that can be copied. Capital promotes the development of an industry, but capital pursues profits and requires long-term returns on assets. This means that only mature business models can attract capital. For the elderly care industry in particular, since it is more or less an industry for public interest, institutions usually carry through the hard early days with the help of government subsidies. Once they take hold of some rigid demand and form a mature business model, capital will surely come their way. Huichen focuses on operation and management of medium-sized retirement communities, Joyway delivers services to homes, and Cuncao dedicates its services to elderly people in need of assisted living and memory care. All these are mature business models that have weathered the storms of the market and won recognitions from people they served, bringing stable cash flow over the years. This is why they were attracted to investors.

Third, they have standard service systems and institutional framework. For an elderly care institution to expand and deliver services to a larger population, it must have a standard services system and institutional framework. Therefore, investors purchases only those elderly institutions that do have these in place. As we can see from the six M&A cases of the year, Huichen, Joyway, and Cuncao all have got a complete system of standards based on years of experience in the industry. Therefore, a complete standard system is a must for any elderly care institution that wishes to invite strategic investment.

3.2 Overseas M&A Cases

3.2.1 CINDAT and Union Life Acquire the Asset Portfolio of American Senior Housing and Long-Term/Post-Acute-Disease Care Facilities from Welltower

This is a typical case where a Chinese insurance company carries out M&A in cooperation with a domestic fund. CINDAT is a private equity investment institution that aims to guide, support, and protect Chinese capital to make investment abroad. As a co-investor, CINDAT provided services such as due diligence, negotiation, fundraising, risk control, etc., ensuring that the transaction process proceeded smoothly and efficiently to the end. Therefore, CINDAT is more of a financial investor in this case.

Union Life is the other strategic investor in this case. It is one of the first Chinese insurance company that have entered the elderly care industry via international M&A. Union Life aims at becoming a first-class conglomerate in the world holding equities in various industries and it focuses on the three business pillars of finance, health, and cultural tourism. It builds retirement communities and apartment buildings in Wuhan, Nanjing and Shenyang to take its share in the Chinese health care market on the one hand, and one the other, expand its deployment in the industry through international M&As. To ensure that its overseas M&A project proceed smoothly, the company established a dedicated department for such projects, attracting talents experienced in international M&A and having a broad vision to embrace the whole world. Within two years, it has invested about USD 200 million in the elderly care industry in the United States.

This acquisition is a brand new move of Union Life for its overseas expansion in the health care industry. Its US subsidiary, Union LLC, set a joint venture in cooperation with CINDAT and Welltower to acquire Welltower's 39 retirement communities distributed across 13 states of the United States. We believe this acquisition, in addition to adding to Union Life's overseas assets in the industry, was made to facilitate the company's IPO because more overseas assets will help it meet the requirements for getting listed on the main board of the Chinese stock market in terms of assets and profits, pushing the company closer to a public offering. For sure, whether this acquisition will be successful depends on how well Union Life can rally up the assets and operate and whether it can bring the experience of American retirement communities back to China, adapt it to local conditions, and turn its investment ultimately into assets that generate returns.

3.2.2 China Oceanwide Acquires Genworth Financial, Inc

On October 24, 2016, China Oceanwide announced its acquisition of Genworth Financial, Inc., a large US finance and insurance conglomerate, with USD 2.7 billion. It then submitted application for this to CFIUS in April 2017. China Oceanwide is a multinational conglomerate engaged in real estate, finance, energy, and comprehensive investment. It holds equities or has investment in a number of listed companies, including Oceanwide Holdings (000046.SZ), Minsheng Holdings (000416.SZ), China Oceanwide Holdings (00715.HK), China Minsheng Bank (600016.SH and 01988.HK), Lenovo Holdings (03396.HK, etc. China Oceanwide's acquisition of Genworth is a typical case of overseas M&A. It is both an investment project for financial gains and a strategic move into the finance and insurance field. Besides the purchase of Genworth's equities, China Oceanwide also promised to provide USD 600 million at or before the time of maturity to repay its debts that matures in 2018 and invest USD 525 million in its life insurance business in the US. In response, Genworth promised to invest USD 175 million in its life insurance business in the US. After the transaction is completed, Genworth will be a wholly-owned subsidiary of China Oceanwide while continuing with its current business portfolio and independent operation.

Genworth is the largest long-term care insurance company in the US, it also engaged in life insurance and annuity business. As a Fortune 500 company, it is No. 77 on the Fortune list of the global insurance industry. Established in 1871 as Virginia Life Insurance, the company now has 3865 employees, with branches in the United States, Canada, Australia, Mexico, and India. Data show that by June 30, 2016, Genworth had total assets of USD 108.2 billion, including USD 77.6 billion of investable assets, and the net asset was USD 17 billion.

China Oceanwide's acquisition of Genworth paves the way into the long-term care insurance market of China, bringing in experience and business models from the United States into China to secure market share. To ensure that this acquisition will finally succeed, China Oceanwide should focus on governance mechanism after taking over Genworth. It should have regular discussions with the board of Genworth on the company's strategy, operation, and finance, so as to minimize financial and operational risks and improve profitability.

3.2.3 Anbang Insurance Group's Acquisition of 24 Retirement "Communities" Under Retirement Concepts of Canada

This case is an extension of Anbang's strategic investment in the real estate industry in Canada. Anbang marched into the Canadian real estate market in 2015, first acquiring 70 York Street Toronto with CAD 110 million and then taking over Bentall Centre in central Vancouver with CAD 660 million. Anbang has acquired one commercial real estate project after another in Canada. However, in this case, what it acquired was not a real estate project as before, but a project that will push it into the health and elderly care industry in the country.

Retirement Concepts is a local family business in Canada, running the largest hospice franchise of British Columbia, which includes 24 retirement "communities". After this acquisition, Retirement Concepts will still keep a small part of its equities and remain in charge of the operation of its hospices.

From this case we can see that Anbang does not rush to assign senior management to the acquired company or bring it into its own management system soon after the acquisition. Instead, it takes things easy and slow to ensure success. With the access, it takes over Retirement Concepts' retirement "communities" and properties, keeps their operation and management stable, and start strategic cooperation in regard to operation model, standardized services and other fields where synergy and collaboration may be formed, so as to complete integration progressively.

3.2.4 Summary

These cases of overseas M&A are all carried out by large Chinese insurance companies. As we all know, the elderly care industry requires long-term investment with relatively low profitability and is therefore not very attractive to the capital market. However, insurance companies have large stable cash flow which suits the industry perfectly. By acquiring mature foreign companies in the industry, Chinese insurance companies aims at both financial gains and an opportunity to learn to run elderly care service institutions. The purpose of these acquisitions, besides financial gains, is to provide a new way for the insured to claim life insurance benefits by making a package of insurance and elderly care. Such products will help high-end customers enjoy elderly care abroad, which will be attractive to high-value customers and expand the market of life insurance by solving the problem of final payment.

In terms of post-acquisition integration, common challenges for Chinese companies include the lack of talents for international business operation and the poor structure of integration efforts. These may make it difficult for Chinese companies to fit into foreign markets and to make the best out of the acquired assets. Specifically, for the elderly care industry, there should be detailed plan before the acquisition so as to get the most out of every M&A opportunity to build a talent pool of our own for international operation and integration, turning the advantage of the acquired foreign company into an advantage of our own.

3.3 Smart Elderly Care Companies Favored by Capital

According to the *Action Plan for the Development of the Smart Health and Elderly Care Industry* (2017–2020), smart health and elderly care makes good use of the Internet of Things, cloud computing, Big Data, smart hardware, and other new-generation IT products to effectively and efficiently allocate health and elderly care resources to individuals, families, communities, and service institutions, upgrade relevant services, and improve service quality and efficiency. Smart elderly care companies usually do not emphasize the possession of properties, has total capital in the ten millions, and remain in the phase of round-A financing. They are mostly startups in urgent need of large capital input. This is what a private fund can provide because it usually is in pursuit of new investment projects to diversify its portfolio and spread out risks. Here is list of recent financing progress of some smart elderly care companies and device makers (Table 3).

Private funds are more interested in products and platform that allow them to quit within short period of time. This means, compared with strategic investors in the elderly care industry, private funds are more short term-oriented. Basically, capital pursues profits, while the elderly care industry requires long times before seeing returns on investment. These two are in natural conflict. Therefore, capital favors smart elderly care projects that have online platforms for they see fast growth of traffic once investment comes in, taking hold of market niches, amplifying voice in the

Table 3 Financing progress of some smart elderly care companies

Company/Brand	Round	Amount	Investor
Sankai Technology	NEEQ listed A	/ RMB 12 million	/ Shenzhen Haoshi Dingtai
Xf9.com	B A	RMB 100 million RMB 100 million	Zhenghe Cixi Capital Zheshang Venture Capital
Zaijia.com	B+ B A	tens of millions USD USD 26 million USD 4.4 million	Lightspeed China Partners and Sinovation Ventures, Chengwei Capital Chengwei Capital, Honghai Group and three others Lightspeed China Partners and Sinovation
Ayilaile.com	B A	Tens of millions RMB Millions of USD	Beijing Life Service Industry Fund Zero2IPO Venture Capital
Maimai	A Angel	RMB 30 million Tens of millions RMB	China Merchants Tendence Capital
Beibang Rehabilitation	A	RMB 8 million	SID Venture Capital
Yige Information	Pre-A	RMB 10 million	Tenplus Venture Capital
Huaren Care	Angel	Tens of millions RMB	undisclosed
Ermao Care	Angel	USD 2 million	BlueRun Ventures
Tangdou.com	B (increment) B	USD 5 million USD 15 million	IDG Capital and Vertex Ventures Shunwei Capital
Jianzubao	Angel	USD 11 million	Fortune Capital, Qianjing Rehab, Longest

Source itjuzi.com

industry, holding down competitors, and gaining advantages. For these companies, move fast to gather traffic is the critical point.

For a smart elderly care company that has secured round-A investment with advantageous traffic and survived the early stage, the key lies in how to take firm hold on traffic portals, grab market share, and achieve sustainability. For a smart elderly care company, most customers are companies that run elderly care service institutions who serve elderly people. Therefore, for these companies grow in the market, they must always keep up with the demand of elderly care service institutions, launch in-depth cooperation with them to find out rigid needs of elderly people, speed up product iteration, and build strong competitiveness.

The year 2016 saw a lot of smart elderly care companies expand and grow by attracting investment from PEs and VCs. On the Internet, whoever stands out gets it all. After burning out the investment, the key to survival is to have elderly consumers truly start to use their products through communication and by offering discounts and subsidies, increase the frequency of their use to enhance user adhesiveness, and take market share. It is expected that a few winners will stand out in a number of market niches but we have no idea yet as for who will be the winners.

4 Problems and Challenges

4.1 Poorly Targeted Policies Hard to Implement

Most of the many policies introduced to support financing the elderly care industry do little more than providing guidelines in general terms. For example, they encourage and guide private capital into the elderly care industry, encourage foreign investors to build for-profit elderly care institutions, and encourage financial institutions to support elderly care services institutions. However, there have been few more detailed and substantive rules.

Financial policies for the elderly care industry usually take the perspective of the financial industry, and can sometimes misrepresent the true needs of the elderly care industry. Generally, an elderly care company or project goes through the construction phase and the operation phase. Both phases require large amounts of fund, but policies usually support only the construction phase, not the operation phase. Also, in the elderly care industry, it takes quite a long time for investors to recover their investment and there are not many financial instruments suitable for this model. The policies do not offer support to encourage long-term investment. As a result, the financial support for the elderly care industry is actually poorly targeted and relevant policies are hard to implement.

4.2 Immature Market with Few Financing Channels

Chinese financial market is not very mature and the financial market for the elderly care industry is still in the early stage. Therefore, the structure of the market is unbalanced and with insufficient power to innovate. According to international experience, a mature capital market should enable a good company to raise fund through a variety of channels at any time, allow value investors to get steady returns over the long run, and offer financial products at stable and reasonable prices.

Based on the description of the financial market for the elderly care industry given above, we can see that the dominant player in the Chinese market is the government, while private capital is not deeply involved; the market offers a limited variety of products and only a small number of financing channels. This forces most enterprises in this industry to design only products and services that meet the governments requirement in order to get the meagre subsidy the government offers and survive the difficult initial stage.

A large number of PPP projects and large amounts of money from elderly care industry funds now focus on less-developed regions with good natural environment, we are not sure for the time being whether they will be able to attract people to those places and whether government and private investment will be recovered and gain profits after the service facilities are put into operation.

4.3 Lack of Rational Long-Term Investors

Usually, companies engaged in the real economy divide equity investors into two categories: strategic investors aiming at long-term returns and financial investors seeking short-term gains. Currently most investors on the financial market for the elderly care industry belong to the second category, mainly pursuing short-term gains. However, financial investors are not likely to bring quality assets into the elderly care industry where it takes a long period for any return on investment to come. Therefore, such a market structure is not good for the long-term strategic development of the industry.

The long cycle and low profitability of the elderly care industry make it clear that strategic investors that will stay for long are the better choice. They don't ask for quick returns; instead, they bring capital, talents, standard business models, and various other resources into the industry, identify the rigid demand of the local elderly population, and help the elderly care institutions to provide products and services that satisfy the needs of the elderly and free their children from relevant worries and burdens. Such products and services can then be copied and standardized, and the institution grow into a franchise business. Only in this way can an elderly care service institution stay viable and thrive. Therefore, what the industry really needs is strategic investors.

4.4 Poor Operation Capacity and Difficulty in Absorbing Acquired Assets

From the major M&A cases in the industry over the past years, we can see that the industry is not really in lack of investment. As the market-based interest rate system grows mature in China, what we actually lack is assets instead of money. Large amounts of capital is out there looking for valuable projects to invest in, but it has been difficult for an acquirer to truly absorb the acquired assets after the acquisition. Since the elderly care industry is an emerging industry open for investment only for several years, enterprises in this industry are usually not capable enough to run projects well. As a result, after an acquisition, the quality assets acquired serve only as a symbol of the buyer's entry into the elderly care industry, for the buyer does not actually have the ability to participate in the operation of the acquired concern, and the acquired concern thus usually does not receive the resources they need. As a result, the acquired company finds it hard to add to its value, and the poor operation after the acquisition will dampen market confidence in similar M&A in the future, lowering the valuation in possible future cases and the PE. This will do harm to the market valuation management on the buyers' part.

To solve this problem, there must be a detailed plan before every acquisition so as to make the best out of each opportunity and build an excellent team for the operation of elderly care institutions and relevant M&A cases. Only in this way will a buyer be able to turn the strengths of the acquired companies into its own strengths, building up its market value and influence by forging synergy between operation and capitalization.

5 Future Trends

5.1 The Principle Is to Focus on the Elderly Care Industry Itself and Seek Support from Finance

Finance is by its very nature a tool to invigorate the elderly care market, regardless of whether it is guided by policies or the market. A thriving elderly care financial market relies on a thriving elderly care industry. If we think about finance for the elderly care industry within a timeframe of one year, we should pay attention to fluctuations on the capital market and policy changes. If the time frame extends to three years, the focus should be how well market players fare and how to make deployment from a strategic perspective. If the timeframe is ten years or more, we should be concerned about where the entire industry is going.

In the long run, elderly care enterprises will gain sustainability only with strenuous efforts to grow and with improved efficiency. When this is achieved, the enterprises will need more money and capital will gradually flow towards the elderly care industry and relevant financial programs will then support its further development, forming truly interactive relationships between the industry and finance. In regard to the relationship between the elderly care industry and finance, we must make sure that the former is the end, while the latter is the means. This is how we will promote the healthy development of the financing for the elderly care industry.

5.2 *The Government Will Become More Service-Oriented*

A service-oriented government is a modern government that has the will and ability to deliver services to meet the needs of the public. Elderly care is a concern for both public interest and profit. Therefore, when trying to support finance for the elderly care industry, the government must shift its role towards a service provider.

For the development of finance for the elderly care industry, the government should point out the direction and then allow financial institutions and elder care institutions to do their own job in a market-based way, so as to make the best out of competition and channel capital to the enterprises where it can achieve the best performance. For elderly care institutions that rely on the government as the last resort to survival, the government may act as the owner or fund the construction of these institutions but delegate the operation to private organizations. In this way, the government will need to put in only a small amount of seed money to set up a fund to guide industry forward, and social capital will then join the efforts. Capital will drive social resources and improve the efficiency of elderly care institutions and projects. By shifting towards a service-oriented government, the government will also retreat from the capital market and become a regulator behind the scene. Its job is to ensure that market players follow relevant rules and to prevent systemic risks.

5.3 *PPP Will Be the Mainstream Financing Model*

The PPP model is new for cooperation between government and social capital. It is widely welcomed and now serves as a new approach towards the financing, construction, and operation of elderly care institutions. The core of PPP is for relevant parties to share the benefits and risks and improve efficiency, lowering overall costs and operational risks.

As it has sometimes been said that PPP is not a wedding but a marriage. This means it represents not merely a set of procedures but a long process of investment and operation guided by clear rules. As such, it combines the advantages of the government and of social capital and is thus good particularly for long-term projects that require large investment. The elderly care industry, therefore, is a perfect match and residential areas built specifically for this will become increasingly attractive to investors.

For local governments, investment in PPP projects must not exceed 10% of the annual public budget, so they tend to review proposals for such projects carefully. Currently, the PPP model is adopted mainly for municipal and infrastructure projects where profits are generated through payment by users, government purchase, or government fund to cover the gap. The PPP model cannot be used in highly lucrative industries and the overall ROI should be 6–7%. Elderly care projects are for the benefit of the people while in the meantime, users also pay for the services, making it possible for relevant investment to be recovered. Therefore, local governments usually would like to boost it. PPP will be a major means to fund elderly care projects in the future.

5.4 There Will Be a Surge in M&A and the Capital Market Will Help with the Emergence of an Industrial Leader

According to industrial economic theories, an industry starts with small, dispersed, ill-regulated and poorly performing concerns and reaches maturity gradually, when relevant enterprises are of larger scales. Capital usually catalyzes this shift. From the large number of M&A this year, we can see that all high-quality elderly care projects have been purchased and the capital thus invested in the industry will allow relevant enterprises to grow into franchises and expand rapidly, reaching from one region to the whole country. This will push a number of small and medium-sized enterprises to mature amid market competition, giving rise to regional leaders in the industry. The government will tend to support these leaders and other enterprises will follow their lead. Small enterprises will be acquired by these leaders and capital will ensure that these leaders can focus solely on building up their core competence, not any other resources or capabilities. The capital market will take care of everything else. For both elderly care service platforms and institutions, the capital market will speed up the emergence or industrial leaders.

5.4.1 Listed Companies to Enter the Industry via Long-Term Capital Platforms

As it gets easier to be listed on the main board of the stock market, a company can now get the approval for IPO 420 days after the pre-announcement, much sooner than the previous average of 771 days. Also, it has become common for applicants to pass the review for IPO within one year. Currently, there are a total of 3205 listed companies in the Shanghai and Shenzhen stock exchanges, but only 58, or less than 2% of them are engaged in elderly care. They moved into the industry under the influence of some market trends. We believe for a listed company to reach out into this industry, it must create a platform for long-term financing of their own.

Most listed companies take elderly care as a new business to explore and they actually do not have the resources and capabilities to thrive in the industry. Therefore, one of the most effective ways to get into this industry is to raise money and acquire and absorb a company already in this field. A long-term capital platform within its own organizational structure will give a listed company the ability to raise fund directly or indirectly and carry out strategic M&A and restructuring projects. Thus, they will be able to acquire and absorb mature market players to form their own elderly care business division, just like Yihua did. This is how a listed company explore the emerging elderly care market and spot new opportunities while its existing pillar businesses provide stable cash flow. In this way, the listed company will maintain its value liquidity on the secondary market.

References

Dang, J. (2015). Revolution in an Aged Society: Risks and Prospects of Human Society. Beijing: People's Publishing House.

Yan, X. (2008). A Study on the Status Quo, Devilment Trend, and Investment Opportunities of the Elderly Care Industry in China. Master's dissertation, Xiamen University.

Zhuojun Cao Partner of Hejun Consultant Group, Deputy Director of Hejun Group Health Care Research Center, Registered International Certified Management Consultant, and Fellow of COACFF50. Ms. Cao's research areas include elderly healthcare industry.

Qin Jing Consultant at Hejun Consulting Group, research fellow of the Health and Ageing Research Center of Hejun Group. Ms. Qin's research area is finance for the elderly care industry.

Chapter 9
Bank Offerings of Wealth Management Products: Market Innovations and Policy Guidance

Jianyu Liu and Xuecheng Zhang

Abstract The aim of financial services for the elderly are, in essence, to preserve and increase the value of retail customers' retirement-earmarked assets through effective asset allocation so as to protect the quality of life of residents in their retirement age. Currently, retirement financial products provided by commercial banks are one of the most important tools to this end. China's banking sector has had a late start in the offering of retirement-financing products, and at the regulatory level a standard product regulatory system has yet to be formed. Although some commercial banks have focused their efforts on bringing about innovative pension financing products, there is not yet a mature product system. To bring about further product development, we must first improve the top-level design of the system, develop product entry thresholds, and work more on the market positioning of such products as well as refine customer segmentation. Second, it is necessary to stimulate the vitality of the market by encouraging commercial banks to work actively at such products and to maintain an ample supply of such products at the front end while improving their professional investment management abilities at the back end. Third, we must create greater awareness of the importance of saving for retirement among residents, and guide them into purchasing wealth management products designed to finance old age care from the perspective of long-term asset allocation. Finally, we must promote the healthy and orderly development of the industry through the joint efforts of the government, regulatory authorities, financial institutions and individual residents.

Keywords Wealth management products designed to finance old age care
Old age security products

J. Liu (✉) · X. Zhang
Industrial Bank, Fuzhou, China

K. Dong and Y. Yao (eds.), *Annual Report on Financing Old Age Care in China (2017)*, https://doi.org/10.1007/978-981-13-0968-7_9

1 Introduction to Wealth Management Products Banks Offered to Finance Old Age Care

1.1 Concepts

At present, with wealth management products designed and issued by commercial banks to finance old age care in China, customers are encouraged to hold these products for a long term for the purpose of long-term asset enhancement. Mature asset allocation strategies are typically adopted with these products to keep product risks within a reasonable range. These products are mainly sold to customers seeking to plan for retirement.

Within the industry, specific product categories have yet to emerge in the market. However, some commercial banks have started to provide specific product definitions in the course of product distribution. Most retirement financial products have the following characteristics: first, the investment period is longer, mostly more than three years, with no design for liquidity in the short term. Second, the total amount of investment is larger, with investment in some products cumulative. Customers are encouraged to hold their investments for the long term. Third, the purpose of such investment is long-term earnings, and risk and investment strategies are tailored to the customer's age.

In terms of market development, changes in the structure of the population and of population wealth have objectively resulted in the accumulation of wealth in the middle-aged and elderly segments of the population. Thus, we will certainly see commercial banks pay more attention to the development of pension wealth management products based on their future target markets and intended customer bases. Internally, the long-term feature of wealth management products designed to finance old age care can also help commercial banks to optimize their asset and liability structure. This will be the intrinsic motivation for commercial banks to develop wealth management products to finance old age care in the future.

1.2 The Environment in Which These Products Emerged

1.2.1 Gaps in Coverage by Basic Pension Insurance and Insufficient Coverage by the State

In China today, retirees mainly depend on pension insurance, or what is known as the Pillar I in retirement funding, for their old age. However, basic pension levels are low, leaving retirees open to greater risks in terms of basic subsistence and little guarantee of quality of life. Further, due to overall system design issues, in most provinces and cities, pension systems are in a highly tenuous position. The problem of the basic pension gap in some provinces has become increasingly serious. For example, in 2015, six provinces including the three northeastern provinces, Shaanxi, Qinghai and Hebei were unable to balance their pension insurance accounts. Heilongjiang Province, which had spent all of the surpluses from previous years, was forced to apply for the last line of defense for social security in the country, a subsidy from the central government via the National Social Security Fund. The lack of coverage by basic pension insurance has prompted residents to allocate their retirement assets through major financial institutions such as banks, and has provided the banking industry with space for the further development of financing old age care.

1.2.2 Slow Development of Supplementary Pension System

Compared to pillar 1 retirement funding (basic pension insurance), pillar 2 funds (annuities operated by private enterprises) can only be operated by corporations with the capabilities to do so. By the end of 2016, there are 76,300 enterprises across the country that have established enterprise annuity programs with a total participation of 23.24 million staff. This means that the vast majority of employees across the country do not have access to such programs. The total funds accumulated in these programs reach RMB 1.11 trillion, with value of assets per capita at RMB 47,600. In this regard, retirement assurance for covered workers is rather limited. The occupational annuity program is a program that has just been started in 2016. Given the small number of employed individuals covered by Pillar II funds (enterprise-based funds) across the country, the coverage of such funds is severely inadequate. At the same time, a Pillar 3 funding system (i.e., tax deferment for the individual taxpayer) has yet to be established in China. There is a lack of diversity in terms of retirement funding options, and residents are looking at growing challenges in ensuring their life quality after retirement.

1.2.3 Residents' Growing Awareness of the Importance of Pension Reserve

The younger members of the population are facing growing family-support burdens due to the aging population and the 4-2-2 household structure (i.e., a working couple supporting the needs of two children and four parents) that is the result of the one-child policy. As such, residents are paying increasing attention to pension reserve. What's more, with the reform and opening-up policy that has been implemented for more than 30 years, the economy has developed and provided the general public with real dividends, and most individuals have already transitioned from being comparatively well-off to the middle class. Now, with idle assets available, it is also possible for individuals to allocate their assets for retirement.

1.2.4 Strategic Business Transformation by Commercial Banks

The population will continue to age at a growing pace, and this is the social reality that domestic commercial banks will need to face in the coming decades. Furthermore, there will also be major changes in the structure of economy and of industry, and there is room for growth for retirement financial products and services. Commercial banks will find it necessary to undergo a strategic transformation and to seek transformation and breakthrough in the field of retirement finance. Such a move will also be an important pillar for sustainable and healthy development. The traditional product-centric model of differentiated marketing has failed to meet the increasingly diversified customer demands in the area of retirement assets. Commercial banks must shift from a product-centric to customer-centric business strategy instead. Providing financial services that meet the needs of elderly customers in a rapidly-ageing society will be an important direction for commercial banks and the one that they cannot afford to ignore. Wealth management products designed to finance old age care are an effective entry point for commercial banks seeking to develop their business of financing old age care. On the other hand, with their long investment cycles and focus on relative returns, wealth management products designed to finance old age care can fully leverage on the strengths of commercial banks in risk control management and also help commercial banks to optimize their own asset and liability structures, reduce operating costs, and mitigate cyclical risks caused by cyclical fluctuations.

1.2.5 Positive Social and Economic Effects Brought by Wealth Management Products Designed to Finance Old Age Care

Vigorous efforts at developing the retirement wealth management product business is a useful move by commercial banks to implement inclusive finance while steadily promoting business innovation and business compliance. Further, it is also a specific measure that can help establish and improve a modern financial system that meets the needs of the ageing population that is aligned with the CPC Central Committee's call for an active strategic response to the aging of the population. Compared with basic and comprehensive wealth management businesses, wealth management products designed to finance old age care operate over a longer duration and thus allow commercial banks to play to their strengths in asset management even more fully. With the creation of wealth management products to finance old age care through market-oriented means and differentiated product design, commercial banks can meet the asset-allocation needs of middle-aged and elderly customers as well as their needs for asset preservation and enhancement. At the same time, such efforts play a key role in providing residents with new innovative wealth management products designed to finance old age care and in improving the design of the national pension security system, and can thus yield positive social and economic effects.

2 History of Wealth Management Products Designed by Banks to Finance Old Age Care and the Current State of These Products

2.1 History

Over the last decade, commercial banks have started from square one with wealth management products and grown the business to the scale that it has today. To date, [the total value of assets under management] stands at more than RMB 30 trillion or about 30% of the disposable income of domestic residents. Wealth management products designed to finance old age care have been around since the early days of the wealth management product business. The development of such products can be divided into two broad stages.

2.1.1 Beginning (2009–2012): Product Differentiation Driving Initial Development of the Industry

After ten years of development, commercial banks now offer a wide range of financial products in various forms. However, the majority of these products are short-term products with a term of one year or shorter. The key indicator used for measuring the competitiveness of various products is the rate of return. As market segments became more well-defined, the needs of elderly customers in terms of financial products are becoming increasingly clear. First, they require long-term investment products for their retirement planning needs; second, they have specific liquidity requirements in order to cater for emergencies; and third, these customers have a lower appetite for risk. Commercial banks have begun to create wealth management products to finance old age care specifically catered to this market segment based on such needs and preferences in order to become more competitive in the market.

The first retirement financial product in the market offered by the Bank of Communications in 2009 was "De Li Bao Jiu Jiu Tian Li". The product was designed, with the participation of professional investment institutions, to bring the customer steady returns through mid-to-long-term investment, and thus meet the customer's individual mid-to-long-term retirement planning needs. Customers were given flexible withdrawal terms during the product term, thus allowing them to fully meet their liquidity needs. The introduction of this product was an early attempt by the market that worked to further broaden the financial horizons of consumers. Product differentiation was the first step by commercial banks seeking a foray into the field of wealth management products designed to finance old age care. Subsequently, institutions such as the Industrial and Commercial Bank of China (ICBC), China Everbright Bank, China Merchants Bank, the Industrial Bank, and the Bank of Shanghai have also introduced wealth management products designed for retirement planning purposes. In general, at this stage the wealth management products designed to finance old age care available focused purely on bank-facilitated financial management and the savings needs of the elderly, and had not yet been integrated with the other financial needs of the elderly.

2.1.2 Exploration and Innovation (2012 to Date): Targeted Management of Customer Segments Being the Second Stage of Industry Development

With continued marketing efforts, a small and undifferentiated offering of products were no longer sufficient to meet the overall needs for integrated financial services on the part of elderly customers. To this end, commercial banks have worked actively to create and provide integrated value-added services to elderly customers on top of their existing products. For example, the Industrial Bank launched its "An Yu Ren Sheng" service brand catering to elderly customers early 2012, with the brand integrating four dedicated services in one: product customization, health management, legal advisory, and property protection. Products offered by the bank included the Au Yu Retirement Wealth No. 1 RMB-denominated product (a non-guaranteed, floating-rate, and open wealth management product) and the An Yu Bai Fu No. 2 product which is an open-end net-value financial product. These highly differentiated products have been highly sought after by the market and their target customers (elderly customers) since their introduction. Subsequently, institutions including the Bank of Shanghai and China Guangfa Bank have developed more wealth management avenues tailored for the needs of the elderly and have also introduced various integrated wealth management services for customers with retirement planning needs.

At this point, the characteristics of wealth management products designed to finance old age care have become more distinct. These products now have longer term duration, typically carry low risk, and are focused on long-term gains, etc. Further, these products also provide elderly customers with customized value-added services. However, compared to the insurance and funds industry commercial banks have yet to achieve sufficient product differentiation with their wealth management products designed to finance old age care in terms of product forms at the front end as well as investment management on the back end. There is a need to make product features and boundaries clearer and more standardized.

2.2 *The Current State of the Industry*

As China ages with greater rapidity, financial institutions, including the banking sector, have started to pay attention to the field of financing old age care, with the concept gradually becoming a hot topic within the industry. At present, China's financial system is still dominated by the banking industry, with indirect financing as the main financing method. Therefore, we may not ignore the important status and role of the banking industry if we wish to further develop the industry of financing old age care in China. In recent years, various commercial banks—large state-owned banks, joint-stock banks and certain city commercial banks—have started to introduce their own wealth management products designed to finance old age care to the market. Compared to the insurance industry and funds industries banks have come to the product game fairly late, and they are currently still in an early exploratory stage in terms of development. However, they have been doing well in terms of overall development thus far. After the development of the past decade the retirement wealth management product market is now worth more than RMB 100 billion. To date, according to incomplete data among four major state-owned banks and national joint-stock banks a total of nine players have introduced wealth management products designed to finance old age care. Details are shown in the table below.

S. No.	Product name	Product description	How to purchase product/Product operations	Rating of product features
1	De Li Bao Jiu Jiu Tian Li, Bank of Communications	Wealth management product developed by bank and trust company; no fixed term; money management cycle of 575 days; capital-guaranteed, floating-income; all funds raised invested in the Ping An Trust (Bank of Communications Fu Rui Yi Sheng Dividend-Type Single-Fund Trust)	Minimum investment of RMB 50,000; open daily for subscription; redemption and cash dividends available every quarter; redemption is free if returns on date of first dividend is less than 3%	First retirement wealth management product from a bank, thus filling a gap in the medium and long-term bank wealth management product market; quarterly cash dividend will be realized if the basic returns have been obtained, redemption fee will be waived if returns on the first dividend date is less than 3%; redemption fee is fairly high at 1.5%, and if investors redeem the product in the short term there may be a loss in principal
2	Hui Cai RMB-Denominated Retire Without Worries product, Bank of Shanghai	Guaranteed-income bank wealth management products, term of 120 days	Minimum investment of RMB 50,000 with increments of RMB 10,000	Only available to existing BOS clients holding retiree certificates and VIP customers
3	Hui Cai Portfolio Series retirement wealth management product, Bank of Shanghai	Non-guaranteed floating income financial product	Minimum investment of RMB 50,000 with increments of RMB 10,000	Customers aged above 50, and VIP clients
4	Hui Cai Ri Xin Yue Yi No. 1 (RMB-denominated): M6 (retirement) wealth management product, Bank of Shanghai	Wealth management products offered by banks and trust companies; accumulative, product term of 182 days; non-guaranteed, floating-rate product; invested assets [held by] the Shanghai Trust-Shanghai Bank Bond Investment Single Funds Trust established by Shanghai International Trust	Minimum investment of RMB 50,000 with increments of RMB 10,000	Only available to existing BOS clients holding retiree certificates and VIP customers

(continued)

(continued)

S. No.	Product name	Product description	How to purchase product/Product operations	Rating of product features
5	Jin Yi Retirement No. 1/2/3 (2012), China Merchants Bank	Long-term wealth management products with interest calculated intermittently at dates of interest adjustment; management period of 1092 days: No. 1 is a guaranteed, floating-income product while No. 2 and 3 are non-guaranteed floating-income products	Minimum investment of RMB 50,000; investment cycle terminates every 91 days, and returns are paid out on the same day; investors may choose to redeem every three months; principal sums that have reached maturity are transferred to [investor's] account on date of maturity; principal sum paid out at redemption transferred to [investor's] account upon termination of [current] investment cycle	One of few long-term wealth management products on the market; however, three years is still a relatively short time for retirement planning purposes
6	Hua Xia Profit and Enhancement No. 1188 (for elderly customers only, 2012)	Closed non-guaranteed floating income financial product; product term of 125 days	Minimum investment of RMB 50,000 with increments of RMB 1000; generally, customers may not terminate investments early	Similar to general wealth management products
7	Xin Fu Nian Hua debit card for middle-aged and elderly customers only (2011), CITIC Bank	Special product-linked debit card: provides cardholders with elder-friendly products	Elderly clients or their legal supporters can use resident property as collateral to obtain from the bank monthly pension loans of no more than RMB 20,000 at a benchmark interest rate for a period of no more than 10 years. The accumulated loan amount shall not exceed 60% of the assessed value of mortgaged housing	Pioneer in real-estate-based retirement financing; however, product model is not yet mature
8	Ru Yi Ren Sheng series of wealth management products designed to finance old age care, ICBC	Fixed-income bank financial product	Minimum investment of RMB 100,000 with increments of RMB 10,000	Subscription and redemption only once a month, with shortest term at one month; returns after one full year of holding at 4.45%, with provision of a fairly comprehensive array of services spanning asset management, account management, and asset custody services, etc., in a "one-stop" model
9	Ru Yi Ren Sheng I (Types A and B), ICBC	Interests based on days, no-fixed term wealth management product; divided into two types (A and B) based on differing subscription/redemption dates. Subscription/redemption date for Type A is on the third working day of each month and for Type B, the 20th of each month (or the next working day in the case of public holidays). Expected rate of return may be adjusted from time to time based on market conditions and state of product operations	Minimum investment of RMB 100,000, no trading level restrictions	Pension-type wealth management product

(continued)

(continued)

S. No.	Product name	Product description	How to purchase product/Product operations	Rating of product features
10	Ru Yi Ren Sheng II, ICBC	Fixed-investment-by-installment wealth management product designed for large-volume issuance. Divided into two types, collection of financial products and dedicated product, based on way funds have been raised. The collection of financial products is issued by the main branch after its structure has been established, and one may participate with a single lump sum of RMB 2 million; the dedicated product is customized with a minimum investment of RMB 100 million (may come from multiple sources). Product terms mostly longer than three months. Expected rate of return fluctuates with market interest rates and the demand for funds and are specifically based on standard industry quotations, the amount of funds involved, and the term of investment		Pension-type wealth management product
11	Ru Yi Ren Sheng III (Types A, B, C, D, E, and F, RMB-denominated), ICBC	No-fixed-term wealth management product with weekly dividends, designed for investment funds with a specified term of investment; divided into six types based on the investment lock-in period. Open for subscription/redemption every Wednesday (or the following Wednesday in the case of public holidays). The period between two open days is considered to be one investment cycle	The lock-in periods for the six products are 12, 24, 36, nine, 18 and 48 months for Types A, B, C, D, E, and F respectively, and the minimum investment is RMB 100,000, RMB 100,000, RMB 100,000, RMB 50,000 and RMB 50,000 respectively. Funds can be redeemed on any open day after the lock-up period expires. The annualized rate of return for each product may be adjusted from time to time in tandem with market prices, and the expected rate of return at the time of subscription is the only benchmark for the duration of the investment	Pension-type wealth management product
12	Inside the product specifications for Ru Yi Ren Sheng IV (RMB-denominated wealth management product), ICBC	Net-value financial product designed for mid-to-long-term investment, divided into closed net-value financial product of fixed investment by installment and open net-value financial product of non-fixed term based on term of investment. There is no expected rate of return, with actual net gains paid out to the client at the time of term maturity or redemption		Pension-type wealth management product

(continued)

(continued)

S. No.	Product name	Product description	How to purchase product/Product operations	Rating of product features
13	Yi Xiang Yang Guang A and B, China Everbright Bank	Product term of 15 years, with fixed income products at the core of investments and asset allocation based on long-term cycles; capital preservation strategy adopted to control portfolio volatility; all investments were made in fixed income in the initial stage of product establishment, and after cumulative income has reached a certain level asset allocation may be diversified—depending on market conditions—in order to achieve steady growth in product returns. Benchmark rate of return is "one-year bank deposit interest rate + 2%"	Minimum investment of RMB 100,000 with increments of RMB 1000 for individual investors; minimum investment of RMB 500,000 with increments of RMB 10,000 for institutional investors	Different from other simple retirement savings financial products in that it serves as a transition or bridge to retirement and lifelong financial management products and plans, and product shows certain preliminary retirement-planning features
14	Le Xiang Ying Zhi Xi, Shanghai Pudong Development Bank	Guaranteed returns, one-year term, investment returns distributed once every month and principal sum returned upon completion of term	Minimum investment of RMB 50,000, with increments of RMB 10,000	Investment in trust plans, similar to general wealth management products
15	Tong Xiang Ying Xi Yang Hong (Retire with Peace of Mind), Shanghai Pudong Development Bank	Non-guaranteed floating-rate product, two-year term, investment returns distributed once every month and principal sum returned upon completion of term	Minimum investment of RMB 50,000, with increments of RMB 10,000	Investment in trust plans, similar to general wealth management products
16	An Yu Retirement Wealth No. 1, Industrial Bank	Non-guaranteed, floating-rate, open, RMB-denominated product; three-year term	Minimum investment of RMB 50,000 with increments of RMB 1000; customers may sign or terminate contracts each month, with one month regarded as one investment cycle; cycle investment gains are returned to the account stipulated in the investor's contract, and if the investor does not choose to terminate the contract the principal sum and gains will be rolled over into the next investment cycle	For An Yu customers only
17	An Yu Yang Lao Bai Fu No. 2, Industrial Bank	Non-guaranteed, open, net-value financial product; three-year term	Minimum investment of RMB 50,000 with increments of RMB 1000; one quarter is regarded as one investment cycle; advance notice required for subscription and redemption	For An Yu customers only

Case study 1: The Yi Xiang Yang Guang product from China Everbright Bank

a. Product features:

Minimum deposit of RMB 100,000 accepted from individual investors with a product term of 15 years. Dividends are paid on the first day of each month. There are two types of dividends: dividend plough-back and cash dividends. Redemption not available for first six months of product term; however, customers may apply to purchase more units on the fifteenth day of each month after the first full month of the product term is completed. After the first sixth months, investors may apply for the purchase of more units or for redemption on the fifteenth day of each month.

b. Product characteristics:

- Security: focus on fixed-income products with a long-term strategy adopted for asset allocation; capital preservation strategy used to control portfolio volatility; in the initial stage of product establishment, all investment is placed in fixed-income products, and when total income has reached a certain level, investment is then diversified (depending on market conditions) in order to achieve steady growth for the product.
- Liquidity: open for redemption monthly, thus providing sufficient liquidity for retirement customers; six months after the establishment of the product regular redemption will be enabled to meet the cash flow needs of retirement customers; a cash-dividend product (Yi Xiang Yang Guang B) has also been set up for elderly customers to provide them with a supplementary source of income for their day-to-day needs. Yi Xiang Yang Guang A, a dividend plough-back product, seeks long-term returns for elderly customers.
- Returns: the returns are higher than that of the Everbright Retirement CPI index and short-to-mid-term wealth management products offered by banks; when investment returns are lower than the performance benchmark the current year's performance pay is used to make up for difference. This ensures that the bank's interests are aligned with the customer's.
- Long-term: the long product term meets the long-term retirement planning needs of customers; customers with retirement planning needs are provided with one-stop asset allocation service; assets are allocated across broad categories with a long-term perspective, and the focus is on steady long-term gains rather than short-term market rankings and yields.

Case study 2: The An Yu Bai Fu No. 2 product from the Industrial Bank's An Yu line of products

a. Product features:

The An Yu Bai Fu No. 2 product is an open net-value financial product available in three options: a total of three (all of which are non-guaranteed, low-risk products). Minimum investment amount of RMB 50,000 with increases of RMB 1000. Benchmark performance is set at Industrial Bank's one-year fixed deposit interest rate + 1.85% (adjusted each investment cycle). Product term of three years, and customers may apply in advance to purchase more units or redeem their investments on a certain date once every quarter. If the customer fails to make a redemption request within the expected redemption period of an investment cycle, his or her wealth management funds will automatically be entered into the next investment cycle.

b. Product features:

- Low risk: The An Yu Fu Bai No. 2 product is an open net-value financial product that is designed specifically for the wealth management needs of elderly customers. It is a low-risk product that is mainly focused on low-risk assets such as bank deposits, bonds (through repurchase), currency funds, government bonds, policy-oriented financial bonds, and central bank bills.
- High yields: The An Yu Bai Fu No. 2 product has a rate of return that is higher than returns for ordinary wealth management products from the same period.
- Investment flexibility: for subscription, customers can make an application for purchase within the subscription period for the investment cycle in question, and the subscription is confirmed by Industrial Bank on the date of purchase. Product redemption also takes place within a specific period in the investment cycle, with the customer placing an advance application for redemption before the redemption date.
- Diverse investment channels: the customer may purchase the product, make a subscription application, or apply for redemption through various Industrial Bank sub-branches or self-service channels.
- Regular earnings payouts: Industrial Bank pays out the wealth management earnings for the investment cycle on a predetermined payout date for the customer's share of product holdings. This helps customers meet their day-to-day financial needs.

c. Product scale:

By the end of 2016, over RMB 3 billion worth of customer assets have been invested in the An Yu Bai Fu No. 2 product.

2.3 The Specific Characteristics of Such Products

A review of current wealth management products designed by commercial banks to finance old age care shows the following common features:

In terms of product duration, wealth management products designed to finance old age care have relatively long product terms, with some clocking in at more than 10 years. For example, China Everbright Bank offers a series of products in its Yi Xiang Yang Guo product line with product terms of 15 years, a duration that can basically cover customers' asset reserve needs from middle-age to old age. Another example is the An Yu Bai Fu No. 2 product from the Industrial Bank, which operates on three-year investment cycles. This model offers both liquidity and long-term investment potential.

In terms of product type, the majority of wealth management products designed to finance old age care on the market are non-guaranteed and floating-rate products. Only very few products offer customers guaranteed returns. Compared to ordinary wealth management products from the same period, wealth management products designed to finance old age care have fairly competitive returns (in the 4.3–4.9%

range). With certain products, returns for VIP customers and customers with significant investment assets put in are pegged even higher. All products are lower-risk products that meet the investment needs of elderly customers who require greater security while providing them with higher levels of return.

In terms of liquidity, wealth management products designed to finance old age care tend to have longer product terms, and with some products residents are encouraged to place their investment for the long term with lower yields, or redemption fees imposed, for short-term redemption. At the same time, in order to meet any unexpected needs for large amounts of funds, such as illness, products with a term of more than two years are regularly open for redemption and subscription, and dividends are paid out regularly.

In terms of market acceptance, elderly customers continue to become more accepting of wealth management products designed to finance old age care thanks to ever-increasing awareness of the importance of planning for old age. As a result, wealth management products designed to finance old age care have a growing position in the market. To take the Industrial Bank as an example: as of April 2017, the value of market holdings managed under its An Yu product line is in excess of RMB 30 billion.

3 Challenges Faced by the Industry

Objectively speaking, due to issues such as regulatory differences, compared to the insurance and funds industries, the retirement wealth management business in the commercial bank sector is comparatively less developed, both in terms of sales volume and the diversity of products on offer. Wealth management products designed to finance old age care offered by commercial banks are still in the early stages of development. There are many reasons for this state of affairs, both due to regulatory factors and those concerning the commercial banks themselves.

3.1 Regulatory Gap

In the *Guidelines on Financial Support for Pension Services Industry to Accelerate Development* (Y. F. No. 65 [2016]) jointly issued by five agencies including the People's Bank of China, it is stipulated that active efforts have to be taken to develop professional financial products that can serve the retirement needs of residents. Banks, securities firms, trusts, funds, insurance and other financial institutions were encouraged to actively develop differentiated retirement financial products that provide long-term, stable returns and meet the needs of pensioners over the course of their life cycles for investors of varying age groups. At present, the insurance and securities industries have already categorized retirement financial products by specific market segments and have established the corresponding systems of management. For example, the China Insurance Regulatory Commission (CIRC) issued the *Administrative Regulations on Old Age Security Management* (B. J. F. No. 73 [2015]) in 2015, and the China Securities Regulatory Commission (CSRC) has also issued its *Pilot Guidelines on Pension Investment Funds* in May 2017. The aim with the latter document is to standardize operations for retirement security products and retirement fund products. However, such detailed categorization has yet to occur with the banking sector.

3.2 More Improvements Needed for Industry Institutions and Systems

Wealth management products designed to finance old age care are tailored to meet the retirement-planning needs of customers. There is a greater emphasis on product stability and yield levels with these products due to the special attributes of such products and the particular needs of their customers. At present, most wealth management products designed to finance old age care mirror the basic pension insurance fund and annuities in terms of the scope of investment, with most of the investment products limited to investment in bank deposits, guaranteed-earnings products, and guaranteed-capital floating-income products offered by banks. The limited scope of investment and relatively low return levels have made products less attractive [to investors] than they can be.

3.3 To Improve the Awareness of the Importance of Pension Reserve Due to Inadequate Knowledge of Such Products Among Residents

Retirement at home remains a distinctly Chinese mode of retirement due to prevalent attitudes about retirement and the traditional belief in the importance of raising a child as assurance for one's old age. In contrast to the developed nations in the West, in China the financial industry has come into being relatively late, and financial knowledge and awareness of financial issues are weak among the general population. Moreover, a significant proportion of the elderly born before the 1950s and 1960s still focus solely on savings deposits and government bonds [as a means of saving up for their old age]. This has led to a situation where insufficient demand make it difficult for commercial banks to develop a diversified offering of wealth management products designed to finance old age care.

3.4 *Industry Has Developed Rather Late in China, Which Leads to an Insufficient Product Supply*

From the economic perspective, demand is the key determinant of the scale of product supply and product pricing. As awareness of financial issues grows among residents, in recent years the concept of retirement financial products has emerged on the market. However, in general we are still looking at a transitional period. Therefore, due to their comparatively late start, the commercial banks have not accrued sufficient experience with the development of wealth management products to finance old age care. The limited scope of investment has also meant the lack of strong investment targets and a difficulty in expanding and diversifying product lines as well as in expanding the scale of products. Compared with ordinary products, the majority of retirement products are only differentiated by slightly higher yields and longer term periods. At the same time, more work needs to be done to seek out more innovative business models. Further, there needs to be more professionalism in how retirement financial services are being provided.

3.5 *With Varying Product Models, More Innovation Is Needed*

There are currently two kinds of wealth management products designed by commercial banks to finance old age care: in the first category (where most products lie) are products that are wholly developed and established by the banks themselves, and in the second category are joint issues created in partnership with other entities. Examples of products in the second category include trust plan products jointly developed by commercial banks and trust companies. With such products, funding is obtained on the front end through the wealth management product, while trust-plan operations are conducted on the back end. At the same time, commercial banks have also issued products through their subsidiaries. For instance, China Construction Bank retails endowment insurance products issued by CCB Pension as well as sells pension insurance products (such as endowment insurance products) issued by other institutions through the consignment sales model. A clear business model has yet to emerge with broad variance in the way products are organized.

3.6 *Commercial Banks not Very Keen on Such Products Due to How Performance Indicators Are Set up*

Due to business pressure commercial banks usually base their cyclic assessment on the fiscal year. Assessment is also further divided into quarterly assessments and monthly indicators. The pressure exerted by financial indicators means that commercial banks are more willing to engage in business with shorter cycles and which produce gains more quickly. With the long-term asset business, banks also prefer to chase maximum short-term gains through [asset allocation] so as to meet targets based on certain performance indicators. Retirement financial products are obviously long-term asset investments that have a longer payback period, and as such commercial banks are less willing to create such products.

4 Prospects for Wealth Management Products Designed by Banks to Finance Old Age Care

4.1 Bright Future for the Industry

In terms of market demand, China's residents continue to become more aware of the need for retirement planning. Further, young people also face increasingly serious pressure in terms of old age pension pressure due to China's long-term family planning policies and the 4-2-1 or 4-2-2 family structure (i.e., four seniors, two working adults, and one or two children in the household) as a result of the recently-implemented two-children policy. As such, demand among individuals for retirement-planning products and services will also grow steadily. From the supply side, commercial banks are the main avenue for residents to engage in personal asset allocation, and the growing desire among residents to save for old age has led commercial banks to pay more attention to the retirement financing market. Some commercial banks have been effective at introducing products with features that are distinct and well-aligned with the needs of investors to plan for retirement, and have thus performed better in the market.

Therefore, we can say that retirement financial products will become a key product category for banks given the high level of recognition from target customers, the high level of market attention received, the positive product development prospects, and the large size of the potential market.

4.2 Product and Service Are Gradually Broadened

At present, most large state-owned banks and joint-stock commercial banks have launched wealth management products designed to finance old age care, and these products have been well-recognized by middle-aged customers. In particular, these products have become a mainstream asset tool among customers with retirement-planning needs. With the influence of market demand as well as the need to transform their own operations, more and more commercial banks, including small and medium-sized city commercial banks, will become more adept at grasping the needs of the retirement financing market, and we will see a growing array of product types and improved systems of service in this area.

4.3 Net-Value Financial Products May Become Market Mainstream

For most products with stated expected earnings that are on the market, managers have no choice but to opt for low-risk investment options as they have to meet payout requirements. Thus, the possibility of product innovation and diversity is very low. At the same time, with low-risk investment also come lower returns. Steadily declining yields will make products a lot less attractive. As such, we foresee that in the future [industry players] will work vigorously to create new, innovative net-value financial product, broaden the investment scope of products, eliminate the strict limitations imposed by cash payout requirements, and make wealth management products designed to finance old age care more competitive through higher yield levels.

4.4 Deeper Cross-Industry Partnerships

Due to policy and business restrictions, there is a lot of overlap between financial institutions—such as banks, insurance companies and trust companies in terms of business strategy, industry and business scope. However, each industry also has its own unique strengths. Banks have the advantage in terms of sales channels and customer recognition, while the insurance and funds industries have obvious advantages in terms of the scope of investment range and asset management capabilities. Through cross-industry cooperation between commercial banks and the insurance and funds sectors, etc., great complementarity that can bring new development opportunities for wealth management products designed to finance old age care can be achieved.

In addition, a new generation of information technology is driving changes in society as a whole. In the Internet+ era, innovation in financial services has made Internet finance flourish, and cooperation between traditional finance and internet finance in the areas of capital, risk control and financial innovation, etc., is closer than ever. The retirement finance business is no exception, for example, introducing smart investment consulting for customers is also expected to be a new point of breakthrough.

4.5 Potential for Wealth Management Products Designed to Fund Retirement Is Even Greater with Large Banks

Compared with the city commercial banks, large commercial banks have unique advantages in the retirement wealth management business. First of all, these banks have access to critical volume and a significant customer base. The large banks have accrued a large customer base following decades or even a century of development, and this base provides a strong foundation for the development of retirement wealth management services. In particular, for the large banks, the proportion of middle-aged and elderly customers within the customer base is relatively high. Second, large banks also have distinct advantages when it comes to the product offering. Large commercial banks have an advantage in terms of the management of, and innovation with, wealth management products. Their strengths are particularly obvious on the back end in terms of asset supply, investment, and risk control, etc. These are all strengths that aid long-term investment, a hallmark of retirement products. Third, brand influence. Large commercial banks have outlets throughout the country and have a large customer base. With product segmentation they can easily establish competitive barriers. Of course, although in terms of overall size they cannot compete with the large commercial banks, city commercial banks may have a better handle on regional customers' product preferences and thus have an advantage in terms of product design and marketing on the regional level.

5 Recommendations for Future Development

5.1 Across-the-Board Regulatory Standards for More Effective Supervision

At present, China's financial sector is still divided into various industries in terms of both operations and regulation/supervision. With retirement products created, different regulatory standards apply in terms of product entry thresholds, scope of investment, funding and marketing, information disclosure, how capital assets are held, and the matching of investor profiles with the appropriate risk levels/investment instruments. Some differences are relatively significant, and thus pose the hidden danger of regulatory arbitrage. We recommend that the authorities standardize requirements on the regulatory level and establish a general system of product risk monitoring and market data for the market [as well as specific standards on issues such as] the definitions of "qualified investors", rules on how product assets can be invested, market entry thresholds and rules on market exit, etc. Doing so will provide a more effective regulatory environment for the development of wealth management products to finance old age care.

5.2 *Implementation of Various Product Management Mechanisms*

In order to have active participation in the building of a multi-level pension insurance system and to allow commercial banks to play a bigger role in the development of retirement products and elderly care services, we recommend that the authorities introduce management guidelines for retirement financial products with clear stipulations on matters such as purchase amounts, product terms, yield levels, scope of investment for these products. Such a document will provide commercial banks with clearer policy guidelines for the further development of their wealth management products to finance old age care.

From the perspective of inclusive finance, efforts can be made to lower the investment threshold for products and simplify the procedures for risk assessment. At the same time, we can encourage commercial banks to introduce smart investment consulting to provide customers with investment advice for the long term. Product investment terms can be made longer in order to strengthen risk control. At the same time, in order to ensure the preservation and appreciation of retirement assets, [players] should purchase risk-buyout contract from qualified third-party institutions if necessary. To ensure asset preservation and enhancement, we can raise the permitted ratio of non-standardized debt assets for wealth management products designed to finance old age care, and—with reference to the *Guidelines for the Investment Management of Basic Pension Insurance Funds*—expand the scope of investment to an appropriate degree, with investment permitted for stocks publicly traded in the domestic secondary market and for shares of state-owned or state-controlled enterprises funded by state-owned asset management departments, etc.

5.3 *Commercial Banks Should Work on New Organizational Structures to Further Professionalize Their Operations*

We will gradually see greater demands by customers for professional and differentiated products and services as the market for financing individual old age care and asset services becomes even more mature. The financing services for senior care and assets services tend to have a long service cycle, and during this period, the customer's retirement goals, occupational status, income status and asset investment performance are likely to change significantly. As such, the customer service provided will also have to change in tandem, including in the areas of personal retirement planning, investment advisory, product promotion, financial settlement, information reporting, etc. The lack of a professional team and service experience will make long-term operations challenging for the organization.

Thus, commercial banks should establish dedicated departments for financing old age care so that they can mobilize system resources and further integrate forces for the establishment of the organizational structure needed for the provision of specialized services. Those with the resources can consider setting up dedicated companies in this regard. This will allow them to improve upon existing financial services and create new innovative services on a continued basis, thereby promoting the transformation of their operating structures and further developing their dedicated operations for financing old age care.

5.4 Equal Focus on Development and Innovation of Wealth Management Products to Finance Individual Old Age Care

With the market liberalization of interest rates and deepening reform in the capital markets, outstanding funds, brokerage firms and trust institutions may demonstrate stronger asset management capabilities by virtue of their extensive investment and flexible operating mechanisms. This may pose a challenge to the bank's traditional financial product structure, but it can also provide opportunities for cooperation and win-win arrangements with these institutions. We recommend that commercial banks actively cooperate with their counterparts to jointly design and develop wealth management products to finance individual old age care that combine innovative financial assurance with health and wealth management. "Encompassing both breadth and depth" will become a key developmental strategy for wealth management products issued by commercial banks.

5.5 Broaden Customer Base Through Consolidation of and Innovations in Financial Services

Overseas experience tells us that in the future there will be a shift from a focus on product marketing to the marketing of integrated product-and-service offerings. This is a shift from a product-centric approach to a customer-centric approach. Although various financial institutions have already recognized the strong prospects of the individual retirement finance market and have introduced certain wealth management products in this respect, regulatory differences across various industries, overregulation and the immaturity of the capital market have led to comparatively little product innovation and homogeneous service and product offerings. As such, financial institutions often have had to compete by means of primitive methods like pricing. This is not conducive to the sustainable and healthy development of the business.

In the future, commercials can only win over customers and move towards professional investment and business operations by integrating products and services, such as by embedding retirement planning and investment advisory services into the sales of financial products. At the same time, commercial banks can also work on the provision of value-added services, such as by designing and development value-added services in the areas of geriatric medicine, and nursing, tourism and education for the elderly. This will allow elderly customers to enjoy both life protection as well as a higher quality of life.

In short, as the ageing of population accelerates, retirement care has gradually become one of the most prominent and serious issues in China's economic and social development. To solve the problem of providing for the aged, we need the joint efforts of society at large. More importantly, we need a sound system of financial services that would give full play to the resource allocation function of financial institutions within society. The commercial banks are duty-bound to participate in this process. Engaging in the development of retirement finance products and in innovation in this field will allow commercial banks to play to their own strengths and actively respond to the aging of the population. Doing so is also an important means for commercial banks to benefit both themselves and the people, and to realize their own business transformation and upgrading. The prospects for the commercial-banking retirement finance products and services market are promising.

Jianyu Liu is General Manager of the Pension Finance Center, Retail Management Headquarters of the Industrial Bank. He is also a member of the supervising board at the Industrial Bank Consumer Finance Co. Liu holds a master's degree in economics and is a member of the China Aging Finance Forum (COACFF 50) by special invite. His research interest is in the area of financing old age care. X. Zhang is an employee of the Industrial Bank Pension Finance Center. His research focus is in the area of financing old age care.

Chapter 10
The Current State of, Opportunities for, and Trends with Retirement Funds

Bo Sun

Abstract Affected by differences in the development of various capital markets and asset management industries, the quality of market players, and the development state in investment consultancy systems, there are only two main types of supplementary pension products in the overseas market: the general pension product and the dedicated pension product. These various industries and systems are represented by the examples of the United States, Chile, Australia, and Hong Kong. In this article, we analyze the general situation of China's retirement fund market, uncover its growth opportunities and obstacles to further development, and then propose that the dedicated product model be established in China, and that retirement fund products be introduced as early as possible as part of preparations for the coming of the so-called "Pillar 3" and for the liberalization of individual choice for the "Pillar II". At the same time, taking the suggested approach will also provide the appropriate investment tools for citizens to plan for their retirement independently. In this paper, we posit that there should be two types of products in China's retirement funds market: the first being solution-based product products such as target-date funds and target-risk funds, and second, "instrument-based" products that are made of various combination portfolios of stocks, bonds and other types of funds. Such products are structured according to the age of the target investor. Meanwhile, investors should—with the long-term attributes of their retirement funds in mind—broaden their investment to an appropriate degree to include other assets such as overseas assets and alternative assets.

Keywords General products · Dedicated products · Solution-based products Instrument-based products

B. Sun (✉)
Pension Management Department, China Asset Management, Beijing, China

K. Dong and Y. Yao (eds.), *Annual Report on Financing Old Age Care in China (2017)*, https://doi.org/10.1007/978-981-13-0968-7_10

1 Introduction to Retirement Fund Products

Since the introduction of the three-pillar pension system by the World Bank in 1994, many countries have conducted reforms to establish similar systems. It is worth noting that in countries where reforms have yielded significant outcomes, supplementary funds that are mainly within Pillar II and Pillar 3 have seen strong development and have thus helped to mitigate pressures on the first pillar (i.e., government finances) as well as created stronger pension protections for citizens.

In China, it has been more than ten years since the supplementary pension, also known as enterprise annuities,—covering more than twenty-three million employees—have been established. However, policies to marketize the operation of enterprise annuities, which were announced in 2016, have not been truly implemented yet. While the outlines of the Pillar 3 personal pension account have been proposed as early as the 1990s, it has yet to be implemented. Nevertheless, as the population ages at a quicker clip, the model of a single-pillar system of pension support (i.e. through public retirement funds) is confronted with tremendous pay-out pressures and structural deficiencies. Thus, an urgent task for China's pension system is to improve upon the system of supplementary support and promote pension support by means of the enterprise and individual responsibility.

Supplementary retirement funds typically adopt a structure of accumulation with a long fund accumulation span and large accumulation amount; thus facing strong depreciation pressures due to inflation over the entire life cycle, making it more important to focus on value preservation/appreciation and investments. However, there are significant differences across supplementary retirement fund product structures in different countries due to varying degrees of development in capital-market operations and asset-management industry structures, huge variations among the characteristics of enrollees and the degree to which investment consultancy systems are developed, etc. In this paper, we summarize the various product models around the world and seek out models that are appropriate for China's circumstances in order to better preserve and raise fund value and enhance financial security for enrollees.

1.1 Overview of Overseas Retirement Fund Product

Retirement fund products are products set up according to the characteristics, risk appetites and yield requirements of enrollees seeking to plan for old age protection. Generally speaking, if funds for this purpose are invested in a mutual fund, they can only be used for investment purposes. As for international community, retirement fund products, as a product category, do not exist in countries such as the United States and Canada. Instead, investors are allowed to choose from existing mutual-fund products across the entire market. In certain other countries and regions, fund products specially designed for old age security purposes have been established. For these products or certain types of retirement fund products, it is advised that investment funds be used only for the stated category of products. Examples of such countries and regions include Australia, Chile, and Hong Kong. In general, there are two main considerations as to whether to establish dedicated or retirement funds.

The First One Is About the State of Development with the Capital Market and Asset Management Industry. In considering whether to set up a retirement fund product, one will have to consider the characteristics of the capital market, investor behavior, and the state of development with the investment consultancy system in the country in question. Take the United States as an example: typically, with the bull markets of the American stock market last a fairly long period of time, while bear markets last a comparatively short period of time, financial products such as mutual funds will do well and perform steadily over time, and mutual fund products with clear positioning (such as targeted date funds or TDFs) will also develop quickly. Furthermore, within the United States asset management industry, the system of investment consultancy is very well-developed, investors are well-educated and are comparatively experienced in investment. Thus, although there is a great diversity as well as number of financial products in the market, there are not too many restrictions on retirement fund investment, and nor are there too much difficulty of choice or investment risks with individual retirement assets. In comparison, in countries such as Australia and Chile, although the asset market has been growing over the long-term, development has been comparatively slow in terms of investor education, information access, investor decision-making and investment consultancy, etc. If placing no restrictions on pension-fund products in these instances, enrollees will have more difficulty in making choices and may even end up losing their money due to an inability to identify product risks. As a result, first-level filtering needs to be conducted by the government on behalf of the individuals so that they will be able to choose the right products that fit their respective risk appetite profiles and thus better meet their asset preservation/growth needs for retirement.

The Second Is About the Degree to Which the Individual is Able to Make Choices. The 401(k)-plan system in the United States, which falls under the Pillar II, provides individuals with some choices of investment. However, one employee may only make choices within the investment options offered by the employer. That is to say, the employer acts as a trustee and is required to define the scope of possible investments in terms of investment managers and products for its employees. At the same time, with the 2006 Pension Protection Act (PPA) the Qualified Default Investment Alternative or QDIA has been introduced, if the participant does not actively make a choice about how the funds in his or her investment account will be invested, they will be automatically invested in QDIA products, which are mainly targeted risk funds and TDFs. But when it comes to Australia super annuities, individuals enjoy less restriction on choosing investment methods of retirement funds (Zheng and Li 2012). Apart from the choice of products available for one's individual investment account, one also has a choice of investment managers and their products. To a certain degree, expanding the scope of selection for these individual investors may lead to an inability on the part of the individual to choose the right investment manager and products in the market. It is at this juncture that dedicated products have emerged, allowing the individual to choose the fund products that are right for his or her retirement profile; thus making pension-fund investment safer.

1.2 Overview of Retirement Fund Products in China

In recent years, with the increasing number of ageing population and growing attention to this issue, the fund industry has also actively made efforts to create new retirement fund products to meet the investment needs of the people. There have been two main approaches in this regard. On one hand, as early as in 2006, HSBC Jintrust established the first hybrid TDF (targeted at the investor with old age security needs) in China. Dacheng Fund and ICBC Credit Suisse Asset Management (ICBCCS) also issued hybrid- and bond-type TDFs subsequently. On the other hand, in 2012, Tianhong Asset Management launched the first public-offering fund with a focus on old age security. Thereafter, as attention on the issue of old age security continued to grow, a number of similar funds were launched. In fact, more than ten such funds were launched by the likes of HFT Investment Management, China Asset Management, and Manulife Teda Fund Management. As of the end of 2016, the market has witnessed a total of thirteen public-offering funds and five TDFs offered by nine and three companies respectively in this area. The total net asset value of these funds is RMB 23.689 billion.

While market players have been working actively to create and offer new products, policymakers have also been working to promote funds designed for pension purposes. In March 2016, the People's Bank, the China Banking Regulatory Commission (CBRC), the China Securities Regulatory Commission (CSRC), the China Insurance Regulatory Commission (CIRC) and the Ministry of Civil Affairs jointly issued the *Guiding Opinions on Financially Supporting the Accelerated Development of Old Age Service Industry*. In the document, it is stated that China would work vigorously to develop retirement fund products, and encourage individuals to enhance their property income by means of investment in various professional finance products to enhance their ability to provide for themselves in old age. This was the first time retirement fund products had been mentioned on a state level. In May 2017, the CIRC released its Trial Guidelines for Pension-Type Publicly-Offered Securities Investment Funds and sought feedbacks from industry at the same time in what was a sign that retirement fund products were to become a reality.

2 The Current State of Retirement Fund Product Market in China

As stated above, there are two main types of pension-related public-offering funds in China: TDFs and fund products with a focus on retirement. We should note here that in this article, "fund products with a focus on retirement" refer to wealth management tools (public-offering funds) that provide investors with a steady yield, and do not include industry funds in the pension-centered investment industry.

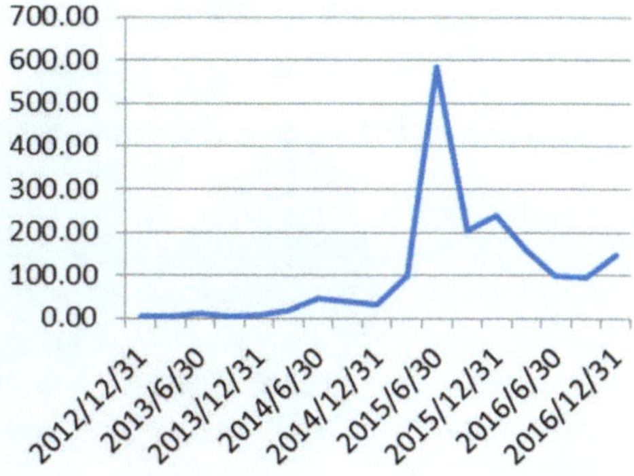

Fig. 1 Total net asset value for funds with a retirement focus (*unit* 100 million). *Source* Wind, accurate as of Dec 31, 2016

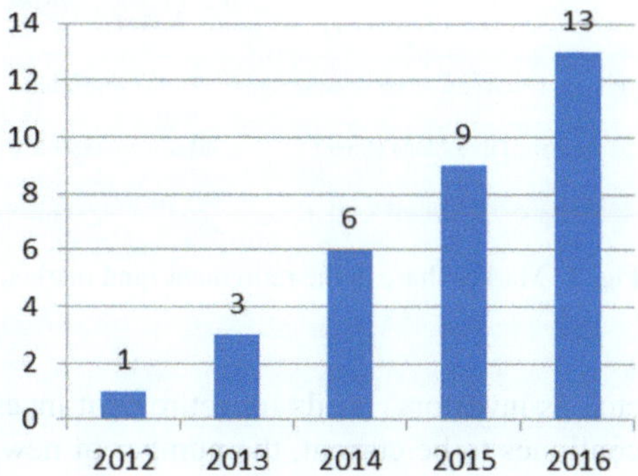

Fig. 2 Number of funds with a retirement focus by year

2.1 *Public-Offering Funds with Focus on Retirement*

In November 2012, Tianhong Asset Management launched the Tianhong Ankang Retirement Fund, the first fund with a focus on retirement needs in the industry. As attention on retirement-related issues continues to bubble up, there has been an increasing number of retirement funds on the market. Since 2015, the number of funds in operation has increased to nine with a total net asset value of nearly RMB 60 billion. However, since September 2015, the size of funds has dipped by nearly 70%. As of the end of 2016, there are a total of thirteen public-offering funds with a retirement focus issued by nine fund management companies on the market. The total net asset value of these funds is RMB 14.299 billion (Figs. 1 and 2).

Fluctuations in the total net asset value of these funds has been significant for three reasons: first, affected by stock market gyrations and losses incurred by various funds, significant and sustained shrinking of fund asset value has been seen in the second half of 2015 and the first half of 2016; second, as institutional investors make up a comparatively high proportion with this category of funds, they were in possession of more than 50% of holdings for more than half of all funds in 2016. When unusual market developments occur, redemption by spooked institutional investors may cause bigger fluctuations in fund size. Third: although the size of such funds has declined dramatically due to market sentiment and the behavior of institutional investors,

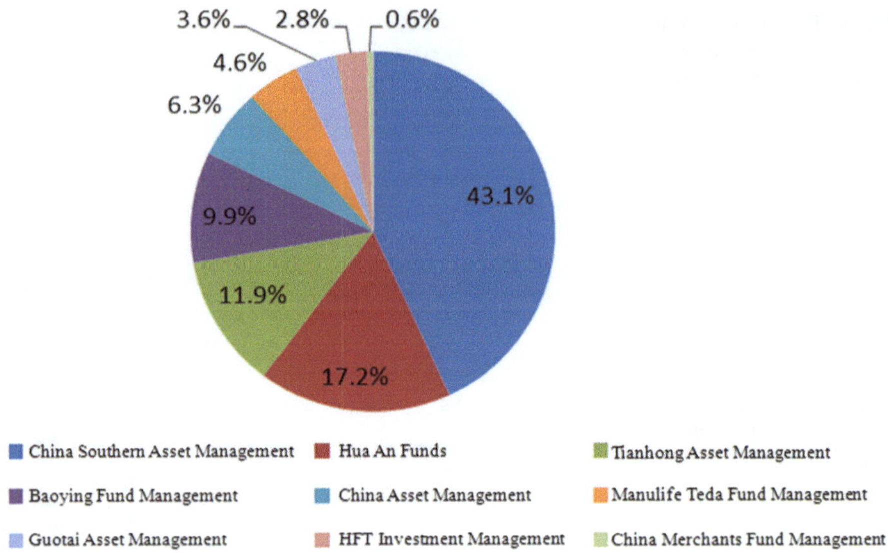

Fig. 3 Market share in the retirement fund market. *Source* Wind, accurate as of Dec 31, 2016

etc., as investors' needs for retirement investment grow and the topic of retirement continues to be current, the number of new retirement funds that were launched in Q2 and Q3 of 2016 has risen and we are also seeing a rebound in fund value.

Of the nine fund management companies that offer retirement fund products, China Southern Asset Management runs the largest fund with a net asset value of RMB 6.375 billion or 43.1% of the net asset value of the thirteen such funds in the market. This is followed by the funds managed by Hua An Funds, Tianhong Asset Management, Baoying Fund Management, and China Asset Management at 17.2, 11.9, 9.9 and 6.3% of total net asset value in the market respectively. The funds managed by the remaining four companies are smaller with an asset value of around RMB 1.707 billion or 11.5% of the market total (Fig. 3).

(1) **Fund Types**

In terms of the **subject of investment**, all thirteen funds in this area are hybrid funds that focus mainly on fixed-yield assets as a way of maintaining stable fund yield. Among them, eleven out of the thirteen funds have a cap of 30–40% for stock investments. Only HFT Investment Management and China Merchants Fund have a far higher cap of 95% of all holdings. In terms of **investment strategy**, some of these funds use the Constant Proportion Portfolio Insurance (CPPI) strategy and the Variable Proportion Portfolio Insurance (VPPI) strategy favored by annuities investment. Firstly, a portfolio heavy on fixed-yield assets provides a safety cushion before the proportion of equity-type assets is raised gradually. Some other funds adopt a more orthodox approach to asset allocation, basing their decisions on macroeco-

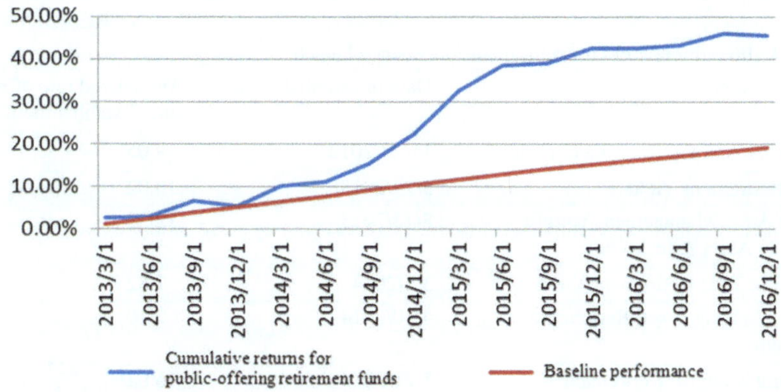

Fig. 4 Cumulative return for retirement funds, 2012–2016. *Source* Wind

nomic analysis and asset allocation models and selecting individual securities for investment to increase yields.

In terms of the **performance benchmarks** used, the majority of these funds used the one/three-year fixed deposit-plus approach while others have adopted the weighted stock and debt composite index approach.

(2) **Investment Yields**

As of Dec 31, 2016, the average weighted average rate of return for retirement funds is 10.50%, with an annualized volatility level of 1.09%. The yield is higher than performance benchmarks (to take the example of the one-year fixed deposit interest rate + 2%) (Fig. 4).

In addition, yields also vary from fund to fund, mainly due to the dates of establishment and asset allocation ratios involved. The table below shows that a total of six funds was launched prior to 2015, and the average annualized return of these funds since establishment stands at 10.74%; for the total of five funds launched since 2015 (with a minimum operating time of one full quarter), the average annualized rate of return is only 1.92%. China Merchants Fund has a negative annualized rate of return as it was launched comparatively late and owned high level of stock holdings in the portfolio. It is the only retirement fund with a negative rate of return (Table 1).

(3) **Asset Allocation**

The primary function for retirement funds is to provide a steady yield for investors. Thus, in terms of asset allocation, the focus is primarily on fixed-income assets and currency assets. Fixed-income and currency assets make up for 60–90% of total assets with these products. Stock holdings typically make up less than 10% of total assets with the exception of funds managed by HFT and China Merchants Fund. However, such holdings never make up more than 30% of total assets in these two instances (Fig. 5).

Table 1 Investment yield for retirement funds since launch

Name of fund	Date of establishment	Annualized rate of return since establishment (%)
Tianhong Ankang Retirement Fund	11/28/2012	9.05
HFT Retirement Yield	5/29/2013	10.02
China Asset Management Yongfu Yanglao Asset Allocation	8/13/2013	12.32
Manulife Teda Retirement Yield	3/5/2014	7.82
Guotai Ankang Fixed Retirement Payments	4/30/2014	9.20
Baoying Xiangrui Retirement	5/21/2014	16.02
Tianhong Puhui Capital-Guarantee Retirement	5/27/2015	6.45
Baoying Xiangtai Retirement	5/29/2015	2.62
Hua An Tianyi Retirement	6/16/2015	2.51
China Merchants Kangtai Retirement	2/4/2016	−2.19
China Southern Asset Antai Retirement	9/22/2016	0.22

Source Wind, and excludes fund products that have yet to operate for at least one full quarter

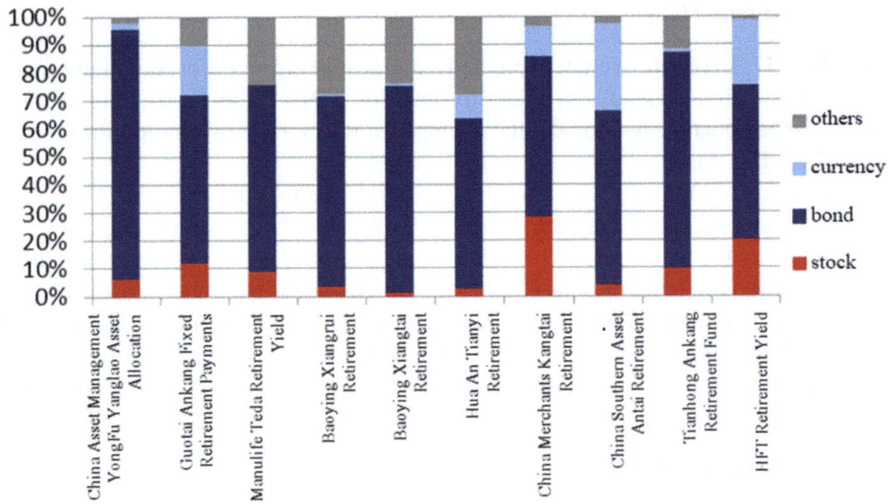

Fig. 5 Asset allocation for retirement funds. *Source* Wind, correct as of Dec 31, 2016. Data for three funds unavailable

In terms of the stability of the asset allocation ratio, fluctuations were greater with the funds that were launched in the early days, mainly during the 2015 bull market when asset allocation shifted to a greater focus on equity-type assets. In

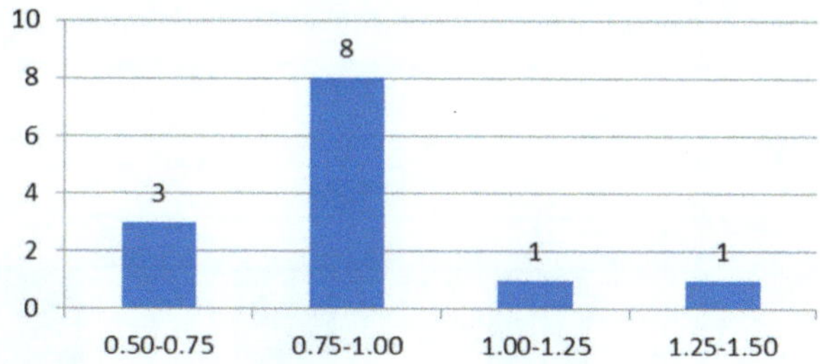

Fig. 6 Management fee rates charged by various retirement funds (%). *Source* Wind, correct as of Dec 31, 2016

recent years, funds managed by Guotai, HFT and China Merchants Fund have also seen greater shifts towards stock holdings, while fluctuations have been smaller with Baoying, Manulife Teda, and Tianhong. Fluctuations in funds managed by China Asset Management and China Southern Asset fall between these two ends.

(4) **Fee Structures**

Management fees for retirement funds fall into two ranges, 0.5–0.75% and 0.75–1%, with 0.9 and 1% the most common and the average rate being 0.90%. Management fees tend to be higher with more flexible solution-based funds while funds that focus more on steady yields have lower management fees (Fig. 6).

(5) **Investor Profiles**

Theoretically, retirement funds are targeted at individual investors looking to plan for their old age or with lower risk appetites. Looking at the profile of fund enrollees at the present, however, it can be seen that institutional investors make up a significant part of the investor base for these funds while individual investors are comparatively few.

Of the ten funds that have made public disclosures to date, as of the end of 2016, there are six funds where more than 50% of holdings are held by institutional investors, with the majority in the 80–90% range. These funds tend to be launched earlier and see fluctuating levels of institutional holdings, which were comparatively low in early 2015 and then rose rapidly by mid-2015 as institutional investors sought to reap the gains of the then-bull market. In addition, funds where more holdings are held by institutional investors also tend to fluctuate more in terms of fund size. When changes occur in the market environment or when bad news is received, similar actions by institutional investors at the same time can impact funds in the form of large-scale redemption.

There are four funds where less than 50% of fund holdings are held by institutional investors. They include two funds where nearly 100% of holdings are held by individual investors. This type of funds tends to have been launched relatively late. As the size of these funds grows, the possibility of participation by institutional investors will also increase. The Tianhong Ankang Retirement Fund is a rather special case here: it was launched earlier than the others in this group, but it still enjoys a fairly high proportion of individual investors perhaps due to its strengths in internet sales channels, despite fairly significant fluctuation in the proportion of institutional holdings (Fig. 7).

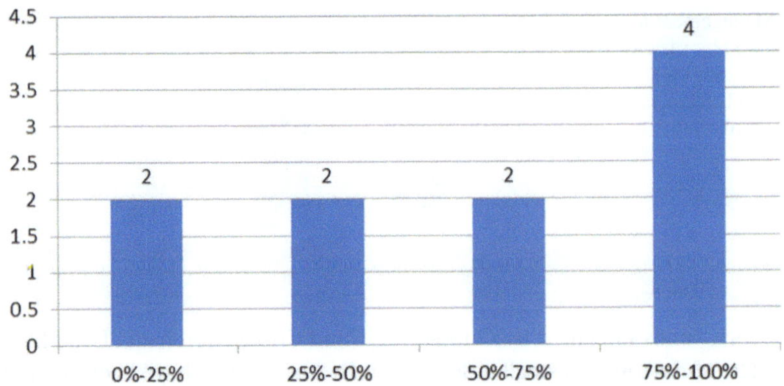

Fig. 7 Shares of retirement fund holdings held by institutional investors. NB: 1. *Source* Wind and various annual fund reports, correct as of Dec 2016; 2. Investor holdings ratio data for three funds unavailable

Table 2 TDFs in China's mutual fund market

Name of security	Date of establishment	Fund type	Offering size	Value of assets under management
Dacheng Wealth Management 2020	9/13/2006	Hybrid	11.13	25.74
HSBC Jintrust 2016	5/23/2006	Hybrid	29.22	2.50
HSBC Jintrust 2026	7/23/2008	Hybrid	3.35	0.81
ICBCCS Tianfu	10/31/2013	Bond	3.99	45.60
ICBCCS Tianyi	8/10/2011	Bond	5.21	19.27

Source Wind and the official web sites of the various fund management companies

2.2 *Target Date Funds (TDFs)*

HSBC Jintrust launched the first TDF in the industry on May 23, 2006. As of the time of writing, there are a total of five TDFs in China's mutual fund market, including three of the more traditional hybrid TDF product type (two by HSBC Jintrust and one by Dacheng Fund) and two more conservative bond-type funds, both managed by ICBCCS. As of March 3, 2017, the total value of assets under management in TDFs in China has reached RMB 9.39 billion. However, compared to overseas TDF markets, China's TDF market has developed rather slowly. At the same time, as funds of funds (FOFs) were introduced relatively late to date in China, there is no FOF-type TDF in domestic market (Table 2).

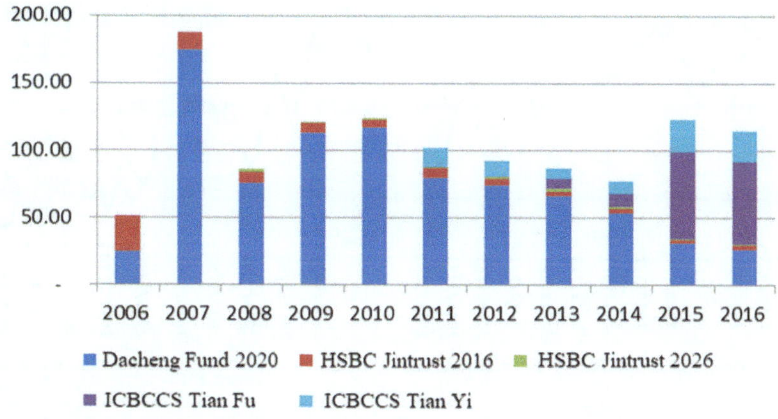

Fig. 8 Fund size of TDF products in China over the years

Historically, hybrid TDFs grew quickly in the infancy stage, mainly due to exuberant growth in the stock market in 2007. With the 2008 financial crisis and stock market crash, the size of hybrid TDFs shrank dramatically due to their previous position in equities and significant fund withdrawals by investors. Moreover, with the target dates of two hybrid TDFs approaching, they are becoming less compatible with investors' life-cycle needs, exerting an impact on fund size. The size of the bond-type TDFs launched in 2011 has on the other hand grown over the years mainly because returns for the more conservative TDF type were especially high in 2014 with a bullish bonds market, pushing the scale of assets under management to a new high as well. To date, the fund size of the two bond-type TDFs has exceeded that of the other three hybrid TDFs (Fig. 8).

(1) **Asset Allocation**

Asset allocation for the three hybrid TDFs over time has been consistent with the planned decline in the proportion of equities within total holdings. For the two bond-type TDFs, as the decline intervals are shorter at three and five years, asset allocation is a dynamic process during the operating process of the fund. Compared to hybrid TDFs, these funds are less aligned with the life-cycle characteristics of investors (Fig. 9).

In addition, over the course of the TDF operating period, asset allocation ratios have not fully shifted over time in accordance with the preset decline curve limits. For instance, during the operating period of Dacheng Wealth Management 2020 product, the proportion of equity-type assets hit bottom on four occasions, in 2007, 2008, 2013, and 2016, mainly due to market gyrations and portfolio adjustments. Equity holding proportions for the two products managed by HSBC Jintrust also declined significantly on multiple occasions. The two bond-type TDFs managed by ICBCCS have seen less drastic adjustments in their equity positions and fluctuations, due to the nature of the funds.

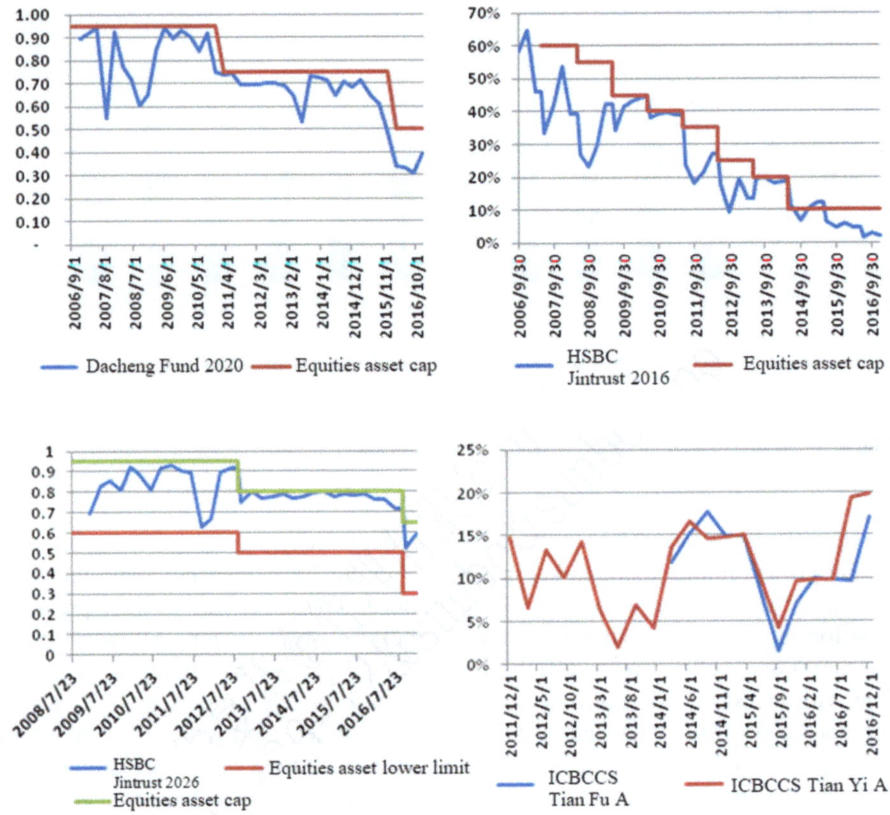

Fig. 9 Asset allocation in TDFs in China

(2) **Investment Yields**

For the three hybrid TDFs, as they started out with comparatively high levels of equity assets in their early days, their performance in this period was also more closely linked to the performance of the Shanghai Shenzhen CSI 300 Index (SHSZ300); thus seeing greater fluctuations in terms of returns. As the target date presses closer, fluctuations in hybrid TDF returns become smaller. At the same time, the correlation with the SHSZ300 also weakens. Although the preset equity position for bond-type TDFs is lower, the historical risk-return profile of these products has been even more similar to the SHSZ300. This is perhaps due to higher returns from automatic equity asset management and higher returns from bond assets in 2014 (Fig. 10; Table 3).

(3) **Fee Structures**

There is significant variance in fee rates across these five funds. The variance is the greatest among the three hybrid funds: the normal management fee rates for the hybrid fund managed by Dacheng fund and the HSBC Jintrust 2026 fund are 1.2 and

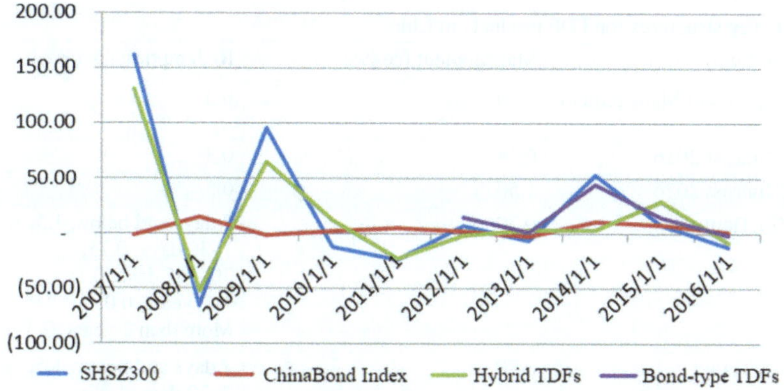

Fig. 10 Historic rates of return on TDF products in China. *Source* Wind

Table 3 Rates of return on TDF products in China

Name of fund	Date of establishment	Cumulative return (%)	Total annualized return (%)
Dacheng Wealth Management 2020	9/13/2006	146.56	8.92
HSBC Jintrust 2016	5/23/2006	172.01	9.65
HSBC Jintrust 2026	7/23/2008	111.52	9.00
ICBCCS Tianfu	10/31/2013	63.80	15.53
ICBCCS Tianyi	8/10/2011	101.60	13.22

Source Wind

1.5% respectively, while the fee for the HSBC Jintrust 2016 fund stands at a mere 0.38% (a rate lower than fees for hybrid funds and even lower than bond-type funds).

As for redemption fees, as TDFs are designed for the purposes of asset allocation and investment management for individual investors over his/her life cycle, the longer the investment period, the more likely that asset allocation can be performed in an optimal manner, and the more likely that a long-term risk premium can be obtained. However, the three hybrid TDFs do not induce investors to invest for the long term through their redemption fee rates. On the other hand, the two bond-type TDFs employ a tiered redemption fee model, that is, redemption within a short period will incur a higher punitive redemption rate while redemption following a longer period will incur a lower, or even zero, redemption fees. This way, investors are encouraged to invest for the long term (Table 4).

(4) **Investor Profiles**

From the perspective of investor profiles, with the three hybrid TDFs that were launched earlier, they are held mostly by individual investors with comparatively few holdings held by institutional investors. In the ten years since the Dacheng Wealth Management 2020 product was launched, institutional investors have always held

Table 4 Fee structures for TDF products in China

Name of fund	Management fee (%)	Redemption fee (%)
Dacheng Wealth Management 2020	1.20	0.3
HSBC Jintrust 2016	0.38	0.3
HSBC Jintrust 2026	1.50	0.5
ICBCCS Tianfu	0.70	7 days and below, 1.5; 7–30 days, 0.75; 30–365 days, 0.1; 1–2 years, 0.05; More than 2 years, 0
ICBCCS Tianyi	0.70	7 days and below, 1.5; 7–30 days, 1.25; 30–180 days, 1; 180–365 days, 0.8; 365–730 days, 0.6; 730–1460 days, 0.4; More than 1460 days, 0.2

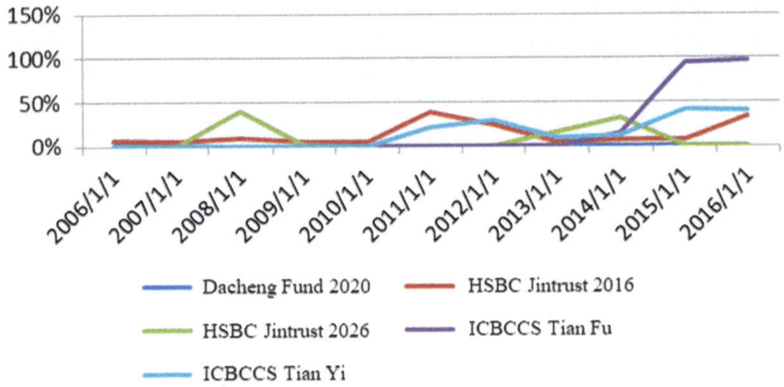

Fig. 11 TDF products in China broken down by investor types over time. *Source* Wind

less than 10% of total fund holdings, while the two funds managed by HSBC Jintrust holdings by institutional investors have never crossed the 40%-mark. On the other hand, institutional investors possess significantly higher levels of holdings in the two bond-type TDFs. In particular, with ICBCCS's Tianfu Fund institutional investors held nearly 90% of all holdings in 2015 and 2016 (Fig. 11).

2.3 Conclusion

(1) **Publicly Offering Funds with a Retirement Focus**

Overall, this category of funds is still in an early stage of development. First of all, the history of these funds has been relatively short and they have yet to be widely recognized by investors. The first retirement fund was launched in 2013, and by the end of 2016, only thirteen such funds with a total asset value of RMB 14.2 billion have been launched by nine fund managers. This is only 0.15% of total assets held in all publicly offered funds. Secondly: the retirement focus is not explicit with these funds, which are unable to actually meet the pension needs of the individual. Retirement funds should be more oriented towards individual investors. However, to date, certain funds have a heavy institutional bias and are thus unable to truly align themselves with the life-cycle needs and risk appetites of individual investors. Thirdly: there is a lack of diversity among these funds in terms of suitability for various risk appetite profiles. Although retirement funds are meant for investors' old age planning, due to the varying ages and risk appetites of investors today, more conservative CPPI/VPPI investment strategies have been adopted by most funds, leading to lower returns. On one hand, this is not in line with the positioning of supplementary pension system that requires funds to provide investors with higher returns over the long term, and on the other hand, these funds are also unable to meet the investment needs of those with higher risk appetites.

(2) **Target Date Funds (TDFs)**

Overall, among the existing few TDF products, product design has been based on overseas models in terms of product structure and asset allocation. However, when it comes to the actual design of the fund ratio curve and product period, etc., there are still significant differences between these funds and their overseas counterparts. Specifically:

1. Changes to the fund ratio occur more frequently. As the fund market in China took off fairly late and investors have not fully developed the habit of long-term investment, the first TDF in China—the HSBC Jintrust 2016—chose to structure the funding ratio curve over a period of ten years. That is, the fund opens with an equities position of 60% of total holdings, and then a downward adjustment will be made every year. By 2016, the equities position has been adjusted to 10%. The downward adjustment in equities holdings has also taken place yearly in the case of the two bond-type funds (Fig. 12).
2. Each product lasts a comparatively short period. Vanguard of the United States is the largest asset manager in the TDF market in terms of market share, and its flagship retirement TDF covers investors retiring from 2010 to 2060 at five-year intervals. As for China, insufficient coverage by TDFs can be seen at present. With the two products launched by HSBC Jintrust, the target dates are set at 2016 and 2026, while Dacheng Fund's product only sets 2020 as the target date.

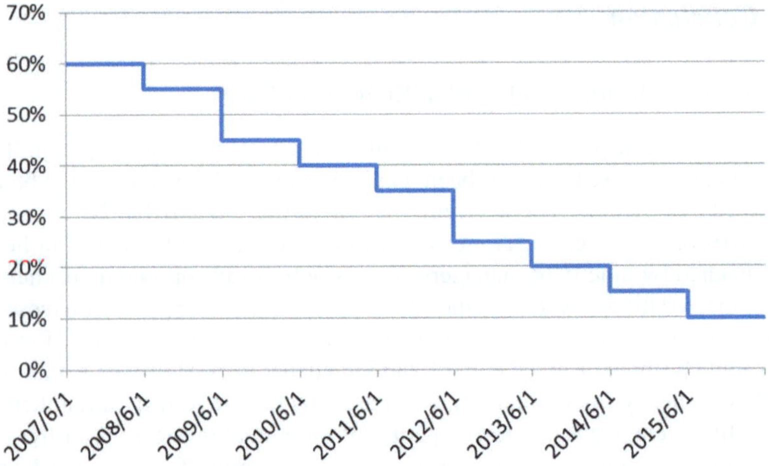

Fig. 12 Preset asset allocation levels for HSBC Jintrust 2016 fund. *Source* Data collated from HSBC Jintrust web site

3. With regard to the two bond-type TDFs, although the equities position has been reduced over time during the operating period, the fund still is not aligned with the life-cycle characteristics of investors fundamentally. Rather, asset allocation is being frequently shuffled within a short fund period, and its proportions, adjusted on a constant basis as well. To a certain extent, this has weakened the fund's ability to provide for investors' old age needs (Fig. 13).

3 Opportunities and Challenges for Retirement Funds in China

3.1 Opportunities

(1) **Vast Room for Market Growth of Pension Asset Management**

Chinese people have seen their wealth grow dramatically over the past three decades of sustained high-speed economic growth. According to a Credit Suisse report, in 2016, domestic household wealth in China totaled more than RMB 150 trillion, and according to data from the Boston Consulting Group, the Chinese wealth management market is predicted to have a compound growth rate at a yearly average of more than 15% between 2015 and 2020, and that by the year 2020, the total value of resident individual investable assets will be more than RMB 2 trillion.

On the other hand, China's population is also ageing at an increasing pace. According to the National Ageing Development and Pension System Building Plan during the 13th Five-Year Plan, by the year 2020, there will be around 255 million individu-

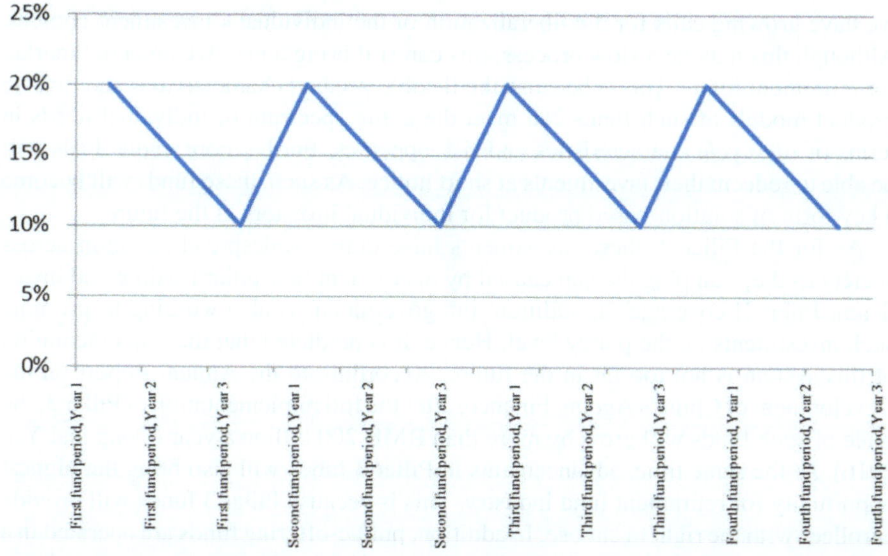

Fig. 13 Asset allocation ratio for ICBCCS's Tianfu fund. *Source* Data collated from ICBCCS web site

als (or 17.8% of the total population) aged more than sixty. The Office of the National Committee on Ageing has predicted that by the year 2030, the elderly population in China will exceed more than 350 million or around 25% of the total population. At the same time, the pension system in China needs further improvements since its pension payout levels are low, which in turn have given rise to the need for individuals to invest for retirement. Therefore, the continued accumulation of wealth among citizens as well as their growing needs for old age investment form a strong economic basis for the future development of the retirement fund industry.

(2) **Pillar II and Pillar III Provide Vast Room for Development of the Retirement Fund Industry**

In Pillar II occupational pensions, the employer acts as a trustee and provides enrollees with a wide range of options of investment products so as to encourage them to accumulate pensions through contributions and self-investment. Such system emphasizes on the equality of individual ownership and individual responsibility for retirement funding. Within the existing institutional framework in China, there are currently no stipulations on the individual right to choose and to make decisions. In practice, within a single enterprise, employees of all ages and varying risk appetites receive the same level of returns. On one hand, such an approach has led to comparatively conservative fund operations that tended towards short term investment, which may harm market competition for fund operations; and on the other hand, it has also made competition between different fund types more difficult as well as undermined individual's right to choose the funds that is right for his/her specific needs. Thus, we have growing calls for the liberalization of the individual's investment choices. Although this may be a slow process, this can still bring a massive potential market for retirement funds. This is because the flexible product characteristics and diverse product models of such funds can meet the entire spectrum of individual needs in terms of life-cycle characteristics and risk appetites. Furthermore, individuals will be able to redeem their investments at short notice. As such, these funds will become a key form of solution-based product for individual investors in the future.

As for the Pillar 3, these investments have drawn widespread attention across society as they can plug the gap caused by insufficient first-pillar funding and insufficient Pillar II coverage. In addition, the government is also working to promote such investments on the policy level. Hence, it is predicted that the implementation of this system is not too far in the future. According to the Annual Report on the Development of China's Ageing Finance, after the full implementation of Pillar 3, the scale of such funds will grow by more than RMB 200 billion a year (Dong and Yao 2016). At the same time, advancements in Pillar 3 funds will also bring the biggest opportunity for retirement fund industry. This is because Pillar 3 funds will provide enrollees with the right to choose. In addition, public-offering funds are operated in a transparent manner, offer flexible redemption options, and have great product diversity, making them a key component in the development of Pillar 3 pension system. These funds will become the main choice for individual old age planning over time: for instance, mutual funds make up almost 50% of all individual retirement account (IRA) plans (i.e., Pillar 3 plans) in the United States.

(3) **Diverse Array of Publicly Offered Funds Lays the Foundation; the Launching of FOFs Creates More Opportunities**

The Chinese publicly offered fund market has been in operation for nearly twenty years. By the end of 2016, there are more than three thousand such funds on the market with the total value of assets under management at RMB 9.18 trillion. They enjoy a diverse array of categories, including stock funds, bond funds, hybrid funds, currency funds, and QDII funds. The fund industry is capable of satisfying the old age investment needs of different types of investors in accordance with the market characteristics, investor risk appetites, and investor life-cycle characteristics of the Chinese capital market.

Furthermore, the introduction of funds of funds (FOFs) has also provided a great opportunity for retirement fund industry. The objective of retirement funds is to enhance the value of pensions through effective asset allocation over the long term in alignment with specific investor needs and in response to market changes. The introduction of FOFs not only allows retirement funds to share the best investment research and management resources, but also provides the basis for further development of products that are aligned with investors' long-term financial needs, such as TDFs and target risk funds (TRFs). Moreover, FOF-type retirement funds can significantly mitigate return fluctuations, an important consideration in pension planning. Meanwhile, such funds can also provide investors with more targeted investment choices that allow for better pension planning by optimizing asset allocation choices (Fig. 14).

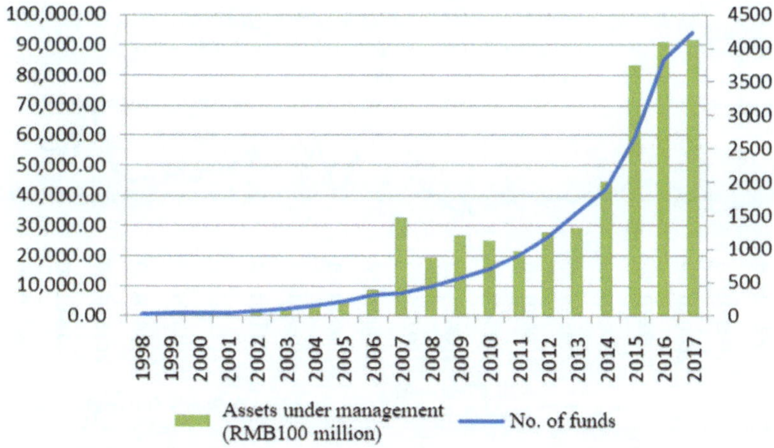

Fig. 14 No. of products and value of assets managed within the fund industry. *Source* Wind

Table 5 The stock index and returns on equity funds

Time interval	Shanghai composite index Average annualized rate of return (%)	Equity funds across the whole market Average annualized rate of return (%)	Inflation rate (%)
Last one year	−12.31	−11.39	2.00
Last 3 years	16.66	21.59	1.80
Last 5 years	9.28	11.89	2.12
Last 10 years	12.17	18.54	2.93
Last 20 years	14.88	22.04	1.88

NB: 1. Data from Wind;
2. The returns for equity funds across the market is for a period that is actually shorter than twenty years. The annualized return rate for equity funds in the last twenty years is the average annualized rate of return for period since equity funds emerged in the market

(4) **Capital Market Brings Steady Returns Over the Long Term**

The management of publicly offered funds mainly focuses on stocks and bonds in the secondary market. Traditionally, equity investment in the secondary market bears higher risks and is thus not suitable for pension investments. However, from the long-term perspective, China's stock market is capable of bring relatively stable returns. Retirement funds are different from short-term funds in that they have a long temporal view and can bear risk better over the short term. That is, with these funds, the investor is able to allocate long-term assets through long-term investment in order to gain long-term risk premiums commensurate with the characteristics of long-term capital (Table 5).

Statistics show that although in the last year, returns on China's stock market and equity funds across the market have been negative, but in the long run, the average

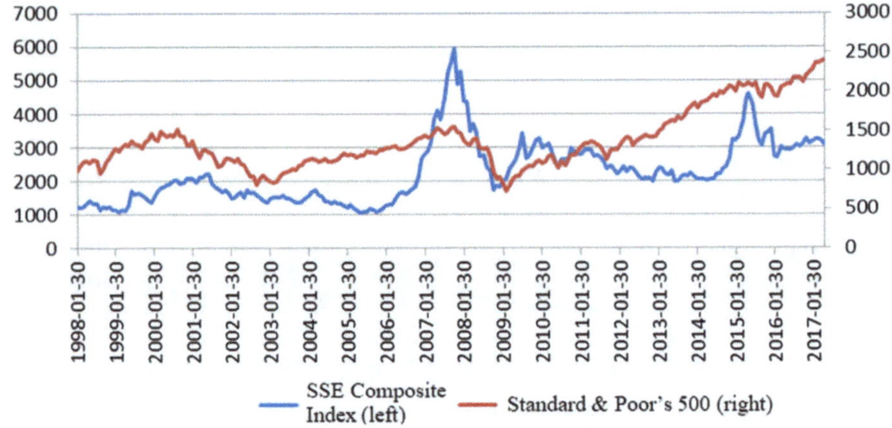

Fig. 15 Historic trends for Chinese and American stock markets

annualized rate of return in China's stock market is as high as 14.88%. Since the establishment of open-to-the-public equity funds, the average annualized rate of return on these funds across the market is 22.04%. Thus, although fluctuations in China's capital market can be dramatic in the short term, it is capable of bringing stable returns to investors over the long run. Furthermore, retirement-focused funds are a classic form of long-term investment that allows investors to win a long-term risk premium by means of trading time for space.

3.2 *Challenges*

(1) **The Issue of Long Bear-Market Periods and Short Bull-Market Periods**

In contrast to the United States stock market where bull markets last a long time and bear markets, a shorter time, in China, the situation is just the opposite. From the illustration, it can be seen that in the last twenty years, the Standard and Poor's 500 index has maintained steady increases over the long term and declines in the short term. The situation is the exact opposite with the Chinese stock market: to take the Shanghai Composite Index as an example, the stock index always shows a steady decline over the long term, with swift growth occurring in short spurts and then reversing themselves in a similarly quick fashion (Fig. 15).

It is also indicated that there are significant differences in the month-to-month fluctuations in the two stock markets, with fluctuations (both increases and decreases) significantly higher in the Chinese market compared to the American market (Fig. 16).

Due to the aforementioned characteristics of China's stock market, although good returns are still possible over the long term. The money-making potential of short-term investments is not significant. This is an obstacle to the further development of

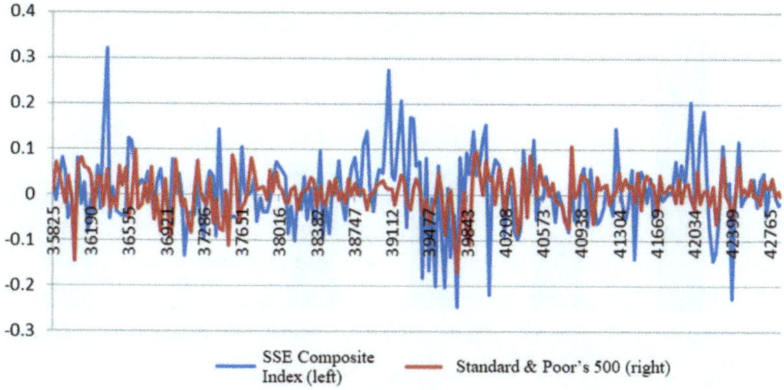

Fig. 16 Returns on key indices in Chinese and American markets by month

retirement fund products to a certain extent. Currently in China, individual investors have yet to acquire the concept or habit of long-term investment, and regard the short-term performance of the product as a key consideration while making investments. Should retirement-focused funds launched at a bad timing and suffered losses in the early days of their operations, it may lead to a loss of investor confidence that will in turn trigger early redemption and the inability to realize long-term investment. Such situations may places even more pressure on the fund issuer, i.e., the investment manager, to perform even better in the area of investment research.

(2) **Investment Consultancy Lags Behind**

The system of investment consultancy in China has yet to be fully developed compared to the U.S. and Europe. Firstly, investors have not developed a mature attitude towards investment and place low confidence on wealth management. Moreover, with fluctuations in the capital market turn more volatile, it is quite difficult to fully understand about asset management products with no guarantee on capitals (as exemplified by funds). Secondly, as investors become increasingly professional and show greater investment needs, they will demand for a more diverse array of products—including funds, futures, commodities, and overseas assets—, and thus also have higher requirements for investment consultants. Thirdly, under the agent model, funds are traded on commission. As such, investment consultants tended to recommend to investors easy-to-sell products with higher commission rates rather than help them conduct asset allocation and investment in accordance with his or her actual needs.

Although the fund industry has been growing for almost two decades and boasts over two hundred million investors, much of the investment is still in currency and bond funds. The number of investors experienced in investing in a diversified array of instruments is still very small. Given that retirement funds come in many forms and also offer products accustomed to various risk appetites, it is especially important that the industry is equipped with professional investment consultants who are able to perform deep needs analysis and come up with the right plan so that investors will

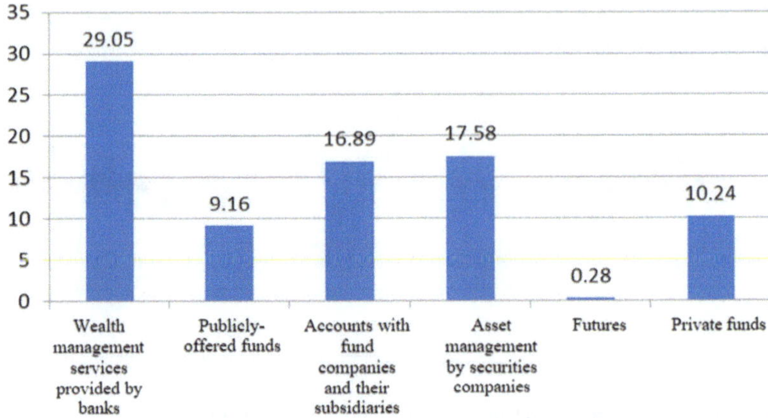

Fig. 17 Asset management by type in the capital market. *Sources* Asset Management Association of China, Banking Industry Wealth Management Registry Center

be able to allocate their assets in the optimal manner and invest wisely in accordance with their pension needs. Therefore, the slow development of investment consultancy system and the developmental issues that have emerged are another obstacle to the development of the retirement fund industry.

(3) **Fierce Competition from Other Financial Products**

Currently in China's asset management market, the total value of assets management is RMB 83.2 trillion, with the top three choices being wealth management services offered by banks, asset management services by securities companies, and dedicated asset management services by fund managers. Individual investors tend to invest with banks and publicly offered funds for their investment needs (Fig. 17).

Wealth management services provided by banks are the primary avenue of investment for Chinese residents. Data in the Annual Report on the China Banking Industry Wealth Management (2016) shows that the industry had launched around 200,000 wealth management products with around RMB 168 trillion raised altogether in 2016. By the end of that year, there are 74,200 products offered by 497 banking institutions, with the total remaining value of RMB 29.05 trillion in operation on the market. The majority of newly-launched products were low-risk products; bonds, bank deposits, and the money market instruments were the main solution-based products.

Statistics from the CIRC demonstrates that by the end of 2016, the total value of retirement funds and other assets under management by insurance companies had reached[1] RMB 377.9 billion. Although the current scale of assets under management

[1]"Other asset under management": refers to asset management services provided by insurance institutions apart from enterprise annuity and old age security services. Examples include third-party asset management (including policy/non-commercial business) and pension products allocated by external investment managers or external trustees. Data from the CIRC cannot be separated from data for old age security services at this point in time.

is still modest, retirement assurance products have been endowed with the characteristics of wealth management services by banks thanks to low entry thresholds and broad scope of investment, etc., as a result of system design. At the same time, these products are superior to wealth management products offered by banks in terms of entry thresholds and scope of investment. As such, these products have been popular with the market and have become a strong competitor to retirement funds.

(4) **The Idea of Fund Investment for Retirement Has Yet to Be Developed**

The United States' pension system is mainly based on Pillar II and Pillar 3 pension. Here, market-oriented investment helps to enhance pension returns for citizens. Publicly offered funds make up for 50% of assets invested in Pillar II and Pillar 3 pension assets. However, compared with the United States, China has not developed the idea of funding one's retirement through investment and the right business ecology.

First off, due to lower risk appetites, Chinese investors tend to invest in financial products with lower levels of risk such as bank deposits and wealth management products. According to an annual report from the Asset Management Association of China (AMAC), in 2015, bank deposits of every Chinese household totaled RMB 55.19 trillion, accounting for 63.7% of its total investment; the value of stocks directly held by individuals was RMB 16.21 trillion while the value of wealth-management holdings directly held by individuals was RMB 23.5 trillion. However, the total value of individual holdings in publicly offered funds was RMB 3.2 trillion or only 3.7% of the total. In addition, according to AMAC, in the year 2015, there were over 180 million active publicly offered fund investor accounts with a total of RMB 840 million worth of assets under management. Growth in this area mainly comes from currency market funds with a share of over 54% of all assets in publicly offered funds (Fig. 18).

Overall, whether from the perspective of resident investment in general or in terms of how funds have been invested, individual investors in China tend to be conservative and do not have adequate knowledge of the role that funds play in pension planning. The lack of an understanding on how funds can help one in providing for themselves after retirement will make it more difficult for a retirement fund ecology to develop, leaving the market with a limited choice of investment mainly in low-risk products such as insurance and wealth management products. For the long term, personal pensions cannot achieve full market-oriented operation that brings about will not higher yields and thus fails to play their role as a supplementary "pillar".

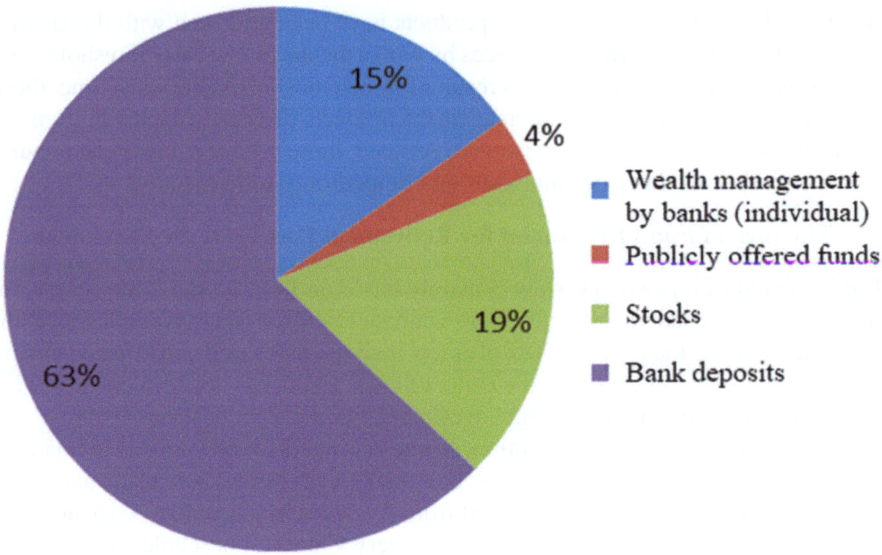

Fig. 18 Key areas of financial investment for Chinese households. *Source* Annual Report on China Securities Investment Fund Industry (2015)

4 Recommendations for the Future Development of Retirement-Focused Funds in China

4.1 Positioning

Based on China's current situation, it is recommended that the retirement funds cover two key areas: to prepare for a broadening of Pillar II and Pillar 3 pension, and to meet citizens' independent pension planning needs.

First, with the boost from preferential tax policies, the primary objective for retirement products is to make full preparations for the advent of Pillar 3 personal pension and the improvements on Pillar II enterprise annuities. Second, as a supplementary pillar to China's pension system, Pillar III must be able to resist inflation, and more importantly, increase asset accumulative value to enhance old age security abilities of each individual through optimal asset allocation. Although currently Pillar 3 plans have yet to be tabled and are clouded with some uncertainties in system design, based on the developmental nature of such plans and overseas experience, we can say that retirement plans can be tailored to meet the specific needs of individual investors and allow for flexibility in asset allocation given the diversity of fund types available, flexibility of product operations, and the higher levels of returns over the long term from such funds. At the same time, managers of the retirement funds should be prepared to liberalize individual investors' choice within the Pillar II and allow them to choose the right allocation.

Second, with ever-strengthening financial supervision, managers of publicly offered funds should work actively to harness the strengths of their products and explore the independent pension management needs of the population. As supervision over wealth management services offered by the banking sector intensifies, banks may launch more products without capital guarantee, which helps change the current situation where banks pay out guaranteed returns only, forming the main trend for bank financing. Under such circumstances, publicly offered funds will be able to enjoy more opportunities. Since its establishment in 1998, the fund industry has accrued a fair bit of experience and first-mover advantage in the area of floating-income product management. Apart from that, the industry also boasts professional investment research that offers individual investors with a diverse array of customized and targeted investment solutions, which will comprehensively uncover investors' old age demands and match their individual risk appetites. By doing so, the industry will be able to become even better at preserving and increasing asset values and controlling risks.

4.2 Product Models

As stated above, certain countries have adopted the dedicated product model. What should be noted here is that "dedicated" is in reference to the various types of supplementary pensions available. This is because both Pillar II occupational pensions and Pillar 3 personal pensions generally adopt the accumulation model and the investment period can last for decades. Objectively speaking, there exists the need for asset preservation and value increasing through market investment. On the other hand, supplementary pensions are generally plans introduced with the guidance of specific government policies to encourage citizens to participate in these plans. Certain enrollees, however, may not be equipped with the basis and capabilities for independent investment perhaps due to the state of development of the capital market and/or their limited knowledge of financial investment. Under such circumstances, certain countries have introduced the dedicated product model that on one hand makes investment easier for citizens, and on the other hand, better serve their needs in terms of asset value preservation and enhancement by clarifying requirements for these products. As for citizen's independent pension investment (excluding pension assets), the product model does not exist in that each individual investor can choose freely whether to invest in retirement funds or other fund products in accordance with his or her needs.

Although enrollees of China's Pillar II occupational pensions have yet to be able to fully exercise the right of investment choice, and the Pillar 3 personal tax-deferred pension plans have yet to be implemented, it is critical for the industry to plan ahead and establish their policies as soon as possible.

Overall, China should adopt the dedicated product model approach. In fact, in May 2017, the CSRC sought public feedbacks on its Trial Guidelines for Open-to-the-Public Securities Investment Funds with a Pension Planning Orientation, which has laid the policy foundation for such a model to a certain extent. In general, there appear to be three key reasons:

First, China's capital market is a relative latecomer that is less mature. On the other hand, the economy has shifted into a "new normal", and as economic growth slows, fluctuations in the capital market have grown. As such, the general population may be exposed to greater risks to their assets should the general product model be adopted. Second, for a long time, China's general population has favored wealth management tools that yield a steady income, such as bank deposits, as their main investment tool. With a limited understanding of professional finance knowledge and fund investment, adopting the dedicated product model can help mitigate poor decision-makings. Third, from the aspect of industry development, the number of fund management companies in China is on the rise. However, they differ in terms of understanding retirement funds and applying investment strategies, even as product types proliferate. Furthermore, investors have not been sufficiently educated and the system of investment consultancy has yet to be well developed. Developing a dedicated product model can thus help to mitigate the issues caused by information asymmetry and the difficulty in making choices in an environment where individual investment competencies are lacking and the number of product types on the market continues to grow.

4.3 Product Types

There are two approaches to choose a retirement fund. The first is to establish a fund product called a solution-based product that is endowed with clear pension management characteristics and where assets are allocated by the fund manager, covering mainly on TDFs and TRFs. The second approach targets fund products with a weaker pension management focus but have a stronger tool orientation, which means the participant is responsible for asset allocation by choosing various funds to allocate his/her investments and provide for old age. These can be known as instrument-based products. More details on how these two products are designed below:

(1) **Solution-Based Products**

solution-based products are designed to provide investors with a diverse array of professional investment portfolios through only a single investment method to meet their old age investment needs. Fundamentally, these are a kind of "one-stop" old age investment solutions. In international communities, TDFs are increasingly favored for old age investment purposes. They have been recognized as qualified default investment alternative (QDIAs) by the Pillar II 401(k) plan scheme in the United States and the Pillar II workplace pension scheme in the United Kingdom. In Chile, TDFs are a default selection item for individual retirement accounts.

Overall, the FOF approach is taken by most TDF and TRF products. In 2016, China released the *Guidelines for the Operation of Publicly Offered Securities Investment*

Funds No. 2: Guidelines for Funds of Funds, laying the policy foundation for TDFs and TRFs. What we need to underline here is that the greatest strengths of TDFs include the flexibility to match the varying asset allocation preferences of enrollees at different life stages and the possibility of investing a greater proportion of funds into equities-type assets at the early stages in order to harness the long-term characteristic of retirement funds for higher returns. This is why stocks make up a higher proportion of TDF assets in the United States (generally more than 80% of all assets, with an average level of around 90%). As for China, although in the short term, fluctuations in the capital market can be severe, in the long-term, returns are fairly good. Thus, fund managers should be allowed to set their opening equities position at 80% of all assets, providing fund management institutions with more flexibility.

(2) **Instrument-Based Products**

Instrument-based products are not designed for old age investment purposes per se and are mainly used as components in a personal retirement-planning portfolio. We should note here that as China's investment consultancy industry is still not very mature and investment/professional knowledge is still lacking among most of the population, there is a need to make the appropriate arrangements for investors so that investment risks can be brought under control and thus better meet the objectives of old age investment. In this respect, we can learn from the design of Chile's individual retirement account system, where proportion caps on equity-type assets are based on the age of the participant. That is, the older the participant and the closer he or she is to retirement, the lower the cap on equity positions. This aligns the overall investment with the individual's ability to bear risk.

The specifics of the plan can be found in the table below. On one hand, instrument-based products have been categorized into five tiers based on the proportion of equities within total assets and the level of risk involved. At the same time, investors are divided into four groups by age: under forty years old, forty to fifty years old, fifty to sixty years old, and older than sixty years old. Investors aged under forty are allowed to invest in all retirement funds, while those aged forty to fifty are not allowed to invest in products classified as high-risk products. Investors aged fifty to sixty are only allowed to invest in products with moderate-to-low levels of risk, while those aged above sixty are only allowed to invest in low-risk products (Table 6).

4.4 *Scope of Investment*

It can be seen from overseas countries that there are fewer restrictions on supplementary pensions compared to public pensions and the scope of investment is also broader: apart from traditional assets like stocks and bonds, "other assets" have also been gaining popularity over time. As of late 2015, in the Organisation for Economic Co-operation and Development (OECD) nations, 15.93% of all supplementary investments for old age purposes were made in the "other assets" category,

Table 6 Equities proportion caps in ordinary retirement funds and availability to investors

Risk rating	Fund type	Equities cap (%)	Equities lower limit (%)	Under 40 years old	40–50 years old	50–60 years old	More than 60 years old
High-risk	Stock funds	95	80	Available	Not available	Not available	Not available
Higher risk	Mixed, with tilt towards stocks	80	50	Available	Available	Not available	Not available
Mid-level risk	Mixed, with tilt towards bonds	50	20	Available	Available	Available	Not available
Lower risk	Bond funds	20	10	Available	Available	Available	Available
Low-risk	Pure bond-based fund	0	0	Available	Available	Available	Available

including loans, real estate, insurance policies, hedge funds, private equity, structured products, and alternative public offerings.

Domestically, asset management products that bear similarities to retirement funds include old age security products from the insurance industry and pension products supervised by the Ministry of Human Resources and Social Security. The similarity between the two is that both non-standard assets such as trusts and infrastructural debt programs are included into the scope of investment. On one hand, diversified investment can help to diffuse risks, and on the other hand, the pricing and cost attributes of non-standard assets help to reduce fluctuations in product net value.

Apart from that, if we look at the market environment for retirement funds, it is reflected that Pillar II and Pillar 3 of the national pension system or retirement savings of the people both face competition from the aforementioned products. If the corresponding products are only to be launched for publicly offered funds, they will not attract individual investors. Based on the experiences of other countries, China can expand the scope of retirement-focus products in a targeted manner and at an appropriate pace while considering factors such as the standards, the scale, and the long-term nature of these funds. Firstly, it is advisable to permit a certain ratio of assets be invested in the Hong Kong and overseas markets within the existing scope of publicly offered funds. Currently, capitals in National Social Security Fund accounts and insurance funds may be invested overseas, and the results have been pleasing. Secondly, we can, based on the existing practice with retirement fund products and retirement assurance products, invest a certain proportion of funds on "other assets" that are comparatively more mature (such as trusts and gold) and are within a defined acceptable risk range. Thirdly, we can accelerate the introduction of real estate investment trusts (REITs) and include this instrument in the investment scope. In fact, following the enactment of the Pension Protection Act in the United States in 2006, among the thirty-three TDFs classified as QDIAs, more than 70% of investment portfolios were allocated based on REITs. Fourthly, we should consider introducing private-public partnerships (PPP) into the scope of investment. Currently, policymakers are working hard to promote the asset securitization of PPP projects, and the listing and transfer of PPP-based asset-backed security (ABS) products have already occurred on both the Shanghai and Shenzhen exchanges. In general, PPP projects have a long investment life cycle and steady returns. Therefore, they are better suited for long-term old age investment purposes. Fifthly, we should consider including assets listed on the National Equities Exchange and Quotations (NEEQ) in the scope of investment. Although trade on NEEQ is not very active and lacks of liquidity, for the long term, there is a fair bit of room for growth in this area. Further, given the long-term nature of old age investment, there is comparatively little need for liquidity. Therefore, a certain proportion of funds can be invested in NEEQ assets as a means of further diversifying assets and diffusing risks.

4.5 Supporting Measures

The First One is to Promote the Development of Investment Consultancy Industry. According to the *Report on the Individual Fund Investors Survey (2015)* by the CSRC, the top two information that individual investors wish to learn about old age investment and its related products. On one hand, professional investment consultants can work to uncover investors' needs and outline the right investment plan, thereby formulating optimal asset allocation and reasonable investment. On the other hand, they can also aid in mitigating information asymmetry between investors and investment managers. Thus, vigorous efforts to develop the third-party investment consultancy industry should be promoted to develop retirement fund products.

The Second Measure Is to Launch Targeted Products to Encourage Long-Term Holdings. Before retirement funds are officially incorporated as a method of investment of Pillar 3 personal pensions and as part of the scope of investment for Pillar II occupational pensions, they were targeted at individual investors seeking to save up for retirement. At that time, they were directly competing with wealth management tools offered by banks. Thus, on one hand, it is our recommendation that fund managers review the fee structures of retirement funds overseas (generally in the range of 0.5–07%) and set lower management fees in order to encourage investor participation. In the meantime, they should also adopt a tiered fee model where management fees decrease as the holding period grows longer, surrendering part of the profits to investors to instill more vitality to such funds. At the same time, for solution-based products like TDFs, full product benefits can only be realized with long-term operations. Thus, one can consider closing the fund for a certain period so that no one can redeem it back.

The Third One Is to Establish Professional Standards for Fund Managers and Investment Managers. Retirement funds are designed for the steady appreciation of investor monies for old age investment purposes. As such, significant public attention is paid to these funds for them to propel the finance for old age care. As a result, standards should be more stringent than even for publicly offered funds to push retirement funds forward. On one hand, fund companies should be required to comply with certain demands, such as a minimum level of assets under management, a diverse product line, and stable company operations, etc. On the other hand, minimum entry requirements for investment managers seeking to manage retirement funds should be adopted, such as a certain degree of investment management experience with publicly offered term funds, the National Security Fund, and enterprise annuities plans, etc. Another possible rule would be that investment managers may not be replaced except under extraordinary circumstances, and should such replacements are required, sales of the fund must be halted in the meantime.

References

Dong, K., Yao, Y. (2016). *Annual report on the development of finance for old age care in China*. Beijing: Social Sciences Academic Press (China).

Zheng, B., Li, Y. (2012). *Lessons from the Australia's 20-Year-Long reform of its superannuity system and experience in countering Crises. Comparing economic and social systems.*

Asset Management Association of China. (2015). 2015 Annual report on China Securities Investment Fund Industry. Asset Management Association of China web site. http://www.amac.org.cn/.

Bo Sun holds a Ph.D. in management science and is a postdoctoral fellow of finance. He is also a invited member of the China Aging Finance Forum. Sun conducts research on financing old age care as a member of the Pension Management Department of China Asset Management. The opinions contained in this article are solely reflections of the writers and do not in any way represent the views of China Asset Management.

Chapter 11
Retirement Communities: Continuing Exploration to Meet Growing Social Demand

Liying Feng

Abstract As China's elderly population continues to grow rapidly, so do needs for elderly care services. The central government has introduce a number of policy measures designed to boost development the service industry, of course retirement community forms an integral part. In this chapter, we first examine concepts related to retirement community, then review the history of retirement communities in China, the needs for such communities, and the current policy environment. We also offer an analysis of the state of development of retirement communities in the year 2016 as well as issues facing the industry and development trends. Finally, we look at how finance can support the development of retirement communities in China.

Keywords Retirement community · Development model · Financial services

China's population is aging rapidly and the size of the elderly population is growing dramatically. At the same, due to the effects of the one-child policy, households are unable to support the elderly the way traditional households did. Retirement communities can provide the elderly with a number of retirement-related products and services and meet their retirement needs, rendering a period of rapid development for the industry.

1 Introduction to Retirement Community

1.1 The Concept of the Retirement Community

In academic a number of definitions for "retirement community" are in use. According to Liu (2012), head of the National Development and Reform Commission Institute of Investment, "retirement community" refers to a community which occupies a fairly large area featuring senior housing (apartments), matching public services and

---

L. Feng (✉)
CCB Pension Management Co., Ltd., Beijing, China

K. Dong and Y. Yao (eds.), *Annual Report on Financing Old Age Care in China (2017)*, https://doi.org/10.1007/978-981-13-0968-7_11

facilities and a fairly complete system of social services to provide elderly residents with the day-to-day care as well as mental and emotional support. According to Ji and Liu (2016), head of the Research Center for Social Security of National Small Towns, a retirement community is a community that is built specifically to serve the elderly and is in fact suited for that very purpose. Any such community must be equipped with dwelling and matching public facilities suitable to meet the psychological and physical needs of the elderly, and a system for providing professional products and services tailored for those in retirement. In this chapter, we draw from the above and use as working definition of retirement community one that is: (a) designed to satisfy the physical and psychological needs of residents; (b) equipped with various public service facilities as well as a system of services that are appropriate for elderly residents; and (c) capable of providing elderly residents with a myriad of services including day-to-day nursing and care, rehabilitation and medical services, health management services, and leisure and entertainment services. The retirement community should ensure that elderly residents receive day-to-day care and have their quality-of-life and mental/emotional needs adequately met.

1.2 Types of Retirement Communities

In China, retirement communities are still in development. However, we already have developed the preliminary outlines of what a complex, well-rounded retirement community might look like. Retirement communities can be categorized into two types based on the length of stay: day-to-day communities and "migratory-bird" communities. Functionally speaking, they can also be divided into ordinary residential communities (already in existence), the new-type integrated communities, nursing homes, continuing-care retirement communities (CCRCs), and holiday resorts for retirees, the last of which belongs to what we call a "migratory-bird" retirement community. In this article, we will expound on various types of retirement communities from the functional perspective.

The ordinary residential communities that are already in existence are residential communities remodeled by real estate companies, with basic facilities upgraded, and services appropriate for the elderly added. These communities provide elderly residents with services such as food and beverage, cultural entertainment, housekeeping, and healthcare services, meeting the day-to-day needs of residents as well as the needs of the aging population in general.

The new-type integrated communities are "elder-friendly properties" where elderly residents live together with younger residents in the same community. The majority of such communities, which come together with a number of facilities offering a diversity of services—including activity centers for the elderly, rehabilitation centers and healthcare centers—are built around the city. Much attention is paid to shape a sense of community within the area. In addition, integrated communities allow elderly residents to spend more time with their children, who can also care for their parents more easily. Moreover, separate living arrangements can also help to reduce conflicts due to differences in living habits.

Nursing homes mainly care for elderly residents with greater needs, such as those of an advanced age, those who are incapacitated or semi-incapacitated, and those who living with dementia. As these residents require more nursing care, nursing homes are also equipped with more specialized nursing facilities and equipment. They can generally be found within cities due to easier access to various healthcare resources.

Continuing-care retirement communities (CCRCs) are a kind of modern integrated retirement community that originated in the United States. These communities, mostly private, provide services tailored to elderly residents in various age groups. Customized facilities and services cater to residents' self-care, nursing and healthcare needs of the residents, while other age-appropriate on-site activities provide residents with outlets for self-actualization.

Holiday resorts catering to retirees are largely located in tourism hot spots with impressive scenery and pleasant climates. Fundamentally, these communities provide holiday services with a specific orientation towards the needs of older customers who are still healthy and active. These communities meet elderly residents' need for quality of life through the integration of elderly-friendly facilities and services designed for healthy living and regular rehabilitation, etc.

2 An Analysis of the Need for Retirement Communities in Society

As the Chinese population continues to age at an ever-quicker pace, the population of the elderly keeps growing as well, driving the rapid development of consumption needs too, especially needs for retirement communities.

2.1 Need for Retirement Communities Caused by Population Aging and Changes in Household Structure

By the end of 2016, there are 231 million people in China aged sixty and above (16.7% of the total population), and 150 million persons aged sixty-five and above (10.8% of the population).[1] The United Nations forecasts that the proportion of the elderly within the general population will continue to grow in China, and that by the year 2060, the population of those aged sixty-five and above will peak at around 420 million,[2] meaning China is about to enter a period of rapid aging (Fig. 1).

At the same time, as the standard of living and levels of healthcare continue to improve, average life span in China is also becoming longer. Data from the sixth

[1]Source: National Bureau of Statistics data.

[2]Statistics from the United Nations: https://esa.un.org/unpd/wpp/.

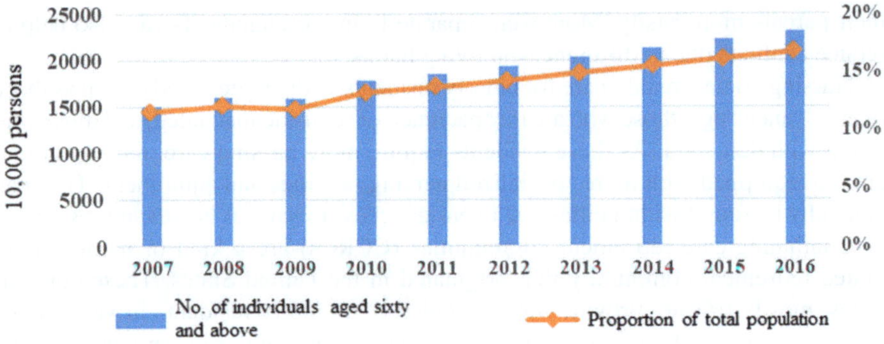

Fig. 1 Absolute and relative size of China's elderly population, 2007–2016. *Source* Web site of the National Bureau of Statistics

national census show that the average life expectancy for Chinese citizens in 2010 was 74.9 years. The number is projected to rise to 79.0 by the year 2030.[3] This means more elderly will need more diverse kinds of support for longer. On the other hand, adaptation to the one-child policy means that Chinese households have become smaller and less capable of supporting elderly family members. Typically, it falls on two working-age adults to provide for four dependent elders and one dependent child, which can be a significant. This has also led to a rise in the proportion of "empty nesters" and elderly people living alone. Intergenerational alienation has also made the traditional model of elder support in the home even more challenging. Under such circumstances, there is an urgent need to develop retirement communities to plug the gap that has resulted households' diminishing capacity for elder support.

2.2 *Income Growth and Changing Attitudes Aiding Diverse Development*

Currently, the group of people that can be considered as "the elderly" are the first to be affected by, and to benefit from, the reforms of China's economic system. Individuals in this age group, who are currently the key source of demand for retirement community facilities and services, have accumulated a certain amount of wealth and are thus capable of paying for such services and facilities. In particular, in tier-one cities like Beijing and Shanghai where the proportion of the elderly population is the highest and where there is a comparatively high concentration of high-income individuals, the need for high-end retirement community has emerged and continues to grow. This will promote retirement communities to transfer into a market with huge purchasing power.

[3]Source: The Healthy China 2030 Plan released by the Communist Party of China Central Committee and State Council in October 2016.

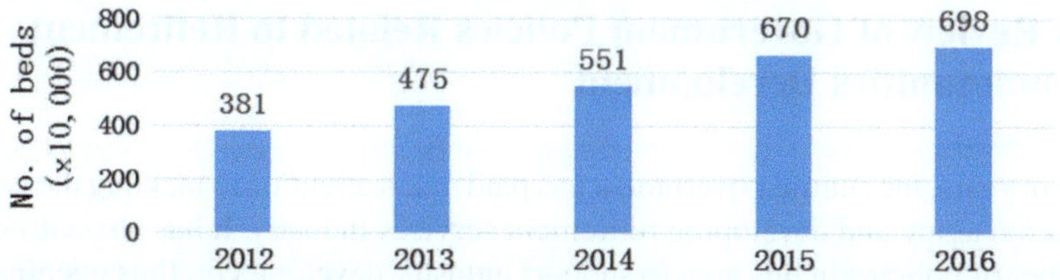

Fig. 2 No. of beds in retirement facilities in China, 2012–2016. *Source* http://www.mca.gov.cn

At the same time, a growing number of younger aged people generally enjoy higher levels of income and education, and demand more and better hardware in retirement residences as well as its supporting facilities. Meanwhile, they also attach great importance to services such as housekeeping, healthcare, healthy living, and entertainment. On the other hand, in modern households, adult children are also more receptive of the idea of having their parents live in retirement facilities where there is more professional care and means for emotional/mental fulfillment. This has driven consumer demands among the elderly for professional retirement community services. It has been forecasted that the elderly market in China will be worth some RMB 900 million by the year 2020 and around RMB 1.06 trillion in the year 2050. The market potential is massive. Diverse products and differentiated services targeted at elderly people in different age groups will become a mainstream development in retirement communities in the future.

2.3 *Tremendous Demands for Retirement-Related Services and Facilities*

Facing strong social demands, the development in retirement-related services and facilities has lagged behind despite the huge potential. Data from the Ministry of Civil Affairs show that as of the end of 2016, there are 374,000 eldercare institutions of various kinds in China with 6.98 million beds available. That works out to 30.2 beds per 1000 elderly persons.[4] However, this is a 30–50% shortfall compared to the target of thirty-five to forty-five beds per 1000 elderly people as stipulated under the 13th Five-Year Plan. This is also some way behind the standard of fifty to seventy beds in developed countries. Moreover, there is also the problem of uneven resource distribution since most eldercare services, facilities and institutions are located in the more advanced cities. At the same time, currently there are only over 50,000 certified eldercare technicians across China. This represents a severe shortfall in professional resources, given that the Ministry of Civil Affairs' target for the year 2020 was to have six million such technicians in the population (Fig. 2).

[4]Source: http://www.mca.gov.cn/.

3 A Review of Government Policies Related to Retirement Communities Development

In recent years, the central government has paid much attention to tackling the issue of population aging and developing retirement services industry. It has also introduced a number of policies in this area to support industry development, thus opening up a window of opportunity for the industry.

3.1 Main Trajectory of Development Under the 13th Five-Year Plan

The year 2016 marks the beginning of China's 13th Five-Year Plan. A number of policies on retirement services industry and developing retirement communities, which together form a strong policy constellation, has been introduced.

In the *Outline of the 13th Five-Year Plan for the National Economic and Social Development of the People's Republic of China* formally passed in March 2016, it was stated that a complex, well-rounded system of retirement services is to be established centered on the residence and the community, with institutional supplementary aid, the work will be done to promote the integration of healthcare services with eldercare services. In the *13th Civil Affairs Development Five-Year Plan* (MCA No. 107 [2016]) issued in July [of that year], healthcare institutions are encouraged to extend their services to each household, urban and rural communities, and nursing homes. This is meant to offer a solution to the current shortage of integrated services in retirement communities and hospitals in China.

"*The 13th Five-Year Plan for the Development of the National Old Age and Pension System*" (National Development No. 13 [2017]) issued by the State Council in February 2017 contains the overall plan for improving the system of eldercare services. Specific tasks listed in the document are: strengthening household and community healthcare services; making eldercare institutions more effective; promoting the integration of healthcare and eldercare services; and enabling the emergence of a prosperous market of senior citizen consumers.

3.2 Market Development Facilitated by Policies on Financial Services

The strategic significance of "financial service-supported eldercare" is becoming increasingly clear. In March 2016, the People's Bank of China, the China Banking Regulatory Commission (CBRC), the China Securities Regulatory Commission (CSRC), the China Insurance Regulatory Commission (CIRC) and the Ministry of Civil Affairs jointly issued the Guiding Opinions on Accelerating the Development of the Finance-Supported Pension Service Industry (PBC No. 65 [2016]), the first programmatic document on the integration of eldercare and finance. Directions in the document call for strong financial-industry support for the elderly care services industry, for the establishment of organizations engaged in financing old age care, and for innovation in old age care business models. The document also encouraged the entry of private capitals into the market as a means of diversifying the market to pave the way for the marketization of the retirement community industry.

3.3 Integration of Healthcare and Elderly Care Becomes a Major Theme of Retirement Community

In November 2015, the Office of the State Council issued the Guiding Opinions on Integrating Healthcare with Elderly Care Services document (OSC No. 84 [2015]). In the document, it was stipulated that an integrated system of healthcare and elderly care services and a system of regulations and policies that are compatible with China's specific circumstances should be up and running by the year 2020. Furthermore, it was stipulated that more than 50% of eldercare institutions should be capable of providing healthcare services to residents. The 13th Civil Affairs Development Five-Year Plan released in July 2016 clearly stated that the focus for the coming five years would be developing elderly care institutions that offer integrated healthcare and elderly care services, and that the government would support elderly care institutions in integrating healthcare services through the coordination of healthcare and elderly care service resources.

By the end of 2016, pilot programs in this area have already been implemented in Beijing, Tianjin, Shanghai, Chongqing, Shandong, Hunan, Hubei, Henan, Fujian, Zhejiang, Yunnan, Hainan, Jiangsu, and Ningxia.

3.4 Building of Elderly Care Services Infrastructure Driven by Supply-Side Reforms

The *Opinions on Further Expanding Consumer Expenditures in the Fields of Tourism, Culture, Sports, Health, Retirement Services, Education and Training*, etc., document (G.B.F. No. 85 [2016]) issued by the Office of the State Council and the *Notice on Supporting the Integration and Reform of Social Resources for the Development of Old Age Care Services* (M.F. No. 179 [2016]) issued by a consortium of eleven agencies and ministries including the Ministry of Civil Affairs and the National Development and Reform Commission in November 2016 have both clearly indicated that the shortfall in elderly care facilities would be mitigated under supply-side reforms through harnessing unused land and other idle resources. This approach will serve as a solution to the problem of lacking land resources for retirement communities.

In December of the same year, the Office of the State Council published the *Opinions on the Liberalizing Old Age Care Services Market and Improving the Quality of Old Age Care Services* (G.B.F. No. 91 [2016]) document, in which the Office called for the full liberalization of the elderly care services market and the enhancement of quality standards in this area to further advance the supply-side reforms within the industry, ensuring that basic needs are met and the market may prosper.

In the Opinions on Further Stimulating Social Investments (G.B.F. No. [2017]) issued in March 2017, the Office of the State Council called for deepening supply-side reforms in the social field to further encourage investment in areas such as healthcare, elderly care services, education, culture and sports, which helps expand room for social capitals in this arena. At the same time, the Office also expressed support for the public-private partnership (PPP) model in this area in that it is compatible to the features of retirement community projects, which is low average returns for an extended period of time.

4 The Current State of Development and Problems of Retirement Communities in China

As the central government continues to introduce more policies to support elderly care services industry, a growing number of private institutions started to be engaged in the industry. The dominance of real-estate enterprises, insurance companies and state-owned enterprises in this area will soon be diffused with the entry of a number of private and foreign-invested companies. The elderly market is one that has drawn the attention of various forms of capital. In addition, there have also been innovations in terms of retirement community investments and operating models, enabling more diverse and integrated services.

4.1 The Current State of Development

4.1.1 Real Estate Concerns: Identifying Development Trajectories and Accelerating Innovation and Transformation

Real estate enterprises enjoy an advantage in terms of development and marketing for retirement community projects. However, for enterprises that have difficulty in follow-on project operations and management, they have mainly partnered with professional elderly care institutions to accumulate customer numbers and industry experience. As such, they are not expected to turn in strong profits in the early period. In 2016, a number of key real estate players—including Vanke, Sino-Ocean, the Poly Group, Wanda and Greentown—started to participate actively in examining or harnessing opportunities in the elderly care services industry. Strategically speaking, various companies have established dedicated retirement services departments and outlined clear developmental pathways in order to realize a transformational shift from retirement property to the retirement services industry, and from an asset-heavy business model to an asset-light model. On the operational level, these companies are now paying closer attention to launch products that are more aligned with their strengths and establish a full-fledged system of services. Vanke Hangzhou's retirement services business has consolidated three key product lines (Sui Yuan Jia Shu, the Sui Yuan Nursing Home, and Sui Yuan Home) under the umbrella of the Zhejiang Sui Yuan Retirement Development Co., Ltd. By doing so, Vanke Hangzhou has established a closed industry loop that caters to senior citizen of all age ranges with a full range of eldercare products and services. It has also launched a stream of new business models, services and projects with an emphasis on delivering an array of human-centered and targeted elderly care products and services. As a subsidiary of the Sino-Ocean Group, Sino-Ocean Old Age Care has introduced the "Senior Living L'amore'" brand as an attempt to experiment asset-light business operation models in its elderly care projects. In July 2016, the company launched the first short-term public-service elderly care demonstration project in China, which is the "SENIOR LIVING L'AMORES" apartment. Under this project, the aged are provided with a maximum of seven days and six nights of round-the-clock care free-of-charge, a solution to families whose children have to leave the elderly unattended due to short-term overseas business trip or travel. In May 2016, the Shanghai Qin He Yuan Senior Living Apartments (the first members-only retirement community in China) launched an innovative new service model with its Kang Qiao Ai Yang Home project that integrates healthcare and elderly care services through harnessing the power of smart management technologies.

4.1.2 Insurance Companies: Steady Advance and Focus on Product Development and Innovation

Compared to the real estate industry, which has been working quickly to establish a foothold in retirement services industry, the insurance industry has been far more cautious. By the end of the first quarter of 2016, there are eight insurance companies that have invested in, or plan to invest in, a total of twenty-eight insurance-linked retirement community projects worth over RMB 67 billion in total. (The total actual investment has exceeded RMB 23.7 billion.) There is a high degree of alignment between insurance assets and the retirement products and services industry. However, insurance companies lack experience in real estate development and project management, and there are also stringent restrictions on using insurance assets for real estate development. Given the lack of flexibility with operations and profit models, insurance companies are unlikely to make any breakthroughs in this area. Other than Taikang Life Insurance, insurance companies have primarily participated in the retirement community market by means of direct investment (with direct shareholdings) in the early period. "Taikang Home", as a standout example of an insurance-linked retirement community project, succeeds in the market by practicing the integration of healthcare and elderly care services through its branded replications of Taikang Homes in other areas. The Taikang Home brand entered the southwest China market in 2016, and at the same time, efforts have been made to further consolidate assets on the healthcare end and connect them with other resources. In addition, efforts have also been made to establish partnerships with academic institutions to develop human resources for the long-time development of the brand nationwide. For overseas markets, Taikang Life Insurance has signed a cooperation agreement with Hokusei Real Estate to advance its "healthcare + elderly care" strategy and asset management business internationally. The China Life Insurance Group and China Pacific Insurance have also enhanced their partnerships with healthcare institutions in 2016 in order to promote the integration of elderly care and healthcare services. Apart from that, certain insurance companies have become more circumspect about the building and operation of elderly care projects and returned to their bread-and-butter insurance business where they have instead worked to develop innovative insurance products such as nursing care insurance and "Home for Care". Such efforts have been able to move forward the retirement wealth management insurances on a continued basis as a result, and laid down the financial foundation for future retirement community developments.

4.1.3 State-Owned Enterprises: Diverse Supply Thanks to Active Participation

Certain state-owned enterprises (SOEs), facing strong pressures to transform, have also entered the retirement services market in various ways by making full use of their existing business, capital, and human-resource strengths. To take the case of Beijing for instance: by the end of 2016, there were ten SOEs involved in the building of thirty-four elderly care facilities across the city. Of these thirty-four projects, fifteen are already in operation with a total of 2377 beds. The Beijing Cheng He Jing Old Age Care Station Home Management Group, the fully state-owned eldercare-station management group in Beijing, commenced official operations in October 2016. Beijing is expected to see the opening of nearly two hundred community-based "elderly care stations" in the coming three years. The China North Industries Group Corporation (Norinco) has joined hands with Jiu Hua Xi Xiu, an eldercare services provider, to tackle a range of issues including making showers and baths easier for the incapacitated elderly, in-community rehabilitation for elderly people with chronic diseases, and the challenges that empty nesters face. The Beijing Enterprises Group has partnered with Vanke on the Yi Yua Guang Xi Seniors Apartments project, which is located at the core area of the capital, providing a balance between the environment qualities of the retirement community with its accessibility. The Beijing Capital Development Holding Group has also worked with Cun Cao Chun Hui to form a joint venture that has harnessed community resources and established an O2O healthcare services platform targeted at the elderly population through the "integrated elderly care" model to meet elderly customers' needs.

4.1.4 Resource Integration Through M&As, Efforts at Creating New Profit Models

In 2016, listed companies, SOEs and key private enterprises including China Everbright, Yihua Healthcare, the Beijing Enterprises Group, Fosun, Zhongjin Ruihua and Beijing Capital Development, undertook the integration of competitive advantages and resources by means of acquisitions or joint ventures. In particular, these players were especially interested in retirement community developments. With much of the pioneering work already performed by the likes of Vanke, Poly, Sino-Ocean, and Yihua, the concept of "real estate" will be relegated to the background for retirement communities in the future. Instead, it will serve as a vehicle for healthy retirement services and "elderly care" will become the theme and operational focus when constructing retirement communities. For funders, merging retirement community projects can aid their internal business in restructuring and adjusting. The availability of capital can also bring the business to scale very quickly and win market share. For retirement community projects, acquisitions and mergers can bring access to sufficient funding to improve service quality, implement various operational standards, extend service chain, and for the entity to further hone its core strengths. Through capital integration, both parties are able to reach out to a bigger market with their existing competitive advantages, build a system of services, integrate resources of various types and generate the steam for continued innovation and the search for new, common profit models.

4.1.5 New Market Players Take Over Industry Chain Nodes by Leveraging Their Own Strengths

Thanks to the opportunity created by the central government's liberalization of the retirement services market, in 2016, we saw an even more diverse of new market entrants to the retirement community industry, working to provide professional services at various nodes along the industry chain. Large enterprises have been working to extend their businesses to the retirement products and services industry. For instance, Huawei and China Life Insurance have jointly established the Smart Aging Joint Innovation Laboratory to provide smart technologies and solutions. The Internet of Things Research Center of the Chinese Academy of Sciences has signed a partnership agreement with Wuzhen county government, Zhejiang Province and Chun Xi Tang Elderly care Services Center to establish a comprehensive smart elderly care services platform for Wuzhen. A small number of foreign enterprises like Airbnb have also entered market by signing a memorandum of understanding with Hua Shou Community Retirement Services Development and Promotion Center (established with the approval of the Office of the National Committee on Aging). The two sides aim to bring in advanced business models and practices from the international community so as to develop new and sustainable retirement community models suitable for the Chinese context. Some internet platforms and smart companies have become the smart service-providers to retirement communities as the emergence and popularization of new models such as "healthy retirement" and "smart retirement". These services are clustered around specific services or functions such as smart home care equipment, remote healthcare equipment, fall alarms and location tracking to facilitate the founding of an "internet plus" retirement community.

CCB Pension Management, a professional retirement-focused fund manager and a State Council-approved pilot company, boasts businesses that cover all three pillars of the pension system and the full extent of the industry chain. As such, CCB Pension Management is able to provide customers with professional and one-stop retirement-focused financial services. It is also committed to developing its business across the entire industry chain in areas including the retirement products and services industry, the retirement community industry, the integration of healthcare and elderly care, retirement health and innovative service model in serving the elderly. Since its founding, the company has made full use of its professional expertise in, and focus on, the retirement-focused finance and has looked deeply at how it can help support the development of the retirement community and retirement services industry. On the front end, the company has worked actively at responsible investing while establishing a retirement-focused financial services platform in its mid-office business, as well as creating innovative new pension products on the back end. By doing so, it will provide comprehensive services for industry development, becoming an active explorer of how financial products can be used to support retirement communities and boost development in retirement services industry. As such, the company is set to contribute significantly to the growth of China's elderly care service industry as well as the establishment of a complex and well-rounded old age security system.

4.2 Problems Facing by Retirement Communities

4.2.1 More Policies and Standards Needed

Currently, land prices for retirement community's construction are still fairly high. Although some preferential policies centered on subsidies have been introduced, it also imposes restrictions on social capitals to enter the market in that these policies have strict criteria for who qualifies for such subsidies. Furthermore, policies pertaining to retirement services and related preferential policies mainly emphasize the welfare and non-profit nature of service activities. As such, clarity on the position of private investment and private service operators are quite vague. Thirdly, according to existing state policies, the sales of retirement-related real estate fall under the broader category of "residential real estate sales" with neither any specific policy support nor any explicit restrictions. Fourthly, there is a lack of implementation guidance for retirement services and service operators. Fifthly, laws and regulations concerning the retirement communities have yet to be introduced, calling for government agencies at all levels to improve upon the corresponding laws, regulations and standards as soon as possible to ensure that the retirement community industry develops systematically, professionally, and with industrial scale. In addition, stipulating standards for areas such as land supply, architectural design, financing, taxation and government subsidies can also help the industry to develop in a standardized manner.

4.2.2 Imbalance Between Supply and Demand, Structural Mismatches to Be Tackled

In terms of planning, there is a need to further strengthen the comprehensiveness and cohesiveness of the overall system of retirement services, from home to retirement communities and elderly care institutions. With retirement communities, we are seeing uneven development across regions, mismatch between supply and demand, and a lack of balance in terms of product structure. At present, the comparatively more mature retirement communities target mid to high end of the market and are mostly located in tier-one and tier-two cities with strong demand for old age care and where a strong service industry is already present. On the other hand, presence is far weaker in tier-two and tier-three cities that are also facing the pressures from an aging population. Across China, there are around three million people currently living in retirement communities of various types due to traditional attitudes regarding eldercare and some other factors, which is only 2% of the elderly population. According to the Report on the State of Development of Old Age Care Institutions by China Research Center on Aging, in 2015, the average vacancy rate in elderly care institutions across the country was as high as 48%, and over 30% of these institutions were in the financial red. Mismatch between demand and supply also exists in facilities and services. Given the physical characteristics of the elderly residents, the majority of retirement communities are focused on providing day-to-day care and health services that are supplemented by other supporting facilities and activities. However, there is a certain gap between the actual needs of the elderly and the services provided, and insufficient attention was paid to providing services that cater to the mental and emotional needs of the elderly.

4.2.3 Financing Issue Calls for Greater Integration with Financial Services

Financing has become a major bottleneck in the industry. Currently, there are relatively few types of financing involved, with bank loans making up the majority of such financing. Traditional banks are unable to assist or meet the financing needs of retirement community developers given the comparatively higher costs of building and maintenance, the long payback period, and the comparatively high level of uncertainty with such projects. This means that a broader array of financing channels will have to be established together with innovative financing methods so as to attract large enterprises, insurance companies, fund companies, overseas funds, and private capital to enter the industry. Methods such as private finance initiatives (PFIs) and the build–operate–transfer (BOT) should also be adopted to attract more funds and diffuse risks. As the old age care industry matures with a complete financial eco-system formed by the activities of developers, investors, operators, players may wish to look into introducing the real estate trust investment fund (REIT) instrument as they seek out more innovative profits and operational models.

4.2.4 Low Integration in Industry-Chain Requires Strong Cross-Industry Partnerships

The retirement community industry in China is still in an early stage of development, and the environment in general still needs to be improved. We have yet to see many cases of success and profits. Outstanding issues include: little industry-chain integration and lacking of clear industry standards; unclear market positioning, and incomplete market segmentation of senior customers. In addition, there is little variety in residential products and services offered with few standards implemented, and at the same time, supporting facilities and service capabilities also need to be further improved. Sufficient attention has to be paid to psychological counseling, education and leisure, hospice and other services for the elderly, and in cases whether these services have been put in place they may not have been effectively implemented; as for the integration of elderly care and healthcare services, there is the question of how to balance the distribution of medical and nursing resources, and there is also the issue of effectively meeting the healthcare needs of elderly individuals at different stages. Another question is how internet technologies can be harnessed to realize the integration of the retirement community industry chain. As the real estate focus fades out with the retirement community business, we will see more in-depth cooperation across various industries related to the retirement-community business as well as more research in the area.

5 Prospects for Retirement Communities in China

5.1 Introducing the Concept of the Consumer Life Cycle and Innovative Retirement-Community Models

The needs of the elderly across various age ranges will become even more differentiated with the continued improvement in material living conditions and healthcare and longer life expectancies. In response to this trend, there will be a greater focus on the "living community + travel" model for comparatively young and active elder people, on catering to elderly individuals of different ages, and on the "multi-generational" living model. Mixed-age communities will emerge, and the concept of individual life cycle will be integrated into the design and planning of future communities. Various parts of the community will be designed to cater to specific needs, and more innovations will occur to create more diversified offerings. All these developments will achieve covering the whole range of elderly consumers in the market and cater to those with varying physical and mental needs, and there will be an array of products and services that cater to younger and more active elder people as well as those closer to the end of life, such as palliative care services.

5.2 Chained-Brand Operators Offering Standardized and Human-Centered Products and Services

Rising incomes and changes in attitudes regarding old age care will provide the elder with greater autonomy of choices with regard to how their retirement will be spent. For most elderly individuals, having access to day-to-day living and ancillary (e.g., healthcare) products and services that meet a set of standards is a basic criterion when choosing a retirement community. In the future, large chained-brand retirement community clusters across the country will reach a certain scale in their operations. The standardization of facilities and standards in these clusters can help reduce the cost of operation and management, and at the same time aid in the building of the brand. At the same time, the positioning of institutions specially catering to those who are incapacitated, living with dementia, or who require rehabilitation services will become even clearer, and the healthcare and nursing services delivered by such institutions will also become even more human-oriented and professional. It is possible for us to see the emergence of retirement community projects that house elderly residents with special needs with warmth and dignity in the future.

5.3 Replacing Traditional Attitudes and Models of Elderly Care with More Integrated and "Smart" Models

As the proportion of elderly citizens within the general population continues to rise, social attitudes towards the elderly are also changing. There is now greater recognition of the elder people's value and more attention has been paid to the psychological changes of the elder individual. In terms of the retirement communities design, there will be less focus on designing simply "barrier-free" spaces. Instead, the focus will be on more multi-functional, integrated and human-centered designs that have a less confining impact on the cognition and behaviors of the elderly residents, models that address the sense of psychological imbalance in the elderly, and sketches that encourage them to be more mobile to engage more in mutual assistance and cooperation so that they may live more positive emotional lives. At the same time, with continued technological advancement and the growing ubiquity of high-tech equipment, the retirement community will become ever smarter and more efficient so that residents will live in ever greater ease and comfort.

6 Possible Means of Financial-Service Support for Retirement Communities

In contrast to the development and sale of traditional real estate and the ownership and operation of general commercial property projects, retirement communities form a three-dimensional concept with endogenous needs and integrate the concept of development cycle with the demand for resources integration. On one hand, there is a need for deep integration with various kinds of financing at various stages of planning, development, holding, operation, service, and withdrawal, etc. On the other hand, a community project will push forward the integration various products and services together such as retirement housing and facilities construction, consumer goods for the elderly, financial services and insurance products, healthcare services, education, entertainment and recreation through capital; thus promoting the development of the entire retirement products and services industry. Experience in overseas markets tells us that mature retirement communities can also provide a sustainable cash flow and steady returns. Effective profit models and vehicles along every node of the industry chain can become the source of projects for the capital market, providing it with a wide array of financial products. This will enable the deep integration of retirement community development and operations with financial services; therefore making such integration an inexhaustible source of energy for the development of retirement communities.

In the spirit of the Guiding Opinion on Accelerating the Development of the Finance-Supported Pension Service Industry document, which was jointly released by five agencies and with the aid of industry experience to date, we can consider the following approaches in integrating financial services with the development of retirement communities.

6.1 Harnessing the Financing Function to Create Innovative Financial Services

Bank loans are a key source of funds for the retirement community industry, and financial institutions should work actively to create innovative and appropriate credit policies in view of the large scale of investment required, the long payback cycle and relatively stable operations. Depending on the specific situation, it may be appropriate to extend loan periods, launch revolving loans, implement an annual review system or staged payments, or adopt other repayment methods. Players can also explore various financing mechanisms and models that are suitable to PPP old age care projects with participation by government, financial institutions, and private capital, such as through credit guarantees, discounted government loans, government subsidies and acquisitions. Financial resources can be leveraged, and institutions, encouraged to place long-term and sustainable capital investment so as to form a diversified, multi-channel, and high-efficiency system of industry investment, inducing greater financial support by encouraging financial institutions to engage in equity investment, mezzanine financing, and shareholder lending, etc.

6.2 Consolidating Industry Chain by Leveraging the Middleman Role of Financial Services

The retirement community industry is linked to a broad range of products and services and requires long spectrum of financial cycles. However, at present, domestic real estate developers, insurance agencies, private equity funds, and internationally renowned pension investment operators have not been able to build industry consolidation in terms of the development and operation of retirement community projects. As a result, financial institutions should work to consolidate the entire industry chain, and harness their middleman role through deeper integration of the industry with financial at key nodes so as to realize the "fiancialization" of the retirement community industry at all stages, from investment to development, holding, operations, service, management and withdrawal. This will help form a complete financial ecological chain and boost the development and operation of retirement communities. On the other hand, the "bundling" approach can be taken to support the market-oriented operation of elderly care institutions, retirement facilities, rehabilitation and care services, housekeeping services as well as upstream and downstream services that are closely related to retirement communities in what is a virtuous industry cycle. This will support the establishment of multi-region, differentiated and chained-brand retirement communities and realize the integrated development of the financial and retirement services industries.

6.3 Focusing on the Financial-Services Needs of the Elderly Community to Introduce Forward-Looking and Innovative Financial Products

Resources for the retirement community industry chain can be consolidated through introducing industry-related products such as various wealth management products, reverse mortgaging, and the securitization of retirement properties. Elderly care institutions can withstand more risks through developing insurance products such as liability insurance. In areas close to retirement communities, financial institutions can work to optimize their operations and remodel their outlets to make them more elder-friendly, such as employ dedicated staff and establish green service channels for the elderly. With regard to current credit and insurance product restrictions on senior citizens, financial institutions and retirement communities can work together to develop financial products that meet the needs of the retiree's life cycle and provide financial products that benefit retirement-community services. Financial institutions can also make use of network and mobile internet technology to create new general and special financial products that are suitable for older consumers. Integrated card/member services can be enhanced to make customers' access to living, healthcare, cultural and entertainment services in retirement communities more convenient. Financial institutions can develop thoughtful and more secure financial services for customers with advanced age and the incapacitated/semi-incapacitated elderly by using fingerprint recognition or facial recognition technologies for their financial products.

References

Liu, L. (2012). Developmental issues and counter-measures with retirement communities. *Macroeconomics*. (1).

Ji, X., Liu, X. (2016). Reviews and counter-measures of issues with the development of retirement communities in China. *Research on local governance*. (1).

China Business Journal Press. (2016). *White paper for the development of the retirement industry in China*. Beijing: China Business Journal Press.

Wang, X. (2016). A study and reflection on real estate development based on the retirement community model in the United States. *Urban development studies*. (5).

Liying Feng is the president of CCB Pension Management Co., Ltd., executive deputy director of the China Banking Association Pension Business Professional Committee, member of the China Society of Social Insurance Social Insurance Fund Investment Management Committee, core member of the China Ageing Finance Forum, licensed Class II Psychological Counselor, Registered Senior Human Resources Professional, and Senior Economist. Her research interests are in the areas of human resource management and pension asset management.

Chapter 12
PPP: New Ways of Financing for Elderly Care Industry Amid Supply-Side Reform

Lan Zhang

Abstract Because of the supply-side reform, the implementation of the new model of urbanization, and the increasingly serious population ageing, Chinese elderly care industry will witness great prospects and become a key area supported by national policies. The elderly care industry is generally characterized by large input, long payback period, low profit margin and strong nature of public welfare. The traditional elderly care system in China that is mainly undertaken by the government and supplemented by private forces is a heavy fiscal burden on the government, and it failed to create a situation that encourages private investors to actively engage in developing the elderly care industry. Based on that, this article, centered on the unique property right structure and operation model of PPP (public private partnership), objectively analyzes why the PPP model is suitable for supporting China's elderly care industry development, and introduces the background, status quo, prospects and positive effects of this approach as well as the challenges it faces. It also offers innovative measures and suggestions on how to effectively apply the PPP model, in the endeavor to explore ways of supporting China's elderly care industry development through this approach.

Keywords PPP · Public-private cooperation · Elderly care industry

1 PPP Profile

Public Private Partnership (PPP) was initiated in Britain in the 17th century and developed into maturity in advanced western economies. The World Bank defined PPP as an arrangement in which "a private sector and a government body sign a long-term contract on the provision of public facilities and services. The private sector bears substantial risks and management responsibilities and the government body pays it according to its performance assessment". In China, the General Office

L. Zhang (✉)
Industrial Bank of China, Beijing, China

K. Dong and Y. Yao (eds.), *Annual Report on Financing Old Age Care in China (2017)*, https://doi.org/10.1007/978-981-13-0968-7_12

of the State Council forwarded the *Notice of the Guiding Opinions on Promoting PPP in Public Service* (G. B. F. No. 42 [2015]) issued by the Ministry of Finance, National Development and Reform Commission and People's Bank of China in 2015. The Notice defined PPP as the arrangement in which "the government selects through competition a private party with the capability of investment and operation management. The two sides sign a contract and clarify the rights and responsibilities on the principle of equal consultation. The private party provides public services as the government pays it according to the performance assessment and ensures reasonable profits for it." In addition to the General Office of the State Council, the Ministry of Finance and NDRC also issued different definitions of PPP.

To implement PPP, it's very important to make a sound system and top-level design and create a business atmosphere and partnership featured by equality between the government and the private party. PPP requires the government and private party to share both risks and profits and pay attention to the full-life-cycle management of the project, especially its operation, maintenance and a rational design of the contract. For the government, PPP is good for accelerating the transformation of government functions and improving the quality and efficiency of public finance in supporting infrastructure and public services construction; for private parties, this model is good for vitalizing private capital, integrating private investors in investment, design, construction and operation, lowering the total input and raising their profitability.

The Operating Guide on PPP (trial) stipulates that the full life cycle of PPP projects can be divided into five stages—project identification, preparation, procurement, execution and transfer, and there are three payback mechanisms—paid by government, paid by user and Viability Gap Funding (VGF). The internal rate of return (IRR) of private capital should be determined in a reasonable way through competition in view of the characteristics of the elderly care industry, and be adjusted dynamically according to the changes in market interest rate. The project operation model includes Operation and Maintenance (O&M), Management Contract (MC), Build-Operation-Transfer (BOT), Build-Own-Operation (BOO), Transfer-Operation-Transfer (TOT) and Rehabilitate-Operation-Transfer (ROT).

2 An Overview of PPP Support for Elderly Care Industry

2.1 Background

After the *New Budget Law* and the *Opinion of the State Council on Strengthening the Management of Local Government Debts* (G. F. No. 43 [2014]) were issued in 2014, the financing mechanism for local government has seen continuous improvements. Recently, the Ministry of Finance issued the *Notice on Prohibiting Local Government from Illegal Financing in the Name of Government Purchase of Service*

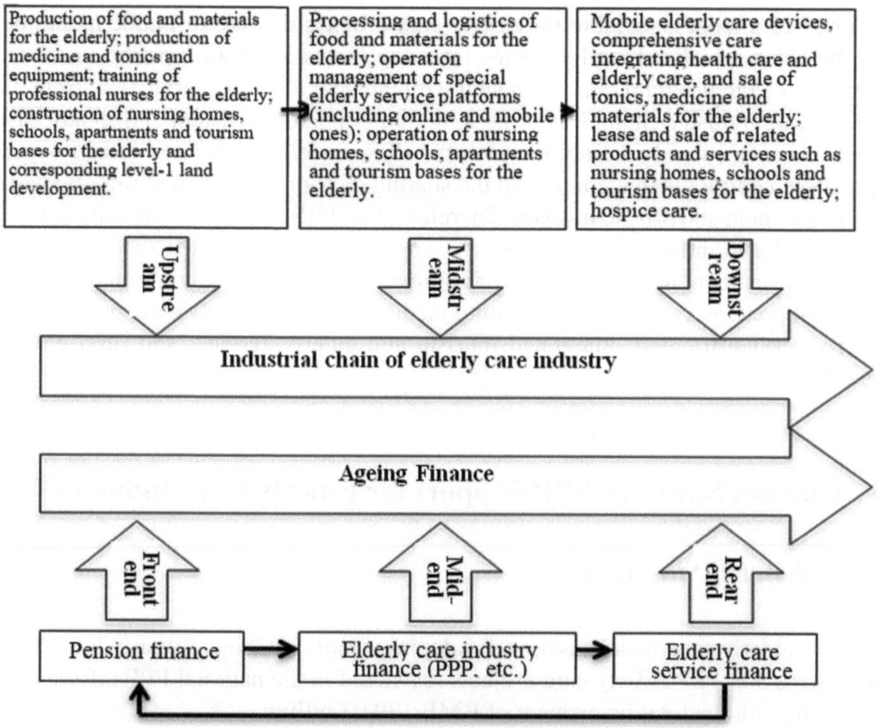

Fig. 1 Scope and boundary of elderly care industry and finance for the industry

(C. Y. No. 87 [2017]), which was aimed to address the "crowding-out effect" on the fast development of PPP model due to local government's attempt to circumvent the government purchase of service. To date, PPP has become the only proper approach for the government to support public services through commercial operation (Fig. 1).

2.2 *Integration of PPP and Elderly Care Industry*

The elderly care industry is not only a livelihood undertaking that concerns the welfare of hundreds of millions of people, but also a rising industry with tremendous potential. It is a comprehensive industrial chain that provides the elderly with the facilities, care and health services and other special products and materials that meet their special needs, and is an indispensable part in their material and cultural life that covers their clothing, food, housing, traffic, medical service, health care, entertainment, study and wealth management.

The PPP model is suitable for elderly care projects that are of public nature but can be commercialized, and schemes featuring long cooperation period and large investment, and program that fits in well with the operation and service sector in the elderly care industry chain. Featuring long duration and consistent and steady cash flow, this sector can be combined with the PPP model that stresses full-life-cycle operation, contract management and the sharing of both interests and risks between the government and private investor. Therefore, the PPP model can be mainly applied to support basic and mid-level elderly care services, with the priority to nursing homes of large investment and a high level of commercialization, large community elderly care, comprehensive services integrating medical care and elderly care, professional elderly service training, integrated tourism and elderly service, and rural elderly service.

3 Current Status of PPP Support for Elderly Care Industry

3.1 General Situation

The PPP elderly care model has been developing rapidly in China. By early June 2017, there were 303 PPP elderly care projects registered in the national PPP information platform, with the total investment of RMB 179.07 billion.

In terms of single-project investment, it ranges from RMB 6 million to thirteen billion[1] and the projects are evenly distributed in different ranges, with fifty-one projects in the range above RMB 1 billion, eighty-one in the range of RMB 0.3–1 billion, ninety-five in the range of RMB 100-300 million, and seventy-six under RMB 100 million.

In terms of project period, PPP elderly care projects usually range from ten to thirty years. There are only eleven projects with the period of over thirty years or whose period hasn't been determined yet, totaling the investment of RMB 2.85 billion. The 128 projects in the period of twenty to thirty years (including thirty years) have the total investment of RMB 97.12 billion, the 117 projects in the period of ten to twenty years (including twenty years) have the total investment of RMB 65.78 billion, and the forty-seven ones in the period of ten years or less have the total investment of RMB 13.32 billion.

Of all the PPP elderly care projects in the database, there are thirty-three national demonstration projects with the total investment of RMB 37.19 billion, whose number and capital accounting for 10.9 and 20.8% of the total respectively; and there are thirteen provincial demonstration projects with the total investment of

[1]The Heishan elderly care center on Dayu Street of Beijing's Mentougou district has the smallest investment for a single PPP project, and the Jiaxiang Jiudingshan project in Jining city of Shandong province, which integrates elderly service with ecological governance, has the largest investment for a single PPP project and is a national demonstration project integrating health care and elderly care.

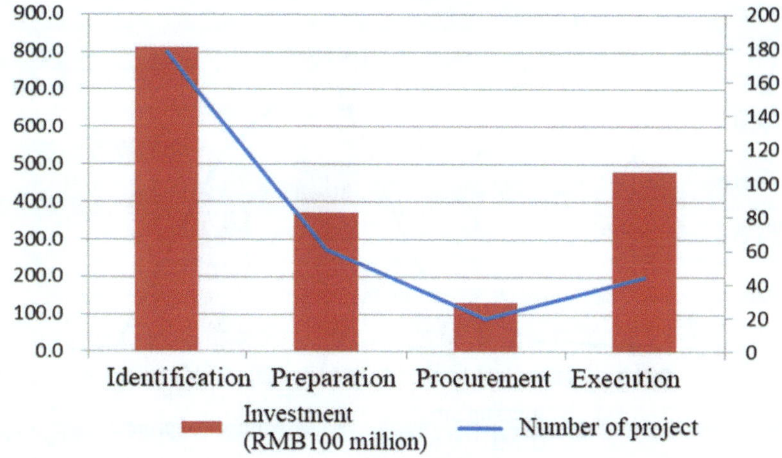

Fig. 2 Stage of elderly care projects in the national PPP information platform (As of early June 2017)

RMB 10.36 billion, whose number and capital accounting for 4.3 and 5.8% of the total respectively. Of the national demonstration projects, ten brought in private capital through open bidding, twenty-two through competitive consultation, and one through competitive negotiation.

3.2 Execution

PPP project generally has four stages - identification, preparation, procurement and execution. Of all PPP elderly care projects currently in the database, 178 are in the identification stage with the total investment of RMB 81.06 billion, sixty-one are in the preparation stage with the total investment of RMB 37.04 billion, twenty in the procurement stage with the total investment of RMB 13.02 billion, and forty-four in the execution stage with the total investment of RMB 47.95 billion. Projects in the identification stage account for more than 50% and are quite uncertain whether they will be successfully implemented or not, and those in the procurement and execution state only take up a small proportion, with the number and capital accounting for 21.1 and 34% respectively. The number is slightly lower than the average delivery rate of PPP projects in all industries, but as far as capital is concerned, the delivery rate of PPP elderly care projects is on a par with all-industry average (Fig. 2).

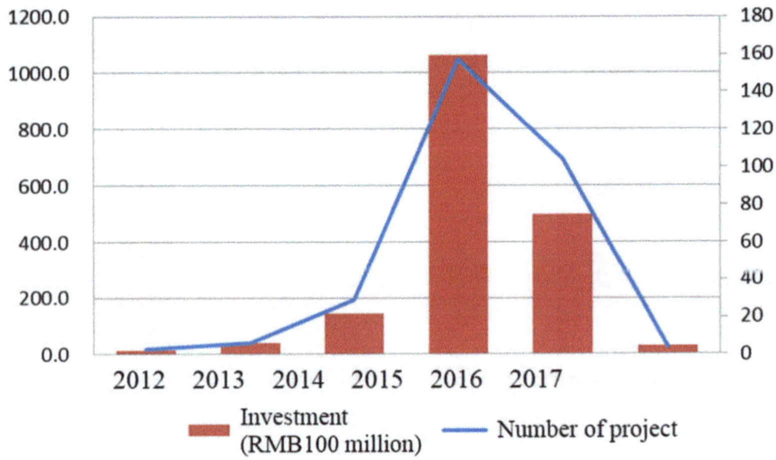

Fig. 3 Time of initiation of elderly care projects in the national PPP information platform (As of early June 2017)

3.3 *Time of Initiation*

PPP elderly care projects were first put in the platform in 2012 and came to a period of high-speed development in 2015–2016. Altogether 266 projects were launched in two and a half years, which amounted to the investment of RMB 158.89 billion, accounting for nearly 90% of all the projects in the database. Suppose the delivery rate of PPP elderly care projects is 26.58%, about sixty-four of the 239 projects that are currently in the identification and preparation stage will be implemented in the next two years. Since there are already sixty-four PPP elderly care projects in process, it is foreseeable that China will have at least 128 such projects, either in procurement or execution stage, in 2019 (Fig. 3, Table 1).

3.4 *Regional Distribution*

Currently, the PPP model has been implemented for elderly care in twenty-four provinces and regions, but regional distribution has obvious characteristics. Shandong, Guizhou and Henan provinces rank among the top three both regarding the number of project and investment amount. They each have forty-seven, forty-two and twenty-six projects and the investment amount of RMB 59.11 billion, RMB 21.39 billion and RMB 18.91 billion, which registered nearly 40 and 56.67% of the total respectively. Shandong, Henan, Jiangsu, Hunan, Hubei, Jiangxi, Yunnan, Shaanxi, Xinjiang, Qinghai, Liaoning and Jilin all have national demonstration PPP elderly care projects; Beijing, Xinjiang and Inner Mongolia have relatively more projects but the investment on each single project is small; Hunan and Jilin own relatively fewer

Table 1 Time of initiation and stage of elderly care projects in the national PPP information platform

Year	Identification		Preparation		Procurement		Execution	
	Number of project	Investment (RMB 100 million)	Number of project	Investment (RMB 100 million)	Number of project	Investment (RMB 100 million)	Number of project	Investment (RMB 100 million)
2012	1	6.8	0	0	1	5.1	1	3.9
2013	3	8	2	31.1	1	1.2	0	0
2014	20	89.1	3	19.8	1	5.1	5	31.7
2015	94	498.2	28	136.2	9	62.3	26	367.7
2016	59	197.5	25	166.2	8	56.5	12	76.2
2017	1	11	3	17.1	0	0	0	0
Sum	178	810.6	61	370.4	20	130.2	44	479.5

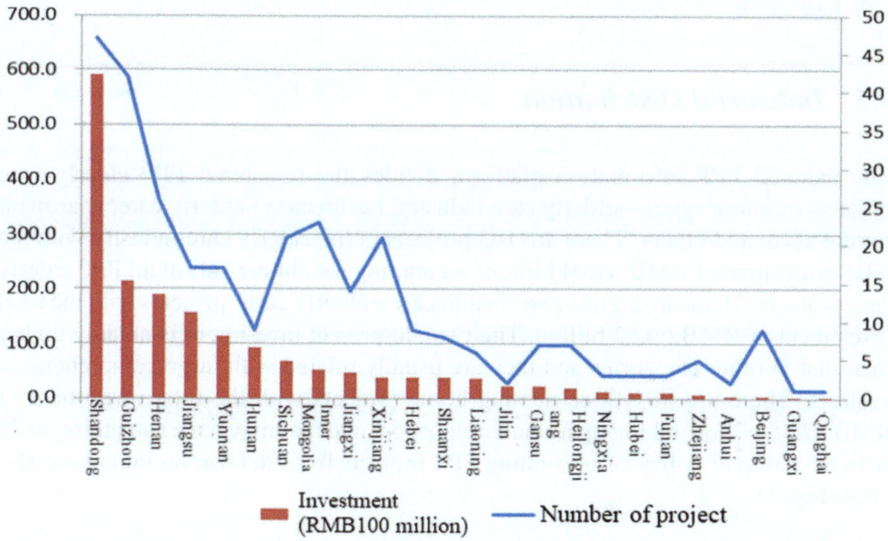

Fig. 4 Regional distribution of elderly care projects in the national PPP information platform (As of early June 2017)

PPP elderly care projects but the single-project investment is large; and Shanghai, Tianjin, Shanxi, Guangzhou, Hainan, Chongqing and Tibet haven not applied the PPP model in the elderly care sector yet (Fig. 4).

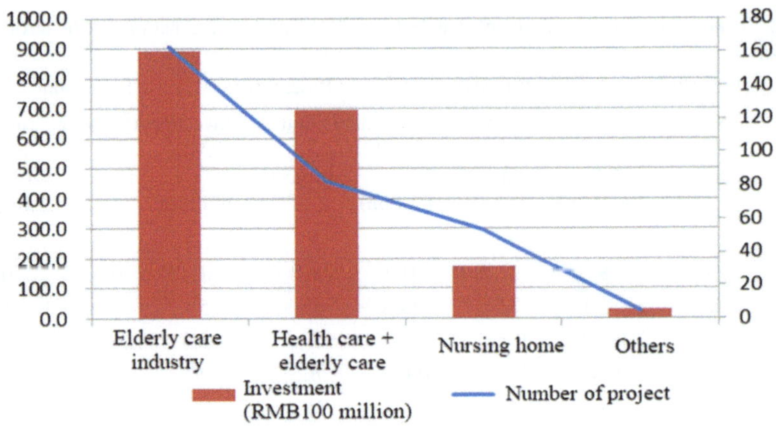

Fig. 5 Sector distribution of elderly care projects in the national PPP information platform (As of early June 2017)

3.5 *Industrial Distribution*

The national PPP information platform divides the registered PPP elderly care projects into four types—elderly care industry, health care + elderly care, apartment for the aged, and others. There are 163 projects in the elderly care industry with the total investment of RMB 89.04 billion, accounting for almost half of all PPP elderly care projects. There are eighty-two "health care + elderly care" projects with the total investment of RMB 69.62 billion. Their single-project investment is notably higher than that in other categories and they are usually related with large comprehensive projects. There are fifty-three nursing home projects with the total investment of RMB 17.48 billion, taking up a small proportion, and that may have something to do with the national policy of preventing PPP projects from deforming into real estate ones (Fig. 5).

3.6 *Payback Mechanism*

There are three payback mechanisms for PPP projects—paid by government, paid by user and Viability Gap Funding (VGF). Of all the PPP elderly care projects in the database, 204 are paid by users, totaling the investment of RMB 123.79 billion and accounting for about 2/3; eighty-nine adopt the approach of feasibility allowance, totaling the investment of RMB 50.75 billion and accounting for a little less than 1/3; and only ten are paid by the government, totaling the investment of RMB 4.53 billion

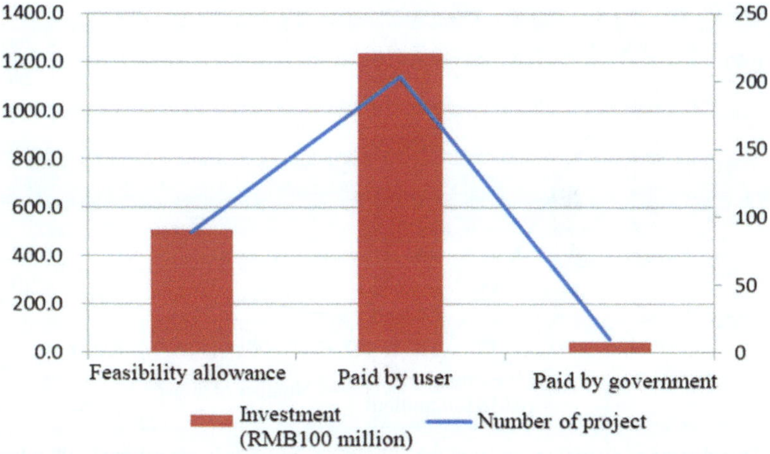

Fig. 6 Payback mechanisms for elderly care projects in the national PPP information platform (As of early June 2017)

and the number and capital investment accounting for only 3.3 and 2.5% respectively. The ten government-paid PPP elderly care projects were mostly initiated in 2015, eight of which are in the identification stage with high uncertainty at the operation level (Fig. 6).

3.7 Form of Initiation

The national PPP information platform only revealed how the non-national demonstration PPP elderly care projects are initiated. Over 80% of them are initiated by the government and only twenty-seven are initiated by private investors, and all the twenty-seven projects adopt the payback mechanism of "paid by user" or "feasibility allowance".

3.8 Operating Model

BOT and BOO are the most common operation models for PPP elderly care projects. There are 160 BOT projects with the total investment of RMB 102.41 billion, the number and capital both accounting for over half; and there are 90 BOO projects with the total investment of RMB 57.68 billion, the number and capital both accounting for around 1/3. Besides, the other models such as TOT, ROT, TOT + BOT, O&M and MC are also applied for PPP elderly care projects but only take up a small proportion. This indicates that PPP elderly care projects are mostly newly built while the renovation

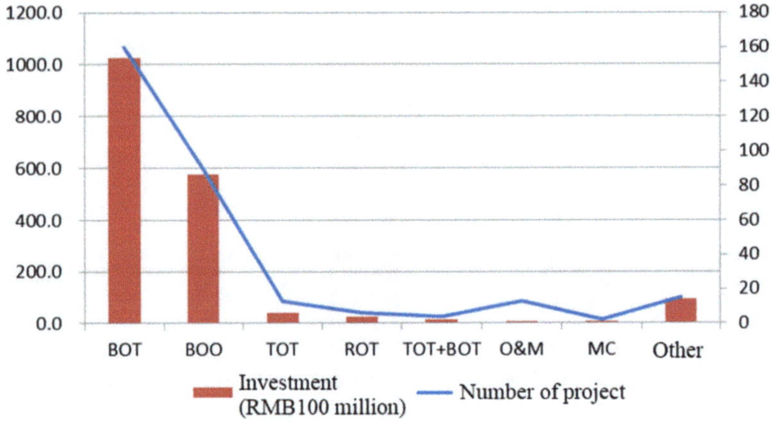

Fig. 7 Distribution of operation model of the elderly care projects in the national PPP information platform (As of early June 2017)

of existing projects or utilization of idle resource is quite rare. Different operation model concerns different property right, accounting and tax arrangement, and special attention shall be paid to taxation during project transfer (Fig. 7).

3.9 Supporting Policies

In the current elderly care service market in China, there are two types of private elderly care institutions—profit-oriented and nonprofit. The former is registered at the industrial and commercial authority and the property ownership is based on the nature of the registered legal entity. The latter is registered at civil affairs authority and, according to the *Provisional Regulations on the Registration and Management of Private Non-enterprise Units*, the property and profits of their elderly care service facilities are public property and cannot be disposed of as dividends. The fee of non-profit elderly care institutions, either public or private, is usually administered by the price bureau of the government.

As far as tax is concerned, private non-profit elderly care institutions basically enjoy the same treatment as public ones. In other words, they are entitled to the same tax reduction and exemption policies concerning income tax, business tax (which was replaced by VAT after April 1, 2016), land value increment tax, land use tax, property tax, vehicle and vessel tax, urban maintenance and construction tax and educational surtax. Moreover, no VAT would be levied on the immovable properties and the transfer of land use right during the asset restructuring of these institutions.

Regarding operation allowance, governments in different places and at different levels have different practices. At present, the main practice is bed allowance, and the allowance standards vary according to the ownership of project properties,

Table 2 Policies for for-profit and non-profit elderly care institutions

Type	Non-profit	For-profit
Land	Fifty-year use right of special-purpose land for elderly care with inseparable property right. The land can be allocated but not for sale and its designated purpose shall not be changed	Forty-seventy-year use right of commercial or residential land, the property right or use right of which can be sold separately
	No or little land-transferring fee is needed	The land is acquired through bidding, auction or listing and all reasonable fees should be paid
Housing	No more than forty square meters; no more than five-year lease	No more than twenty-year lease
Registration	Civil affairs authority, private non-enterprise	Registered at the industrial and commercial authority and approved by the civil affairs authority
Allowance	Lump-sum construction allowance and operation allowance according to the number of beds	Usually no allowance
Tax	Business tax, corporate income tax and administrative charges are exempted	Business tax is exempted and administrative charges are halved
Energy fee	Civilian standard for water, electricity, gas and heating fees	Civilian standard for water, electricity, gas and heating fees
Profit distribution	Profits cannot be distributed as dividends, assets cannot be privatized, and no branch can be set up	No limitation
Insurance	Comprehensive responsibility insurance and employer responsibility insurance for elderly care. The government should bear a certain proportion of the premium	Comprehensive responsibility insurance and employer responsibility insurance for elderly care. The government should bear a certain proportion of the premium
Charge	Subject to government-set pricing guidelines	Subject to market force
Star rating	Determined by the civil affairs authority	Not included in the scope of rating

which can be divided into three types—public elderly service project, private elderly service project of government investment and property right, and private elderly service project of non-government property right. Generally speaking, the operation allowance is higher for those projects of government property right because they are subject to the government's price regulation. As to water, electricity and gas charges, the same standard is applied for private and public elderly care service organizations (Table 2).

4 Significance of Supporting China's Elderly Care Industry with PPP and Current Difficulties

4.1 Significance

(1) Improving the fiscal management system in the elderly care industry

Establishing the cross-year budget balance mechanism, implementing mid- and long-term fiscal plan and management and formulating a financial report that fully reflects the government's asset and liabilities is an important part of creating a sound modern fiscal system. Given the long period of PPP projects, the local government has to change from the annual budget management to the mid- and long-term fiscal plan. There are not only specific regulations on the execution and procedures of government purchase, but a full-life-cycle cooperation mechanism is also created to even out the local government's annual expenditure where the project is located and strengthen the local government's control of its fiscal bearing capacity (Zhou 2016).

(2) Fostering enterprises experienced in operating elderly care project

China lacks a group of enterprises that are able to carry out professional operation and full-life-cycle management in the elderly care industry, which seriously impedes the industry from in-depth development. With the trial operation and promotion of PPP elderly care projects, it is possible to foster a group of PPP companies specialized in project investment and operation in this industry, and these companies can engage in new PPP projects as private investors. This kind of continuation and penetration is good for the rapid spread of the expertise, experience and skills of the elderly care industry and the cultivation and growth of professional elderly care personnel. Going forward, with the extension and restructuring of the industrial chain, these elderly care companies may be integrated into industry leading backbones, listed companies or corporate groups that will lead the development of Chinese elderly care industry.

(3) Strengthening the operation management and maintenance of elderly care projects

When supporting the new-type modernization with PPP model, China is faced with the following dilemma: more importance is attached to construction than operation; land urbanization is faster than population urbanization; the PPP model is well implemented in the infrastructure sector but not so well in the public service sector, and a mature and imitable pattern has not been established. This dilemma is to some extent attributed to the fact that there are not so many assets in the public service sector. In fact, the PPP model stresses operation, contract design and full-life-cycle management, which can effectively make up for the shortcoming of "more importance to construction than operation" in the elderly care industry. Promoting the PPP model in elderly care sector and discussing a feasible PPP model in the public service sector can help resolve the current dilemma in China's new-type urbanization drive and create a multi-layered and multi-channel elderly care supply system.

(4) Creating an equal and win-win government and business environment for developing elderly care industry

The equal and win-win government and business environment is reflected in their sharing of risks and interests. The PPP model can optimize the distribution of the risks and benefits that may arise in the full-life-cycle operation of the project between the government and private investor. Their risk managing ability is measured with the ability to reduce the probability of risk occurrence and minimize the consequences, and by their benefits correspond to the risks they bear.

(5) The project identification and proving mechanism regulates the development of elderly care industry

At present, most PPP elderly care projects in China are still in the identification stage and have to undergo a lot of design and proving. Truth comes from practice. The preliminary work of project identification and proving can lay a solid foundation for further establishing and improving the PPP elderly care project assessment system, developing a mature and feasible commercial model for this industry, and determining its boundary. It will also provide plenty of reserve projects and practice opportunities for the flourishing of the elderly care industry in the future.

(6) Reasonable payment mechanism helps make fiscal subsidy more accurate

The PPP model and the precise use of fiscal subsidy are in a relation of causality and complementarity. On one hand, the precise use of fiscal subsidy is crucial for enhancing the user's paying ability and promoting the healthy and steady development of PPP elderly care projects. On the other hand, with the development of PPP elderly care projects, we can introduce private investment and raise the ratio of user payment in order to shift the indirect fiscal subsidy to direct subsidy and make its use increasingly more efficient and precise. At the moment, the "paid by user" approach takes up a high proportion in PPP elderly care projects, which has mitigated the government's spending pressure while boosting the development of this industry.

4.2 Current Difficulties

(1) Lengthy construction process, slow payback, limited appeal to investors

Elderly care projects tend to require hefty initial investment, have slim profit margin and take a long time for investment to be recouped. The elderly care industry in China is still in its infancy, and in search of clearly-defined and effective business models and profit models. Meantime, most projects cannot realize cash flow balance in the short term. Besides, the PPP elderly care projects in China are mostly paid for by users and operate on the free or relatively cheap land or land for public welfare undertakings provided by the government. They tend to have limited appeal to private investors.

(2) Slow progress, low delivery rate

Based on past experience, the PPP projects in China have a low delivery rate of 20%-30%. In other words, there are not many PPP elderly care projects that are finally signed and put into action. As a matter of fact, the low delivery rate has been one of the key reasons why PPP model has developed so slowly in China. It reflects a series of problems - the private investors are not fully mobilized to participate, the process of project negotiation and contract signing is too complex, and the process of project proving should be improved.

(3) Elderly care project and real estate project are hard to differentiate; PPP project database is the only way of certification.

Unlike real estate projects that feature short period, high frequency and fast progress, elderly care projects require professional operation and involve a large amount of manpower and materials, so they may easily turn into real estate projects. That is why it is important to pick out the elderly care project and establish a clear business model in this sector. At present, the standard of certifying PPP elderly care project is whether it is included in the PPP project database of the Ministry of Finance or National Development and Reform Commission. For one thing, the clear division and explanation of their project database by the Ministry of Finance and NDRC is extremely important, otherwise the local government may be confused or find it hard to make a decision when applying for project inclusion. For another thing, the continuous improvement of the project database itself and the accurate classification of industries is also critical. Currently, the criteria and assessing methods for the inclusion of PPP projects in the database should be perfected urgently, and a more scientific and objective assessing system is yet to be established to discern quality elderly care projects.

(4) Weak development, uneven industrial and regional distribution

In terms of industrial distribution, to prevent and control local debt risks, the *Guide on Proving the Financial Bearing Capacity of PPP Project* (C. J. No. 21 [2015]) provided that "local government should allocate part of the annual budget for all PPP projects in the year, which should take up no more than 10% of the general public expenditure" (hereinafter referred to as the "10% red line"). The governments at various levels and in different regions have not specified the definite ratio and limit of investment in each industry or sector within the 10% red line. Some areas build infrastructure on a large scale and spend most of the budget in the 10% red line on that, but pay little heed to the development of elderly care, which falls in the category of public service.

In terms of regional distribution, the PPP model still is not supportive enough for the elderly care industry. Only twenty-four provinces and regions implement this model to the elderly care industry, and regions like Shanghai, Tianjin, Shanxi, Guangzhou, Hainan, Chongqing and Tibet have not done that yet, indicating obvious regional differences. Shanghai has not adopted the PPP model for elderly care industry mainly because it has a powerful finance resource that offers strong fiscal support for this sector, so it does not have an urgent need for private capital. But in some other regions, the local government has little understanding of PPP and does little or nothing to promote this model. Even in provinces where PPP elderly care projects have been carried out, the development of elderly care industry in rural areas lags way behind than that in urban areas.

(5) Classification is not sufficiently fine-grained and cannot meet the diverse demands for elderly care

At present, the national PPP information platform divides the registered PPP elderly care projects into four types—elderly care industry, health care + elderly care, residential facilities for the aged, and others. This is an extensive way of division, which emphasizes material input, neglects mental care, and does not pay enough attention or give enough input to elderly care service and project operation. Moreover, in practice, the elderly care industry and the "health care + elderly care" sector are overlapping and mixed to some extent. In the future, these sectors need to be further divided, and some sub-sectors such as vacation-style elderly care, rural elderly care and training of elderly service personnel will be added to diversify this industry.

(6) Inadequate financing leads to low self-liquidating ratio for most projects

At present, most PPP projects rely on bank loan for financing. As PPP project companies are usually newly established with little operating experience and past financial data, banks would require the debtor to provide mortgage, pledge, guarantee and other credit enhancements. However, the land and above-ground structures of elderly care projects are generally public assets that cannot be used as collaterals. As the banks do not have full recourse on them, they will set a high demand on the project's self-liquidation ability. Most of the PPP elderly care projects launched by local governments so far are paid by users, but they can hardly achieve cash flow self-balance, which means their future cash flow revenues cannot fully cover the cost. That is why PPP elderly care projects are not attractive enough for private investors and their financing is difficult.

(7) Land supply is insufficient and form of supply needs further innovation and regulation.

The land supply and planning is critical for the development of elderly care industry and a good site is good for the upgrade of relevant facilities and consumption. Therefore, the local governments should be guided to provide land for elderly care projects based on holistic, complete and appropriate arrangements. The form of land supply can be diverse and should be compliant with the law, such as allocation, transfer, lease, and equity investment by contributing land at a proper price. While guaranteeing and strengthening the land supply for elderly care industry, we should also take effective measures to prevent the loss of state-owned assets and curb the phenomenon that private investors would conduct "land arbitrage" through the elderly care industry. It is expressly stated in the *Notice on Jointly Announcing the Third Group of PPP Demonstration Projects and Accelerating Their Construction* (C. J. No. 91 [2016]) that the PPP model is not suitable for level-one land development projects. Even for PPP elderly care projects that involve both level-one and level-two land development, private investors should consult with the local government about the return on investment and terms of payment, and the amount of return should not be linked with the income from the transfer of land use right.

5 Suggestions for PPP Support for Elderly Care Industry

PPP is not purely a means of project financing, but a comprehensive instrument of project management. It is not the only operating model for the elderly care industry, but is an innovative and important model based on property right structure other than the government-funded non-profit elderly care projects and purely private ones. To implement the PPP model in the elderly care industry, there should be a mature business model and the project's investment attraction has to be continuously strengthened. In light of the problems and challenges mentioned above, five major measures have to be taken to promote the extensive and effective application of the PPP model in the Chinese elderly care industry. They are improving the financing approach, selecting projects scientifically, intensifying operating management, integrating and fostering new business forms, and perfecting the auxiliary policies.

5.1 *Improving the Financing Approach*

(1) Opening up financing channels

To fully exert the guiding and driving role of government investment, local governments can support and guide private investors to engage in PPP elderly care projects in the way of authorized operation, land contribution, investment allowance, fund contribution, guarantee subsidy and subsidized loan according to the specific conditions of each project. To exert the leveraging role of fiscal fund, local governments should be encouraged to set up guiding fund for elderly care industry and support PPP elderly care projects consistent with the general direction of this industry through equity, credit or the combination of both. They are also urged to engage in such projects by contributing capital or equity in the form of land or existing assets at a discounted price.

As to private investors, local governments should actively guide and help PPP elderly care projects to get the special construction fund from the China Development Bank and Agricultural Development Bank of China. They should bolster eligible insurance fund, industrial investment fund, private equity fund and trust products to form consortiums with eligible and professional elderly service providers or operators and invest in PPP elderly care projects as private investors. The local government will actively guide financial institutions to set up elderly care industry fund or acquisition fund and give key support to a group of elderly service projects that can be commercialized. They will encourage private investors to foster comprehensive elderly care groups across regions and industries by means of merger, restructuring and export of service, technology and brand, and cultivate brand-name, professional and large-scale elderly service chain organizations. They will also encourage the development of enterprise bond, corporate bond and special-project bond to establish and improve a diverse and multi-layered financing system for the elderly care industry.

(2) Increasing project liquidity

There are three ways to determine the ultimate holder of PPP elderly care projects through the design of financial structure. One is to support those projects with fiscal fund or charity fund like the welfare lottery, or the government provides low-cost land for elderly care institutions' long-term use. The government is the ultimate holder of PPP projects in this case. The second way is to promote the free flow and transfer of equity and creditor's right of PPP projects through the PPP property right transaction center, whereby the equity and creditor's right will generally circulate among large organizations. The third way is to realize the ownership of PPP elderly care projects by all through the securitization of PPP assets or REITs. The second and third ways realize the circulation of PPP projects in the level-two transaction market based on their future right to earnings. This means that after the elderly care project operates for a while, the capital can be vitalized through asset securitization or REITs, or through the circulation of equity or creditor's right at the PPP property right transaction center. In this way, the initial shareholders and creditors will step out so that the elderly care project can have a higher level of liquidity. Generally speaking, the PPP agreement can include the guarantee that the government will ensure the minimal amount of usage and the cash flow is relatively stable. This can dispel the investor's concerns, ensure the project's financing feasibility and resolve the risk of unstable demand. Long-term and relatively steady future right to earnings is an important precondition and guarantee for the liquidity of PPP elderly care projects.

(3) Increasing credit-enhancing measures

We support financial institutions to enhance financing credit for PPP by utilizing the future right to earnings, the government service purchase agreement, and the mortgage or pledge of intangible assets like intellectual property right, on the premise of independent decision and controllable risks. We also support private investors to set up financing guarantee companies either independently or in conjunction with financial institutions, and provide various forms of loan guarantee services for elderly care enterprises, projects, and social organizations.

5.2 Selecting Projects Scientifically

(1) Rigorous and thorough proving

A new surge of PPP appeared at the end of 2014 and this model has spread ever since at a speed never seen before. To lower government debt, some local governments blindly promote the PPP model in the infrastructure and public utility sector, which leads to a string of bad phenomena. For instance, the preliminary proving, including the assessment of the PPP project's worthiness and fiscal bearing capacity, is too perfunctory, no appropriate calculation of the amount of fiscal subsidy needed by the project and the term and arrangement of payment is conducted, and the fiscal payment responsibility for the project is not included in the fiscal budget and the mid- and long-term fiscal plan. Therefore, we need to continuously perfect the methods of proving the worthiness and assessing the fiscal bearing capacity of PPP elderly care projects, and put in place a sound PPP expert review mechanism to truly fulfill the review and supervisory responsibility for the project by collecting the opinions of experts both inside and outside the industry. Projects that did not pass the review cannot implement the PPP model.

(2) Continuous assessment throughout the project

The tracking, monitoring and performance assessment of projects already in process is of great importance for PPP projects in the elderly care industry. On one hand, while carrying out the PPP elderly care projects, we need to continuously summarize the mature and feasible model of commercial operation and profit making, pinpoint successful experience, and cultivate demonstration cases for the later comers to learn from and draw on. On the other hand, a relatively solid system of external supervision and management and project performance assessment should be established. We should establish a supervisory and management system for the elderly care industry integrating the government, the market and private investors, strengthen the full-process supervision of project companies, and specify their term of service provision, type of elderly services, number of elders served, and the level and standards of elderly care. We should also engage the public in supervising and evaluating project performance, accept supervision from all sides, and make sure the performance assessment is meaningful and substantial.

5.3 Strengthening Operation Management

The reason why the PPP model is promoted in elderly care projects is because of the government resource and the private investor's professional and efficient operation management. By introducing the private investor, the project is more cost-effective and efficient than if it is operated and managed by the government alone. The elderly service industry is highly professional and commercialized, so it is suitable to be operated through the PPP model. There are also specific requirements on the operating qualification and professional competence when selecting the private investor, and the contents, terms and standards of the services it provides are clearly stated in the contract, otherwise elderly care project can easily turn into real estate or other types of projects.

The elderly care industry in China has just started, its rate of return is rather low, and a mature business model has not been formed yet, so market organizations engaged in this industry are still making their own explorations. As a result, there is no brand-name and large-scale elderly service chain providers in the Chinese market today. There are some small nursing homes though. Cui Cao Chun Hui has been built in some areas in China and has operated successfully for a while now, but while these small elderly care institutions can run a retirement community well, they cannot reach the threshold set by the government for introducing private investors and implementing the PPP model due to the limited scale. Therefore, we should make greater efforts to cultivate large and professional elderly service operators in the future, and pay close attention to the listing of large elderly care groups or the shift of large listed companies toward the elderly care industry. On the other hand, attention should be paid to the existence and development of small and quality nursing homes too. We should actively create a favorable business environment for them, and the eligibility for private investor should be more focused on the quality of operation and service than on scale.

5.4 *Integrating and Fostering New Business Forms*

Nursing homes alone cannot meet the elders' growing wish and demand for a happy life. In addition, pure elderly care projects only have a low return on investment that barely exceeds 10%. In Japan, the operation of nursing homes can just make ends meet and it is the other businesses that make profits for such projects. Therefore, we should encourage the elderly care institutions to cooperate with medical and health care organizations, support the creation of a full-life-cycle elderly care industrial chain "with health management as the basis, elderly care as the core and medical service as the supporting force", and foster the new "elderly care plus" businesses centered on elderly care along with recreation, health care, sports, medical service, education, culture and entertainment, and online services. Such a comprehensive package can not only increase the profit margin of elderly care service and consequently reduce the fiscal pressure, but can also maintain the non-profit nature of elderly care institutions, thus driving the development of basic elderly care industry through the integration and extension of the industrial chain.

Besides, given the general trend of destocking, many discarded or idle training centers, hotels, hospitals, cadre's sanitariums and commercial properties can be renovated and upgraded into elderly service organizations through the PPP model, which will not only reduce the stock properties, but also put them into efficient use. Special attention should be paid to the changed usage of properties in downtown areas. In some cities where there is a large stock of commercial properties that are hard to lease, the government can offer certain property right, fiscal subsidy or tax policy to help transform those idle or poorly operated properties in downtown areas.

5.5 *Improving Auxiliary Policies*

First, we should give elderly care institutions reasonable tax and fee preferences. Especially after the business tax is replaced by VAT, the study of VAT on profit-oriented old age care institutions and the design of corresponding tax reduction and exemption policy is particularly important. For example, should we reduce or exempt the VAT on the bed charge or rent of elderly care institutions, on the everyday consumption of the elders living there, or on both? These questions require more prudent design and discussions among multiple parties.

Second, we should connect the PPP project database of the Ministry of Finance and NDRC, so that they can ensure each other, meaning the Ministry of Finance can ensure the project's government procurement and payment, while the NDRC can ensure the project's feasibility study and project establishment. This will make PPP elderly care projects much more attractive for private investors.

Third, we should enlarge the coverage of rural elderly service and raise its quality. The lump-sum construction subsidy and later the bed-based operation subsidy for elderly care service organizations can be appropriately inclined to those in rural areas, and more efforts should be made to further urge private investors to engage in rural elderly care construction and service, aiming for the balanced development of the elderly care industry between urban and rural areas.

Fourth, we should make the settlement of medical insurance more convenient. Medical care is an indispensable part of elderly service. Local governments at all levels and in all places should actively coordinate to incorporate the elderly care institutions, "healthcare + elderly care" facilities or retirement communities that are built in PPP model in the local medical insurance system, and make the medical insurance settlement ever more convenient and timely.

Fifth, we should create and design more auxiliary insurance products. The elderly service industry targets a special and high-risk group and needs to be guaranteed by a range of auxiliary insurance products, such as life insurance, accident insurance, long-term nursery insurance and liability insurance of elderly care institutions, so as to relieve these institutions of their concerns and worries.

Reference

Zhou, L. (2016). *How to operate PPP projects*. Beijing: Law Press.

Lan Zhang doctor at the University of International Business and Economics, visiting scholar at Ohio State University, post-doctor at the doctor's work station of the Industrial Bank of China and the mobile station of the Financial Institute of Chinese Academy of Social Sciences, and a young researcher of the China Aging Finance Forum. She specializes in PPP and new type of urbanization. The paper only represents personal opinions, not the opinions of the employer.

Chapter 13
"Home for Care": Localized Exploration for Niche Pension Approach

Dong Zhang and Bo Sun

Abstract As a supplementary pension approach, "home for care" already caught extensive attention in China more than ten years ago, and private organizations, government bodies, banks and the insurance sector have all carried out a series of practices and explorations. But in general, the public demand for this approach is largely restricted due to traditional ideas and many scruples, and the financial institutions are neither capable nor willing enough to finance this approach owing to a string of risks. Besides, the auxiliary policies haven't been fully formulated and the institutional environment isn't mature enough, so the "home for care" approach has developed quite slowly in the country. According to foreign experience, public support and recognition, government engagement and legal guarantee, mature industrial form, and diverse product design are all important guarantees for the development of "home for care" and are worth drawing on and improving. In the future, "home for care" will be a niche approach in China, but the potential market is not to be underestimated. We should specify the government functions, improve the institutional environment for this approach, encourage the cooperation of multiple parties, better "home for care" products, promote the idea of pension diversification, and deepen the rational understanding of "home for care", so as to make full preparations for its long-term development.

Keywords Home for care · Reverse mortgage · Traditional ideas · Systemic risks · Institutional environment

As a mature supplementary pension approach adopted around the world, "home for care" first appeared in the Netherlands and was most mature and well-developed in the United States. It has also developed rapidly in the United Kingdom, France, Singapore and Japan. After decades, this approach has become a mature financing channel and a

---

The paper only reflects their personal opinions, not the opinions of the employer.

D. Zhang (✉)
Renmin University of China, Beijing, China

B. Sun
Pension Management Department, China Asset Management, Beijing, China

K. Dong and Y. Yao (eds.), *Annual Report on Financing Old Age Care in China (2017)*, https://doi.org/10.1007/978-981-13-0968-7_13

relatively effective supplementary pension approach in western countries, and plays an important role in addressing population ageing and meeting the diverse elderly care needs.

With the rapid economic and social development in China, elderly care demands have become increasingly diverse. Due to new trends such as the ageing of population and downsizing of families, the supply of elderly care is facing a range of challenges. Against such a background, developing more pension approaches is the common goal of the government and the market, and socialized pension approaches such as "home for care" came into being.

1 Overview of "Home for Care"

1.1 What Is "Home for Care"

"Home for care" refers to a way in which the elderly finance their own old age care by converting part of the equity in their homes into cash. It is an effective way of helping those elders that have property but lack money to spend.[1] After years of experience, different forms of "home for care" have emerged in different countries, including both financial models and non-financial models. Examples of the former are reverse mortgage and housing-based pension and life insurance, and those of the latter are raising funds to support one's old age care by selling, swapping, leasing or gifting one's residence. Among them, reverse mortgage is the most popular and typical one. The central idea is that the home owner mortgages the housing property right to the bank or insurance company, and the corresponding financial institution performs a comprehensive evaluation of the actual value of the property, the owner's age and life expectancy, and the future depreciation or appreciation. In return, the home owner can receive a certain amount of pension from the institution regularly or receive services from a nursing home. The institution cannot obtain the property right of the housing and dispose of it until after the owner passes away.

The essence of "home for care" is to turn the housing properties owned by the elders from asset into cash through financial or non-financial operations. This makes it possible for these properties to serve the dual function of being a place of dwelling as well as a source of fund to support old age care, thus complementing the elderly care system on the economic or service level. In short, it means "trading home ownership for old age care".

[1] "Home for Care" can be understood in the general sense and the narrow sense. In the narrow sense, it means "home for care" for housing, and in the general sense, it means any action to obtain elderly care income or service based on the self-owned house. The concept of "Home for Care" in this paper is an improvement based on the definition by Xu Shunting, etc.

1.2 Applicable Conditions

As a supplementary option of elderly care, "home for care" needs a series of conditions. First, the elder should own the house and have full property right, which is the precondition for mortgage, sale or lease. Housing of limited property right, such as benefit housing distributed by the company or settlement housing with exchanged property right due to demolition, isn't applicable for the "home for care" approach. Second, the elder has a stable family structure without legacy concerns. The "home for care" approach is particularly suitable for "empty nester" and "DINK" elders, but it's also an option for "4-2-1" families (with four grandparents, two parents and a kid) with average economic condition. Third, the housing is relatively valuable and usually located in urban or suburban areas. This kind of housing has large room for appreciation and is easy to sell, so it's suitable for financial models like "home for care". On the contrary, low-value housing located in rural areas is hard to sell and therefore not so applicable for "home for care". Fourth, the elder is rich in housing but poor with cash. Generally speaking, the financial model of "home for care" isn't universally applicable. It's only suitable for the middle- or low-income group that has housing with independent property right and doesn't involve or care about the housing inheritance.

2 Review of "Home for Care" Policy and Practices of It in China

2.1 Review of "Home for Care" Policy in China

"Home for Care" is a new type of elderly care approach that caught attention and was implemented overseas several decades ago. It first caught attention in China in March 2003, when Meng Xiaosu, then chairman of China National Real Estate Development Group Corporation, submitted a report titled *Suggestion on Providing the Life Insurance Service of Reverse Mortgage* to the State Council, regarding which the then Premier Wen Jiabao gave instructions. Since then the concept of "home for care" has received extensive attention. In August that year, the China Insurance Regulatory Commission and the then Ministry of Construction jointly carried out a survey and submitted the *Report on Matters Concerning the Initiation of Reverse Mortgage* to the State Council, in which they affirmed the great importance of bringing "reverse mortgage for seniors" to China. In the following decade, different industries and organizations have all conducted explorations in that area, but no specific guiding opinions or policy paper has ever been issued.

In September 2013, the State Council issued *Several Opinions on Accelerating the Development of Pension Services Industry*, which, for the first time on the state policy level, proposed to "carry out pilot implementation of endowment insurance based on housing mortgage". This marked that "home for care" officially became a subject supported and guided by the national policy, and China would make more explorations and practices and find a "home for care" model suitable for our national conditions.

After that, various departments have issued a number of measures and documents to promote "home for care" (see Table 1). In 2014, the China Insurance Regulatory Commission issued the *Guidelines on Carrying out Pilot Project of Endowment Insurance Based on Reverse Mortgage for Seniors*, which said that from July 1, 2014, elders aged above 60 who have housing with independent property right can choose the "home for care" approach featuring reverse mortgage for seniors in the four pilot cities of Beijing, Shanghai, Guangzhou and Wuhan. In March 2016, the State Council approved the *Opinions on Key Work of Deepening the Economic System Reform in 2016* submitted by NDRC, which included the trial implementation of endowment insurance based on reverse mortgage for seniors and reflected the close attention to "home for care" work. In July 2016, the China Insurance Regulatory Commission issued the *Notice on Extending the Term and Enlarging the Scope of Trial Implementation of Endowment Insurance Based on Reverse Mortgage for Seniors*, whereby the term of the trial implementation was extended to June 30, 2018 and the scope was further expanded.

2.2 Practices of "Home for Care" in China

After the "Home for Care" model represented by "home for care" received policy support in 2003, relevant departments and the market have conducted a series of studies and practical explorations. Since 2005, this approach has been implemented in some cities and regions on a trial basis and on various scales. At the moment, the elders themselves, the local governments and market organizations are all prudent with the "home for care" business, but current practices and trial implements have provided ample samples and experiences for further improving this model. Current explorations for the "Home for Care" model in China can be divided into four types, each dominated by private organizations, by the government, by banks and by insurance companies respectively (see Table 2).

Source: based on the public documents mentioned in the report.

2.2.1 "Home for Care" Launched by Private Organizations

The Tang Shan Liu Yuan Nursing Home in Nanjing is one of the representative "home for care" projects initiated by private organizations. It began to explore the "home for care" business in 2005. Elders aged above 60 without family who have a housing property of more than 60 m^2 with independent property right in Nanjing can mortgage their housing at their own will and move to live in the nursing home after notarization. The nursing home will lease the mortgaged house and charge the living expenses from the rent, and the remaining rent will be at the elder's disposal.

Table 1 Origin of "Home for Care" in China and change of relevant policies

Time	Document	Main contents
March 2003	Meng Xiaosu submitted the *Suggestion on Providing the Life Insurance Service of Reverse Mortgage* to the State Council, regarding which Premier Wen Jiabao gave instructions	The practice of "reverse mortgage" in developed countries is based on the private house of the elders and offers lifetime social security services for them. This is worth promoting in China
August 2003	China Insurance Regulatory Commission and the then Ministry of Construction submitted the *Report on Matters Concerning the Initiation of Reverse Mortgage* to the State Council	It affirmed the great importance of bringing "reverse mortgage" to China, but called for risk assessment
September 2013	The State Council issued *Several Opinions on Accelerating the Development of Elderly Care Service Industry*	Endowment insurance based on reverse mortgage was carried out on a trial basis
June 2014	China Insurance Regulatory Commission issued the *Guidelines on Carrying out Pilot Project of Endowment Insurance Based on Reverse Mortgage for Seniors*	From July 1, 2014, elders aged above 60 who have housing with independent property right can choose the "home for care" approach in the four pilot cities of Beijing, Shanghai, Guangzhou and Wuhan for the trial period of two years
March 2016	NDRC issued the *Opinions on Key Work of Deepening the Economic System Reform in 2016*	Trial implementation of endowment insurance based on reverse mortgage would be promoted
July 2016	China Insurance Regulatory Commission issued the *Notice on Extending the Term and Enlarging the Scope of Trial Implementation of Endowment Insurance Based on Reverse Mortgage for Seniors*	The term of trial implementation was extended to June 30, 2018 and the scope of trial implementation was expanded to municipalities directly under the central government, provincial capital cities (or capital city of autonomous regions), municipalities with independent planning status, and some prefecture-level cities in Jiangsu, Zhejiang, Shandong and Guangdong

Table 2 Explorations for "Home for Care" in China

	Conditions for application			Product features	
Type	Typical project	Age requirement	Housing requirement	Form of disposal	Form of elderly care
Dominated by private organization	Tang Shan Liu Yuan Nursing Home, Nanjing	Above 60	More than 60 m^2, independent property right	Mortgaged lease, property right belongs to the nursing home in the end	Living in the nursing home
	"Housing bank for elderly care", Beijing	Above 60	None	Rent from leasing the original housing, no change in property right	Living in elderly service center
Dominated by government	"Housing-based self-service elderly care", Shanghai	Above 65	Independent property right	Sale and leaseback, property right is given up	Renting the original housing
	Hubin Sub-district, Shangcheng District, Hangzhou	Above 60	Independent property right or public housing	Lease or sale of housing	Living in nursing home or rental apartment
Dominated by bank	Pension mortgage loan of CITIC Bank	Above 55/special application	Independent property right and with a second housing property	Mortgage loan, principal and interests are paid in time	No limitation
Dominated by insurance company	"Happy "home for care" program" of Happy Life	60–85, widowed or the only child is lost	Independent property right	Pension from mortgaged housing, property right belongs to the institution in the end	Living in the original housing or leasing it and living in nursing home

The property right of the house will belong to the nursing home after the elder passes away. According to survey, only four elderly people adopted this "Home for Care" approach in the end owing to the rigorous conditions, and they quit later due to the nursing home's poor credibility and internal economic disputes. The first attempt at "Home for Care" in China was a failure.

The "housing bank for elderly care" of Beijing is another exploration for "Home for Care" launched by private organizations after the attempt in Nanjing. It was jointly launched by Beijing Shou Shan Fu Hai International Elderly Service Center and Zhong Da Heng Ji Real Estate Agency in October 2007. Elders aged above 60 can apply to live in the elderly service center. After they live there, the center will lease their original house and the rent will be used to cover their expenses at the center, but the ownership of the housing property right will not change. After a half-year trial implementation, less than ten elderly people adopted this approach, and they left in the end due to a series of reasons, including the lack of credibility of this kind of purely commercial model (Chen 2013).

2.2.2 "Home for Care" Launched by the Government

The "housing-based self-service elderly care" in Shanghai is the first "Home for Care" model tried by the government, and was launched by the Shanghai Housing Provident Fund Management Center in 2007. Elderly people aged above 65 can choose to sell their house with property right to the Shanghai Housing Provident Fund Management Center, get the full payment and the property right is transferred to the Center. Then the Center will lease their house back to them at market price, and the elders can pay the rent in lump sum according to the term of lease without paying any other expense. The housing will be used as urban low-rent housing after the lease expires or the elder passes away. The essence of this model is sale and leaseback, and the original house owner obtains pension from the difference between the house value and the rent. The advantage of this model is that it is guaranteed with government credibility and the elders can continue to live in a familiar environment, but the disadvantage is that it's hard for the elders to accept the transfer of housing property right, and they may also face the risk that the payment for the house isn't enough to cover their elderly care expenses and the house price will go up. Elderly people of only five families adopted this model till the end of 2008 when the trial implementation ended, and the program had to terminate in 2010 for various reasons.

As a typical "Home for Care" program dominated by the government, the Hubin Sub-district in Shangcheng district of Hangzhou City put forth four "Home for Care" options for elders with no income and children and the solitary ones with no family in 2008. The first option is that solitary elders who have housing can choose to live in the nursing home through the neighborhood's arrangement, and the neighborhood will lease their original housing and use the rent to cover their everyday expenses. The second option is that solitary elders who have housing can choose to live in the nursing home through the neighborhood's arrangement, and the neighborhood will sell their original housing and use the payment to cover their everyday expenses. The third option is that that solitary elders who have housing can choose to live in the nursing home through the neighborhood's arrangement, and the housing authority will take back their original public housing and subsidize them at market price. The fourth option is leasing the elder's original housing that's located in a good area and renting another housing property in a poor area instead, and the price difference is at the elder's disposal. Elders of four families adopted the first option, but the other three options haven't been implemented yet. The Hangzhou model is attractive because it designs several options for the elders to choose from independently regarding key issues like the housing property right.

2.2.3 "Home for Care" Launched by Banks

In 2011, CITIC Bank took the initiative to carry out the "Home for Care" business in Beijing and Shanghai. The applicants should be aged above 55 or their legal supporter aged above 18 should jointly apply to the bank for the "Home for Care" loan, and the certificate of a second housing property should be submitted too. The bank will entrust a professional organization to evaluate the property, and provide the applicant with a loan no more than 60% of the housing price for elderly care, which will be paid monthly with the monthly amount no more than RMB20,000. The term of the loan is no more than 10 years, during which no interest rate discount will be provided, and the principal and interests should be paid in full when the term matures, otherwise the bank will dispose of the housing property. The Industrial Bank launched the "Home for Care" business in 2013, too, based on its "Pleasant Life" program, according to which customers aged above 50 or their adult children can apply for house-based loan of no more than RMB300,000 for the term of no more than three years. When the two banks initiated this business, many people came to inquire, which reflected the demand for "Home for Care", but not many people eventually adopted this bank-dominated model due to the many restrictions, lack of interest rate preference, and concerns over risks.

2.2.4 "Home for Care" Launched by Insurance Companies

In March 2015, Happy Life's "happy "home for care" program" was officially approved by China Insurance Regulatory Commission and became the first "home for care" product dominated by an insurance company. This product targeted elders aged 60–85, especially widows, widowers and those who lost their only child. Eligible elders can mortgage their property to Happy Life. After the property is evaluated and notarized, the two sides will sign an insurance contract, and the elders can choose to continue living in their own house or live in the nursing home while entrusting the insurance company to lease the house. According to the contract, the insurance company should provide the elders with old age insurance within the specified term and the amount of the pension isn't affected by the fluctuation of the house price. After the elders pass away, the insurance company will have the right to dispose of the mortgaged house, and the income will first be used to pay for the elderly care expenses, while the remaining part will go to the elder's inheritor. If the income isn't enough to cover the elderly care expense, the insurance company should make up for the shortfall. An important precondition for this model is that the insurance company has powerful risk diversification and actuarial technology. Data show that by June 30, 2016, 57 elders of 42 families participated in the trial implementation and completed the insurance underwriting procedures. The enrollees were aged 71.6 on average and the average monthly pension for each family was about RMB9071, with the maximum of RMB20,000 (Mo 2016).

2.3 *Evaluation of "Home for Care" Market in China*

2.3.1 Demand: Potential Demand for "Home for Care" Emerges Amid Economic and Social Transformation

First, with the change of population structure, weakening of family functions, increase of empty nesters and elders who lost their only child, the traditional approach of elderly care is facing many challenges and the emerging approach of "Home for Care" has become a new way to meet the diverse elderly care demands. Because of population ageing, families in China tend to get smaller and with fewer children. According to data from the National Bureau of Statistics, the average family size in China has shrunk from 4.33 people during the first census in 1953 to 3.10 people during the sixth census in 2010, which will further shrink to 2.61 people in 2030 and 2.51 people in 2050 (see Fig. 1). This phenomenon will continue to exist and will largely impair the family function of elderly care. On the other hand, due to the family planning policy and other factors, there are more empty nesters and elders who lost their only child in China. There were more than 100 million empty nesters in 2013 and at least a million families that had lost their only child in 2012, the latter increasing at the rate of around 76,000 families per year.

Second, the old age security system is on a low level and diverse approaches are to be explored. According to the data of previous census and sample surveys, the income of the elderly group mainly comes from labor, pension and provision by other family members. As population ageing aggravates, more elderly people will

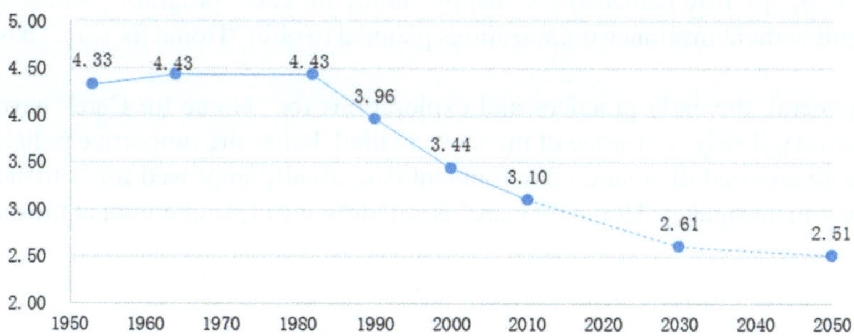

Fig. 1 Family size in previous censuses and future forecast. *Source* Data of 1950–2010 is based on previous census; data after 2010 is in reference to the forecast made by the group that studies the strategy for China to deal with population aging

lose their working ability, and their continuous labor income will not be guaranteed. At the same time, the ever nuclear family structure weakens the providing ability of other family members, while the amount of China's current basic old age insurance is limited and the supplementary endowment insurance hasn't been fully established. As a result, we should urgently develop diverse elderly care approaches and raise the level of elderly care.

Third, self-owned housing takes up a large proportion and the value of housing property keeps growing. According to the *Research Report of China Household Finance Survey 2015*, housing accounts for 69% of the family assets in China as opposed to 30% in the United States. According to the 2010 survey of the situation of elderly people in the urban and rural areas of China, 75.7% of urban elders had their own house with property right.[2] Thanks to the brisk real estate market in recent years, the housing price has kept rising, so has the value of housing properties. Housing becomes an important component of the family assets of urban residents, which provides the basic condition for "Home for Care".

2.3.2 Supply: Explorations for "Home for Care" Have Been Made Continuously and the Approach Has Drawn Extensive Attention in the Market

After the concept of "Home for Care" was introduced to China in 2003, organizations of different natures have carried out explorations actively, including explorations by private organizations represented by the Tang Shan Liu Yuan Nursing Home in Nanjing and the "housing bank for elderly care" program in Beijing, those by the Shanghai Housing Provident Fund Management Center and on the Hubin Subdistrict of Hangzhou's Shangcheng district, and "Home for Care" products designed by CITIC Bank, Industrial Bank and Bank of Shanghai. Moreover, after the China Insurance Regulatory Commission issued the *Guidelines on Carrying out Pilot Project of Endowment Insurance Based on "Home for Care" "Home for Care" for Seniors* in 2014, Happy Life launched the "happy "home for care" program", while several other endowment insurance organizations planned to offer "Home for Care" business too.

In general, the early practices and explorations for "Home for Care" have progressed very slowly, and some of them even failed, but as the supportive policies are getting clearer and the market environment is gradually improved for both sides of the housing mortgage, "Home for Care" is still drawing close attention in the market.

[2]Source: http://politics.people.com.cn/n/2012/0710/c1001-18486623.html.

3 Problems and Challenges Faced by "Home for Care" in China

"Home for Care" is not only a new approach of elderly care, but also an innovative financial product and an effective means of switching the housing's function between elderly care and living. It is of great importance for China to deal with the population ageing and ensure the provision of elderly care through multiple channels. After this model, which is already quite mature in many foreign countries and was introduced to China more than ten years ago, explorations and practices of it have been made in different regions and industries, but the progress is very slow in general for the main reason of weak demand, insufficient supply and immature institutional environment.

3.1 Public Demand Is Limited Due to Traditional Ideas and Systematic Concerns

First, the traditional idea of elderly care and the practice of leaving legacy to children make "Home for Care" less acceptable. Home-based elderly care is still dominant in China and the idea of bringing up children to support parents in their old age is deeply rooted. If the elders mortgage their house, either they still live in it but give up the property right posthumously, or directly give up the property right and obtain pension to live in the nursing home, or live in the original house and their children have the priority to redeem it after the elders pass away according to their elderly care expenses, it's not only hard to accept for the elders themselves, but also brings a lot of mental pressure for the children. In the meantime, China has the tradition of parents leaving some legacy for the children. A house doesn't just have the residential function, but also carries the family history and tradition. It doesn't just have economic value, but also symbolizes the emotional bond between the older and younger generations. These traditional ideas and practices constitute an important reason why very few "Home for Care" programs have been successfully implemented so far.

Second, the credibility of organizations increases the demanders' concerns over "Home for Care". On one hand, the "Home for Care" approach has a long mortgage period, and it just started in China, so there is no mature business model or a well developed legal system to guarantee the elders' rights and interests. The current trial implementation of "Home for Care" in China is mostly undertaken by commercial organizations such as banks or insurance companies. If the organization goes bankrupt due to poor operation or its "Home for Care" business terminates because it cannot meet the expectation, it may cause immense losses to the demanders and make them concerned. On the other hand, once the elders mortgage their property to the loan supplier and move to live in the nursing home that the loan supplier provide or cooperate with, the service quality at the nursing home cannot be guaranteed as the mortgage contract is already signed.

Third, the anticipation for housing price rise reduces the demand for "Home for Care". Ever since the economic crisis in 2008, the Chinese real estate industry has been growing at an ever faster pace. Real estate development has accelerated, housing price has kept rising, and the growing momentum hasn't been fundamentally changed in recent years. As people expect the housing price to go up further, their demand for "Home for Care" has been largely reduced for fear of potential losses. Some trial projects of "Home for Care", such as the "happy "home for care" program" of Happy Life, promised that if the housing price continues to rise, the increased value will be inherited by the elder's inheritor, whereas the risk of housing price reduction will be borne by the company. This policy that obviously deviates from the risk-sharing principle is a measure to attract customers when the product is first launched and won't be a regular mechanism.

Besides, an important step for housing mortgage is evaluation, but the housing evaluation market in China isn't very mature at the moment. Potential customers not only need to bear the risk of unfair evaluation, but also the high evaluation cost, which adds another obstacle to the implementation of "Home for Care".

3.2 Financial Institutions Have Insufficient Supply Ability and Will Due to a Series of Risks

First of all, market and technological risks are hard to expect, which undermines the commercial organization's drive for engaging in "Home for Care". There are several types of market risks, including real estate bubble, interest rate risk and longevity risk. Real estate bubble is highly uncertain as it is closely related with the future economic development and the trend of the real estate industry. What with the macroeconomic trend and what with the national policy, it may undergo unexpected fluctuations anytime, and commercial organizations will have to bear the risk of housing price reduction in a long period once the "Home for Care" contract is signed. Therefore, most commercial organizations are very prudent about the "Home for Care" business. The interest rate risk mainly refers to the market interest rate fluctuations. If the actual interest rate is much higher than the contractual rate, the lender will face the risk that the loan and accrued interests exceed the value of the mortgaged house. If the actual interest rate is much lower than the contractual rate, the borrower may pay back the loan in advance and end the contract. Longevity risk means that if the elder lives much longer than expected, and the mortgaged housing property isn't enough to cover the principal and interests, the commercial organization cannot recover the shortfall from the financer or inheritor, but has to bear the elder's longevity risk. Commercial organizations have to address these risks through scientific and reliable actuarial means. However, as there are many uncertainties regarding the housing price evaluation, the elder's life expectancy and the interest rate fluctuation, commercial organizations are faced with major technological risks, and that dampens their drive for engaging in "Home for Care".

Second, the difficulty in solving the cost risks increases the pressure for organizations to provide "Home for Care" products. The operation of "Home for Care" program is extremely complicated. According to international experience, it generally requires the engagement of multiple parties including the bank, insurance company, investors and relevant intermediary organization, which can work together to lower the cost through their supplementary strengths. However, the *Securities Law of the People's Republic of China* and the *Law of the People's Republic of China on Commercial Banks* stipulate the "separate operation and regulation" of financial institutions, which restricts the cooperation among the different parties to a large extent and significantly increases the implementing cost of "Home for Care". Besides, the mortgaged house also faces natural risks. If the mortgaged house is hit by natural disaster, the commercial organization will suffer losses too, and if the commercial organization buys insurance for the house, that means extra cost.

Third, commercial organizations face a series of moral risks when engaging in "Home for Care". On the one hand, the high house evaluation and short life span of the elder is more beneficial for the commercial organization, but it's easier to evaluate the house than the elder's life span. In fact, elders that expect to live long are more likely to engage in "Home for Care" than those in poor health condition. On the other hand, after the two sides sign the contract, the ultimate ownership of the house belongs to the commercial organization. Therefore, if the elders choose to live in their original house, they will cut the expense on its maintenance in order to maximize their own benefit, which will impair the house's future evaluation.

3.3 Auxiliary Policies Are Underdeveloped and Institutional Environment Needs Improvement

Because of the complexity and specialty of "Home for Care", both the supplier or lender and the demander or borrower face a series of risks, which have to be resolved with the help of laws and policies, thus creating a stable and mature institutional environment. However, at the moment, the auxiliary laws and policies in support of "Home for Care" in China are far from able to solve those risks.

First, the policies and laws concerning "Home for Care" are not well developed, which impedes the development of this approach. On one hand, there aren't definite laws to support "Home for Care" in the country. In recent years, different departments have put forth suggestions on developing "Home for Care" in the form of guiding opinions and notice, but there are no specific implementing rules to guarantee the interests of either side. In comparison, in developed countries like the U.S., their Housing Law and Banking Law contain detailed provisions on "Home for Care", which guarantees the legal rights and interests of both sides. On the other hand, some policies and legal provisions in China, such as the 70-year property right of house, seriously limit the housing value when it's being evaluated for "Home for Care". Although the Property Law provides that the property right will automatically extend when it expires, there are no definite standards and conditions for the extension and payment for it. That is the biggest obstacle for commercial organizations to engage in "Home for Care".

Second, inadequate government regulation dampens people's trust in "Home for Care" products. The "Home for Care" approach is in the trial stage in China. Relevant departments put forth opinions of support but didn't set specific regulatory rules. As a result, different organizations have largely different explorations for this approach and are all in the stage of "crossing the river by feeling the stones". The lack of definite, objective and fair regulations on the mechanism of access, operation, evaluation and contract performance makes the promotion of "Home for Care" difficult.

Third, the immature institutional environment for "Home for Care" impairs the foundation for transaction between the supplier and the demander. On the one hand, housing evaluation is an important step for promoting "Home for Care", but the real estate evaluation organizations in China are not well regulated and highly credible ones are lacking. This impairs the foundation for "Home for Care" transactions. On the other hand, the "Home for Care" approach involves housing mortgage and resale, which requires a flexible and advanced level-2 real estate market. The Chinese level-2 market has progressed to some extent in recent years, but it's not well developed and has such irregular situations as uneven qualifications, asymmetrical information and low credit. The obstacles in terms of institutional environment seriously impede the promotion of "Home for Care".

4 Outlook on the Future Trend of "Home for Care" in China

4.1 "Home for Care" Targets a Small Group but the Potential Market Should not Be Underestimated

Either in terms of its design or its practice in China and abroad, "Home for Care" is a niche product that targets elders who have independent housing and had lost their only child or their children live far away from home. Of the eligible potential customers, only 3% eventually choose this approach even in the United States, where the "Home for Care" business is most developed, and the participation rate in Britain is only 0.2% (Li 2016). Although "Home for Care" is a niche business, its potential demand is not to be underestimated, especially given the "4-2-1" family structure in China and the conflict between fixed housing property and the difficulty in meeting the elderly care demand. "Home for Care" is one of the effective ways to solve this conflict. Compared with other countries, the housing possession rate in China is 87%, much higher than America's 65.4%, Britain's 70% and Japan's 60%, creating the basic condition for promoting this approach. By the end of 2016, there were

231 million elders in China aged above 60, and their urban-rural ratio was 44:56,[3] meaning there were about 102 million elders living in the urban area. At present, the per capita housing area in Chinese cities is more than 33 m^2,[4] and 75.7% of the elderly urban residents have their own housing, so they have about 3366 million m^2 of housing area in total. According to the latest data from the National Bureau of Statistics, the average price of commercial housing in China was RMB6473/m^2 in 2015, which means the housing possessed by elderly city dwellers is worth almost RMB22 trillion. Suppose 1% of the elders are willing to engage in "Home for Care", that will be a market of RMB220 billion. As population ageing becomes more serious and the traditional concept of elderly care gradually changes, the "Home for Care" market may further expand.

4.2 *Cooperation Between Banks and Insurance Companies Is Good for the Development of "Home for Care"*

The most typical form of "Home for Care" is reverse mortgage, which is characterized by the design of mortgage product for the fixed housing assets through a risk diversification mechanism. This involves two most important steps—risk control and financial credit. Therefore, any "Home for Care" product designed by a single party, either the bank or the insurance company, has many defects and is costly. While banks have plenty of capital and solid mortgage experience, they are inexperienced in controlling the life risks. Similarly, while insurance companies are good at risk control, they lack the experience in financial credit. Their cooperation is a feasible thought for the design of "Home for Care" product, while the government will provide policy support and regulation during the operation of the product, so as to ensure its credibility. Besides, private organizations have neither the advantage nor the credibility to run "Home for Care" products, and their prospects in this aspect are limited.

4.3 *Inheritance Tax May Become an Important Booster of "Home for Care"*

An important reason for the popularity of "Home for Care" in developed countries is their high inheritance tax. In the United States, the Federal Estate Tax adopts the progressive tax rate in excess of specific amount. If the child inherits the legacy including the housing property, he/she has to pay inheritance tax varying from 18 to 50% after the debts, funeral expense and other exempted expenditures are deducted from the legacy. But if the elder decides to adopt "Home for Care", the cash he/she receives is

[3]Source: calculated based on data of the sixth census.

[4]Source: http://finance.sina.com.cn/roll/2016-10-19/doc-ifxwzpsa8223864.shtml.

exempt from any tax. China issued the *Provisional Regulations on Inheritance Tax (Draft)* in 2004, but the inheritance tax hasn't been launched yet for various reasons, although the exploration in that aspect has never stopped in relevant departments and regions despite the arguments. Once the inheritance tax is launched, the "Home for Care" product will become an effective tool of tax evasion because it is usually exempt from tax. Therefore, it is foreseeable that inheritance tax may give a strong impetus to the "Home for Care" approach.

4.4 Supporting the Development of Elderly Service Industry with PPP Will Be a Great Opportunity for "Home for Care"

An important reason for the difficulty in developing "Home for Care" in China is the backward development of the elderly service industry. In particular, due to reasons like service quality and regional distribution, some nursing homes have idle beds but some are overcrowded, which is one of the reasons why some elderly don't accept "Home for Care". Great importance has been attached to the development of the elderly service industry in recent years. In 2013, the State Council issued the *Several Opinions on Accelerating the Development of Elderly Service Industry*, which expressly supported private investors in operating nursing homes. In 2015, ten central ministries and commissions jointly issued the *Opinions on Encouraging Private Investors to Engage in the Development of Elderly Service Industry* (M.F. No. 33 [2015]), which encouraged the construction or development of nursing homes in PPP model and supported the development of elderly service industry by private investors. A systematic and sound elderly service industry can ensure the service quality for the elders after they choose "Home for Care" and may offer an important opportunity for the promotion of this approach.

5 Thoughts and Suggestions on "Home for Care" in China

5.1 Clarifying Government Function and Improving the Institutional Environment for "Home for Care"

As one of the many ways of elderly care, "Home for Care" has a strong public nature, involves the interests of multiple parties, and its operating mechanism is very complex, so the government plays a crucial role in the orderly development of this approach. On one hand, there should be specific laws supporting the standard and orderly development of "Home for Care", and legal obstacles such as the limited property right should be cleared away. On the other hand, the top-level design for this approach must be strengthened, detailed policies and rules must be formulated and favorable measures adopted, and the government should effectively regulate the engaged parties. Meanwhile, the government should actively foster the agencies that provide evaluation, guarantee, legal and financial services to make the "Home for Care" approach more credible. Only when the government takes an active part and fosters a good market order can we set the fixed housing value flowing and make it one of the important elderly care options for the elderly group.

5.2 Encouraging Cooperation Among Multiple Organizations, Improving "Home for Care" Products

The design of "Home for Care" products is related with a number of variables, including the evaluation of property value, trend of real estate price, customer's life expectancy and market interest rate. To overcome the difficulties in promoting this approach, we need to give play to the strengths of the government, insurance companies and banks in a coordinated way, in order to lower the operating cost of the approach. At the same time, when designing "Home for Care" products, we should pay close attention to the needs of different elderly groups and provide them with diverse options.

5.3 Promoting the Idea of Diversified Elderly Care, Deepening the Rational Understanding of "Home for Care"

Because of the Confucian tradition, the idea of home-based elderly care is deeply rooted in China, but as population ageing becomes more serious and the "4-2-1" family structure is increasingly dominant, the family function of elderly care has weakened. The social security system is continuously improved in recent years and has played an important role in safeguarding people's life and promoting economic and social development, but it's far from able to meet the people's ever more diversified needs for elderly care. Therefore, exploring diversified elderly care approaches is of special importance.

Generally speaking, "Home for Care" has its potential in China. We can carry out trial projects as the government issues more supportive policies, and a variety of "Home for Care" products can be designed for the potential groups that have the demand, such as empty nesters and solitary elders in big cities. On that basis, we should keep drawing lessons and summarizing experience, reform and improve the product design, and make full preparations for the long-term development of the "Home for Care" approach.

References

Xu, S., (2016). "Difficulty in Promoting "Home for Care" in China and Study of Countermeasures." Master's thesis, Jiangxi Normal University.
Chen, J., (2013). "Beijing: First Attempt at 'Housing Bank for Elderly Care' Fails." *Workers' Daily 3.*
Li, Y., (2016). ""Home for Care": Current Status, Problems and Selection of Paths." *China Real Estate 25.*
Mo, K., (2016). "On the Universality of Innovation of Elderly Care Financial Products Based on "Home for Care"." *Finance & Economy 19.*

Dong Zhang doctor of management at Renmin University of China and a young researcher of the China Aging Finance Forum, specializing in pension policy.

Bo Sun doctor of management, post-doctor of finance, guest member of the China Aging Finance Forum. He works in the Pension Management Department of China Asset Management, specializing in financing old age care.

MIX
Papier aus verantwortungsvollen Quellen
Paper from responsible sources
FSC® C105338

If you have any concerns about our products,
you can contact us on
ProductSafety@springernature.com

In case Publisher is established outside the EU,
the EU authorized representative is:
Springer Nature Customer Service Center GmbH
Europaplatz 3, 69115 Heidelberg, Germany

Printed by Libri Plureos GmbH
in Hamburg, Germany